UNDENIABLE

THE SURVEY OF HOSTILITY
TO RELIGION IN AMERICA

2016 EDITION

Editorial Team

Kelly Shackelford
Chairman

Jeffrey Mateer
Executive Editor

Justin Butterfield
Editor-in-chief

Candice Lundquist
Julie Hennighausen
Stephanie Phillips
Assistant Editors

Past Contributors

Michael Andrews
Bryan Clegg

FIRST LIBERTY

UNDENIABLE
THE SURVEY OF HOSTILITY
TO RELIGION IN AMERICA

2016 Edition

Kelly Shackelford, chairman

Jeffrey Mateer, executive editor

Justin Butterfield, editor-in-chief

Candice Lundquist, Julie Hennighausen, and
Stephanie Phillips, assistant editors

This publication is not to be used for legal advice. Because the law is constantly changing and each factual situation is unique, First Liberty Institute and its attorneys do not warrant, either expressly or impliedly, that the law, cases, statutes, and rules discussed or cited in this publication have not been subject to change, amendment, reversal, or revision. If you have a legal question or need legal advice, please contact an attorney. First Liberty Institute's attorneys may be contacted by going to www.firstliberty.org, selecting the "Contact" menu option at the top of the page, and then selecting "Request Legal Help."

First Liberty Institute
2001 W. Plano Parkway, Suite 1600
Plano, Texas 75075
(972) 941-4444

TABLE OF CONTENTS

FIRST LIBERTY

HOSTILITY TO RELIGION HARMS EVERY AMERICAN

Driven from every other corner of the earth, freedom of thought and the right of private judgment in matters of conscience direct their course to this happy country as their last asylum.

—Samuel Adams, August 1, 1776

Hostility to religion in America is rising like floodwaters, as proven by the increased numbers of cases and attacks documented in this report. This flood is engulfing ordinary citizens who simply try to live normal lives according to their faith and conscience. It is eroding the bedrock on which stand vital American institutions such as government, education, the military, business, houses of worship, and charity. It has the potential to wash away the ground that supports our other rights, including freedom of speech, press, assembly, and government by consent of the people.

Since 2012, First Liberty Institute (formerly Liberty Institute) has documented and publicized this rising tide of hostility to religion in America. First Liberty Institute is the largest legal organization in America with the exclusive mission of protecting religious freedom for all our citizens. So it is important for us to know the scope of the problem, and we are glad to share what we learn with our fellow Americans, including our nation's leaders in Congress and beyond.

In this 2016 edition of our annual study *Undeniable: The Survey of Hostility to Religion in America,* First Liberty Institute's team of researchers, led by a Harvard-trained constitutional attorney, documents a continuing increase in the number of incidents hostile toward religion.

The flood is a national problem. Every American should share in the concern for at least three reasons:

First, individuals and families are being hurt. The attacks you will read about in these pages are sweeping away small businesses, careers, and ministries. Behind the legalities are tears, anguish, and the denial of basic human tolerance, compassion, and common decency. It's time for a national rejection of politically correct cruelty based on discrimination against traditional American forms of faith.

Second, the attacks injure us all. The animus toward religion springs from a relatively small but powerful sector of society composed of influential people and organizations who consider active faith as irrelevant at best, and dangerous to essential social progress at worst. As a result of such hostility to religion:

- Good employees are being unlawfully fired, and productive businesses recklessly harmed;

- Valuable public servants are being aggressively driven from their fields;

- Ministries, churches, and chaplains are being threatened or restricted from fulfilling their spiritual callings.

The flood is curtailing help for students, the elderly, the sick, the poor, orphans, addicts, and the homeless. It is even endangering efforts to show compassion and comfort to current and former members of our military, jeopardizing morale and thus our national security.

One must ask: Is America prepared to sacrifice the benefits of open religious activity on the altar of modern political correctness? Noted social historian Dr. Rodney Stark of Baylor University undertook a comprehensive analysis of the positive impact of religion in the United States in reducing crime, improving education, bettering mental and physical health, increasing employment, and reducing welfare. He conservatively estimated the benefit to be at least $2.67 trillion per year.[1] Other scholars confirm this overall assertion. Can we afford to ignore such research and toss away the blessings of free religious exercise?

Third, freedom of religion is foundational to all other freedoms. From the beginning of the colonies and continuing until today, immigrants came to America for religious freedom. Freedom of religious conscience is part of a person's core identity, and embedded in America's cultural DNA. Further, religious freedom is in the First Amendment because all other freedoms rest upon it. Without the concept of a higher authority to make government accountable to unchanging principles of justice, all other freedoms are at risk of being violated, redefined, or revoked by government. As the Declaration of Independence says, all men are "endowed by their Creator with certain unalienable Rights . . . . That to secure these rights, Governments are instituted among Men."

---

1 Stark, Rodney, *America's Blessings* (West Conshohocken, PA, Templeton Press, 2012, Kindle ed. 85%)

The good news is that the vast majority of the hostility to religion you will read in this survey is unlawful. It succeeds only because of its own bluff and the passivity of its victims. Hostility to religion can be defeated in the legal system—but only if challenged by Americans like you. When you stand up, First Liberty Institute and your fellow Americans will be standing with you offering legal assistance, research, and decisive help.

Kelly Shackelford
President, CEO, and Chief Counsel
First Liberty Institute

FIRST LIBERTY

EXECUTIVE SUMMARY

An age is called Dark not because the light fails to shine, but because people refuse to see it.

James A. Michener, Space

Abstract

Hostility to religious expression in America continues to grow at an alarming rate. The hostility is growing in the areas of:

- The "Public Arena" of public places, government, and the workplace.

- The "Schoolhouse" of education, from K–12 through higher academia.

- "Churches and Ministries," in which one might expect hostility to be the least.

- The "Military," which includes our service members, veterans, and their memorials.

More than 1,200 cases are documented in this 2016 edition of Undeniable, yet this is not an exhaustive accounting. These cases include past years' cases but show a clear expansion during this past year. Quantitatively and qualitatively, the hostility is undeniable. And it is dangerous.

Attacks in Four Key Social Sectors

The title of this survey, *Undeniable: The Survey of Hostility to Religion in America,* exemplifies its purpose: to bring to light the increasing acts of hostility to religion in such a way that even the most uninformed and skeptical person cannot deny that we in America are facing an unprecedented assault on our First Freedom. With each edition, *Undeniable* unfortunately continues to grow rapidly.

Here is a summary of the more detailed documentation of hostility that you will find in this volume, categorized by the four key sectors of society:

I. Attacks in the Public Arena

This category covers all attacks on exercising religious liberty in public locations, government, the marketplace, and the workplace.

This past year has seen high-profile attacks on religious liberty in the public arena as people of faith have been fired, refused employment, or fined for privately praying in the sight of others, for wearing religious attire, and for speaking out about their religious beliefs.

The following are some of the most significant areas of hostility, and legal cases in this category:

Attacks on Companies and Ministries that Oppose Providing Insurance Coverage for Abortion-Inducing Drugs

- *Burwell v. Hobby Lobby Stores, Inc.*
- *Holland v. U.S. Department of Health and Human Services*
- *Insight for Living Ministries v. Burwell*
- *Christian and Missionary Alliance Foundation, Inc. v. Burwell*
- *Little Sisters of the Poor v. Burwell*
- *Priests for Life v. Burwell*

The period under survey has seen the government continue its threats against religious nonprofit ministries that refuse to fund abortion-inducing drugs as required by Obamacare's "HHS Mandate." The HHS Mandate is a federal regulation that requires any company that provides group health insurance to also fund insurance coverage for abortion-inducing drugs such as Plan B (the "day-after pill") and Ella (the "week-after pill"). Many nonprofit ministries with religious convictions against funding abortions are being forced to sue the government to avoid having to either violate their religious beliefs or go out of business. While Hobby Lobby, last year, was able to successfully challenge the HHS Mandate's application against closely-held for-profit companies in *Burwell v. Hobby Lobby Stores, Inc.*, that ruling did not extend to religious nonprofit organizations, which have now become the target of the government's attacks.

The cases cited above are representative of the over 100 lawsuits filed by both for-profit companies and nonprofit ministries that oppose the federal government's forcing them to fund abortion-inducing drugs against the organizations' religious beliefs.

Attacks on Ten Commandments Displays

- *Van Orden v. Perry*
- *McCreary County v. ACLU*
- *Prescott v. Oklahoma Capitol Preservation Commission*
- *American Atheists v. Thompson*

These cases involve challenges to Ten Commandments displays at the Texas capitol, in a courthouse in Kentucky, and at the Oklahoma capitol. The U.S. Supreme Court heard both the Texas and the Kentucky cases at the same time and held that the Texas display is permissible because there were other, secular monuments around it, while the Kentucky display is impermissible because there were insufficient secular displays nearby. First Liberty Institute successfully defended the Oklahoma Ten Commandments display at the federal court level, but the Oklahoma Supreme Court held that the Ten Commandments display violated the Oklahoma Constitution in a state court proceeding.

Attacks on Public Invocations
- *Town of Greece, New York v. Galloway*
- *Atheists of Florida, Inc. v. City of Lakeland, Florida*

These cases involve challenges to legislative assemblies' opening with prayer. In *Marsh v. Chambers,* a 1983 U.S. Supreme Court case on legislative prayer, the Court noted that Congress has opened with prayer since the founding of the United States and Congress hired a chaplain to give these opening prayers the same week that it passed the First Amendment. Despite the historical evidence and the U.S. Supreme Court's holding that legislative prayer is constitutional, threats and lawsuits challenging these prayers are growing more frequent. In *Atheists of Florida, Inc. v. City of Lakeland, Florida,* the Eleventh Circuit Court of Appeals followed the Supreme Court's decision in *Marsh v. Chambers* and upheld a city commission's opening each meeting with a prayer. In *Town of Greece, New York v. Galloway,* however, the Second Circuit Court of Appeals rejected the Supreme Court's decision in *Marsh v. Chambers* and struck down legislative prayer. The Supreme Court reversed the Second Circuit in a landmark decision upholding the historical practice of legislative prayer and ensuring that government cannot censor the content of a prayer.

Attacks on Public Speech and Expression
- *Eric Walsh v. Georgia Department of Public Health*

In 2014, the State of Georgia enthusiastically hired Dr. Walsh as a senior official in the State's Department of Public Health. After conducting a review of sermons Dr. Walsh had preached at his local church, the State terminated him. Dr. Walsh filed a charge of discrimination with the Equal Employment Opportunity Commission against the State for unlawfully terminating him based solely on his religious beliefs.

- *Barton v. City of Balch Springs*

In *Barton v. City of Balch Springs,* city officials told senior citizens at a senior center that they could not pray before their meals, listen to religious messages, or sing gospel songs because religion is banned in public buildings. After the senior citizens filed a lawsuit, government officials told the senior citizens that if the won their lawsuit their meals would be taken away because praying over government-funded meals violates the "separation of church and state."

- *Roman Catholic Diocese of Austin et al. v. City of Austin*

The City of Austin, Texas, passed an ordinance on Good Friday in April of 2010 requiring pregnancy resource centers that oppose abortion and certain forms of birth control to post false and misleading signs at their front entrances. Facilities that provide abortions, however, were not required to post any signs or disclaimers. First Liberty Institute, then Liberty Institute, representing three such faith-based pregnancy resource centers brought a federal lawsuit to prohibit the City of Austin from requiring the posting of false and misleading signs. A federal district court held that Austin's ordinance was unconstitutional, and Austin was forced to pay almost a half-million dollars as a result of their violation of the pregnancy resource centers' constitutional rights.

II. Attacks in the Schoolhouse

Attacks on religious liberty in the schoolhouse comprise the second broad category of hostility to religion chronicled in Undeniable 2015. These cases primarily involve school officials prohibiting students or teachers from sharing their faith or exercising their religious free speech rights. Many of these cases arise because of the misinformation that secularist organizations send annually to school officials, threatening lawsuits unless the school officials stamp out all religious expression within the school. While this type of attack on religious liberty has been common for decades, these attacks are now occurring with increasing frequency. The following are some of the most significant recent attacks on religious liberty in the schoolhouse:

- *High School Football Coach Suspended for Praying to Himself*

Coach Joe Kennedy is head coach for the Bremerton High School junior varsity football team and an assistant coach for the varsity team. After a football game in 2008, Coach Kennedy waited until the game ended and the players cleared the field, then he walked to the fifty-yard line, took a knee, and thanked God for his players. Coach Kennedy continued to do this for seven years. In 2015, however, Bremerton High School suspended Coach Kennedy for giving a prayer after a football game. First Liberty Institute stepped in to defend Coach Kennedy's right to give a prayer under the First Amendment, federal law, and extensive legal precedent.

- *Substitute Teacher Fired for Handing a Bible to a Student*
Walt Tutka, a substitute teacher for the Phillipsburg School District in New Jersey, said, "The first shall be last, but the last shall be first," to a student coming last through a door. The student asked Tutka several times about the source of the quote. Tutka eventually used his personal Bible to show the quote to the student. At the student's request, Tutka gave the student the Bible. Upon learning that Tutka had given a student a Bible, the school district terminated Tutka for distributing religious literature on school grounds. First Liberty Institute stepped in to assist Tutka and filed a complaint with the Equal Employment Opportunity Commission (EEOC), asserting that the school district's firing on Tutka was religious discrimination. The EEOC agreed, determining that there was reasonable cause to believe that the Phillipsburg School District discriminated against Tutka "on the basis of religion and retaliation."

- *Matthews v. Kountze I.S.D.*
The Kountze High School cheerleaders wanted to display encouraging messages to the football players of both KHS's team and the opposing teams. The cheerleaders decided that the best way to encourage the players was to write Bible verses on the "run-through" banners that the football players run through at the beginning of each game. The Freedom From Religion Foundation discovered that the cheerleaders were writing Bible verses and sent a letter to Kountze I.S.D. demanding that the school district stop the cheerleaders. The superintendent of Kountze I.S.D. then banned any student group, including the cheerleaders, from bringing signs with religious messages to sporting events. The cheerleaders sued the school district to protect their free speech and religious liberty rights. A state district court judge held that the cheerleaders' speech is protected and may not be censored by the school district. The case is on appeal.

- *Morgan v. Swanson*

Public school officials told Jonathan Morgan, a third-grader in Plano, Texas, that he could not include a religious message in the goodie bags that he was bringing to the "Winter Party" to share with his classmates. School officials prohibited other children at the school from distributing pencils that stated "Jesus Is the Reason for the Season" and "Jesus loves me this I know for the Bible tells me so." A government school official ordered another student to stop distributing tickets to a Christian drama and to discard the remaining tickets. In a fractured en banc opinion, the U.S. Court of Appeals for the Fifth Circuit stated that the students are protected by the First Amendment but that their protection was not clearly enough established to award damages against the school officials involved.

- *Pounds v. Katy I.S.D.*

A Houston-area school district banned religious items at Christmas and Valentine's Day cards that contained religious content, merely because they were religious. When one student was asked what Easter meant to her, she was told that she could not say, "Jesus." A federal court held that the Katy I.S.D. violated the students' constitutional rights because of its hostility to religion.

- *Schultz v. Medina Valley I.S.D.*

Angela Hildenbrand, the valedictorian of her class, wanted to say a prayer during her graduation ceremony from Medina Valley High. A fellow student from an agnostic family filed a suit to prevent Hildenbrand from praying. The federal district court judge issued an order prohibiting Hildenbrand from using words like "Lord," "in Jesus' name," and "amen." The U.S. Court of Appeals for the Fifth Circuit reversed the ruling and allowed the prayer. On June 6, 2011, Hildenbrand gave her speech, which included a prayer.

III. Attacks Against Churches and Ministries

The third broad category of hostility to religion that is covered by this survey is attacks against churches and ministries. Only five years ago, the idea that the federal government would argue before the Supreme Court that it could regulate churches to the extent of determining who a church may choose as its pastor was unthinkable, yet the government made that very argument—effectively arguing that the religious liberty clauses of the First Amendment are meaningless—in *Hosanna-Tabor Evangelical Lutheran Church*

& School v. EEOC. Not only did the government, for the first time, argue that it may regulate churches and determine qualifications for pastors, but the past ten years have seen an explosion in cases involving local governments discriminating against churches, particularly in the local governments' use of zoning laws and granting of permits.

The following cases illustrate this new front in the secularists' war on religious liberty:

- *Hosanna-Tabor Evangelical Lutheran Church & Sch. v. EEOC*
A private Christian school fired Cheryl Perich, a minister and a teacher at Hosanna-Tabor Lutheran School, for threatening to sue the school after she was asked not to return because she had narcolepsy. Perich sued under the Americans with Disabilities Act. In response, the school argued its right to hire or fire Perich based on the "ministerial exception," which legally protects the rights of churches to select its religious leaders without government interference. The Justice Department argued that the "ministerial exception" does not exist and the government may regulate churches' selection of pastors. The U.S. Supreme Court unanimously upheld the ministerial exception and specified that government regulation of the hiring and firing of ministry leaders would violate both the Free Exercise Clause and the Establishment Clause.

- *Opulent Life Church v. City of Holly Springs, MS*
Opulent Life Church in Holly Springs, Mississippi, wanted to move into a larger facility because it had nearly outgrown its present meeting place. Once the church found a new property, however, it also discovered that the city would not grant a permit for the church to move into the new property without getting permission of 60 percent of all property owners within a one-quarter mile radius of the proposed site—a requirement that applied only to churches and to no other type of facility or business. Opulent Life Church sued the City of Holly Springs for violating the Constitution and the Religious Land Use and Institutionalized Persons Act, which prohibits zoning ordinances from discriminating against churches. After the Fifth Circuit ruled in favor of the church, the case settled, and Opulent Life Church is now free to move into its new property.

- *Schneider v. Gothelf; Highlands of McKamy IV and V Community Improvement Association v. Gothelf; City of Dallas v. Gothelf*

The members of Congregation Toras Chaim, a small Orthodox Jewish congregation in North Dallas, met at a home in their neighborhood that was the only site available to the congregation within walking distance of each member—an important consideration because the members cannot drive on the Sabbath. David Schneider, a neighbor of the home in which the congregation met, filed a lawsuit against Congregation Toras Chaim, claiming that the congregation's use of the home for religious worship violated the homeowners' association's (HOA) restrictive covenants. Schneider then became president of the HOA and brought the HOA into the lawsuit as an additional plaintiff against the small congregation. First Liberty Institute successfully defended Congregation Toras Chaim, winning a victory under both federal and state religious protection laws. Now, however, the City of Dallas has filed a new lawsuit against Congregation Toras Chaim, attempting to require the congregation to spend considerable resources acquiring additional parking and renovations that are unreasonable for the small size of the congregation. First Liberty Institute continues to represent Congregation Toras Chaim against the city.

- *Barr v. City of Sinton*

The City of Sinton, Texas, completely banned Pastor Barr's Christian organization, which provides housing and religious instruction to men who have been released from prison for misdemeanor offenses, from existing anywhere within its city limits. In a landmark decision, the Texas Supreme Court applied the Texas Religious Freedom Restoration Act to rule in favor of Pastor Barr and his ministry.

- *HEB Ministries, Inc. v. Texas Higher Educ. Coordinating Bd.*

Texas passed a law forcing all seminaries to get state approval of their curriculum, board members, and professors. The State fined Tyndale Seminary $173,000 for using the word "seminary" and issuing theological degrees without government approval. The ministry filed a suit to prohibit the government's attempts to control religious training. Both the district court and the court of appeals upheld the law. Finally, after nine years of suffering and losses, the Texas Supreme Court reversed and held that the law violated the First Amendment and the Texas Constitution.

IV. Attacks in the Military

Attacks on the religious liberty of active and retired members of the U.S. military has continued to grow over the past year. While religious liberty and open religious sentiment in the armed forces goes back to the Continental Army and was formalized in the administration of President Thomas Jefferson, even military chaplains are now subject to attack and persecution for following their religious beliefs. Religious freedom in the military is protected by the U.S. Constitution, Department of Defense regulations, service branch regulations, and case law. Nevertheless, recent attacks on our service members' religious freedom ignore this law and tradition. The following are samples of the attacks documented in this survey:

Attacks on Religious Belief and Thought

- *Navy Chaplain Investigated for Providing Counseling According to His Religious Beliefs*
- *Air Force Master Sergeant Punished for Christian Beliefs*

These cases represent attacks on religious belief and thought in the military as virtually a thought crime. In one case, Navy Chaplain Wes Modder, a decorated military hero with an exemplary 19-year service record, was investigated and faced dismissal for cause and a Naval Board of Inquiry because he provided pastoral counseling consistent with his religious beliefs about sexual conduct outside of marriage. First Liberty Institute stepped in to defend Chaplain Modder, and the charges against him were dropped.

In the second case, Senior Master Sergeant Phillip Monk, a 19-year Air Force veteran at Lackland Air Force Base in San Antonio, Texas, returned from deployment and found that he had a new commander who was an open lesbian. Sergeant Monk's commander asked Sergeant Monk what he thought about same-sex "marriage." Sergeant Monk initially refused to answer, stating that his views on same-sex "marriage" were irrelevant to his job. When Sergeant Monk's commander insisted that he tell her what he thought, Sergeant Monk affirmed that he believed in the biblical view of marriage. Sergeant Monk's commander then relieved him of his duties and had him reassigned, despite Sergeant Monk's spotless record. When Sergeant Monk reported the retaliatory religious discrimination, Air Force investigators charged him with the crime of making false official statements. First Liberty Institute stepped in to assist Sergeant Monk. The Air Force dropped their charges and awarded Sergeant Monk the Meritorious Service Medal.

Attacks on Veterans Memorials

- *Salazar v. Buono*
- *Trunk v. City of San Diego*

These cases each represent a lawsuit demanding that a veterans memorial be torn down because it includes a cross. In *Salazar v. Buono,* the memorial was saved after Congress transferred the land to private ownership and the Supreme Court upheld the constitutionality of the land transfer. In *Trunk v. City of San Diego,* the U.S. Court of Appeals for the Ninth Circuit held that the veterans memorial is unconstitutional, but the federal government has now transferred the memorial and land upon which it sits to a private party.

Attacks on Religious Speech

- *Rainey v. U.S. Department of Veterans Affairs*
- *Pentagon Removes Chaplain-Created Video Tribute to First Sergeants*

These cases illustrate the growing pattern of censorship of religious speech within the active military. In *Rainey v. U.S. Department of Veterans Affairs,* the director of the Houston National Cemetery informed a pastor, Scott Rainey, that he could not pray "in Jesus' name" at a Memorial Day service. Following the filing of a lawsuit, First Liberty Institute attorneys discovered that the U.S. Department of Veterans Affairs had a policy that funerals at national cemeteries could not include religious content. Government officials told grieving families who wanted a religious funeral that the service could not reference God. A federal district court held that the government could not dictate prayers at memorial services and funerals, and the U.S. Department of Veterans Affairs agreed to change its policy at all national cemeteries to allow the families' wishes regarding religious content to be followed.

In the second example, an Air Force chaplain wrote a poem to honor First Sergeants, patterned off of the popular Dodge Ram commercial, "God Created a Farmer." The poem was adapted into a video. The video was posted on the official Joint Base McGuire Dix YouTube site; however, it was quickly removed after someone complained about the video. The alleged offense of the video was the language, "On the eighth day, God looked down on His creation and said, 'I need someone who will take care of the Airmen,' So God created a First Sergeant."

There Is Hope, If . . .

While the 2016 edition of *Undeniable: The Survey of Hostility to Religion in America* shows that attacks on religious liberty are dramatically increasing in the United States, both in the frequency and in the severity of the attacks, this survey also shows that those persons and organizations who stand up for religious liberty win when they fight. As more and more Americans become aware of the growing attacks on religious liberty and what their rights are, they can stand and turn back the tides of secularism and hostility that have so eroded our religious liberty rights, our First Freedom.

ATTACKS IN THE PUBLIC ARENA

FIRST LIBERTY

Abercrombie & Fitch Refuses to Hire Woman Because of Her Religious Attire

EEOC v. Abercrombie & Fitch Stores, Inc., 135 S. Ct. 2028 (2015)

Samantha Elauf, a Muslim woman, sought employment at Abercrombie & Fitch. As a practicing Muslim, Elauf wears a headscarf. Abercrombie & Fitch imposes a "Look Policy" on its employees to maintain a consistent image across stores. Abercrombie & Fitch determined that Elauf's headscarf—like all other headwear—was not permitted by its "Look Policy." Because of Abercrombie & Fitch's determination, it refused to hire Elauf. The Equal Employment Opportunity Commission brought a lawsuit on Elauf's behalf against Abercrombie & Fitch. The lawsuit went to the U.S. Supreme Court, which held that Abercrombie & Fitch's refusal to hire Elauf because of her religious attire violated her rights under Title VII of the Civil Rights Act of 1964.

Religious Convictions Trump Government Mandate to Fund Abortifacient Drugs

Burwell v. Hobby Lobby Stores, Inc., and Conestoga Wood Specialties Corp. v. Burwell, 573 U.S. ___ (2014)

In implementing the Patient Protection and Affordable Care Act, also known as "Obamacare," the Department of Health and Human Services issued a mandate (the "HHS Mandate") that requires every organization, except churches, that provides group health insurance to provide, directly or indirectly, for abortifacients such as Plan B (the "day-after pill") and Ella (the "week-after pill"). Hobby Lobby Stores, Inc., and Conestoga Wood Specialties Corp., for-profit Christian organizations, objected to being forced to fund these abortifacients. Hobby Lobby and Conestoga Wood sued the federal government and argued that the HHS Mandate violates these organizations' religious liberty rights. The U.S. Supreme Court held that closely-held for-profit corporations like Hobby Lobby and Conestoga Wood are entitled to religious liberty protections and do not have to fund abortifacient drugs if doing so would violate sincerely held religious beliefs.

Right to Pray Before Government Meetings Without Government Censorship Protected

Town of Greece, New York v. Galloway, 134 S. Ct. 1811 (2014)

The Town of Greece, New York, was sued for opening town board meetings with a prayer. The district court upheld the prayers, but the Second Circuit reversed, holding that the prayers "impermissibly affiliated the town with a single creed, Christianity," because most of the prayers before the town board—along with most of the churches in the town—were Christian. The

U.S. Supreme Court reversed the Second Circuit and held that the prayers are constitutional and that the government cannot interfere in the content of the prayers or require an artificial diversity of religions. The Supreme Court made clear that the government cannot require "non-sectarian" prayers but must allow each person who prays to pray according to that person's conscience.

World War I Veterans Memorial Preserved from Being Demolished
Salazar v. Buono, 130 S. Ct. 1803 (2010)
A former U.S. Park Service employee filed a lawsuit objecting to the World War I Mojave Desert Cross Veterans Memorial. In 2010, overturning a decision of the Ninth Circuit, the U.S. Supreme Court ruled that the Mojave Desert Cross Veterans Memorial could remain and the land could be transferred from the U.S. government to the Veterans of Foreign Wars in order to preserve this veterans memorial. After a remand of the case to the federal district court, the Plaintiff (represented by the ACLU) and the U.S. government entered into a settlement paving the way for completion of the land transfer.

Right of Local Communities to Choose Which Monuments to Display Protected
Pleasant Grove City et al. v. Summum, 555 U.S. 460 (2009)
After Pleasant Grove City, Utah, rejected Summum's offer to place a religious monument reflecting The Seven Aphorisms of Summum in a local public park, the organization filed suit. The Tenth Circuit Court ruled in favor of Summum, arguing that cities must allow all privately donated monuments in public areas, regardless of the monument's message or purpose, or not allow any monuments at all. In 2009, the Supreme Court overturned the Circuit Court's decision, ruling in favor of a city's ability to choose whether or not a monument could be erected on city property.

Prisoners' Religious Freedoms Protected
Cutter v. Wilkinson, 544 U.S. 709 (2005)
Current and former Ohio prison inmates filed suit when prison officials would not accommodate their exercise of religion. The lower courts split over whether the government needed to accommodate the inmates' exercise of religion. The Supreme Court's ruling indicated that the government's accommodation of individual exercise of religion did not violate the Establishment Clause.

Texas Ten Commandments Monument Allowed to Remain
Van Orden v. Perry, 545 U.S. 677 (2005)
An atheist filed suit against the State of Texas to have the Ten Commandments

monument on the grounds of the state Capitol removed. The Fraternal Order of Eagles donated the monument many years ago to the State of Texas as a symbol to battle against juvenile delinquency. SCOTUS held (declining to use the notorious *Lemon* test) that this did not violate the Establishment Clause.

Ten Commandments Displays in Kentucky Ordered Removed
McCreary County v. ACLU, 545 U.S. 844 (2005)
The ACLU filed suit to challenge Ten Commandment displays in three Kentucky county courthouses, seeking to have the displays removed. Both the Sixth Circuit of Appeals and the U.S. Supreme Court ruled that the Ten Commandments displays were unconstitutional.

"Under God" in the Pledge of Allegiance Does Not Violate the Establishment Clause
Elk Grove Unified School District v. Newdow, 542 U.S. 1 (2004)
Atheist Michael Newdow filed suit to remove the words "under God" from the Pledge of Allegiance. Newdow's daughter attended public elementary school where students recited the Pledge as part of the morning activities. Newdow filed suit claiming that his daughter was injured because she was compelled to witness her teacher lead her classmates in a ritual where they proclaimed there is a God and that our nation is under God. The Supreme Court held that Newdow lacked standing to challenge the constitutionality of the district's court policy in federal court.

Government Cannot Discriminate in Public Displays Solely on the Basis of Religious Viewpoint
Capitol Square Review & Advisory Board v. Pinette, 515 U.S. 753 (1995)
The Ohio State Capitol Square Review Board refused a permit to a group wanting to display a cross during the 1993 Christmas season, so a lawsuit was filed, seeking an injunction requiring the board to issue the permit. The District Court granted the injunction, the Sixth Circuit affirmed, and the Supreme Court held that issuing such a permit did not violate the Establishment Clause.

ACLU Challenges Christmas and Hanukkah Displays
County of Allegheny v. ACLU, 492 U.S. 573 (1989)
The ACLU filed a lawsuit against the county stating two of the county's holiday displays were unconstitutional. One of the displays was a Nativity scene at the county courthouse. The other display was a menorah placed alongside a Christmas tree at the City-County Building. The Supreme Court held that a menorah in front of the City-County Building for a seasonal display did not

violate the Establishment Clause, though the Nativity scene in the county courthouse did.

Christmas Display Challenged for Including Nativity Scene
Lynch v. Donnelly, 465 U.S. 668 (1984)
In a Pawtucket shopping district, there was an annual Christmas display owned by a nonprofit organization. The display included a Santa house, a Christmas tree, a "Seasons Greetings" banner, and a Nativity scene, which had been a staple of the display for over forty years. A lawsuit was filed to challenge the display, specifically the inclusion of the Nativity scene. The U.S. Supreme Court held the display did not violate the Establishment Clause.

Prayer Before a Legislative Meeting Challenged and Upheld
Marsh v. Chambers, 463 U.S. 783 (1983)
A member of the Nebraska legislature filed suit challenging the longstanding practice of employing a chaplain to pray before the opening of each legislative session, claiming the practice was unconstitutional. The District Court of Nebraska enjoined the chaplaincy practice, and the Eighth Circuit affirmed. The Supreme Court reversed, holding that legislative prayers do not violate the Establishment Clause.

Alabama Forces Native American Inmate to Cut Hair
Knight v. Thompson, 796 F.3d 1289 (11th Cir. 2015)
The Eleventh Circuit Court of Appeals upheld an Alabama prison policy requiring male inmates to keep their hair short. Alabama refused to grant an exception for Native American inmates to wear long hair in accordance with their religious beliefs. Even though the Supreme Court in *Holt v. Hobbs* found that a prison must permit a Muslim inmate to grow a beard, the Eleventh Circuit sided against the Native American inmate.

County Commissioners Ordered to Stop Prayers
Lund v. Rowan Cty., No. 15-1591 (4th Cir. July 27, 2015)
Rowan County Commissioners have been sued for opening meetings with an invocation or a moment of silence. A district court ruled against the city commissioners, even though the Supreme Court recently affirmed the constitutionality of non-coercive legislative prayers in *Town of Greece v. Galloway.* The county is appealing the lower court's decision to an appellate court.

California Threatens 10,000 Year-Old Native American Practices
Pit River Tribe v. BLM, 793 F.3d 1147 (9th Cir. 2015)
A Native American Tribe has challenged twenty-six geothermal leases in California's Medicine Lake Highlands national forests. For at least 10,000 years, members of the Pit River Tribe have used the area for religious activities, such as vision quests, prayers, and ceremonies. The geothermal development projects threaten the continued use of their land at the lake and highlands.

Florida Prisons Deny Navajo Religious Observer Venison and Religious Headband
Schlemm v. Wall, No. 14-2604 (7th Cir., Apr. 21, 2015)
The Florida Department of Corrections denied David Schlemm, a follower of the Navajo religion, venison for him to celebrate the Ghost Feast, a religious celebration. The department of corrections also denied Schlemm access to a religious headband. Schlemm filed a lawsuit against the secretary of the Florida Department of Corrections to defend his religious liberty rights. The U.S. Court of Appeals for the Seventh Circuit held that the Florida Department of Corrections violated Schlemm's religious rights and ordered that he be provided with venison for the Ghost Feast and a religious headband.

Use of "In God We Trust" on Currency Challenged
Newdow v. Peterson, No. 13-4049 (2d Cir. 2014)
Newdow filed a lawsuit challenging the use of the phrase "In God We Trust" on U.S. currency. The U.S. Court of Appeals for the Second Circuit held that including "In God We Trust" on coins and bills does not violate the First Amendment or the Religious Freedom Restoration Act.

Muslim Inmate Denied Access to Religious Literature and Ability to Fast
Wall v. Wade, 741 F.3d 492 (4th Cir. 2014)
Officials in the Red Onion State Prison refused to allow Gary Wall, a Muslim, to participate in Ramadan because he could not produce literature to substantiate his claim to be a practicing Muslim. Wall could not prove that he was a practicing Muslim because his property was confiscated during a prison transfer. Prison officials also did not permit him to follow the ritual fasting required by his Islamic beliefs. The U.S. Court of Appeals for the Fourth Circuit has allowed Hall's lawsuit against the prison to proceed.

Native American Inmate Denied Ability to Perform Religious Ceremony
Native Am. Council of Tribes v. Weber, No. 13-1401, 2014 WL 1644130 (8th Cir. 2014)
When the South Dakota Department of Corrections (SDDOC) changed its

policy to completely ban the use of tobacco by Native American inmates during their religious ceremonies, an inmate brought a lawsuit against the discriminatory ban. The U.S. Court of Appeals for the Sixth Circuit found in the inmate's favor and affirmed the district court's order against the SDDOC granting injunctive relief for the burden on Native American inmates' religious freedom.

Prison Officials Refuse to Even Attempt Religious Accommodation
Yellowbear v. Lampert, 741 F.3d 48 (10th Cir. 2014)
Yellowbear sought use of a sweat lodge on the prison property in order to practice his religion. When prison officials made no sincere effort to accommodate his request for such activity, Yellowbear sought relief under the Religious Land Use and Institutionalized Persons Act. The U.S. Court of Appeals for the Tenth Circuit allowed Yellowbear's suit to continue.

Jewish Inmate Denied Kosher Diet and Prayer Group
LeBaron v. Spencer, 527 Fed. Appx. 25 (1st Cir. 2013)
The U.S. Court of Appeals for the First Circuit allowed a Messianic Jewish inmate to proceed with his First Amendment and RLUIPA challenges seeking a sufficient kosher diet and access to a Messianic synagogue and group prayer. This case is currently pending.

Company Director Fired for Religious Conversion
Mariotti v. Mariotti Building Products, Inc., No. 11–3148 (3d Cir. 2013)
Mariotti Building Products, a Pennsylvania business, ousted one of its director-officers following his religious conversion. The Third Circuit Court of Appeals held that Title VII provides no protection to director-officers from religious discrimination.

Security Officer Prohibited from Wearing Religiously-Mandated Clothing
Finnie v. Lee County, Miss., 541 F. Appx. 368 (5th Cir. 2013)
After working as a security officer for a juvenile detention center in Lee County, Mississippi, for almost four years, Crystal Finnie began following the Pentecostal faith, which required her to wear skirts instead of pants. However, Finnie's employer refused to accommodate her request for a religious exemption from the dress code. The EEOC filed a lawsuit on Finnie's behalf, but the court dismissed all of her claims.

IRS Refuses to Allow Three-Inch Ceremonial Knife But Permits Pocket Knives

Tagore v. United States, 735 F.3d 324 (5th Cir. 2013)

After being hired by the IRS, Kawaljeet Tagore was baptized into the Sikh religion and began wearing a small, blunted sword called a kirpan in accordance with the religion's requirements. However, the three-inch blade was half an inch longer than allowed under the "pocket knife exemption" for knives allowed in federal buildings. Tagore applied for a security waiver, but his application was denied. The IRS then fired Tagore when she continued to adhere to her religious requirements by wearing the kirpan. Tagore subsequently brought a lawsuit for the IRS's failure to accommodate her religion, but a Texas federal court ruled against her. Upon appeal, the Fifth Circuit Court of Appeals remanded the case back to the district court to assess whether Tagore's sincere religious beliefs prohibit her from wearing a kirpan that adheres to federal requirements.

Bus Driver Fired for Keeping the Sabbath

Antoine v. First Student, Inc., No. 11–31126 (5th Cir. filed Apr. 10, 2013)

Robert Antoine, a Seventh-day Adventist school bus driver, requested to not work on Friday nights to observe the Sabbath. Antoine's employer, First Students, Inc., did not follow up with its offer to swap shifts. When Antoine failed to report for work on Friday nights, he was relieved for absenteeism. Antoine brought a religious discrimination suit against his former employer. The case is currently pending.

Government Attempts to Deport Family Fleeing Persecution for Religious Beliefs

Romeike v. Holder, No. 12-3641 (6th Cir. 2013)

The U.S. Justice Department revoked asylum granted to a Christian family from Germany. The family fled to the United States to avoid a Nazi-era law meant to eliminate philosophies and religions inconsistent with state ideology by banning primary education outside public schools. When the Romeike family tried to homeschool its kids to provide religious education, it was slapped with oppressive fines and German authorities forcibly removed the children to public school. The U.S. federal government opposed the family's asylum in the U.S., arguing that parents do not have a fundamental right to choose their children's education, even when public schools insist on a curriculum offensive to the family's religious beliefs. The Sixth Circuit Court of Appeals accepted the government's arguments, and the Supreme Court refused to hear the Romeike's appeal. Following the Supreme Court's denial of the appeal, the Department of Homeland Security suddenly reversed its decision and permitted the Romeikes to remain in the United States.

Muslim Inmate Preventing from Having a Beard While Other Inmates Are Allowed Beards

Holt v. Hobbs, 509 Fed. Appx. 561 (8th Cir. 2013)

Gregory Holt is a Muslim inmate in a prison operated by the Arkansas Department of Corrections (ADC). Because of his Muslim beliefs, Mr. Holt sought permission to maintain a short beard. ADC refused to allow Mr. Holt to have a short beard, even though ADC does allow inmates to have beards for other purposes, such as skin conditions. Mr. Holt challenged ADC's refusal to permit him to grow a beard under the Religious Land Use and Institutionalized Persons Act, which was designed to stop religious discrimination against prisoners. The U.S. Court of Appeals for the Eighth Circuit rejected Mr. Holt's claim, but the U.S. Supreme Court has agreed to hear the case.

Christian Banned from Distributing Bibles During Gay Pride Festival

Johnson v. Minneapolis Park & Recreation Bd., 729 F.3d 1094 (8th Cir. 2013)

Every year, Twin Cities Pride, a LGBT advocacy group, hosts a gay pride festival in a public park in downtown Minneapolis. Subject to city approval, vendors of all kinds are allowed to set up booths in order to sell their wares to the public. However, when Brian Johnson, an evangelical Christian, requested a booth to distribute Bibles, the city denied his application and proceeded to pass an ordinance that limited the distribution of materials in booths and throughout the park. Johnson then filed a lawsuit to request an injunction against the discriminatory regulation. In a 2–1 decision, the U.S. Court of Appeals for the Eighth Circuit reversed the district court's original denial of Johnson's request.

Prayers Before City Council Meetings Challenged

Rubin v. City of Lancaster, 710 F.3d 1087 (9th Cir. 2013)

The city of Lancaster, California, invites all religious congregations in the community to volunteer up to three times per year to give a non-proselytizing, non-disparaging invocation before city-council meetings. Representatives from four different religious traditions have participated. Two persons brought a lawsuit challenging the prayers. A federal district court in California upheld the invocation policy, and the Ninth Circuit Court of Appeals affirmed, holding that the prayers are permisible and the government cannot censor the persons who pray before the meetings.

Clothier Refuses to Hire Muslim Because Her Headscarf Violates Company "Look Policy"
E.E.O.C. v. Abercrombie & Fitch Stores, Inc., 731 F.3d 1106 (10th Cir. 2013)
Samantha Elauf, a practicing Muslim, interviewed for a model position at an Abercrombie & Fitch retail store in Tulsa, Oklahoma. Although Elauf's initial interviewing score with the store manager justified an offer of employment, the manager informed Elauf that they would not hire her because her hijab (a religious headscarf required for modesty purposes) conflicted with the store's "look policy." Elauf filed a lawsuit for Abercrombie's failure to provide a religious exemption, but the U.S. Court of Appeals for the Tenth Circuit reversed the district court's initial decision for Elauf and instead ruled in Abercrombie's favor.

Atheist Group Sues Florida City for Refusing to Censor Prayers
Atheists of Florida, Inc. v. City of Lakeland, Florida, 713 F.3d 577 (11th Cir. 2013)
A group called the Atheists of Florida sued the City of Lakeland, Florida, for opening each city commission meeting with a prayer. The city sent invitations to pray to all of the religious groups in the city. Atheists of Florida argued, however, that the prayers violated the Establishment Clause because some of the persons who prayed did so "in the name of Jesus Christ" or to "the Father, Son and Holy Spirit." A federal district court held that just because some of the persons invited to pray give Christian prayers, it does not mean that the city's policy violates the Establishment Clause. The Eleventh Circuit Court of Appeals affirmed.

Christians Stopped from Sharing Their Faith at a Festival Without a Permit
Bays v. City of Fairborn, 668 F.3d 814 (6th Cir. 2012)
Two Christian men were prevented from presenting the gospel at a Festival in Fairborn, Ohio, because they did not have a permit. The Sixth Circuit held that the policy was unconstitutional because it was not narrowly tailored to serve a significant government interest.

Atheist Sues to Stop Grant for Restoration of Cross
Sherman v. Illinois, 682 F.3d 643 (7th Cir. 2012)
An atheist sued Illinois claiming a violation of the Establishment Clause when the Illinois Department of Commerce and Economic Opportunity granted $20,000 to a nonprofit group to restore a 111-foot-tall Latin cross. The court dismissed the claim for lack of taxpayer standing.

Atheist and Agnostic Group Sues City to Remove Ten Commandments Display

Red River Freethinkers v. City of Fargo, 679 F.3d 1015 (8th Cir. 2012)

In 1961, the Fraternal Order of Eagles—a nonreligious organization—donated a Ten Commandments monument to Fargo, North Dakota. The city installed it on city property. In 2002, forty-one years later, the Red River Freethinkers, a group dedicated to promoting atheistic and agnostic views, sued the city after the city declined to accept a monument donated by the Freethinkers. The Freethinkers claimed the Ten Commandments display and the city's decision not to accept the Freethinker's monument constituted a violation of the Establishment Clause. A federal district court dismissed the lawsuit, but the Eighth Circuit Court of Appeals reversed the district court, allowing the case to continue.

Christian Counselor Fired for Referring Homosexual Clients to Other Counselors

Walden v. Centers for Disease Control & Prevention, 669 F.3d 1277 (11th Cir. 2012)

A Christian counselor for the Center for Disease Control (CDC), Marcia Walden, was fired because she refused to lie about why she was referring clients with same-sex relationship problems to other counselors. Walden told a homosexual client that her personal values would interfere with the client/therapist relationship, never mentioning her religious objections. In response, the client complained to the CDC that Walden was homophobic. Walden reiterated to her supervisors that she had no problem counseling homosexual individuals, but her religious beliefs prevented her from conducting relationship counseling for those in homosexual relationships. Her supervisors suggested that she lie to homosexual clients and tell them she did not have much experience with relationship counseling. Walden refused to lie about why she was referring clients and was ultimately fired for not "altering her approach." The Eleventh Circuit rejected claims that Walden's free exercise rights were violated under the First Amendment, affirming the district court's summary judgment ruling against her.

Prayers Before Forsyth County Board of Commissioners Stopped for Being Too Christian

Joyner v. Forsyth County, North Carolina, 653 F.3d 341 (4th Cir. 2011)

The Fourth Circuit Court of Appeals struck down a county policy permitting any community religious congregation to lead invocation at the Forsyth County Board of Commissioners because too many of the prayers being offered were Christian.

Religious Tracts Banned from Arab Festival

Saieg v. City of Dearborn, 641 F.3d 727 (6th Cir. 2011)

Dearborn, Michigan, instituted a new policy prohibiting the distribution of leaflets in and around the Arab International Festival. Saieg, founder of the Arabic Christian Perspective (ACP), wanted to distribute religious tracts to Muslims at the festival. Dearborn provided ACP with a booth at the festival from which to distribute tracts, but prohibited Saieg from distributing tracts outside of the booth. The Sixth Circuit held that Dearborn's restrictions on distributing flyers in and around the festival violated Saieg's free speech rights.

Ohio Judge Sued for Having Poster of the Ten Commandments

DeWeese v. ACLU of Ohio, 545 U.S. 1152 (2005)

American Civil Liberties Union of Ohio Foundation, Inc. v. DeWeese, 633 F.3d 424 (6th Cir. 2011)

In 2001, the ACLU of Ohio sued Judge DeWeese for displaying a poster of the Ten Commandments in his courtroom. In July 2004, the U.S. Court of Appeals for the Sixth Circuit upheld the decision of a lower court that ruled that the poster was unconstitutional. In June 2005, the Supreme Court refused to hear the case, allowing the ruling of the Sixth Circuit to stand. Following these cases, Judge DeWeese hung a replacement poster, which contrasted "moral absolute" principles, as expressed in the Ten Commandments, with "moral relativist" principles. The Sixth Circuit again ruled that the poster was unconstitutional.

Atheist Group Sues to Stop the National Day of Prayer

Freedom from Religion Foundation, Inc. v. Obama, 641 F.3d 803 (7th Cir. 2011)

The Freedom from Religion Foundation sued to have the National Day of Prayer declared unconstitutional. The district court held that declaring a National Day of Prayer violates the Establishment Clause and prohibited such declarations. The Seventh Circuit reversed.

Christian Banned from Distributing Religious Flyers at Mt. Rushmore

Boardley v. U.S. Dept. of the Interior, 615 F.3d 508 (D.C. Cir. 2010)

Boardley, a Christian evangelist, brought a lawsuit against the U.S. Department of the Interior for restricting him from passing out gospel tracts at Mt. Rushmore National Park. The appellate court found the national park policy against distributing materials was overbroad and unreasonable.

Atheists Sue to Stop Use of the Phrase, "So Help Me God" in Presidential Oath
Newdow v. Roberts, 603 F.3d 1002 (D.C. Cir. 2010)
Michael Newdow and approximately thirty other atheists filed suit to challenge the phrase "so help me God" when used in the oath at the presidential inauguration. The federal district court dismissed the lawsuit, and the D.C. Circuit affirmed.

Nurse Forced to Participate in Late-Term Abortion Against Her Religious Beliefs
Cenzon-DeCarlo v. Mount Sinai Hospital, 626 F.3d 695 (2d Cir. 2010)
A nurse at Mount Sinai Hospital in New York was forced to participate in a late-term abortion against her conscience and religious convictions. She was threatened with severe penalties including termination and loss of license if she refused to participate in the abortion. Following a request from her attorneys, the U.S. Department of Health and Human Services investigated the hospital for civil rights violations. Mount Sinai Hospital now has a policy that no person can be forced to participate in an abortion against that person's conscience.

Vermont Resident Denied Religious Message on License Plate
Byrne v. Rutledge, 623 F.3d 46 (2nd Cir. 2010)
Vermont resident Byrne applied for a "vanity" license plate that had a combination of letters and numbers that could be interpreted as a Bible verse. The state refused to give Byrne that license plate because of the religious content. Byrne filed suit against the state commissioner. The Second Circuit found that the state was wrong to limit Byrne's ability to put religious content on his license plate and that there was no legitimate government interest served by their action.

"Under God" Challenged in Texas Pledge of Allegiance
Croft v. Perry, 624 F.3d 157 (5th Cir. 2010)
The Crofts, parents of school-age children, challenged the phrase "under God" in the Texas Pledge of Allegiance. The district court and the Fifth Circuit both held that the Texas Pledge was constitutional.

Jewish Inmate Denied Kosher Meals
Moussazadeh v. Texas Department of Criminal Justice, 364 Fed. Appx. 110 (5th Cir. 2010)
Max Moussazadeh, an observant Jew incarcerated in the Texas prison system, brought suit against the state for its failure to accommodate his religious

beliefs by providing kosher meals. Mr. Moussazadeh argued that the state unlawfully restricted his right to religious exercise under the Religious Land Use and Institutionalized Persons Act (RLUIPA). Since Mr. Moussazadeh filed his lawsuit, he has been relocated to a facility that serves kosher meals.

ACLU Sues to Censor Historical Documents from County Courthouse
ACLU of Kentucky v. Grayson County, 591 F.3d 837 (6th Cir. 2010)
The ACLU challenged a county courthouse display containing various historical documents about the founding of America and the Ten Commandments. The district court censored the use of the Ten Commandments in the display, but the Sixth Circuit reversed, holding that the Ten Commandments display does not violate the Establishment Clause.

Atheist Sues to Stop Pledge of Allegiance Recitations in Daughter's Classroom
Newdow v. Rio Linda Union School District, 597 F.3d 1007 (9th Cir. 2010)
A parent of a student in Rio Linda Union School District, California, sued to prohibit the recitation of the pledge by all students in her child's classroom. A self-professed atheist, the parent acknowledged that her child had never said the pledge. The court below held that the recitation of the Pledge of Allegiance violated the Establishment Clause and prohibited its recitation. However, the Ninth Circuit overruled that decision on March 11, 2010, because the purpose of the pledge was patriotic, not an attempt to impress a religious doctrine on anyone.

Atheist Group Sues to Remove Memorial Crosses Placed in Memory of Fallen Patrolmen
American Atheists, Inc. v. Duncan, 637 F.3d 1095 (10th Cir. 2010)
An atheist group filed suit in federal court claiming that allowing the Utah Highway Patrol Association to erect memorial crosses bearing its logo on state property in memory of fallen patrolmen violated the U.S. Constitution. The Tenth Circuit held that the crosses violate the Establishment Clause.

Couple Fired and Evicted for Having a Picture with a Religious Reference
Dixon v. The Hallmark Companies, Inc., 627 F.3d 849 (11th Cir. 2010)
Daniel and Sharon Dixon managed an apartment complex. In the apartment office, the Dixons placed a stained glass piece of artwork that had a picture of lilies and contained the words "Consider the lilies... Matthew 6:28." The Dixons' supervisor, upon seeing the stained glass artwork, fired the Dixons and evicted them from their apartment for being "too religious." The Dixons sued, and the case settled.

Pharmacy Appeals to Supreme Court to Protect Conscience Rights
Stormans, Inc. v. Selecky, 586 F.3d 1109 (9th Cir. 2009)
The Stormans family, who run Ralph's Thriftway in Olympia, Washington, have religious beliefs against dispensing abortion-causing drugs. The Ninth Circuit, however, has ordered the pharmacy to dispense these drugs. The Stormans have appealed to the Supreme Court to protect their right to follow their conscience rather than be forced to be complicit in ending a human life.

ACLU Sues to Remove Ten Commandments and Mayflower Compact from Courthouse Lawn
Green v. Haskell County Board of Commissioners, 568 F.3d 784 (10th Cir. 2009)
James Green and the ACLU filed a lawsuit to have a monument of the Ten Commandments and the Mayflower Compact removed from the Haskell County courthouse lawn, claiming that the monument violated the Establishment Clause. The monument was erected at the request of a resident of Haskell County, who wanted to honor the historical and legal traditions represented by the monument. The county has a longstanding policy and practice of permitting citizens of Haskell County to display monuments on the county courthouse lawn. The Tenth Circuit Court of Appeals held that the monument violated the Establishment Clause.

"Orthodox Catholic" Inmate Denied Kosher Meals
Guzzi v. Thompson, No. 07-1537, 2008 U.S. App. LEXIS 11531 (1st Cir. 2008)
Rosario Guzzi, an inmate at a Massachusetts prison, sued the facility after it denied his request to provide kosher meals in keeping with his "orthodox Catholic" faith. The district court found that Catholicism does not require kosher meals and ruled against Guzzi. The First Circuit Court of Appeals vacated the lower court's decision, holding that the court had overstepped its bounds in interpreting what constituted "orthodox Catholicism."

Cobb County Commission Sues to Stop Opening Prayers
Pelphrey v. Cobb County, Georgia, 547 F.3d 1263 (11th Cir. 2008)
A group of taxpayers sued Cobb County, Georgia, because the Cobb County Commission and the Cobb County Planning Commission open in prayers that often include references to particular religions. The Eleventh Circuit Court of Appeals held that under *Marsh v. Chambers,* opening legislative assemblies with prayer is constitutional and that theologians, not courts, should determine what is a "sectarian" prayer.

Harris County, Texas, Sued to Remove Bible from Monument to Philanthropist

Staley v. Harris County, Texas, 485 F.3d 305 (5th Cir. 2007)

A lawsuit was filed against Harris County to have a Bible removed from a portion of a monument dedicated to a prominent and charitable citizen, William S. Mosher. The monument was donated and erected by the Star of Hope Mission, a Christian outreach organization that assists the homeless and jobless in the Houston area. The district court ordered the Bible be removed from the monument and the Court of Appeals panel agreed before the case became moot.

Man Arrested for Preaching Without a Permit

Hood v. Keller, 229 Fed. Appx. 393 (6th Cir. 2007)

A man was arrested for publicly preaching without a permit. He filed a lawsuit seeking declaratory and injunctive relief, compensatory damages, costs, and attorney's fees from public officials for violating his First Amendment rights to freedom of speech and free exercise of religion.

Faith-Based Child Services Provider Denied Children Because of Religious Content

Teen Ranch, Inc. v. Udow, 479 F.3d 403 (6th Cir. 2007)

A faith-based child services provider filed suit against the Family Independence Agency (FIA) when the FIA decided to discontinue referring children to the provider based on its incorporation of religion into its programming. The district court ruled in favor of the FIA. On appeal, the court affirmed, stating that funding for placements of children with Teen Ranch would violate the Public Act and the Establishment Clause.

Minister Threatened with Arrest for Preaching Loudly in Public

Deegan v. City of Ithaca, 444 F.3d 135 (2nd Cir. 2006)

The city of Ithaca, New York, warned a minister that he would be arrested if he persisted in preaching loudly in the public commons. The minister sued for First Amendment violations and the court ruled in favor of the city on summary judgment.

Davidson County Sued to Remove Religious Imagery from County Seal

Lambeth v. Board of Commissioners of Davidson County, North Carolina, 407 F.3d 266 (4th Cir. 2005)

A pair of attorneys filed suit claiming that a display of the National Motto on the Davidson County Governmental Center violated the Establishment Clause.

The Fourth Circuit held that the display did not violate the Establishment Clause under the *Lemon* test.

ACLU Sues to Remove Ten Commandments Display
ACLU Nebraska Foundation v. City of Plattsmouth, 419 F.3d 772 (8th Cir. 2005) (en banc)
The ACLU filed suit complaining that the city's Ten Commandments display violated the Establishment Clause. The display was donated to the city in 1965 by the Fraternal Order of the Eagles. The district court ordered the display removed, determining that it promoted religion. The Eighth Circuit reversed the district court in an en banc decision.

School Board Sued for Displaying Ten Commandments Monuments
Baker v. Adams County / Ohio Valley School Board, 86 Fed. Appx. 104 (6th Cir. 2004)
A school board erected Ten Commandments monuments bought by a county ministerial association, and a suit was filed, challenging the constitutionality of the monuments. The school board added other historical documents relating to the development of American law and government to the displays, but the lawsuit continued anyway. The court ordered that the monuments be removed.

Employee Fired from Hewlett-Packard for Having Scripture in His Cubicle
Peterson v. Hewlett-Packard Co., 358 F.3d 599 (9th Cir. 2004)
A 21-year HP employee was fired for refusing to remove scriptures from his office cubicle opposing homosexuality that he posted in response to a company poster hung in the office that depicted a homosexual employee and sought to encourage tolerance.

Chester County Sued to Remove Ten Commandments Display
Freethought Society v. Chester County, 334 F.3d 247 (3rd Cir. 2003)
A lawsuit was filed to challenge the Ten Commandments display on the county courthouse facade, but the court allowed the display to remain.

Preacher Prohibited from Speaking on Public Sidewalks Without a Permit
Sewell v. City of Jacksonville, 69 Fed. Appx. 989 (11th Cir. 2003)
Reverend Wesley Sewell stood at the local post office on a public sidewalk to share his Christian faith with those who passed by. He used limited amplification: a single ten-inch speaker. He was told he could not use his speaker and that he would have to get a permit to share his faith on the public sidewalk. Police directed Sewell to the director of Parks and Recreation, who

told him that no written application or guidelines existed for issuing a permit. Nonetheless, the director said Sewell could only preach in one location with the volume set so low that only people who approached him could hear his message. A lawsuit was filed to protect Rev. Sewell's right to share his beliefs without excessive restriction.

Chief Justice of the Alabama Supreme Court Sued for Displaying Ten Commandments
Grassroth v. Moore, 335 F.3d 1282 (11th Cir. 2003)
Alabama Supreme Court Chief Justice Roy S. Moore installed a Ten Commandments monument in the state's judicial building. A lawsuit was filed to challenge the display and the monument was forcibly removed.

Richmost County Sued to Remove Ten Commandments from County Seal
King v. Richmond County, 331 F.3d 1271 (11th Cir. 2003)
A small group of citizens filed suit and claimed that the 130-year-old seal of the Superior Court of Richmond County violated the Establishment Clause and was unconstitutional because the image included a portrayal of the Ten Commandments tablets. The Eleventh Circuit held that the display of the seal did not violate the Establishment Clause under the *Lemon* test.

Kentucky Biblical Heritage Display Attacked as Unconstitutional
Adland v. Russ, 307 F.3d 471 (6th Cir. 2002)
The governor of Kentucky signed a resolution that permitted public school teachers to display the Ten Commandments in their classroom. He also authorized the display of the Ten Commandments monument on Capitol grounds as part of a display that would showcase Kentucky's Biblical historical heritage. Citizens protested the proposed display and filed a lawsuit to challenge the resolution, and the court determined that the proposal was unconstitutional.

Mt. Soledad Veterans Memorial Ordered Torn Down
Paulson v. City of San Diego, 294 F.3d 1124 (9th Cir. 2002)
A citizen challenged the constitutionality of a memorial in Mount Soledad Natural Park, which is owned by the City of San Diego. The court found that the city violated the California Constitution by keeping the cross-shaped memorial and forbade the city from maintaining the cross. A stay of the dismantling of the cross was won at the U.S. Supreme Court.

Religious Group Demands Display of Their Monument with Ten Commandments Monument

Summum v. City of Ogden, 297 F.3d 995 (10th Cir. 2002)

The Summum Church asked the City of Ogden to replace a Ten Commandments display that the Fraternal Order of the Eagles had donated to the city with a monument to the Summum religion. The church filed a lawsuit. The Tenth Circuit held that the city discriminated against the church by displaying the Ten Commandments but refusing to display the church's monument and that the city's alleged concern for avoidance of an Establishment Clause violation did not justify rejection of the church's monument.

ACLU Attacks Christmas and Hanukkah Display in New Jersey

ACLU of New Jersey v. Township of Wall, 246 F.3d 258 (3d Cir. 2001)

The ACLU, along with some citizens, filed a lawsuit to challenge a holiday display consisting of a Nativity scene with traditional figures, a lighted tree, urns, candy cane banners, a menorah, and signs commenting on celebrating diversity and freedom. The Third Circuit held that the plaintiffs lacked standing because they failed to show a non-economic injury resulting from the display and that the plaintiffs failed to show that the city spent any money on the display. Vacated and remanded.

ACLU Attacks Ohio State Motto, "With God, All Things Are Possible"

ACLU of Ohio v. Capitol Square Review and Advisory Bd., 243 F.3d 289 (6th Cir. 2001) (en banc)

The ACLU filed a lawsuit challenging Ohio's motto, "With God, All Things Are Possible." On a rehearing en banc, the Sixth Circuit held that display of the motto did not violate the Establishment Clause.

Indiana ACLU Stops Indiana from Replacing Vandalized Ten Commandments Display

Indiana Civil Liberties Union v. O'Bannon, 259 F.3d 766 (7th Cir. 2001)

The Fraternal Order of the Eagles donated Ten Commandments plaques to communities across the U.S. in the 1950s, including one to the Indiana Statehouse in Indianapolis, which was destroyed in 1991 by a vandal. An Indiana State Representative planned a replacement monument consisting of the Ten Commandments, the Bill of Rights, and the Preamble to the Indiana Constitution, but a lawsuit was filed challenging the proposed monument on the grounds that it would establish religion. The Seventh Circuit held that setting up the monument would violate the Establishment clause.

Indiana Ten Commandments Display Attacked
Books v. City of Elkhart, Indiana, 235 F.3d 292 (7th Cir. 2001)
A lawsuit was filed in objection to a Ten Commandments display at the Elkhart's Municipal Building, claiming the display violated the Establishment Clause. The Seventh Circuit struck down the display.

ACLU Attacks Holiday Display Representing Several Holidays
ACLU of New Jersey v. Schundler, 168 F.3d 92 (3d Cir. 1999)
The ACLU filed suit to challenge a holiday display, which included a Nativity scene and a menorah, claiming the display violated the Establishment Clause. The Third Circuit (Alito, J.) held that the display did not violate the Establishment Clause because the city modified the display to include Kwanzaa symbols, a sled, Frosty the Snowman, and Santa Claus.

Lawsuit Challenges Closing Government Offices for Good Friday
Granzeier v. Middleton, 173 F.3d 568 (6th Cir. 1999)
County courthouses and administrative buildings were closed on Good Friday. Plaintiff sued, declaring such a practice unconstitutional. The Sixth Circuit Court of Appeals found that there was a valid secular purpose in closing on Good Friday and that there was no excessive entanglement of religion between church and state.

Indiana Good Friday Closing Upheld Against Challenge
Bridenbaugh v. O'Bannon, 185 F.3d 796 (7th Cir. 1999)
A citizen filed suit to challenge the Indiana policy of allowing state employees to observe Good Friday as a day off with pay, claiming that the policy established religion. The Seventh Circuit Court of Appeals held that this did not violate the Establishment clause.

ACLU Attacks Holiday Display Because It Contains a Nativity Scene
ACLU v. City of Florissant, 186 F.3d 1095 (8th Cir. 1999)
The ACLU filed suit to challenge a holiday display at the city Civic Center in Florissant, Missouri, on behalf of a resident who was offended by the inclusion of a Nativity scene in the holiday display. The Eighth Circuit held that the display did not violate the Establishment Clause.

Public School Sells Ad Space but Bans Ten Commandments in Ads
DiLoreto v. Downey Unified School Dist. Bd. of Education, 196 F.3d 958 (9th Cir. 1999)
A school's baseball booster club raised funds by selling ads on the baseball field fence for $400. Mr. DiLoreto, CEO of Yale Engineering, bought an ad

that he wanted to use to display the Ten Commandments, but the sign was rejected and Mr. DiLoreto's money was returned. A lawsuit was filed to protect Mr. DiLoreto from viewpoint discrimination. The Ninth Circuit held that the board's decision to reject the ad was a permissible content-based limitation and not viewpoint discrimination.

Lawsuit Challenges Statute of Aztec God as First Amendment Violation
Alvarado v. City of San Jose, 94 F.3d 1223 (9th Cir. 1996)
The City of San Jose installed and maintained a sculpture of Quetzalcoatl, an Aztec god, to commemorate the Mexican and Spanish contributions to the city's culture. When people began to bring flowers and burn incense at the sculpture, citizens filed a lawsuit claiming the sculpture violated the Establishment Clause, but the court upheld the sculpture.

Teacher Sues to Stop Good Friday Closure
Metzl v. Leininger, 57 F.3d 618 (7th Cir. 1995)
A teacher filed suit in objection to a policy that allowed teachers to take Good Friday off with pay, claiming the practice violated the Establishment Clause. The Seventh Circuit Court of Appeals held that state law requiring closures on Good Friday violated the Establishment clause.

Edmond City Seal Declared Unconstitutional for Having a Cross
Robinson v. City of Edmond, 68 F.3d 1226 (10th Cir. 1995)
Plaintiffs filed suit to challenge the use of a Latin or Christian cross on the Edmond city seal, which was adopted in 1965 by a competition through the city council and the local newspapers. The cross reflected the historical importance of the Catholic Church in the development of the Southwest, but the court held that the seal established religion and struck down the use of the cross.

ACLU Attacks Menorah Placed in Plaza for Hanukkah
Americans United for Separation of Church and State v. City of Grand Rapids, 980 F.2d 1538 (6th Cir. 1992)
Americans United for Separation of Church and State filed suit to prevent a menorah from being placed at Calder Plaza during the Hanukkah celebration, claiming the placement of the menorah established religion. The court agreed, determining that the city appeared to be endorsing religion because of the display. On a rehearing en banc, the Sixth Circuit held that the display did not violate the Establishment Clause.

Lawsuit Attacks Austin City Insignia for Including a Cross
Murray v. City of Austin, 947 F.2d 147 (5th Cir. 1991)
The Society of Separationists filed suit challenging Austin's city insignia because it included a cross, but the court upheld the city's insignia against the censorship attempt.

Illinois Cities Sued to Ban Use of Cross in City Seals
Harris v. City of Zion, 927 F.2d 1401 (7th Cir. 1991)
The Society of Separationists and some other plaintiffs challenged the use of religious symbols on city seals in Rolling Meadows and Zion, Illinois. The Rolling Meadows seal contained a Latin cross and was adopted in 1960. Zion's seal contained a Latin cross and a dove carrying a branch and was adopted in 1902. The court ordered the cities to stop using the long-standing seals, holding that the use of the religious symbols in the seals violates the Establishment Clause.

Annual Christmas Display Banned for Tell About Jesus
Doe v. Small, 934 F.2d 743 (7th Cir. 1991)
A city's annual yuletide display included sixteen large paintings showcasing events in the life of Jesus Christ. A lawsuit was filed to eradicate the religious expression from the public square and end the yuletide display. The court struck down the long-standing tradition of including the pictures, finding that such a display endorsed religion and violated the Establishment Clause.

Italian Cultural Festival Banned from Including Italian Mass
Doe v. Village of Crestwood, 917 F.2d 1476 (7th Cir. 1990)
A long-standing tradition of the Village of Crestwood's "A Touch of Italy" festival was to include an Italian mass, but a citizen filed suit challenging the mass tradition. The Northern District of Illinois granted an injunction preventing the mass. The Seventh Circuit affirmed.

Lawsuit Leads to Banning of Hanukkah Display
Kaplan v. City of Burlington, 891 F.2d 1024 (2d Cir. 1989)
A lawsuit challenged a city's menorah display during the month of December, and the court struck down the display of the menorah on the grounds that such religious expression violated the Establishment Clause.

ACLU Attacks Nativity Scene
ACLU v. City of Birmingham, 791 F.2d 1561 (6th Cir. 1986)
The ACLU filed suit to expel a Nativity scene from the annual holiday display

at city hall, claiming it violated the Establishment Clause. The Sixth Circuit held that the display violated the Establishment Clause.

Lawsuit Challenges Nativity Scene
Mather v. Village of Mundelein, 864 F.2d 1291 (7th Cir. 1989)
Rachel Mather challenged a holiday display in front of Village Hall in Mundelein, alleging that the display's inclusion of a Nativity scene gave her a sense of inferiority because she was Jewish. The Seventh Circuit held that the display did not violate the Establishment Clause.

Lawsuit Attacks School District for Allowing Religious Expression for Cultural Heritage
Florey v. Sioux Falls School District, 619 F.2d 1311 (8th Cir. 1980)
A lawsuit was brought, alleging that policy statement and rules adopted by the Siouz Falls School District regarding religious expression during holiday celebrations violated the Establishment Clause and the Free Exercise Clause of the First Amendment to the United States Constitution. The Eighth Circuit Court of Appeals held that the school district could adopt rules permitting the observance of holidays having both a religious and a secular basis. These rules permitted religious symbols, music, art, literature, and drama to be taught as part of the instruction in the cultural and religious heritage of the holidays.

ACLU Sues County over Courthouse Nativity Scene
Freedom From Religion Found. v. Franklin Cty., No. 1:14-cv-02047-TWP-DML (S.D. Ind. Sept. 23, 2015)
The American Civil Liberties Union of Indiana filed a lawsuit against Franklin County for allowing a Christian Nativity scene on its courthouse lawn. The lawsuit was dismissed as moot because the county passed an ordinance allowing residents to erect their own displays outside the courthouse, regardless of the displays' point of view.

Health Care Center Retaliates Against Nurse Who Asked for Religious Accommodation
EEOC v. N. Mem'l Health Care, No. 0:15-cv-03675 (D. Minn., filed Sept. 16, 2015)
North Memorial Health Care, based in Robbinsdale, Minnesota, withdrew a job offer to Emily Sure-Ondara after she requested an accommodation to allow her time for her religious practices. Although she told the hospital that she was willing to work without the accommodation if necessary, the center withdrew her job offer entirely. The Equal Employment Opportunity Commission commented that federal law protects the right of job applicants

to request a religious accommodation without fear that it will lead to retaliation.

Employee Fired After Posting Comment About Religious Beliefs
Banks v. Rapid Glob. Bus. Sols., Inc., No. 2:15-cv-12455-GAD-EAS (E.D. Mich., filed July 10, 2015)
After Ford Motor Company posted an article on its intranet about making the company more pro-LGBT, Thomas Banks posted a comment to the article respectfully disagreeing with the company's stance. He commented that he believed that an automotive manufacturer should not be endorsing or promoting immoral sexual conduct. He also voiced his concerns about the policy's effect on Christians in the workplace. In response to the comment, Banks was immediately terminated. He has since filed a lawsuit against Ford and Rapid Global Business Solutions to protect his civil rights.

County Clerk Sued to Compel Her to Violate Conscience
Cato v. Lang, No. 4:15-cv-00491-A (N.D. Tex., filed July 6, 2015)
Katie Lang, a county clerk in Hood County, Texas, was sued for not issuing a marriage license to same-sex couple James Cato and Jody Stapleton. Lang clarified that although she was unable to issue the license due to her faith-based beliefs, other employees in her office would issue marriage certificates. Although the plaintiffs received a marriage license from one of the other employees, they did not drop their lawsuit against Lang.

Police Force Muslim Woman to Remove Religious Headscarf
Aldhalimi v. City of Dearborn, No. 2:15-cv-12337-DPH-MJH (E.D. Mich., filed June 30, 2015)
Maha Aldhalimi, a devout Muslim, was arrested by a police officer for an unpaid parking ticket. When she was taken to the police headquarters in Dearborn, Michigan, she was forced to remove her headscarf for a booking photo even though she informed them that doing so in front of male, non-family members would be a serious violation of her sincerely held religious beliefs. Aldhalimi filed suit against the city for failing to provide any religious accommodations.

Florida Department of Corrections Denies Kosher Diet to Jewish Inmates
United States v. Florida Department of Corrections, No. 2012-cv-22958 (S.D. Fla., Apr. 30, 2015)
For years, the Florida Department of Corrections refused to provide kosher meals to Jewish inmates. The United States Department of Justice was forced to file a lawsuit against the Florida Department of Corrections under the

Religious Land Use and Institutionalized Persons Act to force the department of corrections to provide the kosher meals. A federal district court held that denying the kosher meals violated Jewish inmates' religious rights.

Firefighter Fired for Writing Book Advocating for Biblical Marriage

Cochran v. City of Atlanta, No. 1:15-cv-00477-LMM (N.D. Ga., filed Feb. 18, 2015) Atlanta Fire Chief Kelvin Cochran, a firefighter since 1981, was fired for publishing a men's devotional book for a Baptist church group. Through his book, he wanted to help Christian men who struggle with issues of sexuality. Cochran affirmed that love is the foundation of his Christian faith, and he is willing to die for anyone as a part of his job. Although an investigation concluded that he has never discriminated against anyone, Cochran was suspended and ordered to attend sensitivity training before being terminated.

American Humanist Association Sues Baxter County, Arkansas, Over Nativity Scene

American Humanist Association v. Baxter County, Arkansas, No. 3:14-cv-03126-TLB (W.D. Ark., filed Dec. 23, 2014)
Baxter County, Arkansas, has, for at least fifteen years, displayed a Nativity scene along with a series of secular Christmas displays such as a Santa Claus, reindeer, and a Christmas tree. The American Humanist Association filed a lawsuit to ban Baxter County from displaying the Nativity scene.

Doctor Wins Settlement Allowing Her to Choose Not to Participate in Abortions

Fernandes v. City of Philadelphia, No. 2:14-cv-05704 (E.D. Pa., filed Oct. 7, 2014)
Dr. Doris Fernandes, a Catholic physician working in Philadelphia's District Health Center, was fired for refusing to prescribe contraceptives or abortion-causing drugs. Patients seeking these drugs would be transferred to another physician at the clinic. In 2013, Dr. Fernandes was terminated after refusing to obey an order to begin prescribing contraceptives. Following a lawsuit, Dr. Fernandes received a settlement in which the city agreed to respect the deeply held religious beliefs of medical providers.

Dunkin' Donuts Settles Lawsuit After Discriminating Against Seventh-day Adventist

EEOC v. Citi Brands, LLC d/b/a Dunkin' Donuts Bakery, No. 1:14-CV-00236-MOC-DLH (W.D.N.C., filed Sept. 11, 2014)
After telling Darrell Littrell that he could begin work at a Dunkin' Donuts plant the next day, Littrell replied that working on that day would conflict with his beliefs about the Sabbath as a Seventh-day Adventist. The manager

immediately rescinded the employment offer. After Littrell filed suit for religious employment discrimination, the company offered to pay him $22,000 to settle the lawsuit out of court. The settlement also includes injunctive relief prohibiting the company from discriminating on the basis of religion in the future.

Austin Ordinance Requires Pregnancy Resource Centers to Post False and Misleading Information
Austin Lifecare v. City of Austin, No. 1:11-cv-00875-LY (W.D. Tex. June 23, 2014)
The City of Austin, Texas, passed an ordinance compelling Pregnancy Resource Centers to post a misleading sign on their doors stating whether they have a full-time medical director on-site, even if the center is not opened full-time, and whether they are licensed by the state, even though there is no license available for Pregnancy Resource Centers. A federal district judge held that the ordinance violated the constitution, and Austin was forced to pay almost $500,000 in attorneys fees.

Kentucky Prison Forces Jewish Inmates to Shave Heads in Violation of Religious Beliefs
Price v. White, No. 5:13-cv-00076, 2014 U.S. Dist. LEXIS 70133 (W.D. Ky. May 22, 2014)
A Jewish inmate of the Kentucky State Penitentiary was forced to shave his head on a weekly basis, in violation of his religious beliefs. The case was dismissed because the inmate was transferred to a different facility.

Humanist Group Sues to Stop Prayers at County Commissioners' Meetings
Hake v. Carroll County, Md., No. 13-1312, 2014 WL 2047448 (D. Md. May 15, 2014)
http://christiannews.net/2014/04/12/maryland-county-commissioners-agree-to-obey-court-order-to-halt-prayers-in-jesus-name/
The American Humanist Association (AHA) brought a lawsuit against the Carrolton County Commissioners in Maryland in an attempt to quell the commissioners' prayers prior to meetings. A federal district court ordered an injunction barring them from using specific language, but the commissioners chose to follow their religious beliefs rather than follow the decree. The AHA consequently filed a motion for contempt of court, but the injunction and the motion were dismissed upon the Supreme Court's decision in *Town of Greece, New York v. Galloway.*

Muslim Inmate's Religious Books Confiscated
Payne v. Duncan, No. 3:13-cv-2203, 2014 WL 1653136 (M.D. Pa. Apr. 24, 2014)
Joshua Payne, an inmate at the Pennsylvania Department of Corrections

(PDC), had several books that he used to help him study Islam. When PDC authorities confiscated and discarded his books after a cell search, Payne brought a lawsuit. A Pennsylvania district court dismissed Payne's claim because he failed to allege "that he was actually prevented from exercising any religious right."

Prison Allows Religious Meetings Except for Jewish Inmate
George v. County of Westchester, NY, No. 13-cv-4511, 2014 WL 1508612 (S.D.N.Y. Apr. 10, 2014)
Prison authorities denied access to congregational religious services to a Jewish inmate even though other religions were allowed to meet regularly. This lawsuit is ongoing.

Prison Limits Inmate Access to Religious Books
Ind v. Colorado Dep't of Corr., No. 09-cv-0537, 2014 WL 1312457 (D. Colo. Mar. 31, 2014)
Jacob Ind, an inmate at the Colorado Department of Corrections (CDOC), used numerous books to study the Bible and his religious faith after his conversion to Christian Separatism while in prison. However, prison authorities passed a rule that inmates could only have two books during administrative segregation. Ind sued for the burden that CDOC put on the free exercise of his religious practices, and a Colorado federal district court found in Ind's favor.

Muslim Bus Driver Fired for Refusing to Attach Logos to Religious Headscarf
Lewis v. New York City Transit Auth., No. 04-cv-2331, 2014 WL 1343248 (E.D.N.Y. Mar. 31, 2014)
Stephanie Lewis, a practicing Muslim, was employed by the City of New York as a bus driver. However, she was transferred to a bus depot and ultimately terminated after she refused to attach company logos to her khimar (a long headscarf required by her religion). Lewis then brought a lawsuit against the city for their failure to adequately accommodate her religion. This case is ongoing.

Lawsuit Challenges County Commissioners' Prayers Referencing Jesus
Hake v. Carroll County, 2014 U.S. Dist. LEXIS 40476 (D. Md. Mar. 25, 2014)
http://americanhumanist.org/system/storage/2/35/9/5068/Carroll_County_PI_Order.pdf
http://americanhumanist.org/news/details/2014-06-american-humanist-association-files-summary-judgment
A federal district court in Maryland granted a preliminary injunction barring

Carroll County Commissioners from offering "sectarian" prayers at council meetings. The Board of Commissioners previously agreed to not say the words "Jesus," "Jesus Christ," "Savior," "Prince of Peace," or "Lamb of God." The plaintiff in the case argued that the prayers offered at meetings required him to act in violation of his religious rights. The court decided that the commissioners could offer nonsectarian prayers that do not invoke a particular deity associated with a specific faith or belief. American Humanist Association is currently seeking a permanent injunction on prayers at city council meetings.

Muslim County Employee Subjected to Years of Harassment Before Being Fired
Aboubaker v. Washtenaw, No. 2:11-cv-13001 (E.D. Mich. Feb. 27, 2014)
Ali Aboubaker, a Muslim, worked as a maintenance engineer for Washtenaw County, Michigan, for seventeen years before being fired because of his race and religion. During those seventeen years, Aboubaker was harassed by his employer because of his beard, which is required by his religious beliefs, and his head covering and called a "terrorist." A jury awarded Aboubaker $1.2 million because of the discrimination that he endured. The county is appealing.

NYPD Sued for Maintaining Surveillance on Persons Because of Their Religion
Hassan v. City of New York, No. 2:12-cv-03401 (D.N.J. Feb. 20, 2014)
A group of New Jersey Muslims filed a lawsuit against the New York Police Department (NYPD) for being subject to surveillance based solely on their religion. The NYPD used video surveillance, photographs, and a human mapping system to track the daily lives of Muslim residents. The NYPD continued to track every aspect of the plaintiffs' lives even after they found no leads to terrorism. A federal district court dismissed the lawsuit.

Muslim Inmate Sues Prison for Banning Him from Prayer Services
Dixie v. Virga, No. 2:12-cv-2626, 2014 U.S. Dist. LEXIS 5892 (E.D. Cal. Jan. 16, 2014)
Because prison officials believed that an altercation had taken place at a prayer service, James Dixie, a practicing Muslim, was not allowed to continue attending Jumu'ah prayer services with the general population of the prison. Dixie filed a lawsuit against the prison, arguing that keeping him from Jumu'ah prayer services substantially burdens his religious beliefs. A California federal

magistrate recommended permitting Dixie to proceed in his claims, and this case is pending.

Muslim Inmate Subjected to Public Strip Searches in Violation of His Religious Beliefs

Strickland v. Van Lanen, No. 13-cv-1127, 2014 U.S. Dist. LEXIS 873 (E.D. Wis. Jan. 3, 2014)

Melvin Strickland, a Wisconsin state prisoner, alleges that the practice of strip searches in locations without privacy violated his sincerely held religious beliefs as a Muslim. When he requested appropriate accommodation, asking only to be searched in privacy, prison officials told him to "man up." A Wisconsin federal district court has approved the proceeding of his complaint, and a case is pending.

Muslim Inmate Denied Halal or Kosher Meals

Strickland v. Texas Dept. of Criminal Justice, No. 3:10-cv-411 (S.D. Tex. Dec. 23, 2013)

A Muslim inmate brought a discrimination lawsuit against prison officials when they denied his request for halal meals or the kosher diet that was provided to Jewish inmates. This case is ongoing.

Muslim Inmates Prohibited from Growing Even Short Beards to Satisfy Their Religious Beliefs

Strong v. Livingston, No. 2:12-cv-106, 2013 WL 6817095 (S.D. Tex. Dec. 20, 2013)
Hickman-Bey v. Livingston, No. 2:13-cv-266, 2013 WL 6890767 (S.D. Tex. Dec. 31, 2013)

Prison authorities refused to allow Muslim inmates to grow one-quarter inch beards in order to conform to their religious mandates. The inmates brought lawsuits for the prison's failure to accommodate their religious needs, and a federal court issued a preliminary injunction allowing the inmates' beards.

Muslim Inmate's Library Time Conflicts with Religious Observance

Simmons v. Adamy, No. 08-cv-6147, 2013 WL 6622907 (W.D.N.Y. Dec. 17, 2013)

Alphonso Simmons, a Muslim prison inmate, requested certain times to access the jail library. When the prison authorities scheduled his access times to conflict with his observance of Ramadan, Simmons brought a claim for burdening his practice of his religion. A New York federal district court ruled in favor of the prison.

Federal Government Sues Florida for Florida's Refusal to Grant Kosher Diet for Inmates

United States v. Sec'y, Florida Dept. of Corr., No. 12-22958, 2013 WL 6697786 (S.D. Fla. Dec. 6, 2013)

The U.S. Department of Justice brought a lawsuit against the State of Florida for its blanket denial of kosher foods to prisoners. A federal district court granted a preliminary injunction that ordered the Florida Department of Corrections to provide a kosher diet for all prisoners with sincerely held religious beliefs that require such a diet.

Lawsuit Challenges Strip Searches of Muslim Inmates Attending Religious Meetings

Warrior v. Gonzalez, No. 08-00677, 2013 WL 6174788 (E.D. Cal. Nov. 20, 2013)

An inmate brought a claim against prison authorities for their policy of strip-searching Muslim inmates attending religious meetings during Ramadan. The strip searches included invasive body cavity examinations and were not imposed on any other religious groups. This case is ongoing.

Jewish Police Officer Fired for Violating No-Beards Policy

Litzman v. New York City Police Dept., No. 12-4681, 2013 WL 6049066 (S.D.N.Y. Nov. 15, 2013)

Fishel Litzman, a member of the Chabad Lubavitch Orthodox Jewish movement, was hired as a probationary police officer by the NYPD. Although the Department had an existing religious exemption to its general no-beard policy that beards not exceed one millimeter in length, Litzman filed a request for a further exemption due to his religious requirement of a longer beard. Litzman's request was denied, but he nonetheless continued to wear his beard. As a result, the NYPD fired him. Litzman fought back, and a New York federal district court held that the NYPD violated Litzman's First Amendment free exercise rights. Litzman is now seeking reinstatement.

State Law Bars Children from Seeking Professional Help in Overcoming Unwanted Same-Sex Attraction

King v. Christie, 86 Fed. R. Serv. 3d 1581 (D.N.J. Nov. 8, 2013)

New Jersey Governor Chris Christie signed legislation barring licensed therapists in New Jersey from assisting children in overcoming unwanted same-sex attractions. A lawsuit was filed on behalf of several licensed counselors who provide the now illegal counseling and their clients arguing that the ban violates the religious liberty rights of both the counselors and the clients. A federal district court dismissed the lawsuit.

Christian Employee of the City of Portland Subjected to Extreme Hostility and Harassment

Griffin v. City of Portland, No. 3:12-cv-01591, 2013 WL 5785173 (D. Or. Oct. 25, 2013)

Theresa Lereau, an employee of the City of Portland, severely harassed her coworker, KellyMarie Griffin, about her Christian beliefs with condemnations such as, "I'm sick of your Christian attitude, your Christian [expletive] all over your desk, and your Christian [expletive] all over the place." Griffin brought a lawsuit to stop the persecution, and a federal district court awarded damages and attorneys fees to Griffin due to the extreme hostility towards her religion in her work environment.

Lawsuit Dismissed Challenging Obamacare as Interfering with Parental Rights

Wieland v. U.S. Dept. of Health & Human Services, No. 4:13-cv-1577, 2013 WL 5651391 (E.D. Mo. Oct. 16, 2013)

A federal district court in Missouri held that a state employee and his wife lacked standing to bring a lawsuit alleging that the Patient Protection and Affordable Care Act (Obamacare) unconstitutionally violates their religious beliefs as well as interferes with their parental rights and family integrity due to the fact that it would provide abortifacients to their daughters.

Muslim Employees of JBS Stopped from Using Informal Breaks for Prayer

E.E.O.C. v. JBS USA, LLC, No. 8:10-cv-318, 2013 WL 6621026 (D. Neb. Oct. 11, 2013)

JBS, a meat processing plant with a location in Grand Island, Nebraska, refused to allow its Muslim employees to use their informal breaks for prayer. Instead, JBS insisted that the employees wait until regularly scheduled break times (such as lunch) to conduct their mandatory prayers. The EEOC brought a lawsuit against JBS for its failure to make a religious accommodation for the Muslim employees, but a Nebraska federal district court ruled in favor of the plant.

Prison Denies Muslim Inmate Religious Diet or Shaving Waiver

Nance v. Miser, No. 12-cv-0734, 2013 WL 5530821 (D. Ariz. Oct. 7, 2013)

Prison authorities denied a Muslim inmate's request for a halal diet and a shaving waiver pursuant to the requirements of his religion, even though such requests were granted to adherents of other faiths.

Inmate and Leader of Protestant Prison Group Attacked for Complaint Against Guards

Uduko v. Cozzens, No. 11-13765, 2013 WL 5435207 (E.D. Mich. Sept. 27, 2013)

Okechukwu Udoko, a prisoner in the custody of the Federal Bureau of Prisons and the leader of a prison Protestant faith group, was removed from his leadership position and subjected to false accusations in retaliation for lodging a complaint against prison guards. This case is pending.

Prison Refuses to Provide Jewish Inmate's Saturday Meal on Friday to Keep the Sabbath

Johns v. Lemmon, No. 3:12-cv-232JVB, 2013 WL 5436935 (N.D. Ind. Sept. 27, 2013)

Charles Johns, an observant Jew incarcerated under the Indiana Department of Corrections, requested that his Saturday meals be delivered on Friday so that he could correctly adhere to the mandates of his Sabbath, which is from sundown on Friday until sundown on Saturday. However, the prison authorities refused to accommodate his request, even though other prisoners were allowed to keep precooked food in their cells for consumption at a later time. Johns filed a lawsuit to enjoin the discriminatory treatment, and an Indiana federal district court ordered the prison to accommodate Johns's religious request.

Non-Muslim Inmates Permitted Worship Time While Muslim Inmate Was Refused

Allen v. Mikarimi, 2013 U.S. Dist. LEXIS 126996 (N.D. Cal. Sept. 5, 2013)

A Muslim inmate of San Francisco County Jail was not permitted to have group worship even though non-Muslim inmates were allowed to do so. This case is pending.

Muslim Employee Fired for Refusing to Remove Headscarf

U.S. Equal Employment Opportunity Comm'n v. Abercrombie & Fitch Stores, Inc., No. 11-cv-03162, 2013 WL 4726137 (N.D. Cal. Sept. 3, 2013)

Umme Hani-Kahn, a practicing Muslim, was hired by Abercrombie & Fitch to work as a stockroom employee in San Mateo, California. Although Kahn wore a religious headscarf called a hijab that is not sold by Abercrombie as part of her religious practice, local supervisors agreed to make an exception to its "look policy" by allowing her to continue to wear a hijab so long as it matched company colors. However, several months after she was hired, a district manager informed Kahn that the mere wearing of her hijab was contrary to the "look policy." When Kahn refused to remove her hijab, she was fired. Consequently, Kahn filed a lawsuit, and a California federal district court ruled in Kahn's favor. Abercrombie agreed to revise its "look policy" and pay Kahn $48,000 in damages.

Prison Cancels Muslim Inmate's Religious Diet During Ramadan
Grigsby v. Gaetz, No. 13-579, 2013 WL 4516408 (S.D. Ill. Aug. 26, 2013)
A Muslim inmate's Ramadan diet was cancelled twenty-two days into Ramadan, and prison guards refused to reinstate the inmate's name onto the list of prisoners eligible for the special diet. This case is pending.

Dollar General Fires Seventh-day Adventist Employee for Keeping Sabbath
Webster v. Dolgencorp, LLC, No. 13-0690, 2013 WL 4501461 (D.N.J. Aug. 22, 2013)
Dollar General in Sicklerville, New Jersey, hired Matthew Webster, a practicing Seventh-day Adventist, and agreed to give Webster a religious accommodation that exempted him from working on his Sabbath, which is from sundown on Friday until sundown on Saturday. Dollar General began to schedule Webster for Saturdays, however, and terminated Webster after he continued to exercise his religious faith by honoring his Sabbath. This case is pending.

Messianic Jewish Inmate Denied Kosher Meals
White v. Linderman, No. 11-8152, 2013 WL 4496364 (D. Ariz. Aug. 22, 2013)
Prison authorities refused to accommodate a Messianic Jewish inmate with a kosher diet unless the inmate adequately proved the religious requirements of the faith with outside documentation. This case is currently pending.

ACLU Stops Indiana Art Project Featuring Crosses Decorated by Children
Cabral v. City of Evansville, 958 F. Supp. 2d 1018 (S.D. Ind. July 31, 2013)
The ACLU of Indiana sued the city of Evansville, Indiana, for approving the display of up to thirty-one crosses along a section of the city's riverfront. The city regularly allowed the display of other artwork and sculptures. The exhibition, entitled "Cross the River," would have been decorated by children attending local Vacation Bible School summer camps. A federal district judge held that such a display violated the Establishment Clause.

ACLU Attacks Prayers Before Rowan County Board of Commissioners' Meetings
Lund v. Rowan County, North Carolina, No. 1:13-cv-207 (M.D.N.C. July 23, 2013)
Rowan County Board of Commissioners has operated for over forty years under a policy permitting each board member (on a rotating basis) an opportunity to open the board's meeting with prayer. The ACLU filed a

lawsuit against the county seeking to eliminate this practice because its representatives have largely been Christian, and thus most of the prayers offered have been Christian. A federal district court granted a preliminary injunction stopping the Rowan County Board of Commissioners from opening with "sectarian" prayers.

Hebrew-Israelite Inmate Denied Kosher Diet
Thompson-Jones v. Gossage, 2013 U.S. Dist. LEXIS 100513 (E.D. Wis. July 18, 2013)
Authorities at the Brown County Jail refuse to accommodate a Hebrew-Israelite jail inmate with a kosher diet unless the inmate adequately proves his practice of the faith. This case is currently pending.

Inmates Sue Jail for Confiscating Religious Books
Handzlik v. Lain, 2013 U.S. Dist. LEXIS 96767 (N.D. Ind. July 11, 2013) and *Bray v. Lain,* 2013 U.S. Dist. LEXIS 97269 (N.D. Ind. July 12, 2013)
Inmates at Porter County Jail were allowed to file lawsuits against jail staff alleging, among other complaints, that the staff, without reason, intercepted and confiscated books sent to inmates that were needed to practice their religion. These cases are pending.

Messianic Jewish Inmates Denied Worship Time or Kosher Diet
Alldred v. Keller, 2013 U.S. Dist. LEXIS 97045 (E.D.N.C. July 11, 2013)
Jail authorities refused to allow two Messianic Jewish inmates to worship on their Sabbath and other holy days and refused to provide them kosher meals. This case is pending.

Catholic Inmate Threatened for Writing to Catholic Bishop
Quintero v. Palmer, 2013 U.S. Dist. LEXIS 92831 (D. Nev. July 1, 2013)
Jail authorities disallowed a Catholic inmate from conducting group rosary services. The inmate was additionally threatened with disciplinary action if he continued to write to the local catholic bishop, and the jail mail room rejected his subscription to Catholic reading materials. This case is pending.

New Jersey Car Dealership Refuses to Hire Sikh Unless He Shaves His Beard
E.E.O.C. v. United Galaxy, Inc., No. 10-4987, 2013 WL 3223626 (D.N.J. June 25, 2013)
Gurpreet Kherna, a practicing Sikh, applied for a position as a sales associate with United Galaxy, Inc., a car dealership in Little Falls, New Jersey. Although Kherna was qualified for the position, the dealership informed him that the

job was contingent on the shaving of his beard—an action prohibited by his religion. Kherna chose to honor his faith, and the dealership refused to hire him. The EEOC filed a lawsuit on Kherna's behalf, and the court issued a consent decree giving Kherna $50,000 in addition to other significant relief.

Chevrolet Dealership Challenges Obamacare's Abortifacient Coverage Mandate

Holland v. U.S. Dep't. of Health and Human Svcs., No. 2:13-15487 (S.D.W.V. filed Jun. 24, 2013)

Joe Holland Chevrolet is a family-owned Chevrolet dealership whose stated purpose is "to glorify and honor God by being faithful stewards for all that is entrusted to us." Because of the Holland family's strong religious beliefs regarding abortion, Joe Holland Chevrolet does not want to fund abortifacient drugs like Plan B (the "day-after pill") and Ella (the "week-after pill") as required by Obamacare's HHS Mandate. Liberty Institute is working with Joe Holland Chevrolet to fight the government's requirements that the Holland family's company fund these abortion-inducing drugs.

Lawsuit Seeks to End Prayers at Commissioners Meetings

Hake v. Carroll County, Maryland, No. 1:13-cv-1312 (D. Md. filed May 1, 2013)

The Carroll County Board of Commissioners opens its meetings with prayer. Two county residents sued to end the prayers. When asked, one of the residents argued that the "prayers violate his own right to religious liberties, which is assured in the Free Exercise Clause." The lawsuit is pending in federal district court.

Abercrombie & Fitch Discriminates in Hiring of Muslim Employees

E.E.O.C. v. Abercrombie & Fitch Stores, Inc., 2013 U.S. Dist. LEXIS 51905 (N.D. Cal. Apr. 9, 2013).

The EEOC sued Abercrombie & Fitch for refusing to hire a stockroom employee applicant because of her religious conviction to wear an Islamic head scarf. Although she received a passing score in the interview, she was not hired because Abercrombie determined her head scarf would be inconsistent with its "look policy"—despite the fact that it has made over seventy exceptions to its "look policy" since 2006, including headwear exceptions. The court found in favor of the applicant and awarded her $23,000 in damages.

Muslim Employee of New York City Transit Authority Alleges Discriminatory Treatment
Ahmed v. New York City Transit Authority, No. 1:13-cv-1777 (E.D.N.Y. filed Apr. 3, 2013)
A Muslim employee filed a federal lawsuit against the New York City Transit Authority (NYTA), where he worked as a bus cleaner. The man alleges the NYTA unreasonably refused to accommodate his religious observance of Friday Jumu'ah services and acquiesced to anti-Muslim harassment.

Religious Liberties Group Sues for Right to Meet in Plainfield Village Hall
Liberty Counsel, Inc. v. Village of Plainfield, Illinois, No. 1:12-9485 (N.D. Ill., filed Nov. 28, 2012)
The Plainfield Village Hall is a public forum for community meetings in Plainfield, Illinois, that is open to educational, cultural, and civic groups so long as the meeting has no religious content. Liberty Counsel wanted to reserve a community room to teach about American history from a Christian perspective. The administrator of the Plainfield Village Hall told Liberty Counsel that their request would be rejected because it was "from a Christian perspective." Liberty Counsel filed a lawsuit against the village challenging the village's discrimination against religious use. Plainfield settled with Liberty Counsel and changing its policies to clarify that the "Village does not prohibit an applicant from presenting civic, cultural, educational or informational programs from a religious viewpoint."

Member of East African Hebrew Religion Sues for Right to Wear Religious Headdress
Daniels v. City of N. Charleston, No. 2:12-319, 2012 U.S. Dist. LEXIS 126767 (D.S.C. Aug. 9, 2012)
A municipal court in North Charleston, South Carolina, refused to allow Daniels, a member of the East African Hebrew religion, to wear a religious headdress into its courtroom. Daniels sued the city for violating his rights under the U.S. Constitution and South Carolina's Religious Freedom Restoration Act.

FFRF Sues City for Refusal to Place Atheist Sign Next to Nativity Scene
Freedom From Religion Found., Inc. v. City of Warren, Mich., WL 1964113 (E.D. Mich. May 31, 2012)
The Freedom From Religion Foundation filed suit claiming the city of Warren, Michigan, denied a resident's free speech rights when it refused his request to place a sandwich board sign containing atheistic statements like, "There

are no gods, no devils, no angels ... Religion is but myth and superstition" next to a Nativity scene. The court upheld the city's decision to not allow the atheist to display his sign.

Atheist Group Attacks Florida Ten Commandments Monument
American Atheists, Inc. v. Bradford County, Florida, No. 3:2012-cv-00618 (M.D. Fla., filed May 25, 2012)
American Atheists, Inc. claimed Bradford County, Florida, violated the Establishment Clause by placing a five-foot-tall stone Ten Commandments monument in the courtyard of the courthouse. Following a mediation, the monument was allowed to remain, but the atheist group was permitted to place a monument to atheism several feet away from the Ten Commandments.

Lawsuit Attacks Use of the Lord's Prayer Before Sussex County Council Meetings
Mullin v. Sussex County, 2012 WL 1753662 (D. Del. May 15, 2012)
The Delaware Federal District Court granted a preliminary injunction against the Sussex County Council from opening their meetings with the Lord's Prayer on the grounds that the practice violated the Establishment Clause. However, the court stayed the effectiveness of the injunction for thirty days to allow the parties to come up with a compromise that would allow the meeting to be opened with a prayer in a manner that did not violate the state or U.S. constitutions. The council voted to have a rotation of different prayers read before the meetings to comply with the Establishment Clause.

Pastors Required to Sign Away Constitutional Rights for Permit to Preach
Stand Up America Now v. City of Dearborn, 2012 WL 1145075 (E.D. Mich. April 5, 2012)
Pastors that work with Stand Up America Now applied for a permit to preach to Muslims in Dearborn, Michigan, but were told they must sign away their constitutional rights in order to get the permit. The court sided with the pastors and declared Dearborn's demands unconstitutional.

ACLU Attacks Privately Donated Ten Commandments Monument in New Mexico
Felix v. City of Bloomfield, New Mexico, No. 1:12-cv-00125 (D.N.M., filed Feb. 8, 2012)
In July of 2011, the City of Bloomfield, New Mexico, erected a privately donated Ten Commandments monument in front of their city hall. Less than a year later, the ACLU filed suit in the U.S. District Court of New Mexico to remove the monument.

Lawsuit Stops Virginia County Meetings from Opening with Prayer

Doe v. Pittsylvania County, Virginia, No. 4:11-43, 2012 WL 363978 (W.D. Va. Feb. 3, 2012)

A federal district court in Virginia held that the Pittsylvania County Board of Supervisors violated the First Amendment's Establishment Clause by opening its meetings with Christian prayer.

Christian College Forced to Sue to Avoid Being Forced to Cover Abortifacient Drugs

The Criswell College v. Sebelius, No. 3:12-4409 (N.D. Tex., filed Nov. 1, 2012)

The Criswell College is a nonprofit, Christian college that was going to be forced under Obamacare to indirectly provide for abortifacient drugs such as Plan B (the "day-after pill") and Ella (the "week-after pill"). Liberty Institute worked with The Criswell College to fight the government's requirements that The Criswell College provide these drugs against its religious convictions.

Preacher Forced to Sue to Preach at a Public Festival

Jankowski v. City of Duluth, 2011 WL 7656906 (D. Minn. Dec. 20, 2011)

A federal district court granted a preliminary injunction allowing a preacher to speak at the Bentleyville Tour of Lights festival in Duluth, Minnesota. The preacher sued the City of Duluth for stopping him from preaching at the public festival, claiming that the city's actions were in violation of the First Amendment.

Sixty-Three-Year-Old Nativity Scene Shut Down When Road Commission Refuses Permit

Satawa v. Board of County Road Commissioners of Macomb County, 788 F. Supp. 2d 579 (E.D. Mich. 2011)

A Michigan family erected a Nativity scene display for over 63 years at the median of a county road servicing over 82,000 cars per day. The Freedom From Religion Foundation wrote a complaint to the Road Commission in 2008 on behalf of an anonymous resident to have the display removed. Despite the structure's nine-and-a-half-foot height, bright lights at night, and other structures erected at the site by private organizations, the Road Commission claimed that it was unaware of the display until the complaint. The display was immediately removed for not having a permit, and subsequent applications for a permit were denied. The owners of the display offered to pay for insurance, display a sign clearly stating that it is a private display, and move the display twenty-five feet from the curb. The U.S. District Court for the Eastern District of Michigan held that the denial of the permit was justified by a compelling state interest in traffic safety.

ACLU Sues to Keep Ten Commandments Display Out of School
Doe v. School Board of Giles County, No. 11-435 (W.D. Va. Sept. 13, 2011)
The ACLU of Virginia, working with the Freedom From Religion Foundation, sued a school board because a school had a display of the Ten Commandments. The school board removed the display and replaced it with a page from a textbook that describes the Ten Commandments as the roots of democracy but does not list each commandment.

ACLU Attacks Ten Commandments Display in Dixie County, Florida
ACLU of Florida, Inc. v. Dixie County, 797 F. Supp. 2d 1280 (N.D. Fla. July 15, 2011)
Dixie County permitted a local company to erect a Ten Commandments monument near the county courthouse. The ACLU filed a lawsuit, seeking removal of the monument, damages, and attorney's fees. A federal district court ordered the city to remove the monument.

Police Arrest Proselytizers at a Catholic Festival
Teesdale v. City of Chicago, 792 F. Supp. 2d 978 (N.D. Ill. May 26, 2011)
Police arrested proselytizers at a Catholic festival for disturbing the peace. The U.S. District Court for the Northern District of Illinois held in favor of the proselytizers, allowing them to enter the public streets where the festival was being held, speak to people at the festival, hand out pamphlets, and carry signs within a certain size.

Muslim Taxi Driver Persecuted for Wearing Clothing Required by His Religious Beliefs
Naeem v. Metropolitan Taxicab Commission, No. 4:11-670 (E.D. Mo., filed Apr. 14, 2011)
The Metropolitan Taxicab Commission in St. Louis, Missouri, suspended Raja Awais Naeem's taxicab license because Mr. Naeem wore the attire required by his Muslim beliefs. Mr. Naeem was also ticketed at the St. Louis Airport for wearing his religious garb and threatened with arrest for being at the airport in religious clothing. Mr. Naeem filed a lawsuit alleging that these restrictions on his ability to peacefully wear religious clothing violate his religious liberty rights.

Transportation Authority Prohibits Ad Targeting Persons Leaving Islam

American Freedom Defense Initiative v. Suburban Mobility Authority, No. 10-12134, 2011 U.S. Dist. LEXIS 35083 (E.D. Mich. Mar. 31, 2011)

The Suburban Mobility Authority for Regional Transportation (SMART) prohibited the American Freedom Defense Initiative from running advertisements on SMART buses that stated, "Fatwa on your head? Is your family or community threatening you? Leaving Islam? Got questions? Get Answers!" A federal judge ruled that SMART violated the American Freedom Defense Initiative's First and Fourteenth Amendment rights.

Atheist Group Opposes 9/11 Cross Made from Steel Girders that Survived the Attack

American Atheists, Inc. v. Port Authority of New York and New Jersey, No. 1:11-06026 (S.D.N.Y. 2011)

Atheists sued to stop the erection of the World Trade Center cross. They claim the cross, made of two steel girders that survived the September 11th attack, has become a symbol of religion and thus needs to be removed because it now violates the Establishment Clause. A federal district court in New York dismissed the lawsuit, but the American Atheists are appealing.

Bus Driver Fired for Refusing to Drive Woman to Planned Parenthood

Graning v. Capital Area Rural Transportation System, No. 1:10-523 (W.D. Tex. 2010)

Pastor and bus driver Edwin Graning was fired for refusing to drive a woman to Planned Parenthood. According to federal law, employers must accommodate their employees' religious beliefs. Graning and the Capital Area Rural Transportation System settled, with Graning receiving $21,000.

Professor Denied Position Because He is a Christian

Gaskell v. University of Kentucky, No. 09-244 (E.D. Ky. 2010)

Professor Martin Gaskell applied for the position of Observatory Director at the University of Kentucky, but he was turned down after the hiring committee found out that he was a Christian. Professor Gaskell filed a lawsuit under Title VII alleging religious discrimination. The court found that there was clear evidence of religious discrimination. Gaskell agreed to a settlement of $125,000.

Two Employees Fired for Privately Praying After Work

Shatkin v. University of Texas at Arlington, 109 Fair Empl. Prac. Cas. (BNA) 1559 (N.D. Tex. July 9, 2010)

The University of Texas at Arlington (UTA) fired two women for privately praying for an absent coworker after work. The women sued UTA for violating their religious liberty. The case settled.

FFRF Sues Wisconsin County to Remove Nativity Scene from Courthouse

Freedom from Religion Foundation v. Manitowoc County, 708 F.Supp.2d 773 (E.D. Wis. April 22, 2010)

Freedom From Religion Foundation sued Manitowoc County, Wisconsin, in an attempt to remove a Nativity scene from the front of the courthouse. The county changed the policy about decorations to one in which anyone can put up decorations outside the courthouse. A federal district court found that under the new policy, the Nativity scene did not reflect a governmental endorsement of Christianity.

FFRF Sues to Stop Architect from Adding Pledge of Allegiance and National Motto to Capitol

Freedom From Religion Foundation, Inc. v. Ayers, 748 F.Supp.2d 982 (W.D. Wis. 2010)

The Freedom From Religion Foundation filed suit against Ayers, an architect hired by the Wisconsin capital to put the Pledge of Allegiance and the national motto, "In God We Trust," on the capitol building. The suit alleged that the Pledge and the motto violate the Establishment Clause. The district court found that there was no violation of the Establishment Clause and that the Freedom From Religion Foundation did not have taxpayer standing to bring the suit.

Lawsuit Seeks to Stop Voluntary Recitation of Pledge of Allegiance

Freedom From Religion Foundation v. Hanover School District, 665 F.Supp.2d 58 (D.N.H. Sept. 30, 2009)

Jan and Pat Doe, parents of three children in the Hanover and Dresden school districts, filed a suit to combat the New Hampshire School Patriot Act, which required all school districts to authorize a time for a voluntary recitation of the Pledge of Allegiance. The Does contended that the recitation violated their parental rights, their children's rights, the Free Exercise Clause and the Equal Protection Clause. On September 30, 2009, the court found that the statute was constitutional, did not violate the students' or parents' right under the Free Exercise Clause, and that the act did not violate the student's right under the Equal Protection Clause.

Houston City Council Member Sued for Praying the Lord's Prayer

Staley v. Houston, No. 4:09-3394 (S.D. Tex. 2009)

Houston City Council member Anne Clutterbuck was sued for praying the

Lord's Prayer at the beginning of a council meeting. Ms. Clutterbuck had chosen the Lord's Prayer because she believed it to be inoffensive to persons with various religious views. The court dismissed the case after a motion for summary judgment.

Two Gideons Arrested for Distributing Bibles on a Public Sidewalk
Gray v. Kohl, 568 F. Supp. 2d 1378 (S.D. Fla. June 18, 2008)
Two members of the Gideons' Key Largo Camp were arrested for distributing Bibles on a public sidewalk.

Evangelist Arrested for Speaking About His Faith in Public
Schaffer v. City of Jacksonville, No. 3:07-00053 (M.D. Fla. 2007)
John Schaffer was standing on public property at the Jacksonville Landing shopping center speaking to others about his faith in Jesus Christ. Officers approached Schaffer as he was talking with a passerby and told him to either stop speaking or leave the premises. When Schaffer attempted to tell the officers that he had the constitutional right to speak in public just like any other citizen, he was arrested and jailed overnight.

Man Arrested and Held in Jail for Distributing Religious Tracts on a Public Sidewalk
Baumann v. City of Cumming, Georgia, No. 2:07-0095 (N.D. Ga. Nov. 2, 2007)
Baumann was arrested for distributing religious tracts on a public sidewalk outside the City of Cumming's fairgrounds. It was alleged he had violated a city ordinance requiring parade and demonstration organizers to obtain a permit before engaging in such activities. The permit requirement, however, only applied to private organizations or groups of more than three persons. Baumann's multiple requests to view a copy of the ordinance were denied. After serving two days in jail, he was convicted before a municipal court judge and sentenced to time already served. Baumann was not notified that he would stand trial that day nor was he given the opportunity to obtain legal counsel.

Department of the Interior Employee Harassed for Objecting to Gay Pride Observance
Gee v. Kempthorne, No. 03-432, 2007 U.S. Dist. Lexis 6695 (D. Idaho Jan. 30, 2007)
On June 3, 2000, Kenneth Gee received an email from his boss at the Department of the Interior regarding President Clinton's proclamation encouraging government employees to celebrate and "observe gay and lesbian pride" during the month of June. Mr. Gee responded, notifying his

boss of his sincere religious objection to receiving the emails. Mr. Gee's boss then asked him to retract and delete the email questioning the Department's policy of promoting and celebrating homosexuality. Mr. Gee obeyed the order and deleted the email. Four days later, however, Mr. Gee was formally chastised in a meeting with three supervisors. Mr. Gee's boss informed him that management would review all of his outgoing email and that random checks of his computer and email would be done to ensure his compliance with Department policies. Mr. Gee filed a suit to protect his rights. The court dismissed Mr. Gee's First Amendment and Religious Freedom Restoration Act claims as moot because the Department changed its email policy.

Resident Assistant Prohibited from Leading Dormitory Bible Study
Steiger v. Lord-Larson, No. 05-0700 (W.D. Wis. 2006)
Lance Steiger, a resident assistant at the University of Wisconsin, Eau Claire, was told he could not lead a Bible study in the basement of the dormitory where he was living. He was forced to file a federal lawsuit to protect his right to lead Bible studies in the dorm.

School District Bans Woman from Distributing Religious Literature on Public Sidewalk
Colston v. Crowley I.S.D., No. 4:06-00097 (N.D. Tex. 2006)
Mrs. Colston was banned from handing out religious literature on a public sidewalk in front of a public high school. The school district only allowed her to do so after she filed suit to protect her constitutional rights.

Lawsuit Required to Allow Nativity Scene Next to Menorah
Koenig v. City of Atlantic Beach, Florida, No. 3:05-1244 (M.D. Fla. 2005)
Town Center Park, operated jointly by the City of Atlantic Beach and the City of Neptune Beach, contained a 25-foot-tall Christmas tree and a large, privately provided, menorah. Koenig wanted to display a private Nativity scene in the park, but the request was denied because a Nativity scene is a "religious symbol." Following the filing of the lawsuit, the park permitted the Nativity scene to be displayed.

Lawsuit Challenges Ten Commandments Display in Maryland
Chambers v. City of Frederick, 373 F. Supp. 2d 567 (N.D. Md. 2005)
A Frederick resident objected to the Ten Commandments display in the city park that the Fraternal Order of the Eagles (Eagles) had donated in 1958. In response, the city sold that portion of the park to the Eagles, but a lawsuit was filed anyway. The district court held that the display did not violate the Establishment Clause.

Senior Citizens Banned from Praying or Singing Religious Songs at Senior Center

Barton v. City of Balch Springs, No. 3:03-2258 (N.D. Tex. 2004)

Senior citizens in Balch Springs, Texas, were told to stop praying before their meals, listening to inspirational religious messages, and singing gospel songs in their senior citizens' center because of a new city policy banning religion in public buildings. The citizens sued to defend their right to religious freedom. The Department of Justice also opened an investigation. The seniors were told that if they won their lawsuit, their meals would be taken away since praying over government-funded meals violates the "separation of church and state."

Lawsuit Challenges Ten Commandments Display in Habersham County, Georgia

Turner v. Habersham County, 290 F. Supp. 2d 1362 (N.D. Ga. Nov. 17, 2003)

Citizens challenged the display of the Ten Commandments at the Habersham County Courthouse. The court granted the injunction, ordering the removal of the display.

Lawsuit Challenges Virginia Pledge of Allegiance and National Motto at Public Schools

Myers v. Loudoun County School Bd., 251 F. Supp. 2d 1262 (E.D. Va. Feb. 21, 2003)

A lawsuit was filed challenging the constitutionality of two Virginia statutes, one that required students in public schools to say the Pledge of Allegiance and the other requiring the national motto to be posted at Virginia schools. The District Court held that the Pledge and the county's actions in allowing the Pledge to be said did not violate the Establishment Clause.

Lawsuit Stops Lease of Land to the Boy Scouts

Barnes-Wallace v. Boy Scouts of America, 275 F. Supp. 2d 1259 (S.D. Cal. 2003)

An agnostic family sued San Diego and the Boy Scouts because the city had leased some public parkland to the Boy Scouts. The family claimed the lease violated the Establishment Clause because the Boy Scouts do not allow agnostics to become members. A federal district court in California agreed with the family and held that the lease violated the Establishment Clause.

ACLU Sues to Remove Ten Commandments Display in Tennessee County Courthouse

ACLU of Tennessee v. Hamilton County, 202 F. Supp. 2d 757 (E.D. Tenn. May 3, 2002)

The ACLU filed suit, challenging the Ten Commandments displays in county courthouses. The court granted the injunction holding that it violated the Establishment Clause.

ACLU Sues to Remove Ten Commandments Display in Tennessee County Courthouse

ACLU of Tennessee v. Rutherford County, 209 F. Supp. 2d 799 (M.D. Tenn. 2002)
The ACLU sued Rutherford County to challenge the Ten Commandments display in the county courthouse lobby. The court ordered the display removed.

Indiana ACLU Attacks Proposed Ten Commandments Display

Kimbley v. Lawrence County, Indiana, 119 F. Supp. 2d 856 (S.D. Ind. 2000)
The Indiana Civil Liberties Union filed suit in response to a proposed Ten Commandments display, which had been authorized by state law, seeking to prevent the display. The court granted an injunction to prevent the display, holding that it violated the Establishment Clause.

Lawsuit Forces Public Schools to Remove Ten Commandments Displays

Doe v. Harlan County Sch. Dist., 96 F. Supp. 2d 667 (E.D. Ky. May 5, 2000)
A Harlan student's parents filed suit to challenge the public schools' practice of posting the Ten Commandments in classrooms. In response to the lawsuit, the school district added other historical documents to the displays, but the lawsuit continued. The Eastern District of Kentucky granted an injunction, holding it was a violation of the Establishment Clause.

ACLU Forces City to Remove Cross from City Seal

ACLU v. City of Stow, 29 F. Supp. 2d 845 (N.D. Ohio Dec. 16, 1998)
The ACLU challenged the placement of a cross on Stow's city seal, claiming that the use of such a symbol served as an establishment of religion. The ACLU prevailed in the lawsuit because the court found that a reasonable observer would perceive the cross on the seal as an establishment of religion with the effect of advancing or promoting Christianity. The city was forced to remove the cross.

Lawsuit Ends Sixty-Year-Old Christmas Tradition in Somerset, MA

Amancio v. Town of Somerset, 28 F. Supp. 2d 677 (D. Mass. Nov. 23, 1998)
A Somerset resident filed a lawsuit challenging Somerset's Christmas display, which included a Nativity scene, holiday lights, a wreath, a Christmas tree and a plastic Santa Claus. The display had been a Somerset tradition for sixty years. The court held that the display violated the Establishment Clause.

Lawsuit Forces City to Remove Cross from Water Tower
Mendelson v. City of St. Cloud, 719 F. Supp. 1065 (M.D. Fla. Aug. 23, 1989)
A citizen sued the city claiming an illuminated Latin cross on a city water tower violated the Establishment Clause. The court determined that the cross did violate the Establishment Clause and ordered the cross to be removed from the water tower.

ACLU Attacks Privately-Funded Nativity Scene in Kentucky Capitol Building
ACLU of Kentucky v. Wilkinson, 701 F. Supp. 1296 (E.D. Ky. 1988)
The ACLU filed suit to challenge a Nativity scene in the Kentucky Capitol, seeking an injunction preventing the continued use of the Nativity scene and claiming the Nativity scene was an endorsement of religion. The court denied the injunction on condition that the state put a disclaimer on the display stating that the state intended no endorsement of religion and that no state funds were expended for the display.

Lawsuit Attempts to Stop Texas Christmas Celebration
Soc'y of Separationists, Inc. v. Clements, 677 F. Supp. 509 (W.D. Tex. 1988)
The Society of Separationists filed a lawsuit challenging the "Christmas Carol Program." The program is an annual event in the Texas Capitol. When a Christmas tree is presented to Texas, politicians make speeches, the Texas Public Employees Association presents money to charity, Santa visits, singers perform Handel's Messiah, and two religious carols are performed. The Separationists asserted that the program violates the Establishment Clause and sought a preliminary injunction to prevent the program from occurring. The court held that the State's sponsoring of the event did not violate the Establishment Clause.

Lawsuit Attacks Christmas Display in Westland, Michigan
Doe v. City of Westland, No. 87-74468, 1987 U.S. Dist. LEXIS 15321 (E.D. Mich. Dec. 23, 1987)
Doe, supported by the ACLU, brought a lawsuit to challenge a Christmas display in the Westland central city complex because it included a Nativity scene.

Colorado Forces Bakeries to Make Pro-Same-Sex Marriage Cakes But Allows Bakeries to Opt Out of Making Anti-Same-Sex Marriage Cakes
Mullins v. Masterpiece Cakeshop, Inc., 2015 COA 115 (Colo. Ct. App. Aug. 13, 2015)
Jack Phillips of the Masterpiece Cakeshop in Denver, Colorado, was sued for refusing to participate in a same-sex wedding by crafting a wedding cake. The

owner of the bakery explained that he would be happy to make the couple any other baked item but that he could not promote a same-sex ceremony because of his faith. The couple filed a complaint with the Colorado Civil Rights Commission, which ruled against the bakery. By contrast, the same commission found that three bakeries were not guilty of discrimination when they refused to make a cake with an anti-same-sex marriage message.

Private Farm Sued for Not Hosting Same-Sex Wedding
Gifford v. McCarthy, No. 520410 (N.Y. App. Div. 3d Dep't June 25, 2015)
The owners of Liberty Ridge Farm in Schaghticoke, New York, were sued for politely declining to host a same-sex wedding, based on their religious beliefs, at the farm where they live. The owners offered to permit the couple to view the farm as a potential venue for the reception instead. The New York Division of Human Rights ordered the owners to pay a $10,000 fine and $3,000 in emotional damages to the couple.

St. Louis, Missouri, Prohibits Muslim Cab Drivers from Wearing Religious Attire
Naeem v. Metropolitan Taxicab Commission, No. 1322-CC09365 (Mo. Ckt. Ct., June 22, 2015)
The St. Louis, Missouri, Metropolitan Taxicab Commission (MTC) required all taxicab drivers in St. Louis to follow a dress code. Raja Naeem, a Muslim cab driver, was issued over $800 in citations and had his license revoked because he wore religious attire that the MTC determined was in violation of its dress code. Naeem filed a lawsuit against the MTC, and a judge held that the MTC's refusal to allow religious attire violated Naeem's constitutional rights.

Oklahoma Supreme Court Strikes Down Ten Commandments Monument
Prescott v. Okla. Capitol Pres. Comm'n, 2015 OK 54 (Okla. 2015)
The Oklahoma Supreme Court ruled that a privately-funded Ten Commandments Monument, located at the state's capitol, violated a provision of the state's constitution that restricts government funding to religious institutions. Attorney General Scott Pruitt, who defended the monument, commented that the court came to the wrong conclusion because it ignored the profound historical impact of the Ten Commandments on the foundation of Western Law. The monument had just been restored after being shattered by a citizen.

Ohio Judges Cannot Opt Out of Performing All Marriages Due to Religious Belief

http://www.supremecourt.ohio.gov/Boards/BOC/Advisory_Opinions/2015/Op_15-001.pdf

The Ohio Board of Professional Conduct issued an advisory opinion stating that state judges must marry any couple or opt out of performing all weddings. The opinion also states that judges may not decline to perform marriages in order to avoid marrying same-sex couples based on his or her personal, moral or religious beliefs. Critics of the opinion question why a judge may not opt out of performing marriages in an exercise of his or her religious beliefs in districts where there is no access problem for same-sex couples seeking marriage.

Pastor / Police Officer Fired for Visiting Parishioner in Jail

Fierro v. Park City Mun. Corp., 323 P.3d 601 (Utah Ct. App. 2014)

Michael Fierro was a police officer for Park City, Utah, but also served as a lay pastor for a local Mormon church. When a parishioner from Fierro's church was incarcerated, Fierro obtained special permissions from his superiors to arrange for a visit. However, the Park City Employee Transfer and Discharge Appeal Board decided that Fierro abused his police privileges in the visit and consequently fired him. Seeking to protect his job and his ecclesiastical privileges, Fierro filed a lawsuit. The Utah Court of Appeals found that Feirro fulfilled all the proper requirements in his visit and set aside his termination.

Woman Held for Psychiatric Treatment Because She Prayed and Read Her Bible in a Hospital

Doe v. St. Vincent Charity Medical Center (filed Mar. 10, 2014)

A Cleveland woman became disoriented in the fifteenth day of a water-only fast. After speaking with her mother, the woman went to St. Vincent Charity Medical Center where she was treated for water intoxication. At the hospital, the woman began to pray and read her Bible. A doctor in the hospital asserted that the woman's Bible reading and audible praying were evidence of mental illness. The hospital then kept the woman in the psychiatric ward for five days and attempted to get a court order having her involuntarily committed. The woman, who is a Pentecostal Christian, sued the hospital for false arrest and violation of patient's rights.

Christian Scientist Has Drivers License Revoked for Refusing Blood Test

State v. Milewski, 841 N.W.2d 581 (Wis. Ct. App. Nov. 27, 2013)

Victoria Milewski, a Christian Scientist, was pulled over and arrested under suspicion of driving under the influence of an intoxicant. When asked to submit to a chemical test of her blood, Milewski refused, informing the police that her religion did not permit the intrusion of a needle into her body. Consequently, Milewski was sent a notice of intent to revoke her driving privileges due to her refusal. Milewski filed a lawsuit claiming that her refusal was reasonable, but a Wisconsin state appeals court ruled against her, stating that she failed to actually argue a burden to her religion.

FFRF Sues to End Arizona Day of Prayer

Freedom From Religion Foundation v. Brewer, No. 1 CA–CV 12–0684, 2013 Ariz. App. Unpub. LEXIS 671 (Ariz. App. June 11, 2013)
The Freedom From Religion Foundation (FFRF) filed a lawsuit against the state of Arizona to end the Arizona Day of Prayer. After a U.S. District Court dismissed the suit because FFRF could not show injury, FFRF filed a complaint in a state court alleging violations of the state constitution. The Arizona State Court of Appeals dismissed the lawsuit because FFRF did not have standing to bring the suit.

Christian Photographer Fined for Refusing to Photograph Same-Sex Wedding

Elane Photography, LLC v. Willock, No. 33,687 (N.M. 2013)
A Christian photography company was sued after declining for religious reasons to take a job photographing a homosexual couple's commitment ceremony. The New Mexico Human Rights Commission ordered the photographer to pay over $6,600 in attorney's fees. The New Mexico Supreme Court affirmed, with one justice stating that the photographers "now are compelled by law to compromise the very religious beliefs that inspire their lives." The U.S. Supreme Court refused to hear the case.

Bed and Breakfast Ordered to Rent Rooms to Homosexual Couples

Cervelli v. Aloha Bed & Breakfast, No. 11-1-3103-12 (Haw. 1st Ckt. 2013)
Lambda Legal filed suit against Hawaii's Aloha Bed & Breakfast for refusing to rent a room to a lesbian couple. The Hawaii Civil Rights Commission also intervened in the case against the bed and breakfast. The court held that the bed and breakfast violated Hawaii's public accommodation laws and must rent rooms to homosexual couples.

FFRF Sues to Stop Colorado Governor's 2004 Day of Prayer Proclamation

Freedom From Religion Foundation, Inc. v. Hickenlooper, 2012 WL 1638718 (Co. App. May 10, 2012)
The Colorado Court of Appeals held that the governor's 2004 Day of Prayer

proclamation violated Colorado's constitution because it implied that those who pray enjoy a more favorable political status than those who do not.

Citizen Sues to End Prayers at Town Meetings in Franklin, Vermont
Hackett v. Town of Franklin, No. 77-11 (Ver. Super. Ct., filed May 29, 2012)
A citizen of Franklin, Vermont, regularly attended annual town meetings. The town included prayer in its meetings, often led by a local minister. The citizen sued the town, and the court enjoined the town from continuing such prayers, finding that by including the prayers, the town compelled the citizen to attend religious worship.

Hutterite Religious Community Forced to Provide Insurance to Workers
Big Sky Colony, Inc. v. Mont. Dep't of Lab. and Indus., 291 P.3d 1231 (Mont. 2012)
Labor unions and construction lobbyists in Montana complained that the Hutterites, a religious community, were receiving a "competitive advantage" because—based on 500-year-old religious practices—they did not provide compensation for their workers, including compensation insurance. The Hutterites already provide comprehensive care to all members of the community as part of their religious commitments. Nevertheless, the state responded to complaints by forcing the Hutterites to provide compensation insurance to their workers—an unnecessary and direct threat to the 500-year-old religious practice of holding property in common and not expecting compensation. Because Hutterite beliefs preclude them from participating in the political process, the state legislature never consulted the Hutterite community before passing the law. The Montana Supreme Court upheld the law, but the Hutterites are seeking review by the U.S. Supreme Court.

Commission Rules Bed-and-Breakfast Cannot Refuse to Host Same-Sex Civil Union
Wathen v. Beall Mansion Bed & Breakfast, No. 2011-SP-2486 (Ill. Human Rights Comm'n, Nov. 1, 2011)
Jim Walder, the owner of TimberCreek Bed-and-Breakfast, allowed same-sex couples to rent guest rooms but declined to host a same-sex civil union ceremony in 2011 due to his faith-based beliefs about marriage. He explained to the couple his religious belief against participating in the same-sex ceremony. The Illinois Human Rights Commission ruled that Walder violated an anti-discrimination law and is determining how much to fine him.

Kentucky Statute Attacked for Mentioning Reliance on God

Kentucky Office of Homeland Security v. Christerson, No. 2009-1650, 2011 WL 5105253 (Ky. Ct. App. Oct. 28, 2011)

A Kentucky statute and policy were attacked on state and federal constitutional grounds for mentioning reliance on God. A Kentucky appeals court upheld the statute as a historical reference that does not promote one religion over another.

Illinois Pharmacists Forced to Sue for Right to Refuse to Dispense Abortifacient Drugs

Morr-Fitz, Inc. v. Blagojevich, No. 2005-495 (Ill. Ck. Ct. Apr. 5, 2011)

Pharmacists Luke Vander Bleek and Glen Kosirog filed a lawsuit after Governor Rod Blagojevich issued an "Emergency Rule" stating that pharmacists cannot refuse to fill prescriptions for emergency contraceptives. After a five-year legal battle, an Illinois judge ruled that the "Emergency Rule" violated the First Amendment and the Illinois Religious Freedom Restoration Act.

Lawsuit Attacks Privately-Owned Menorah in Downtown Area of Poughkeepsie, New York

Chabad of Mid-Hudson Valley v. City of Poughkeepsie, 907 N.Y.S.2d 286 (N.Y. Sup. Ct. 2010)

A New York Supreme Court found that a privately owned, eighteen-foot-tall menorah did not violate the Establishment Clause. The decoration is owned by the Chabad of Mid-Hudson Valley, which puts it up in the downtown area of Poughkeepsie, New York, every year. Because the menorah is also displayed alongside other secular Christmas decorations, the court found that the menorah did not violate the Establishment Clause. However, the court maintained that it would be a violation of the Establishment Clause for the city to use its personnel and power to put up the menorah.

Firefighters Harassed for Religious Convictions Against Participating in Gay Pride Parade

Ghiotto v. City of San Diego, No. D055029 (Ct. App. Cal., filed Oct. 14, 2010)

San Diego, California, hosted a "Gay Pride Parade" and demanded that its firefighters participate in their official capacities or face retaliation. Four of those firefighters were Christians who objected to attending the parade because of their religious beliefs. The city threatened the firefighters with disciplinary action if they refused to participate. During the parade, the firefighters were subject to verbal abuse and sexual gestures. The firefighters sued the city and were awarded approximately $30,000.

Political Signs Permitted but Religious Signs Banned in Berkeley County, South Carolina
Moultrie v. Berkeley County, South Carolina, No. 2:10-2584 (D.S.C., filed Oct. 5, 2010)
Berkeley County, South Carolina, required its residents to obtain a permit to place signs in their yards. Political signs and for sale signs were deemed appropriate, but signs that carry a religious message were not. One resident, Moultrie, was cited for having signs with Bible verses on them. Moultrie filed suit against the county alleging violations of free expression, free exercise, and equal protection rights. The case settled.

Evangelist Sues for Right to Preach in California Shopping Mall
Snatchko v. Westfield, LLC, 187 Cal.App.4th 469 (Cal. Ct. App. 2010)
Snatchko wanted to preach the Gospel to shoppers in Westfield, LLC's shopping mall in Roseville, California. After being prohibited from sharing the Gospel to shoppers, Snatchko sued the mall's owner. Snatchko alleged that the restriction violated his First Amendment rights. The California appellate court agreed with him and found the mall's policy to provide stress-free shopping to patrons vague and not a substantial enough interest to take away Snatchko's free speech rights.

Pharmacist Fined for Following Religious Beliefs
Noesen v. Dep't. of Regulation and Licensing, 311 Wis. 2d 237 (Wis. Ct. App. 2008)
A pharmacist was fined over $20,000 and had restrictions placed on his license after he refused to give a patient oral contraceptives because their use is against his religious beliefs as a Roman Catholic.

Lawsuit Attacks South Carolina Ten Commandments Display
Young v. County of Charleston, 1999 WL 33530383 (S.C. Com. Pl. 1999)
A court struck down a city courthouse Ten Commandments display as a violation of the Establishment Clause.

FFRF Sues City of Denver After Pope's Visit
Freedom From Religion Foundation v. Romer, 921 P.2d 84 (Colo. App. 1996)
After the Pope visited Denver for World Youth Day, The Freedom From Religion Foundation filed a lawsuit for an injunction and damages against the City of Denver, council members, and Arapaho County officials. They asserted that using a state park for religious services, temporarily closing the park to the public, and the use of state funds to facilitate the visit violated the First and Fourteenth Amendments. The District Court dismissed the claim.

The Colorado appeals court held that 1) the injunction claim was moot, since the event was already over, and 2) city, county, and state officials could not be sued for damages in their official capacity under §1983.

Lawsuit Attacks Nativity Scene in Waunakee, Wisconsin

King v. Village of Waunakee, 517 N.W.2d 671 (Wis. 1994)
Citizens filed a lawsuit challenging a Nativity scene displayed during the Christmas season, seeking to eradicate the religious symbol from the public square. The Wisconsin Supreme Court held that the display did not violate the Establishment Clause or the Wisconsin State Constitution.

Lawsuit Challenges Georgia Courthouse Ten Commandments Display

Harvey v. Cobb County, 811 F. Supp. 669 (N.D. Ga. 1993), *aff'd per curiam*, 15 F. 3d 1097 (11th Cir. 1994)
Plaintiffs filed suit challenging framed panels of the Ten Commandments and the Great Commandment displayed at the county courthouse. The court concluded that the displays were unconstitutional, but the court allowed a stay so that the county could incorporate nonreligious, historical items, which according to the court would transform the display to fit within constitutional guidelines.

Student Given Failing Grade Because School Refuses to Accommodate Religious Travel

Johnson v. Shineman, 658 S.W.2d. 910 (Mo. App. 1983)
A student received a failing grade in music class because he could not make the final group performance, which was required to pass. The student claimed religious necessity to travel, but the school denied student's request for exemption from final performance. The court held in favor of the school.

Cracker Barrel Did Not Let Worker Attend Sunday Morning Church

http://www.dailypress.com/news/crime/dp-nws-eeoc-filing-20150929-story. html
Darika Jackson filed an Equal Employment Opportunity Commission complaint for religious and racial discrimination against Cracker Barrel Old Country Store in Virginia. The store manager refused to grant a religious accommodation that would have allowed her to attend church on Sunday mornings. After she contacted the corporate office to file a complaint, her hours were reduced and she was terminated.

Courthouse Defends "In God We Trust" Installation

http://www.mcdowellnews.com/news/in-god-we-trust-now-installed-on-county-buildings/article_f48cd5f4-63c8-11e5-85da-b79f3885419c.html

The McDowell County Courthouse in North Carolina has posted the nation's motto, "In God We Trust," over the front entrance. There was no cost to the county to install the sign. Commission Chairman David Walker commented to opponents of the display that the Supreme Court has ruled that the national motto may be displayed on county-owned property.

ExpressJet Suspends Muslim Flight Attendant for Abiding by Faith

http://www.cnn.com/2015/09/05/travel/muslim-flight-attendant-feat/

Charee Stanley, a Muslim flight attendant for ExpressJet, was suspended after refusing to serve alcohol to passengers based upon her religious beliefs. The airline originally agreed to allow other flight attendants on her flights to serve alcohol instead. However, she was suspended after a co-worker complained. The co-worker's complaint also noted that she carried a book with "foreign writings" and wore a headscarf. Stanley has brought an Equal Employment Opportunity Commission complaint for discrimination.

County Clerk Goes to Jail for Not Issuing Same-Sex Marriage Licenses

http://www.nbcnews.com/news/us-news/kentucky-clerk-kim-davis-held-contempt-court-n421126

Kim Davis, a county clerk for Rowan County, Kentucky, refused to issue marriage licenses to same-sex couples. Judge David Bunning ordered her to jail for contempt of court for failing to issue licenses, stating that she would be released only when she agreed to follow his order. Five of the six deputy clerks under Davis testified that they would issue same-sex marriage licenses.

Chick-fil-A Delayed at Denver Airport Due to Owner's Religious Beliefs

https://www.washingtonpost.com/news/volokh-conspiracy/wp/2015/08/21/no-airport-concessions-for-opponents-of-same-sex-marriage/

The Denver City Council questioned a concession agreement with Chick-fil-A at the Denver International Airport due to the owner's religious beliefs. Some councilmembers noted concern with profits made by Chick-fil-A going toward causes with which they disagree. Legal scholars note the potential First Amendment violation of singling out a business for its religious and political opinions.

Belen's Nativity Scene Under Attack Despite Bethlehem Ties

http://www.theblaze.com/stories/2015/08/13/mayor-seething-after-groups-call-to-take-down-nativity-scene-thats-been-in-a-city-park-for-decades/

The Freedom From Religion Foundation has set its sights on removing a Nativity scene in the little town of Belen, whose name translates to Bethlehem. Belen Mayor Jerah Cordova commented that the town takes pride in its name, and the organization does not understand the cultural importance of the display to the town's residents. Since it was first established in 1992, the Nativity scene has been a permanent display in a city park.

FFRF Attacks "In God We Trust" Bumper Stickers

https://www.washingtonpost.com/news/acts-of-faith/wp/2015/08/05/why-officers-are-putting-in-god-we-trust-bumper-stickers-on-their-patrol-cars/
http://www.inquisitr.com/2331894/missouri-sheriff-departments-asked-to-remove-in-god-we-trust/

At least ten sheriff's departments have begun to post bumper stickers of the nation's motto, "In God We Trust," on their patrol cars. The Freedom From Religion Foundation has sent letters to these sheriff's departments calling the nation's motto "inappropriate and unconstitutional." Many departments, including Laclede County Sheriff's Department and the Stone County Sheriff's Office, are not backing down.

"You're Not Welcome Here!" Yelled at Muslim Group

http://dallasmorningviewsblog.dallasnews.com/2015/08/heroes-in-farmersville-muslim-cemetery-fuss-religious-liberty-lovin-baptists.html/

At a city council meeting, the Islamic Association of Collin County, Texas, proposed to build a Muslim cemetery in Farmersville, Texas, to serve the local Muslim community. However, many in the audience made it clear that they wanted to shut out the Muslims community, jeering and interrupting the presentation. One man yelled, "You're not welcome here!" In a written response, Farmersville First Baptist Church pastor Bart Barber urged the town to respect religious freedom for all Americans.

Florida Sheriff Defies "In God We Trust" Bumper Sticker Opponents

http://www.washingtontimes.com/news/2015/jul/27/frank-mckeithen-florida-sheriff-defies-in-god-we-t/?page=all

After an increase in violence against police, Bay County Sheriff Frank McKeithen decided to posted the nation's motto "In God We Trust" on the county's patrol cars. He hopes that the move will help reassure the public that his officers are committed to conduct themselves ethically while on duty.

In response, the American Civil Liberties Union (ACLU) demanded that the sheriff remove the nation's motto, which is also Florida's motto, from the patrol cars. The sheriff simply stated that he was not afraid of the ACLU.

Newspaper Editor Fired for Blog Post About a Bible Translation
http://www.theblaze.com/stories/2015/07/27/how-this-newspaper-editor-reacted-when-he-saw-a-gay-friendly-bible-got-him-fired-but-heres-what-happened-when-he-fought-back/
Bob Eschliman, the editor-in-chief of the Newton Daily News in Newton, Iowa, was fired for a personal blog post sharing his opinions about a Bible translation. Eschliman's blog post was critical of the "Queen James Bible," a translation that rewords only the verses of the Bible that discuss homosexuality. The parties have since come to a settlement agreement.

ACLU Opposes Religious Freedom Protections
http://www.bloombergview.com/articles/2015-07-24/liberals-abandon-religious-liberty
The American Civil Liberties Union (ACLU) has retracted its support of Religious Freedom Restoration Acts (RFRAs), laws designed to prevent the government from oppressing religious people without a compelling justification. Reva Siegel and Douglas Nejaime published an article in the American Prospect magazine attempting to justify liberal groups' modern rejection of religious liberty. According to them, religious freedoms are only for minority religions with "unconventional" beliefs. If you are a Christian or have a divisive belief, you do not deserve protection under their theory.

"Protect Thy Neighbor" Campaign Aims to Force Religious Minorities into Compliance
http://www.washingtonblade.com/2015/07/08/putting-the-religious-right-on-notice/
Americans United for Separation of Church and State launched a "Protect Thy Neighbor" campaign, aimed at preventing states from protecting religious conscientious objectors. The campaign is designed to force religious dissenters into compliance. For instance, Americans United advocates for forcing pharmacists, business owners, and other people of faith who oppose abortion to fund or participate in distributing abortion-inducing drugs.

Christian Bakery Compelled to Bake Same-Sex Wedding Cake or Close Shop
http://dailysignal.com/2015/07/02/state-silences-bakers-who-refused-to-make-cake-for-lesbian-couple-fines-them-135k/
Aaron and Melissa Klein, owners of Sweet Cakes by Melissa in Oregon,

politely declined to design a cake for a same-sex wedding celebration. Although the bakers would bake a cake for the couple to celebrate other events, they could not create a cake endorsing a same-sex wedding due to their religious beliefs. A lawsuit was filed against the bakery, which included a charge against the Kleins for talking about their faith-based reason for declining. The Oregon Labor Commission ordered the bakers to pay $135,000, and the bakery has been forced to close.

U.S. Senator Claims Individuals Do Not Have Religious Freedoms
http://mediatrackers.org/wisconsin/2015/07/02/sen-baldwin-1st-amendment-doesnt-apply-individuals
On national television, Wisconsin Senator Tammy Baldwin stated that individuals and businesses do not have religious freedom and only institutions of faith are protected by the First Amendment. She said that she did not think the freedom to observe deeply held religious beliefs extended far beyond churches, synagogues, and mosques. Her interpretation contradicts the vast majority of case law that the First Amendment applies to everyone, including individuals, businesses, and other organizations.

California Passes Bill Removing Religious Exemption for Vaccines
https://www.washingtonpost.com/news/morning-mix/wp/2015/06/26/the-california-assembly-just-approved-one-of-nations-strictest-mandatory-vaccine-laws/
California removed its religious exemption to receiving mandatory vaccines. Now, all California citizens must receive all required vaccines, even if they have a religious objection to some or all vaccines.

American Atheists, Inc. Sues to Remove Ten Commandments Monument from Florida Courthouse
http://miami.cbslocal.com/2015/06/24/lawsuit-targets-ten-commandments-monument/
American Atheists, Inc. filed a lawsuit to remove a Ten Commandments monument that stands outside a Levy County, Florida, courthouse.

Art Gallery Forced to Close Following Refusal to Host Same-Sex Weddings
http://www.usatoday.com/story/news/nation/2015/06/22/gortz-haus-gallery-closes/29128889/
The Gortz Haus art gallery in Grimes, Iowa, permanently closed after it was fined for refusing to host a same-sex wedding. The owners of the Gortz Haus, Dick and Betty Odgaard, stated that their Mennonite faith prohibited them from hosting the same-sex wedding. To avoid further fines, the Odgaards

decided to stop hosting weddings at the Gortz Haus, which made the art gallery's survival financially untenable.

New York Towns Sued for Discriminating Against Hasidic Jews
http://www.startribune.com/discrimination-lawsuit-against-new-york-village-can-proceed/306698111/
The village of Bloomingburg and the Town of Mamakating, both in New York, blocked construction of housing and a bath used for ritual immersion and purification by Hasidic Jews. The developer filed a lawsuit against the two towns.

Michigan Sheriff's Office Forces Muslim Woman to Remove Headscarf in Front of Males
http://www.wzzm13.com/story/news/2015/06/15/headscarf-removal/71271466/
Fatme Dakroub, a Muslim woman whose faith requires her to wear a headscarf, was forced to remove her headscarf in front of three males after being arrested for driving on an expired license. Dakroub requested that her headscarf be removed only in front of a female officer, but the Oceana County Sheriff's Department refused.

Judge Stops Pittsylvania County, Virginia, Board of Supervisors Prayer Despite Supreme Court Ruling
http://www.roanoke.com/news/politics/judge-urbanski-rules-supervisors-prayers-remain-unconstitutional/article_414209f0-20fd-5b4e-bfae-aaa26e780a2b.html
The American Civil Liberties Union of Virginia sued the Pittsylvania County Board of Supervisors to stop them from opening meetings with a prayer. A federal district court judge held that the board of supervisors' prayers are unconstitutional despite the Supreme Court's opinion in *Town of Greece v. Galloway* holding that opening prayers are constitutional because the prayers in Town of Greece were given by volunteers from the community while the prayers before the Pittsylvania County Board of Supervisors were given by the supervisors themselves. Another Supreme Court opinion, however, *Marsh v. Chambers,* held that a legislative body like the board of supervisors could even hire a paid chaplain to give prayers.

Indiana Pizzeria Attacked for Supporting Traditional Marriage
http://radio.foxnews.com/toddstarnes/top-stories/christian-pizzeria-slammed-by-modern-day-fascists.html
Memories Pizza in Walkerton, Indiana, was forced to close and its owner went into hiding after a local news station asked if the pizzeria would cater

a same-sex wedding. The pizzeria had never been asked to cater a wedding before, but the owner, Kevin O'Connor, said that, because of his religious beliefs about marriage, he would have to refuse if he ever did receive a request to cater a same-sex wedding. The pizzeria has never turned away a customer because of the customer's sexual orientation. A high school softball coach in Concord, Indiana, was suspended after posting an arson threat against the pizzeria on Twitter.

San Antonio Police Cite Woman for Feeding the Homeless, Tell Her, "If You Want to Pray, Go to Church."

http://www.texasobserver.org/feeding-homeless-religious-freedom-restoration-act/

Joan Cheever operates a nonprofit ministry in San Antonio called The Chow Train that serves food to the homeless. San Antonio police issued Ms. Cheever, herself a lawyer, with a citation for serving food without a permit, despite her informing them of the laws that protected her giving out meals. The police officers told Ms. Cheever, "Ma'am, if you want to pray, go to church."

Governor Mocked for Praying to God

http://thefederalist.com/2015/02/25/scott-walker-flap-shows-how-political-media-actively-loathe-christianity/

After Wisconsin Governor Scott Walker noted that as a Christian he seeks God's guidance and comfort through prayer, Freedom From Religion Foundation demanded that Walker's office provide copies of all correspondence between Walker and God. After the office responded that they did "not have records responsive to your request," media journalists mocked Governor Walker by saying that the lack of written correspondence proves that "Walker has not communicated with God."

FFRF Forces Dallas, Texas, to Remove Nativity Scene from Court Square

http://www.gastongazette.com/20150211/new-owner-for-nativity-scene/302119920

The Nativity scene on Dallas' Court Square has been a tradition every Christmas for more than 30 years. But last year, the Freedom From Religious Foundation sent a letter demanding the town remove the display from public property or face possible legal action. Reluctantly, the city was removed the Nativity scene onto private property, despite overwhelming support and organized demonstrations to keep the religious display in the Court Square.

FFRF's Attacks Do Not Prevail Over Ottawa County

http://fox17online.com/2015/02/11/group-asks-ottawa-co-to-remove-religious-sign-from-hager-park/

The Ottawa County Commission voted to reinstall a sign that displayed a Bible verse at a local park after it was removed by the Ottawa County Parks Commission a few months prior. The sign, which displayed Psalm 19:1, reads, "The heavens declare the glory of God: and the firmament sheweth his handiwork." It was originally taken down after the Michigan Association of Civil Rights Activists demanded it be removed and threatened legal action. After its reinstallation, Freedom From Religion Foundation sent a letter condemning the commissioner's decision to display the sign, and the Ottawa County administrator responded the sign is not "as much about the Constitution or the Bible as much as community values."

City in Texas Votes to Keep Prayer in City Council Meeting

http://www.ktre.com/story/28133935/nacogdoches-citizens-fill-city-hall-prayer-stays-in-meetings

For 25 years, the Nacogdoches City Council has traditionally opened all meetings with a non-denominational prayer. However, an objection was recently voiced and so the city met to discuss the issue with advice from Liberty Institute. "There was standing room only," said one resident, in support of upholding the tradition of prayer before meetings. Nacogdoches residents not only brought signs and filled the city hall to capacity, but they also started a movement. The issue prompted many Nacogdoches churches and members to get together and commit to putting crosses in their yards, determined not to back down from their beliefs. When the mayor proposed including prayer as a written policy, not one person objected, and the crowd gave a standing ovation.

Congressional Prayer Caucus Attacked by Humanist Group

http://americanhumanist.org/news/details/2015-02-humanist-group-sends-letter-criticizing-congressiona

In 2005, Congressman J. Randy Forbes gathered a small group from the U.S. House of Representatives who began meeting in Room 219 of the Capitol to pray for our nation. These Members later formed The Congressional Prayer Caucus—an official Caucus of the U.S. House of Representatives—to formally acknowledge the important role that prayer plays in American life and our 200-year history, and to monitor and work to guard the right of individuals to pray. The Prayer Caucus has grown to a bipartisan group of 86 Members dedicated to protecting religious liberty. The American Humanist Association

(AHA) seeks to destroy the group by urging Members of Congress not to join the Prayer Caucus. AHA has sent out at least two post-election letters to newly-elected Members claiming the group "discriminates against nonreligious Americans and regulates them to mere second-class citizens."

FFRF Seeks to Remove a Nativity Scene Displayed for Years
http://www.brainerddispatch.com/news/3668107-constitutionality-park-nativity-scene-questioned
Freedom From Religious Foundation (FFRF) is challenging the constitutionality of a Nativity scene long displayed on Wadena, Minnesota city property. Mayor George Deiss wholly supported the Nativity scene stating, "I believe we need it; I'm going to do whatever I can to make sure that it's out there again." Mayor Deiss said he has received feedback from residents who would like to see the city continue to display the scene. "This is small-town USA and people here still have strong Christian values," he said. "It was heartwarming for me the number of people who stopped me on the street and talked to me or called me or wrote letters to the editor about how supportive they were of still having a Nativity scene in the city of Wadena." The Wadena City Council is set to meet to discuss how to respond to FFRF's threatened lawsuit amid resounding support of the Nativity scene by residents.

Muslim College Students Tragically Killed by "Anti-Theist"
http://ffrf.org/news/news-releases/item/22352-ffrf-condemns-shooting-deaths-attributed-to-purported-atheist
http://www.newyorker.com/magazine/2015/06/22/the-story-of-a-hate-crime
On February 10, 2015, Craig Hicks turned himself in to police after shooting three Muslim college students in the head. Posts on Hicks' Facebook page rail against religion, including quotes like "People say nothing can solve the Middle East problem. Not mediation, not arms, not financial aid. I say there is something. Atheism. –Jr Grover." The Freedom From Religion Foundation (FFRF) was quick to release a statement that Craig Hicks was not a FFRF member after it was reported he "liked" FFRF's Facebook posts.

FFRF Protests Bible in Arizona House Lounge
http://ffrf.org/news/news-releases/item/22324-ffrf-protests-open-bible-in-ariz-house-lounge
Once the Freedom From Religion Foundation (FFRF) heard a Bible was placed in the Arizona House of Representatives' lounge, they threatened the Speaker of the House, demanding the Bible be removed. They protested the "holy book" stating "Legislators should not take inspiration or counsel

from the Bible. Reading this ponderous tome is unlikely to result in thought, let alone legislation, beneficial or acceptable to Arizonans," and suggesting that legislators would be guided to "murder homosexuals." Further, their ranting letter states "the [B]ible is full of nonsense," and mocks Biblical stories and Christian beliefs as "blind faith."

FFRF Attacks Proposal to Place "In God We Trust" on Courthouse

http://www.gastongazette.com/20150205/commissioner-lets-put-in-god-we-trust-on-courthouse/302059919

The Gaston County commissioners unanimously approved the proposal to place the phrase "In God We Trust" on the marquee of the courthouse. All the money to be used for the construction and installation was raised from private donations. Gaston County Commission Chairman Tracy Philbeck supported placement of the national motto on the courthouse, saying, "It honors our heritage and history," and "It's about a demonstration of patriotism and an ideology the country was founded on," and less about encouraging people to "believe a certain way." The proposal survived attack by the Freedom From Religion Foundation (FFRF), who stated that they "certainly oppose this action by the county government," and believe it to be "unconstitutional." However, federal courts have repeatedly upheld the motto's use and the U.S. House of Representatives have even encouraged, by way of resolution, its display in schools and other public institutions.

Religious Objector Refused Internship Over Objection to Social Security Number

http://www.cleveland.com/court-justice/index.ssf/2015/01/federal_appeals_court_says_pot.html

Donald Yeager, an Austintown, Ohio, resident, refused to give his Social Security number to FirstEnergy in Shippingport, Pennsylvania, after he was accepted as the company's student intern. The Christian Fundamentalist disavowed his Social Security number when he turned 18. He believes the number is a "mark of the beast," a reference to a passage in the Book of Revelations. Yeager lost the internship because FirstEnergy would not process his application without a Social Security number. He sued the company, claiming the company violated state and federal laws by discriminating against him because of his religion. The case was dismissed after the Cincinnati-based appeals court pointed out that Yeager's claim fails because "FirstEnergy's collection of Yeager's social security number is a 'requirement imposed by law' and therefore not an 'employment requirement.'"

Arkansas Gun Range Bans Muslims

http://www.opposingviews.com/i/religion/justice-department-monitor-arkansas-gun-range-banned-muslims

The Gun Cave Shooting Range in Hot Spring, Arkansas, declared itself a "Muslim-free zone" and refuses to rent or sell guns to any person of the Muslim faith. The Department of Justice stated that it is "monitoring" the gun range.

Cross in Grand Haven, Michigan, Removed After Threat of Lawsuit

http://nation.foxnews.com/2015/01/08/fifty-year-old-cross-be-removed-after-pressure-atheist

A cross on top of Dewey Hill in Grand Haven, Michigan, was removed after fifty years to avoid a lawsuit from an activist. The Grand Haven City Council voted three-to-two to remove the cross.

Atlanta Fire Chief Fired for Religious Views

http://www.usatoday.com/story/news/nation/2015/01/07/atlanta-fire-chief-fired-gay-comments-book/21378685/

Atlanta fired its fire chief, Kelvin Cochran, because he wrote a book titled Who Told You That You Were Naked? that expressed Cochran's personal religious beliefs about homosexual conduct and same-sex marriage. Cochran filed a lawsuit against Atlanta for wrongful termination.

Washington, D.C., Curtails Religious Freedom Protections

http://heritageaction.com/2015/01/protecting-religious-freedom-d-c/

Washington, D.C., passed two bills that curtail religious liberty protections. One bill, the Reproductive Health Non-Discrimination Act, forces even pro-life employers to cover elective, surgical abortions in their health plans. The other bill, the Human Rights Amendment Act, revokes a 1989 protection for religious schools' religious beliefs about "any homosexual act, lifestyle orientation, or belief." In order to prevent the D.C. laws from taking effect, both houses of Congress must pass a resolution of disapproval and the president must sign it. The U.S. House of Representatives voted to strike down the laws, but the U.S. Senate took no action on the bill.

Blue Ridge, Georgia, Walmart Demands Greeter Stop Saying, "Have a Blessed Day"

http://www.wsbtv.com/news/news/local/walmart-asks-greeter-stop-saying-have-blessed-day/njzWm/

James Philips, a greeter at a Walmart in Blue Ridge, Georgia, greeted persons entering the store with the phrase, "Have a blessed day." Walmart, however, informed Philips that, as a Walmart employee, he could not use that phrase. Following Walmart's decision, a public outcry ensued, and Walmart reversed its decision, allowing Philips to say, "Have a blessed day."

IRS Agent Fired for Wearing Ceremonial Dagger to Work

http://taxprof.typepad.com/taxprof_blog/2014/11/former-irs-agent-settles-claim-.html

After being hired by the IRS, Kawaljeet Tagore was baptized into the Sikh religion and began wearing a small, blunted sword called a kirpan in accordance with the religion's requirements. However, the three-inch blade was half an inch longer than allowed under the "pocket knife exemption" for knives allowed in federal buildings. Tagore applied for a security waiver, but her application was denied. The IRS then fired Tagore when she continued to adhere to her religious requirement by wearing the kirpan. Tagore subsequently brought a lawsuit for the IRS's failure to accommodate her religion, but a Texas federal court ruled against her. Upon appeal, the U.S. Court of Appeals for the Fifth Circuit remanded the case back to the district court to assess whether Tagore's sincere religious beliefs prohibit her from wearing a kirpan that adhered to federal requirement. The dispute ended in a settlement between the former IRS worker and the U.S. government that expunges Tagore's firing from her record, allows her to enter federal buildings with the blade for a period of three years, and awards her lawyers $400,000 for fees and expenses. However, Tagore will be barred from seeking re-employment with the IRS, but may seek work with other federal agencies.

Humanist Group Attacks Display of Student Artwork on Snowplows

http://www.usatoday.com/story/news/nation/2014/11/01/student-artwork-on-citys-snowplows-poses-legal-questions/18352795/

One town in South Dakota decided to feature student artwork on twenty-seven of their city snowplows, including two pieces of art that included religious themes. Siouxland Freethinkers, a group that calls itself a community of agnostics, atheists, humanists, and skeptics, immediately demanded that Sioux Falls take down the students' artwork on the snowplows. The city stood by the artwork display, but included a disclaimer stating, "Any messages or views expressed on the plows are not those of the city or endorsed by the city." Sioux Falls City Attorney David Pfeifle reiterated the city's commitment to keeping the artwork stating, the disclaimer "is sufficient to alleviate any Establishment Clause concerns. We're confident this will pass legal muster."

FFRF Urges Mayor to Cancel 46th Annual Community Prayer Breakfast

http://ffrf.org/news/news-releases/item/21752-ffrf-urges-mayor-to-cancel-city-sponsored-prayer-breakfast

For 46 years, the City of New Albany, Indiana, has held a community prayer breakfast to "come together to celebrate the diversity within God's family." The event is an opportunity to unite citizens of all ages and faiths. Freedom From Religion Foundation (FFRF) called this prayer breakfast "a particularly egregious example of an inappropriate union between government and religion," but City Controller Linda Moeller defended the event, stating, "This is the 46th year; there's a lot of history and tradition behind this breakfast that we do every year. I've been on it for many years and during that time, there are no city funds that are attached to the breakfast. It's self-supporting and run off the ticket sales themselves."

County Offices Received Criticism for Closing on Good Friday

http://ffrf.org/news/action/item/21746-ask-fayette-county-commission-to-end-good-friday-holiday

A Fayette County Commission in La Grange, Texas, closed their offices in observance of Good Friday. Freedom From Religion Foundation (FFRF) immediately sent letters stating that by closing its government office on Good Friday, the Texas county commission violated the Establishment Clause by promoting religion over non-religion. The Texas county attorney replied, "This is the culture that we live in, and most of our people would like to be off on that day." The county attorney invited anyone who has an issue with the county holidays policy to voice his or her concerns at a public hearing.

FFRF Attacks Orlando Police Chaplain

http://ffrf.org/news/news-releases/item/21726-ffrf-protests-many-police-chaplains-nationwide-including-in-orlando

The Freedom From Religion Foundation (FFRF) attacked police, sheriff, and fire department chaplaincy programs in fifteen cities, opposing the use of chaplains to counsel employees, employees' families, victims of crimes, and assist with various other police activities, including death notifications. Cities and counties across the nation are launching new police chaplain programs. One department revived their police chaplain program, stating that they "wanted to bring faith into the organization to help officers and their families cope with the stress of the job." Orlando Police Chief John Mina emailed back the day after receiving FFRF's letter, saying, "I have no intention of discontinuing our Chaplain Program."

Humanist Group Attacks Police and Pastor Alliance Focused on Protecting City

http://americanhumanist.org/news/details/2014-11-police-and-pastors-cant-partner-in-city-sponsored-pr

The Clergy and Police Alliance Program is a coalition dedicated to serving the citizens of Fort Worth, Texas. Their goal is to provide advice, support, and prayer during times of need. The program is not limited to particular religions; they seek to have a representation from every church, denomination, and faith from the City of Fort Worth. However, American Humanist Association warned that failure to terminate the program would result in a lawsuit against the city.

ALAC Legislation Restricts Religious Liberty

http://blog.acton.org/archives/73790-anti-sharia-legislation-can-restrict-religious-liberty-christians.html

Alabama passed a ballot measure that forbids courts, arbitrators, and administrative agencies from applying or "enforcing a foreign law if doing so would violate any state law or a right guaranteed by the Constitution of this state or of the United States." Such "American Laws for American Courts" or ALAC statutes are often dubbed "anti-Sharia" statutes since preventing the encroachment of Sharia, the moral code and religious law of Islam, is usually their primary objective. "Anti-Sharia" laws cannot be written to oppose only Sharia because such measures would be religious discrimination, but opposing Sharia law is unnecessary since state law and the Constitution already trump foreign law. However, Muslim Americans who seek to use Sharia are not asking the American legal system to adopt Islamic rules of conduct, but rather to recognize the norms to which the litigants have already agreed to be bound. By pushing the idea that religious beliefs should be kept private, "anti-Sharia" laws become a threat to all of our religious beliefs.

City Bans 90-Year-Old from Feeding the Homeless

http://dallasmorningviewsblog.dallasnews.com/2014/11/texas-faith-when-is-a-city-ban-on-feeding-the-poor-an-infringement-on-religious-liberty.html/

A 90-year-old World War II veteran and two pastors have fed the homeless in a public park in South Florida. The 90-year-old founded an interfaith volunteer organization, "Love Thy Neighbor," over 20 years ago to help the homeless. However, the City of Fort Lauderdale charged the benevolent 90-year-old with committing a crime due to the city's desire to eliminate the homeless from their city limits. The City passed an ordinance restricting public feedings of the homeless in the city, making it virtually impossible for "Love Thy Neighbor" to operate as it has for decades.

Complaint Filed Against Videographer for Refusing to Video Same-Sex Wedding

http://www.christianpost.com/news/christian-videographer-faces-legal-action-after-refusing-to-work-lesbian-wedding-says-its-against-her-biblical-beliefs-135888/

Courtney Schmackers, a wedding videographer in Bexley, Ohio, was asked to create a wedding video for a same-sex wedding. Schmackers refused to create the wedding video because of her religious beliefs that marriage is between one man and one woman. The couple who requested the video then filed a complaint against Schmackers with the Bexley Area Chamber of Commerce. The chamber of commerce indicated that it would revise its membership policy to ban persons whose religious beliefs do not permit them to participate in same-sex weddings.

FFRF Threat Leads to Revised Holiday Display Policy

http://walpole.wickedlocal.com/article/20140616/NEWS/140617061

After the Freedom From Religion Foundation (FFRF) sent a letter to Walpole, Massachusetts, complaining about a Nativity scene on display at the Walpole Chamber of Commerce, Walpole Selectmen implemented a new holiday display policy that requires all displays to go through a selection process to make sure no displays either advance or inhibit religion, culture, or ethnicity.

Utah Police Officer Put on Paid Leave for Requesting to Not Lead Gay Parade

http://www.slate.com/blogs/outward/2014/06/09/salt_lake_city_police_officer_won_t_protect_gay_pride_parade.html

http://christiannews.net/2014/06/11/suspended-police-officer-requested-to-be-reassigned-from-leading-gay-pride-parade/

A police officer asked for a reassignment after he was told that he would have to lead a gay pride parade. The officer told his superiors that leading a gay pride parade would violate his religious beliefs. He asked if he could protect the parade in another capacity. He was put on paid leave and subject to investigation for refusing to lead the parade. A spokesperson for the police station said the officer must surrender personal beliefs when he assumes his role as an officer. The officer was forced to resign after the media falsely reported that he refused to attend the gay pride parade.

IRS Releases Donor Information for the National Organization for Marriage

http://religionclause.blogspot.com/2014/06/pro-marriage-group-entitled-to-actual.html

The National Organization for Marriage (NOM) is a nonprofit organization that defends traditional marriage and faith groups who uphold traditional marriage. The IRS released, without authorization, a Schedule B list of donors who donated more than $5000 to the organization. The Huffington Post published the donor list that was supposed to be redacted from NOM's tax form. NOM was awarded actual damages.

Judges Banned from Sharing the Bible with Criminal Defendants

http://religionclause.blogspot.com/2014/05/florida-judge-ordered-to-stop-offering.html

http://www.mynews13.com/content/news/cfnews13/news/article.html/content/news/articles/cfn/2014/5/4/osceola_judge_bibles.html

A judge in Osceola County, Florida, was ordered to stop handing out Bibles to criminal defendants. An attorney complained after learning that the judge distributed Gideon Bibles to criminals.

Virginia County Board Told They Cannot Limit Prayers to Clergy

https://www.au.org/media/press-releases/aclu-and-americans-united-say-va-county-board-may-not-permit-only-ministers

The American Civil Liberties Union and Americans United for the Separation of Church and State wrote a letter to the Virginia County Board of Supervisors telling them that the board cannot choose only clergy members for opening prayers. Both groups acknowledged the recent ruling in *Town of Greece v. Galloway;* however, they object to the council using clergy members who mostly represent the Christian faith.

Two Brothers' TV Show Cancelled Because of Their Faith

http://www.cbn.com/cbnnews/us/2014/May/Benham-Twins-HGTV-Flap-Wont-Silence-Our-Faith/

HGTV cancelled the show "Flip it Forward" after the TV station received complaints about David and Jason Benhams' Christian faith. The complaints came after People for the American Way posted David's comments affirming traditional marriage and the pro-life movement on their website, Right Wing Watch.

City Disallows Banners Advertising Christmas Musical

http://aclj.org/free-speech-2/victory-for-religious-free-speech-in-texas

A chapter of the Knights of Columbus in New Braunfels, Texas, obtained permission from the city to display a large banner advertising a musical entitled "Keep Christ in Christmas." However, when several citizens complained that the city's allowance of the banner "violated the separation of church and state," the city ordered the banners to be taken down and amended its policy to prohibit banners that advocated religious beliefs. With the help of a religious liberties group, the Knights of Columbus fought back against the discrimination, and the city agreed to reerect the banners.

Texas Department of Transportation Bans Private Ten Commandments Sign
http://www.libertyinstitute.org/txdot?
Jeanette Golden placed a sign displaying the Ten Commandments on her private property near Hemphill, Texas. When the Texas Department of Transportation ("TXDoT") learned of the sign, however, they deemed it to be an illegal "outdoor advertising sign" and ordered it removed. After attorneys from Liberty Institute sent a demand letter to TXDoT on behalf of Ms. Golden, however, TXDoT rescinded their order, changed their rules on such signs, and agreed that the sign could remain on Ms. Golden's property.

Residents Boycott Store Due to Owner's Belief in Traditional Marriage
http://www.oregonlive.com/portland/index.ssf/2014/04/owners_anti-gay_views_cause_fu.html
Chauncy Childs, owner of Moreland Farmer's Pantry in Sellwood, Oregon, posted commentary on her religious and political opposition to same-sex "marriage" on her personal Facebook page. When neighbors discovered the postings and publicized them, members of the local community called for a boycott of Child's business.

FFRF Complains About Utility Company's Observance of Good Friday
http://ffrf.org/news/news-releases/item/20418-sun-prairie-utility-closes-illegally-for-good-friday-uses-crown-of-thorns-graphic
Sun Prairie Utilities (SPU) in Sun Prairie, Wisconsin, closed for Good Friday and announced its observance on its website with a banner that included a crown of thorns. The Freedom From Religion Foundation (FFRF) accused SPU of constitutional violations and demanded that SPU take the banner down and remain open. SPU removed the crown of thorns, but continued in its Good Friday observance.

ACLU Condemns Jewish Park
http://www.nyclu.org/news/victory-park-hasidic-enclave-kiryas-joel-will-not-segregate-based-sex
The Village of Kiryas Joel, New York, constructed a large public park for the

community, which is comprised predominately of members of the Satmar Hasidic Jewish sect. In accordance with Satmar Hasidic Jewish religious principles, signs divided the park into areas that kept men and women separate. The ACLU heard about the segregation and demanded that the village redact any affiliation with or enforcement of the park signs. The village agreed to remove the signs and gave the ACLU permission to visit the park semiannually to check on compliance.

California Court Refuses Sikh Man for Jury Duty

http://sacramento.cbslocal.com/2014/04/29/sikh-man-barred-from-sutter-county-courthouse-for-refusing-to-remove-religious-dagger/

When Gursant Singh, a practicing Sikh, arrived at the Sutter County Courthouse in Yuba City, California, after being summoned for jury duty, authorities refused to let him into the courthouse due to his kirpan (a small, blunt dagger worn by Sikhs at all times under the requirements of Sikhism). Singh lamented the position of having to choose between breaking the law by not fulfilling his jury duty requirements or following his religion, but ultimately made it clear that he would suffer punishment rather than deny his religion.

Antireligion Organization Demands Removal of Religious Stickers from Post Office

http://ffrf.org/legal/other-legal-successes/item/20790-ffrf-removes-%E2%80%9Csmile-god-loves-you%E2%80%9D-from-post-office-grounds-april-25-2014

The Freedom From Religion Foundation sent a letter to the manager of a U.S. Post Office in Cleveland, Ohio, complaining that a sticker reading "Smile! God Loves You" violated the First Amendment by showing a governmental preference for religion. The Post Office promptly removed the sticker.

Atheist Group Condemns "In God We Trust" License Plates

http://ffrf.org/news/news-releases/item/18803-ffrf-kill-in-god-we-trust-license-plates

http://www.620wtmj.com/news/local/Appleton-Man-Hopes-for-In-God-We-Trust-License-Plates-in-Wisconsin-255569221.html

When the Wisconsin legislature proposed a bill that would permit the issuance of specialty license plates bearing the words "In God We Trust" to help support veterans and police officers, the Freedom From Religion Foundation protested. Nonetheless, the legislature approved the bill.

Software Company CEO Pushed Out for Belief in Traditional Marriage
http://www.theatlantic.com/politics/archive/2014/04/mozillas-gay-marriage-litmus-test-violates-liberal-values/360156/
Brendan Eich, CEO and co-founder of Mozilla, resigned following an uproar over his political donation to California's Proposition 8 (the California bill upholding traditional marriage between one man and one woman) became known.

Atheists Oppose Easter Displays Across America
http://ffrf.org/news/news-releases/item/20370-ffrf-counters-wisconsin-capitol-easter-display
http://ffrf.org/news/news-releases/item/20417-warren-mich-mayor-censors-ffrf-member%E2%80%99s-message-again
http://ffrf.org/news/news-releases/item/20419-nonbelievers-counter-catholic-easter-display-in-daley-plaza
Around the country, the Freedom From Religion Foundation and other anti-religion groups and individuals installed various displays that sought to undermine the religious story behind Easter.

Atheists Pressure Louisiana Representative over Bill Making the Bible the Official State Book
http://www.nola.com/politics/index.ssf/2014/04/louisiana_bible_state_book.html
http://ffrf.org/news/news-releases/item/20364-ffrf-condemns-louisiana-bible-bill
Louisiana Representative Thomas Carmody proposed making the Bible the official state book of Louisiana. However, atheist groups like the Freedom From Religion Foundation criticized the bill, and Carmody scrapped the plan before it could go to a vote.

Atheist Organization Bullies Small Town into Removing Crosses
http://www.foxnews.com/us/2014/04/17/group-protests-illegal-display-easter-crosses-in-ohio-village/
http://ffrf.org/news/news-releases/item/20359-illegal-crosses-rise-again-for-easter
When the Freedom From Religion Foundation heard that the tiny town of Stratton, Ohio, displayed crosses on the town municipal building, it threatened to sue the city for violating the Constitution. Mayor John Abdalla initially removed the crosses, but returned them during the Easter season.

Pharmacy Employee Derided by Supervisor Because of Religious Beliefs
http://nypost.com/2014/04/14/bronx-man-says-muslim-cvs-boss-disliked-his-white-boy-religion/
Nowran Busgith, a practicing Seventh-day Adventist and employee at a CVS Pharmacy in New York, obtained permission to abstain from working on his Sabbath, which is from sundown on Friday until sundown on Saturday. However, when Abdul Salui, Busgith's supervisor, found out that Busgith's time off was tied to his religious beliefs, Salui ridiculed Busgith for adhering to a "white boy religion" and denied all of Busgith's subsequent requests. Busgith filed a lawsuit for Salui's discrimination. This case is ongoing.

Muslim Family Forced to Stop Praying at Empire State Building
http://religionclause.blogspot.com/2014/03/muslim-couple-claims-discrimination.html
A Muslim family was reprimanded for praying on the observation deck of the Empire State Building. A security guard escorted the family off the observation deck and out of the building. The family was praying in an area with little foot traffic. They believe that they were targeted for participating in Muslim prayer while wearing Muslim attire.

FFRF Decries Wisconsin Governor's Tweet of a Bible Reference
http://host.madison.com/ct/news/local/writers/jessica_vanegeren/freedom-from-religion-foundation-asks-scott-walker-to-remove-bible/article_f157ac50-aed5-11e3-b3ea-001a4bcf887a.html
http://ffrf.org/news/news-releases/item/20275-ffrf-to-walker-delete-religious-tweet
The Freedom From Religion Foundation reprimanded Wisconsin Governor Scott Walker for posting a reference to a Bible verse on Twitter. Walker's tweet read, "Philippians 4:13." The Governor did not quote the verse, which says, "I can do all things through Christ who strengthens me." The FFRF claims that the words in the scripture Walker references make Walker sound like a threatening "theocratic dictator."

FFRF Complains About Police Chief's Prayer Walks
https://ffrf.org/news/news-releases/item/20235-police-chief-uses-office-to-blatantly-promote-christianity
Freedom From Religion Foundation sent a complaint letter and an open records request to Birmingham, Alabama, Police Chief A.C. Roper for leading monthly prayer walks in his community. Roper, who is also an ordained

minister, prays for the safety and welfare of the community. The atheist group believes that Roper is using his government position to endorse religion.

FFRF Attacks City Council Prayers Made "In Jesus' Name"
http://crossmap.christianpost.com/news/ohio-city-councilman-refuses-to-stop-presenting-prayers-in-jesus-name-9270
Freedom From Religion Foundation (FFRF) sent a letter to the Cuyahoga Falls city council requesting that they stop praying before meetings. The city council had appointed Councilman Terry Mader as its chaplain. As Councilman Mader's religious beliefs required, he prayed "in Jesus' name." The atheist group claimed that the phrase "in Jesus' name" violates the United States Constitution.

American Humanist Association Fights Roadside Memorial to Killed Pedestrian
http://americanhumanist.org/news/details/2014-03-roadside-cross-in-lake-elsinore-ca-must-be-removed-s
The American Humanist Association (AHA) sent a letter to Lake Elsinore, California, demanding that a roadside memorial in the shape of a cross be removed. The memorial was placed at the site of a fatal accident off of I-15 to commemorate the victim of the traffic accident. The AHA stated that "religious symbols serving as memorials on government property are unconstitutional." Lake Elsinore removed the memorial.

FFRF Opposes Kentucky Governor's Support of Prayer Breakfast
http://www.secularnewsdaily.com/2014/03/ffrf-mix-ham-eggs-not-state-church-2/
The Freedom From Religion Foundation complained that Kentucky Governor Steve Beshear sent invitations to a prayer breakfast from his government email account and posted a link to the nondenominational prayer breakfast on his website. Governor Beshear was asked to cancel the prayer breakfast and remove any posts on the government website that could indicate government sponsorship of the citywide event.

Atheist Group Objects to Unpaid Police Chaplains
http://lacrossetribune.com/news/local/group-claims-la-crosse-police-chaplains-are-unconstitutional/article_e0751c0e-4c14-5bdd-886f-e4009cf6cca4.html
Freedom From Religion Foundation demanded that La Crosse Police terminate its chaplaincy program in which religious persons volunteer their time to serve citizens during emergencies and to support law enforcement officials.

Saginaw City Council Attacked for Opening Meetings with Prayer
http://www.mlive.com/news/saginaw/index.ssf/2014/02/pre-meeting_prayers_by_saginaw.html
Sagniaw City Council routinely issued a prayer before each meeting, but then Freedom From Religion Foundation sent a letter in opposition. Before receiving a demand letter, the Council had never received a complaint.

Atheist Group Attacks Prayer at Mayoral Inauguration
http://freekeene.com/wordpress/wp-content/uploads/2014/02/Keene-NH.pdf
Freedom From Religion Foundation wrote a letter to Mayor Lane in Keene, New Hampshire, objecting to the invocation and benediction given during his inauguration ceremony. Describing prayer in public ceremonies "of dubious legality," FFRF took issue with prayers given in this case by a reverend to solemnize the proceedings.

Religious Group Fights for a Booth at a Public Fair
http://www.gazettextra.com/article/20140211/WC/140219947/1133
Walworth County Fair refused to renew the application for a booth submitted by Peter's Net, a Catholic education group. The group participated in the 2013 Walworth County Fair, following all directives and instructions. Peter's Net objects to the fair's discrimination in denying its application.

Pharmacist Fired After Refusing to Sell Abortifacient Contraceptives
http://www.christiannewswire.com/news/6850273650.html
For six years, Walgreens accommodated Pharmacist Dr. Philip Hall's deeply held religious beliefs, including his strong objection to the dispensation of abortion-inducing drugs. When customers asked for these drugs, he either referred them to another pharmacist there or another nearby pharmacy. However, in August 2013, Walgreens attempted to coerce Hall to violate his religious beliefs. After he was fired, Hall filed a lawsuit in federal court to protect his religious freedom.

Department of Homeland Security's Naturalization Test Recognizes "Freedom of Worship" But Not "Freedom of Religion"
http://www.christianpost.com/news/senator-rebukes-dhs-for-suggesting-freedom-of-religion-is-only-freedom-to-worship-140131/
Senator James Lankford of Oklahoma asked the Department of Homeland Security(DHS) to change its naturalization test to promote "freedom of religion" instead of "freedom of worship." While the First Amendment protects freedom of religion—a stronger protection than mere freedom to

worship—the DHS responded that it chose "freedom of worship" because that phrase is "more inclusive."

FFRF Attacks Religious References in Sherriff's Department's Facebook Page

http://ffrf.org/legal/other-legal-successes/item/19880-ffrf-deletes-religious-postings-from-sheriff-department%E2%80%99s-facebook-page-january-2-2014
The Douglas County Sheriff K-9 unit included some Christian themed posts on its Facebook page. After receiving a complaint from the Freedom From Religion Foundation, the K-9 unit stopped writing religious posts.

Penitentiary Prohibits Jewish Inmates from Wearing Yarmulkes in Public

https://www.aclu.org/files/assets/WDOC%20Kippah%20Letter%201-9-14.pdf
The Wyoming State Penitentiary prohibited Mr. Fisher, an Orthodox Jew, from wearing his yarmulke while out of his cell if not at a religious service. The prison's policy allows inmates to wear their yarmulkes only in their cells or during religious services, in violation of Jewish religious practice.

Atheist Group Complains About Nativity Scene

http://www.heraldmailmedia.com/news/local/hancock-council-of-churches-followed-protocol-in-displaying-nativity-scene/article_46eb2800-5c9b-11e3-aacb-0019bb30f31a.html
When the town council for Hancock, Maryland, approved the erection of a Nativity scene by the Hancock Council of Churches, the Freedom From Religion Foundation protested the display on Establishment Clause grounds. Town Manager David Smith insisted that the display was permissible, but agreed to post a sign disavowing any town association with the Nativity scene.

Hotel Security Guard Vandalizes Guests' Religious Objects

http://www.justice.gov/usao/tnw/news/2013/DEC9Baker.html
http://forward.com/articles/194105/tenn-security-guard-gets-federal-sentence-for-defa/
Justin Baker, a self-professed anti-Christian activist and security guard at Doubletree Hotel in Jackson, Tennessee, discovered religious objects such as the Torah and various prayer books left in a meeting room by overnight guests for a worship ceremony the following morning. Baker spit on the Torah and defaced the books with profanity and phrases including "Hail Satan." Baker was sentenced to five years in prison and required to pay $9,999.99 in restitution damages.

Resident Sues Local County Over Opening Prayers
http://www.mlive.com/news/jackson/index.ssf/2013/12/jackson_county_will_not_back_d.html
Jackson County resident Peter Bormuth filed a lawsuit against the Jackson County Board of Commissioners due to the board's tradition of opening prayers that included the closing phrase "in the name of Jesus Christ, Amen." The county refused to change its tradition and is currently defending against the lawsuit.

North Carolina Groups Oppose School Grants for Low-Income Families
http://www.reflector.com/node/2242447
http://www.wncn.com/story/24741381/nc-judge-hears-lawsuits-over-private-school-grants
When the North Carolina legislature proposed a law that would give financial aid to low-income students wishing to attend private schools, the North Carolina Association of Educators and the North Carolina Justice Center attempted to block the financial aid by claiming that such action violated the state constitution. This case is ongoing.

Groups Seek to Undermine Oklahoma Ten Commandments Monument
http://www.nbcnews.com/news/other/satanists-want-statue-beside-ten-commandments-monument-oklahoma-legislature-f2D11712595
http://rajanzed.com/rajan/index.php/2013/12/10/hindus-interested-in-erecting-lord-hanuman-statue-in-oklahoma-capitol-grounds/
Various groups, including Satanists and Hindus, sought permission to erect displays next to the Ten Commandments monument on the State Capital grounds. The State has ordered a moratorium until the lawsuit regarding the Ten Commandments monument is resolved.

Anti-Religion Advocates Ridicule Christmas Displays
http://articles.orlandosentinel.com/2013-12-09/news/os-festivus-florida-capitol-20131209_1_festivus-pole-chaz-stevens-nativity-scene
When the Florida Prayer Network (FPN) obtained permission to erect a Nativity scene in the Florida Capital, various antireligion groups and individuals pitched in to mock FPN, constructing displays right beside the Nativity scene such as a six-foot tall "Festivus" pole made from empty beer cans and a banner reading: "At this season of the Winter Solstice, we celebrate the Birth of the Unconquered Sun—the TRUE reason for the season."

Utah Attorney General Orders Issuance of Same-Sex "Marriage" Licenses Regardless of Religious Beliefs
http://www.sltrib.com/sltrib/news/57306295-78/county-sex-marriage-office. html.csp
After a federal district court legalized same-sex "marriage" in Utah, several clerks refused to administer the licenses due to religious beliefs. The Utah Attorney General consequently issued a statement that anyone refusing to administer the licenses would be held in contempt of court.

California Citizen Sues to Stop City Council Prayers
http://www.times-standard.com/breakingnews/ci_24818317/prayer-city-judge-narrowly-rules-eurekas-favor
Carole Beaton, a citizen of Eureka, California, brought a broad claim against the city for the city council's regular opening of their meetings with prayer by a paid chaplain and the annual Mayor's Prayer Breakfast. In her lawsuit, Beaton attempted to silence any type prayer whatsoever. A California state court held that the city's prayer practice was permitted, but indicated that Beaton could have successfully challenged the practices if she had narrowed her complaint.

Employees Fired for Refusing to Follow Scientology Mandates
http://eeoc.gov/eeoc/newsroom/release/12-23-13a.cfm
Dynamic Medical Services (DMS), a medical services company in Miami, Florida, ordered several employees to spend half of their workdays attending Scientology courses that involved practices such as staring at someone for eight hours without moving or screaming at inanimate objects. When the employees repeatedly requested exemptions from the classes and ultimately refused to continue attending, they were terminated. The employees filed a lawsuit for the discrimination, and DMS paid the employees $170,000 in settlement.

Restaurant Fires Employee for Religious Observance
http://www.laurinburgexchange.com/news/home_top-news/2550429/Suit-brought-against-Scottish-Foods
http://www.eeoc.gov/eeoc/newsroom/release/12-23-13.cfm
Sheila Silver is a devout Pentecostal woman who wore skirts instead of pants to work in accordance with her religious beliefs. After another company acquired her restaurant, the new owners commanded her to conform to their dress code by wearing pants. When Silver insisted on following her religious convictions, she was fired. The EEOC subsequently brought a lawsuit

on Silver's behalf, and the new owners agreed to settle the suit by paying Silver $40,000.

California McDonald's Fires Employee for Religious Beliefs

http://eeoc.gov/eeoc/newsroom/release/12-20-13a.cfm

McDonald's Restaurants of California, Inc. refused to allow a Muslim crew trainer to grow a beard in adherence to his religion. When the employee refused to compromise on his religious beliefs, he was fired. The employee filed a complaint against the discrimination, and the restaurant agreed to settle by paying the employee $50,000.

"Duck Dynasty" TV Star Suspended for Religious Beliefs

http://www.foxnews.com/entertainment/2013/12/18/phil-robertson-suspended-after-comments-about-homosexuality/

http://www.foxnews.com/entertainment/2013/12/28/duck-dynasty-to-resume-filming-with-phil-robertson-ae-announces/

When Phil Robertson of A&E's "Duck Dynasty" stated that he believed that homosexuality was a sin due to his religious beliefs, A&E suspended him from the show. After a massive national controversy ensued, the network reinstated Robertson and continued the show as before.

Activists Pressure Comedian into Canceling Performance for Catholic Group

http://www.catholicculture.org/news/headlines/index.cfm?storyid=20035

Comedian Bob Newhart was scheduled to perform for Legatus, an organization of Catholic businessmen, but backed out under pressure from the Gay and Lesbian Alliance Against Discrimination who denounced Legatus as a "rabid anti-LGBT organization."

Atheist Group Demands the Removal of Nativity Scene from City Hall

http://www.theblaze.com/stories/2013/12/12/officials-refuse-to-back-down-in-battle-with-atheists-over-florida-citys-nativity-scene/#

When the City of Chipley, Florida, erected their annual Nativity scene display in the city hall, a local reporter contacted the Freedom From Religion Foundation. The FFRF wrote a demand letter to the city council, claiming that the display violated the Constitution and demanding its elimination. City officials refused to remove the Nativity scene but added a decorated Christmas tree in an attempt to balance the display with a secular symbol.

ATTACKS IN THE PUBLIC ARENA

County Officials Block Business Owner from Building Chapel on Private Land

http://www.onenewsnow.com/legal-courts/2013/12/06/vineyards-private-chapel-focus-of-legal-dispute-in-calif#.U5CCoi-Qydw

Reverge Anselmo, owner of Seven Hills Land and Cattle Company in Shasta County, California, built a private chapel on part of his land for use by friends and family. However, officials from Shasta County issued a "Red Tag Stop Order" prohibiting Anselmo from using the chapel.

Police Drag Pro-Life Advocates to Court for Sidewalk Ministry

https://www.thomasmoresociety.org/2013/12/06/breaking-news-cases-dismissed-and-pro-lifers-first-amendment-rights-protected/

Brian Westbrook, executive director of Coalition for Life, and Rita Sparrow, veteran sidewalk counselor, peacefully protested outside of a local Planned Parenthood location in St. Louis, Missouri, on a regular basis. Westbrook maintained a sign offering free pregnancy testing and ultrasounds, while Sparrow sat in her chair and spoke with individuals. Without warning, St. Louis police charged Westbrook with false advertising because he was not personally giving the pregnancy tests but was instead referring patrons to the ultrasound van across the street. Additionally, Sparrow was accused of littering with her lawn chair. Judge Michael Noble of the St. Louis Circuit Court threw the charges out, protecting Westbrook and Sparrow's First Amendment rights.

Senior Center Told to Quit Praying Before Meals

http://ffrf.org/legal/other-legal-successes/item/19742-ffrf-removes-prayers-before-meals-at-south-carolina-senior-center-december-5-2013

The Freedom From Religion Foundation sent a letter to the Simpsonville Activity and Senior Center in Simpsonville, South Carolina, demanding the discontinuation of praying before meals. Director of Recreation Robbie Davis confirmed that "staff at the Simpsonville Senior Center has ceased leading or encouraging prayer before meal functions."

Police Officer Rebuked for Recommending Local Churches

http://ffrf.org/legal/other-legal-successes/item/19882-ffrf-ends-religious-promotion-by-police-december-4-2013

In Toledo, Ohio, the course of a conversation between a citizen and a police officer brought up the topic of churches, and the officer recommended several local churches to the citizen. The citizen complained to the Freedom From Religion Foundation, who complained to the Toledo Police Department. The

Chief of Police confirmed that the officer's supervisor would be told to counsel the officer about his actions.

FFRF Ends Church Discount at New Jersey Restaurant
http://ffrf.org/legal/other-legal-successes/item/19743-new-jersey-restaurant-retracts-exclusive-discount-december-2-2013
When the Freedom From Religion Foundation heard that Aleathea's Restaurant in Cape May, New Jersey, offered a discount to churchgoers, it wrote a letter demanding the elimination of the practice. The restaurant cancelled its discount.

Atheist Group Calls for Shoppers to Boycott Hobby Lobby
http://ffrf.org/news/news-releases/item/19500-ffrf-calls-for-hobby-lobby-boycott
The Freedom From Religion Foundation called for a complete boycott of Hobby Lobby due to the company owners' stand for their religious beliefs regarding the Obamacare contraceptive mandate.

Atheist Group Condemns Local Police Chief's Christian Affirmations
http://christiannews.net/2013/11/26/georgia-police-chief-moves-christian-posts-to-personal-page-following-pressure-from-atheists/
Gary Jones, a police chief in Harlem, Georgia, posted a myriad of messages on the Harlem Public Safety Department Facebook page that included alerts, encouragement, criminal updates, and parenting tips from a Christian perspective. The Freedom From Religion Foundation found out about the Christian nature of some of Jones's posts and immediately sent a demand letter to the department to bring a halt to Jones's messages. Jones eventually submitted and created a separate personal page to continue his posts.

President Obama Omits "Under God" from Public Reading of Gettysburg Address
http://blog.libertyinstitute.org/2013/11/was-president-obama-right-to-omit-under.html
In celebration of the 150th anniversary of the Gettysburg Address, President Obama was scheduled to recreate President Lincoln's famous speech. However, the President declined to visit the official site, opting instead to record a reading of the address that conspicuously left out the words "under God."

U.S. Senate Passes Bill Attacking Religious Liberty

http://blog.libertyinstitute.org/2013/11/us-senate-passes-bill-attacking.html
The U.S. Senate approved and passed on to the House of Representatives the "Employment Non-Discrimination Act" (ENDA), which would affect hiring and firing laws as well as workplace codes of conduct. The ENDA would discriminate against those who believe that homosexual and transgender behavior is wrong based on religious grounds.

Atheist Group Sues California City for Prayers at City Council Meetings

http://ffrf.org/news/news-releases/item/19100-ffrf-sues-over-prayers-chaplain-in-pismo-beach-calif
The Freedom From Religion Foundation filed a lawsuit against the city of Pismo Beach, California, complaining that the appointment of a city chaplain who prayed to the Christian God and led the vast majority of opening prayers at city council meetings was unconstitutional. The city agreed to pay over $47,000 in nominal damages and attorneys' fees, eradicate the practice of praying at meetings, and eliminate the chaplain position.

Shipping Company Suppresses Employee Prayer

http://www.wcpo.com/news/region-northern-kentucky/cair-cincinnati-to-announce-complaint-against-dhl-for-firing-24-nky-muslim-workers-over-prayers
After a DHL Express branch in Kentucky realized that some of its Muslim employees were using their flexible fifteen-minute break periods for prayer, the facility eliminated the breaks. When several employees attempted to continue conducting their prayers outside of formal break times, DHL fired them, even though other employees were allowed to take nonscheduled breaks for activities such as smoking. The employees have filed a complaint with the EEOC for DHL's discrimination.

National Bank Closes Muslims' Bank Accounts

http://dearborn.patch.com/groups/politics-and-elections/p/civil-rights-lawsuit-alleges-huntington-national-bank-discriminates-against-arab-americans
http://dawudwalid.wordpress.com/2013/11/22/civil-rights-advocacy-group-says-banks-closed-more-accounts-of-muslims/
Without explanation, Huntington National Bank suddenly began closing numerous personal and business bank accounts that belonged to individuals who were Muslim or of Arabian descent. After receiving numerous reports of such closures, the Arab-American Civil Rights League launched an investigation and assisted in filing a lawsuit against the arcane discriminatory treatment. The group has also requested the Office of the Comptroller of

the Currency and the Consumer Financial Protection Bureau to investigate similar closures of JPMorgan Chase Muslim customers.

Wholesale Giant Labels Bibles as "Fiction"

http://townhall.com/columnists/toddstarnes/2013/11/19/why-did-costco-label-bible-as-fiction-n1749324

A Costco Wholesale store in Simi Valley placed Bibles in the fiction book section. When confronted, Costco management blamed placement on human warehouse error.

Atheist Scares City into Withdrawing Funding for Annual Christmas Celebration

http://www.theblaze.com/stories/2013/11/18/christmas-was-nearly-canceled-in-this-small-town-after-an-atheist-activists-threat-but-heres-how-people-rallied-to-save-an-annual-celebration/

After an atheist complained to city officials in Spencerport, New York, about the annual holiday celebration, "Christmas on the Canal," which included carols, tree lighting, a Nativity scene, and other festivities, the town told event founder and organizer Elaine Spaziano to remove religious references and secularize the event. When Spaziano refused, the town pulled its sponsorship. However, the community rose up in support of the event and provided the necessary funding to continue the annual celebration.

New Mexico Hotel Fires Muslim Employee for Following Religious Practices

http://eeoc.gov/eeoc/newsroom/release/11-18-13.cfm

Safia Abdullah, a practicing Muslim, was hired for a housekeeping position by MCM Elegante Hotel in Albuquerque, New Mexico. However, Abdullah's supervisor refused to allow her to work unless she removed her hijab. When Abdullah insisted on following her religion by not removing her hijab, she was fired. The EEOC filed a lawsuit on Abdullah's behalf, and the hotel settled the claim.

ACLU Demands That Catholic Hospital Advise Abortions

http://durangoherald.com/article/20131113/NEWS01/131119849/-1/News01/ACLU:-Mercy-anti-abortion-policy-illegal-

After Mercy Regional Medical Center cardiologist Dr. Michael Demos advised a woman to consider abortion due to a possible medical condition, the Catholic hospital's chief medical officer instructed Demos not to recommend abortions in order to uphold the hospital's religious, pro-life stance. The ACLU found out about the issue and demanded that the state Department of Public Health and Environment investigate and end the hospital's policy.

Atheist Group Fights Church Discount at Texas Restaurant

http://ffrf.org/legal/other-legal-successes/item/19292-ffrf-stops-illegal-church-discount-november-8-2013

When the Freedom From Religion Foundation heard that Luna's Friendswood, a Mexican food franchise in Texas, offered a ten percent discount to diners with church bulletins, it threatened the restaurant with a demand letter that called for the discontinuation of the discount. The restaurant owners bowed to the FFRF's demands and stopped the discount.

UPS Fires Jehovah's Witness for Attending Religious Service

http://eeoc.gov/eeoc/newsroom/release/12-3-12a.cfm

http://www.eeoc.gov/eeoc/newsroom/release/11-4-13.cfm

UPS refused to accommodate a request to adjust the start date of a newly hired employee so that he could attend an annual religious service as part of his beliefs as a Jehovah's Witness. UPS fired him after he chose to attend the religious service rather than violate his religious beliefs. The EEOC filed a lawsuit on his behalf, and the UPS agreed to pay $70,000 in a settlement.

Minnesota Attorney Attacks Judges with Anti-Religious Slurs

http://www.twincities.com/crime/ci_24613398/hastings-lawyer-suspended-religious-slurs

Rebekah Nett, an attorney based in Hastings, Minnesota, lashed out at several federal bankruptcy judges in her filings before the court. Nett described the judges with slurs such as "black-robed bigot" and "Catholic Knight Witch Hunter." Nett was suspended indefinitely for her harassment and discriminatory statements.

Muslim Security Guard Fired for Refusing to Shave His Beard

http://seattletimes.com/html/localnews/2021994205_beardlawsuitxml.html

American Patriot Security (APS) hired Abdulkadir Omar, a practicing Muslim, as a security guard in 2009. One day, the APS regional manager, citing the company's grooming policy, commanded Omar to shave his closely cropped beard, even though Omar had never before been told that his beard was not allowed. Omar repeatedly requested a religious exception due to the fact that his religious beliefs required him to have a beard. Nonetheless, APS fired Omar for his desire to honor his religion. Omar then filed a lawsuit against APS for its discriminatory actions, and the U.S. District Court for the Western District of Washington awarded Omar with over $66,000 in back pay.

Atheist Group Pressures Police Department into Forgoing Prayer for the City

http://www.wlwt.com/news/local-news/cincinnati/police-forced-to-withdraw-from-prayer-walks-after-lawsuit-threat/22775768

In Cincinnati, Ohio, local faith leaders joined with members of the Cincinnati Police Department (CPD) to combat violence by making regular prayer walks around the city. The Freedom From Religion Foundation found out about the initiative and promptly sent a letter threatening a lawsuit unless the CPD ended their involvement with the prayer walks. Although the CPD initially wanted to find a way to continue their participation, the organizers agreed that a lawsuit should be avoided, and the CPD consequently withdrew from the group.

Prayer at Luncheon at Atlanta Airport Draws Rebuke

http://ffrf.org/legal/other-legal-successes/item/19137-ffrf-grounds-prayer-at-atlanta-airport

An employee and customer satisfaction luncheon at Hartsfield-Jackson Atlanta International Airport was opened with Bible verses and prayer. When an attendee complained to the Freedom From Religion Foundation, the FFRF wrote a demand letter to the airport with charges of constitutional violations. The airport responded that it took notice of the FFRF's objection and would "abide by all applicable law" in the future.

Department Head Criticized for Providing Devotionals to President Obama

https://www.au.org/blogs/wall-of-separation/publicly-funded-presidential-prayers-former-faith-based-office-director

Joshua Dubois, former head of the Office of Faith-Based and Neighborhood Partnerships, provided regularly emailed morning devotionals to President Obama during his tenure. Even though Dubois composed the messages while off the clock, Americans United for Separation of Church and State condemned Dubois's actions as an inappropriate use of government time and money, as well as an unfit catering to President Obama's religious interests.

Atheist Group Threatens Lawsuit over Police Chaplains Unit

http://blog.al.com/montgomery/2013/10/atheist_group_says_montgomery.html#incart_m-rpt-2

http://www.wsfa.com/story/23780685/montgomery-responds-to-atheist-organizations-demand-it-end-operation-good-shepherd

The Montgomery Police Department in Montgomery, Alabama, has a program called Operation Good Shepherd that dispatches trained clergy to violent crime scenes to help comfort the victims. The Freedom From Religion Foundation (FFRF) and American Atheists Inc. (AAI) threatened to sue the city unless Operation Good Shepherd was disbanded or expanded to somehow include atheists. Montgomery City Attorney Kimberly Fehl refused to succumb to the threats and instead informed the FFRF and AAI that Operation Good Shepherd would continue.

Mennonite Couple Threatened for Refusing to Host Same-Sex "Marriages"

http://www.christianpost.com/news/mennonite-couple-refuses-to-host-same-sex-wedding-files-lawsuit-against-iowa-civil-rights-commission-106308/

Richard and Betty Odgaard, a Mennonite couple from Iowa, own Gortz Haus Gallery, a former church that was transformed into an art gallery. When the Odgaards refused to host a same-sex "marriage" at the Gallery due to their religious beliefs, a claim for discrimination was filed before the Iowa Civil Rights Commission (ICRC). The Odgaards refused to stand for the discrimination against their own beliefs, and responded by filing a lawsuit in the Polk County District Court to enjoin the punitive action levied by the ICRC.

California Train Refuses Transportation to Sikh Student

http://www.davisenterprise.com/local-news/sikh-student-barred-from-bus-over-religious-artifact/

Harsimran Singh, a UC Davis student and a Sikh from Davis, California, attempted to board a local Amtrak for transportation as he had for the past two years. The driver, noticing Singh's kirpan (a small, blunt dagger worn by Sikhs at all times under the requirements of Sikhism), called the police and refused to allow Singh to board the bus. Singh refused to violate his religious beliefs by removing his kirpan, and was consequently barred from the bus.

Restaurant Supervisors Heap Anti-Semitic Harassment on Jewish Deliveryman

http://nypost.com/2013/10/28/anti-jewish-jokes-about-nazi-death-gas-netsman-900k/

For sixteen years, Adam Wiercinski, a Jew with close family ties to the Holocaust, delivered food to Mangia 57, a midtown New York restaurant. During that time, Wiercinski's supervisors subjected him to continual persecution because of his Jewish heritage, joking about Nazi gas chambers and referring to him as a "dirty Jew." Wiercinski finally filed a lawsuit to stop the harassment, and the jury levied a judgment of $900,000 against the restaurant.

Missouri Governor Vetoes Proposed Law Protecting Christmas

http://www.stljewishlight.com/news/local/article_da3ab208-3205-11e3-aa21-001a4bcf887a.html

After the Missouri legislature passed a bill that would prohibit government facilities from banning or restricting the observance of federal holidays (including Christmas), Missouri Governor Jay Nixon vetoed the bill, citing safety concerns. State legislators overwhelmingly voted to override the governor's veto, however, and the bill was passed into law.

Washington State Court Judge Disciplined for Refusing to Perform Same-Sex Weddings

http://www.theolympian.com/2013/10/05/2759870/state-admonishes-judge-over-wedding.html

http://www.cjc.state.wa.us/Case%20Material/2013/7251%20Tabor%20Stip%20FINAL.pdf

Thurston County Superior Court Judge Gary Tabor publicly stated that he would not perform same-sex weddings in his judicial capacity due to his philosophical and religious convictions. In response, the Washington Judicial Conduct Commission levied a sanction against Judge Tabor for violating sexual orientation discrimination laws and required him to choose between violating his religious beliefs by performing same-sex "marriages" in addition to traditional marriages, or abstaining from performing marriages at all. Judge Tabor opted to cease performing marriage ceremonies entirely under the illusory choice.

City Council Member Criticized for Organizing Weekend Prayer Vigil

http://wtvr.com/2013/10/02/aclu-eyes-district-wide-prayer-event-at-richmond-schools/

http://acluva.org/14059/aclu-of-virginia-seeks-information-about-upcoming-prayer-events-in-forty-five-richmond-public-school-buildings-urges-compliance-with-the-constitution/

Michelle Mosby, a city council member for Richland, Virginia, was concerned for the safety of children in the wake of growing violence in schools. Consequently, she organized a community hour of prayer on a Saturday at all Richmond public schools. However, the Richmond ACLU launched an inquiry when it heard of the event and condemned Mosby's identification as a city council member affiliated with prayer and her use of work printers for producing event flyers. Mosby ignored the backlash and carried out the event as planned.

Atheist Organization Targets Religious Contract Workers

http://ffrf.org/news/news-releases/item/18310-us-postal-service-trucks-no-place-for-religious-imagery

The Freedom From Religion Foundation sent a demand letter to the U.S. Postal Service requesting a ban on religious symbols on contract workers' personal vehicles.

Mississippi Judge Ejects Sikh from Courtroom for Wearing a Turban

http://www.huffingtonpost.com/2013/09/27/judge-rimes-sikh-slur-remove-that-rag_n_3998852.html

Jagjeet Singh, a practicing Sikh, was pulled over for a flat tire, harassed by Mississippi Department of Transportation officers, and ultimately arrested for refusing to relinquish his kirpan (a small ceremonial knife that is a mandatory religious article for Sikhs). Once taken to court, Judge Aubrey Rimes of the Pike County Justice Court ejected Singh from the court due to Singh's turban, which Judge Rimes publicly referred to as "that rag." The Department of Justice intervened with an investigation and prompted amendments to the Pike County nondiscrimination policy to protect religious freedom in the future.

Car Dealership Fires Employee for Honoring Sabbath

http://www.sacbee.com/2013/09/27/5775664/maita-chevrolet-pays-to-settle.html

Anthony Okan, a Seventh-day Adventist, was a salesman for Maita Chevrolet in El Grove, California. Mr. Okan notified Maita Chevrolet of his religious beliefs against working from sundown Friday until sundown Saturday. Maita Chevrolet nevertheless repeatedly scheduled Mr. Okan to work during those times. Maita Chevrolet harassed, disciplined, and fired Mr. Okan when he continued to honor his Sabbath. The EEOC filed a lawsuit on Mr. Okan's behalf, and the car dealership settled by agreeing to pay Mr. Okan $158,000, revise its policy manual, and train its personnel on their legal obligations regarding religious freedoms.

Freedom From Religion Foundation Opposes Jewish Holiday Observance

http://ffrf.org/news/news-releases/item/18762-new-york-sukkahs-need-to-stop-obstructing-pedestrians

Every year, practicing Jews place small, temporary booths outside of their homes in which they eat their meals as part of the celebration of the Jewish holiday of Sukkot. The Freedom From Religion Foundation specifically targeted observant Jews from Brooklyn, New York, by complaining to the city's Department of Sanitation Bureau of Legal Affairs that the booths should be banned. Additionally, the FFRF called on other New York citizens to follow suit.

Freedom From Religion Foundation Demands Abolition of Cross from City Seal

http://www.idsnews.com/news/story.aspx?id=94285
Ellettsville, Indiana, has a city seal featuring symbols representing key features of the community: knowledge, industry, unity, and God. When the FFRF discovered the city seal's inclusion of a cross and the words "In God We Trust," they sent a demand letter to the town council that denounced the seal as an unconstitutional violation of the Establishment Clause of the First Amendment. The city council stated that the seal would remain unchanged unless a lawsuit is filed against the town.

Florida Business Attacked for Requiring Accurate Advertising for Anti-Christian Documentary

http://aclj.org/equal-access/victory-for-liberty-defeat-anti-christian-activists
A private business owner in Florida who provided facilities for homeschoolers and community events was approached by a patron who wanted to show a documentary at the business owner's facilities entitled, "Caesar's Messiah: The Roman Conspiracy to Invent Jesus." However, the patron wanted to advertise the film on the business owner's website under the title, "Caesar's Messiah Documentary (History of Christianity)." The business owner refused to post the misleading title and instead required accurate advertising. After the showing, the patron filed a discrimination complaint with the Florida Commission on Human Rights (FCHR) against the business owner for his insistence on honesty. After a religious liberties group stepped in to defend the business owner, the FCHR quickly dismissed the complaint.

Ten Commandments Monument Vandalized in Washington, D.C.

http://www.breitbart.com/Big-Government/2013/09/23/10-Commandments-monument-toppled-in-Washington
http://www.washingtontimes.com/news/2013/oct/29/toppled-ten-commandments-back-in-place-near-suprem/
Faith and Action, a Christian outreach ministry in Washington, D.C., installed a monument of the Ten Commandments on their property, which is behind the U.S. Supreme Court. The monument was situated so that it was visible to the Supreme Court justices as they entered and exited the courthouse. One morning, Reverend Robert Schenck arrived at the Faith and Action building to

find the monument pushed facedown into the dirt; the metal pole supporting the monument had been bent into a 90-degree angle to the ground. Faith and Action repaired the monument and vowed to never yield to persecution.

Sikh College Professor Beaten for His Religion
http://www.huffingtonpost.com/2013/09/22/prabhjot-singh-sikh-columbia-hate-crime_n_3972449.html
Dr. Prabhjot Singh, a Columbia University professor and a practicing Sikh, was attacked by a group of men who believed him to be a Muslim due to his beard and turban. Singh was knocked to the ground and beaten while the men shouted anti-Muslim statements at him.

Atheist Group Calls for Dismemberment of Police Chaplain's Unit
http://www.kob.com/article/stories/S3148086.shtml?cat=500
The Albuquerque Police Department in New Mexico maintains a chaplain's unit, which is mainly composed of volunteers who pray with and counsel police officers and families that are experiencing trauma due to horrific accidents or crimes. The Freedom From Religion Foundation wrote a letter to the mayor calling the chaplain's group "callous" because it doesn't address atheists and requesting the unit's dissolution.

Religious Statues Decapitated in New Jersey
http://philadelphia.cbslocal.com/2013/09/19/religious-statues-decapitated-outside-church-in-gloucester-county/
Nine statues belonging to St. Mary's Malaga in New Jersey were defaced, including the decapitation of statues of Jesus and the Virgin Mary. Local police are investigating the vandalism and considering upgrading the charges to a hate crime.

College Threatens to Expel Student for Observance of Religious Holiday
http://blogs.dallasobserver.com/unfairpark/2013/09/an_orthodox_jew_says_el_centro.php
Hillel Rodin is an Orthodox Jew from Dallas, Texas, who attends nursing school at El Centro Community College. On Rosh Hashanah, the Jewish New Year and one of the holiest days in Judaism, Rodin is prohibited from working, driving, writing, touching money, or using electricity due to his religious beliefs. When Rodin found out that classes would be conducted on Rosh Hashanah, he requested an exception from attending and offered to participate in make-up classes. The school refused to accommodate Rodin's requests and threatened to expel Mr. Rodin if he missed class or was more than fifteen minutes late. However, after Rodin filed a lawsuit, the school

discontinued their religious discrimination and agreed to allow Rodin to make up missed classes at a later date.

Muslim Groups Call for Disciplinary Action Against County Employee for Criticism of Islam

http://www.theblaze.com/stories/2013/09/14/county-employee-faces-discipline-for-post-critical-of-islam-he-made-on-his-private-facebook-page/

John Jamason, a county public affairs staffer for Palm Beach County in Florida, posted a message criticizing Islam on his personal Facebook page. Word spread about the post, and Islamic advocates called for disciplinary action against Jamason. After an investigation, the county decided against punishing Jamason.

Man Attempts to Gun Down Christians for Their Beliefs

http://www.lifenews.com/2013/09/11/man-who-shot-up-pro-life-office-wanted-to-kill-conservative-right-wing-christians/

http://www.breitbart.com/Big-Government/2013/09/19/Convicted-Gay-Marriage-Domestic-Terrorist-Sentences-to-25-Years-in-Prison

Floyd Lee Corkins entered the office of the Family Research Counsel with a semi-automatic pistol and one-hundred rounds of ammunition and began firing on employees before the building manager and police apprehended him. Corkins later verified that he wanted to kill "conservative right-wing Christians." Corkin was sentenced to twenty-five years in federal prison.

College Football Commentator Fired for Belief in Biblical Marriage

http://www.libertyinstitute.org/pages/issues/in-the-public-arena/liberty-institute-confronts-major-network-after-sportscaster-is-fired-for-his-faith

Craig James, a former college and NFL player, was hired by Fox Sports Southwest to join their sports broadcasting team. After one appearance on the air, Fox Sports Southwest fired Craig James. A Fox spokesperson told the Dallas Morning News that James was fired because of his religious convictions that marriage should be between one man and one woman. James had not discussed his views about marriage on the air but two years prior after being asked about his views during a campaign for the U.S. Senate. James retained Liberty Institute as counsel to help him fight back against the discriminatory termination.

City Refuses to Accommodate Messianic Jewish Woman

http://blog.al.com/spotnews/2013/09/messianic_jewish_woman_wins_ba.html

The City of Birmingham, Alabama, required Renee Gunn, a Messianic Jew, to work on her Sabbath, which is from sundown Friday until sundown Saturday.

After the city refused to accommodate her request for an exemption, Ms. Gunn resigned from her position in order to observe her Sabbath. Ms. Gunn then filed a lawsuit. The city agreed to settle the religious discrimination claim by rehiring Ms. Gunn and paying her $80,000 in back pay and compensatory damages.

Anti-Religion Group Opposes State Bill that Safeguards Religious Freedom

http://ffrf.org/news/news-releases/item/18615-quash-orwellian-%E2%80%9Creligious-freedom-amendment%E2%80%9D-in-wis-legislature
The Wisconsin legislature introduced an amendment to the state constitution consistent with Supreme Court precedent that protects religious liberty and the right of conscience for all citizens. The Freedom From Religion Foundation labeled the proposal "Orwellian" and called for its rejection.

Group Demands the Removal of Cross from City Seal

http://www.news-journalonline.com/article/20130903/NEWS/130909828?p=1&tc=pg
Americans United for Separation of Church and State wrote a letter to Mayor Bob Apgar of DeLand, Florida, demanding that the city remove a cross from the 131-year-old city seal. The town refused to bow to the request, and the city's attorney wrote a reply letter outlining the constitutionality of the seal.

Mayor Eradicates Cross from City Seal

http://ffrf.org/legal/other-legal-successes/item/18824-ffrf-complaint-removed-latin-cross-seal-from-public-building-august-30-2013
When the Freedom From Religion Foundation heard that the city seal of Wauwatosa, Wisconsin, contained a Latin-style cross, it called on Mayor Kathleen Ehley to purge the cross from the seal. Mayor Ehley assured the FFRF that they were in the process of replacing the seals, and that the versions displaying the cross were almost extinct.

Atheist Group Threatens Lawsuit over 9/11 Memorial

http://aclj.org/us-constitution/jay-sekulow-princeton-nj-must-not-let-atheists-derail-9-11-memorial-cross
Roy James, the Deputy Fire Chief in Princeton, New Jersey, acquired an iron beam from the ruins of the World Trade Center and proposed using the beam as a 9/11 memorial. When the American Atheists (AA) learned that a cross had been cut into one side of the beam, they called the memorial "grossly offensive" and threatened to sue the city if the memorial were approved.

Atheist Group Pressures County Chairman to Eliminate Religious References

http://whnt.com/2013/08/26/exclusive-atheist-group-calls-for-elimination-of-prayer-at-madison-county-commission/

Dale Strong, the Madison County Chairman in Huntsville, Alabama, opened commission meetings with prayer and included a reference to Joshua 1:9 in his official public biography. The Freedom From Religion Foundation wrote multiple letters to Strong insisting that he eliminate the opening prayers and remove the Bible verse from his biography. FFRF called the prayers "unnecessary, inappropriate and divisive" and stated that Strong was unconstitutionally using "official power to espouse [his] particular religious beliefs." Strong refused to compromise from his position and reaffirmed his commitment to continue his practices until commanded otherwise by the courts.

Atheist Group Harasses County into Removing George Washington Quote from Website

http://ffrf.org/legal/other-legal-successes/item/18645-ffrf-removes-out-of-context-washington-quote-that-puts-down-nonbelievers-august-23-2013

The website for Creek County, Oklahoma, contained a quote from George Washington calling for acknowledgement of God's providence in all things. The Freedom From Religion Foundation complained that the quote disparaged nonbelievers and called for its removal. The county acquiesced and deleted the quote.

City Eliminates Prayer from Anniversary Celebration

http://ffrf.org/legal/other-legal-successes/item/18686-ffrf-ensures-ny-town%E2%80%99s-bicentennial-celebration-stays-secular-august-23-2013

The town of Victor, New York, planned a bicentennial anniversary celebration of the city's incorporation. The celebration was to include a prayer service. The Freedom From Religion Foundation told the town that such prayer would be an unconstitutional government endorsement of Christianity. The town submitted to the FFRF's threat and cancelled the prayer service.

Anti-Religion Group Attempts to Coerce City Counsel into Abandoning Prayer

http://www.thenewamerican.com/culture/faith-and-morals/item/16132-texas-city-stands-up-to-atheists-over-prayers-at-government-meetings

http://blog.libertyinstitute.org/2013/08/liberty-institute-helps-league-city.html

The Freedom From Religion Foundation sent a demand letter to Mayor Tim Paulissen and the city counsel of League City, Texas, calling for the immediate abandonment of the city's tradition of opening counsel meetings with an invocation. Instead of succumbing to the FFRF's threats, Mayor Paulissen retained Liberty Institute for counsel and boldly declared that he and the other counsel members had no plans to stop praying before meetings.

Atheist Groups Demand Halt to Prayers by City Council
http://www.chicoer.com/news/ci_23842557/whats-prayer-got-do-it-local-atheist-group
The Coalition of Reason and the Freedom From Religion Foundation called for Chico, California, to stop opening its city council meetings with prayer. Even though the U.S. Supreme Court declared that such actions were constitutional over thirty years ago, the groups allege that the practice unconstitutionally breaches separation of church and state. Chico City Attorney Lori Barker stated that the prayers are "clearly permitted by law" and that the city will not change its practice until mandated by the U.S. Supreme Court.

San Antonio Proposes Ordinance Limiting All Who Have Ever Held Traditional Views of Sexuality
http://blog.libertyinstitute.org/2013/08/san-antonios-proposed-ordinance-would.html
http://radio.foxnews.com/toddstarnes/top-stories/san-antonio-passes-non-discrimination-law-christians-fear-reprisals.html
San Antonio proposed an ordinance that would ban citizens who have ever held traditional religious views about sexuality from holding public office or performing city contracts and subcontracts. Liberty Institute submitted a letter to the mayor and city council opposing the ordinance and warning of its unconstitutionality. San Antonio enacted a modified version of the proposed ordinance.

ACLU Seeks to Remove Ten Commandments from State Capitol
http://blog.libertyinstitute.org/2013/08/aclu-wants-ten-commandments-monument.html
In 2009, Oklahoma Representative Mike Ritze proposed legislation for a privately funded monument of the Ten Commandments on the Oklahoma state capitol grounds. The proposal received bipartisan support from both the state House of Representatives and the Senate, with former Democratic Governor Brad Henry signing the bill into law. Less than a year after the erection of the monument, the ACLU of Oklahoma filed a lawsuit to have the monument removed, alleging that it constitutes an unlawful "appropriation of public property" in support of religion. The lawsuit is ongoing.

Hotel Refuses to Provide Employee With Religious Accommodation
http://eeoc.gov/eeoc/newsroom/release/7-23-13.cfm
A hotel group that owns and operates the Comfort Inn Oceanfront South in Nags Head, North Carolina, hired Claudia Neal, a Seventh-day Adventist, and agreed to give her a religious accommodation that exempted her from working on her Sabbath, which is from sundown on Friday until sundown on Saturday. After a change in management, the hotel refused to uphold the religious accommodation and fired Neal. After Neal filed a religious discrimination lawsuit, the hotel agreed to settle by paying $45,000 in damages to Neal and implementing policies and training to prevent religious discrimination in the future.

Cell Phone Retailer Refuses to Provide Employee With Religious Accommodation
http://eeoc.gov/eeoc/newsroom/release/7-18-13a.cfm
United Cellular, a Sprint Preferred Retailer headquartered in Irving, Texas, hired Charles Embry, a practicing Seventh-day Adventist, with full knowledge of Embry's need for a religious accommodation exempting him from working on his Sabbath, which is from sundown on Friday until sundown on Saturday. Nevertheless, United Cellular scheduled Embry for weekends and terminated Embry after he continued to exercise his religious faith by honoring his Sabbath. The EEOC has filed suit (*EEOC v. United Cellular, Inc.*, Case No. CV-13-JHE-1207-NE) in the U.S. District Court for the Northern District of Alabama.

Atheist Group Objects to Holocaust Memorial
http://online.wsj.com/article/AP6a74789b5c1748418b33e05294cb1c2f.html
http://ffrf.org/images/Ohio%20Statehouse%20Holocaust%20Memorial.pdf
http://ffrf.org/news/news-releases/item/18172-ffrf-objects-to-religious-symbol-at-ohio-capitol
The Freedom From Religion Foundation complained that the display of a Star of David on a privately funded Holocaust memorial designed by a famed architect and displayed on Ohio statehouse grounds violated separation of church and state. Nonetheless, the Ohio Capitol Square Review and Advisory Board approved the display of the memorial.

Social Media Website Blocks Page About Christian Film
http://townhall.com/columnists/toddstarnes/2013/07/19/why-did-facebook-block-kirk-camerons-new-movie-n1644555
When Christian actor Kirk Cameron created a Facebook page for his newest faith-based film, "Unstoppable," Facebook blocked his page and sent a

message informing him that the content was "abusive" and "unsafe." After his appeals to lift the block were ignored, Cameron alerted over 500,000 fans from his personal Facebook page. Facebook then immediately removed the block without explanation.

Rhode Island Governor Vetoes Bill Authorizing "Choose Life" License Plate

http://www.foxnews.com/politics/2013/07/17/rhode-island-governor-vetoes-choose-life-license-plates/

Governor Lincoln Chafee vetoed a bill that would have authorized the issuance of license plates reading "Choose Life." Half of the issuance cost of each plate would have gone to the CareNet Pregnancy Center of Rhode Island, a Christian organization that offers free pregnancy testing, post-abortion counseling, and information about abortion alternatives. In striking down the bill, Governor Chafee stated that this type of funding would violate the separation of church and state.

YMCA Kicks Pro-Life Students Off Premises

http://townhall.com/columnists/toddstarnes/2013/07/10/ymca-kicks-out-prolife-students-n1637757

Over fifty members of a pro-life organization arrived in Austin, Texas, to peacefully protest at the Texas state capital. In advance of their trip, a local YMCA agreed to allow the students to shower in their facilities between 9 o'clock and 10 o'clock each night. When pro-abortion members of the local YMCA found out about the arrangement, they harassed the YMCA employees into revoking their agreement with the pro-life students.

Freedom From Religion Foundation Denounces Church Discount

http://ffrf.org/legal/other-legal-successes/item/18205-ffrf-keeps-sushi-discounts-secular-july-16-2013

After discovering that Tokyo Japanese Restaurant in Fairhope, Alabama, gave a ten percent discount to diners who brought in their church bulletin, the Freedom From Religion Foundation complained of discrimination and demanded that the restaurant change its practices. The restaurant complied and removed the flyer advertising the discount, clarifying that it respects all people, regardless of religious preference.

Freedom From Religion Foundation Attacks Kentucky Mayor for Religious References

http://ffrf.org/news/news-releases/item/18229-ffrf-seeks-to-stop-mayors-proselytizing

When the Freedom From Religion Foundation found out that Mayor Rita

Stephens of Hawesville, Kentucky, voluntarily wrote regular columns for the local newspaper that made references to God, the FFRF pounced on Stephens, demanding that she "quit using her civic 'bully pulpit' as an actual pulpit." The FFRF's demand letter also called for the immediate termination of prayer as a part of the city government meetings.

Atheist Group Calls for End of Prayer at Local Government Meeting
http://ffrf.org/news/news-releases/item/18244-ffrf-seeks-end-to-divisive-prayer-at-ala-government-meetings
The Alabama Public Service Commission opens its meetings with a prayer led by a member of a church or a friend of one of the commissioners. When the Freedom From Religion Foundation found out, it vehemently objected to the custom and demanded that the Commission cease its practice of prayer.

Atheist Group Continues to Harass U.S. Government About Historical Religious References
http://ffrf.org/news/news-releases/item/18273-ffrf-objects-to-religious-quotations-on-us-passports
The Freedom From Religion Foundation continued its six-year protest against official U.S. passports containing historical quotations from past United States leaders referencing God by sending yet another demand letter objecting to such references. The United States government has not responded.

City Attempts to Block Church Services in Delaware
http://www.usatoday.com/story/news/nation/2013/07/03/religion-protest-at-rehoboth-beach/2486107/
Reverend Robert Dekker, the pastor of New Covenant Church in Lewes, Delaware, requested permission to conduct an eight-week sermon series by a public bandstand on Rehoboth Beach. Despite the fact that the City had allowed other groups to hold meetings on the beach, the mayor repeatedly denied Dekker's appeals. Word of the rejections became public, and members of the community united in support of Dekker. The mayor finally agreed to allow Dekker to hold a one-time meeting on July 4th. Over 1,500 people attended to back the church and rally for religious freedom.

Colorado Court Holds Governor's National Day of Prayer Proclamation Unconstitutional
http://ffrf.org/news/news-releases/item/17846-ffrf%E2%80%99s-%E2%80%9Ccolorado-day-of-prayer%E2%80%9D-victory-appealed-to-state-supreme-cou
The Freedom From Religion Foundation sued Colorado Governor John

Hickenlooper, asserting that his National Day of Prayer proclamations were an unconstitutional endorsement of religion. The state appeals court found that the Governor's proclamations were unconstitutional. Subsequently, Gov. Hickenlooper appealed the decision and the Colorado State Supreme Court has agreed to hear the case.

Idaho Town Forced to Revoke Policy Permitting Any Peaceful Symbols on Water Tower

The city of Roberts, Idaho, removed three crosses adorning the local water tower following a complaint from City resident Joe Cohea, supported by the ACLU. It is Roberts's city policy that anyone may place symbols on the water tower so long as they are not offensive. After Cohea appealed to the ACLU for assistance, the town removed the crosses and replaced them with American flags. Cohea vowed to take legal action should the crosses be replaced, pursuant to his position that "no kind of religious symbol belongs on city property, period."

City Forces Catholic Pizza Shop Owner to Remove Statue from Privately Adopted Median

http://www.wwlp.com/dpp/news/local/hampden/a-virgin-mary-statue-controversy-in-west-springfield

http://www.foxnews.com/us/2013/09/06/virgin-mary-statue-installed-by-pizzeria-owner-on-mass-traffic-island-is/

West Springfield, Massachusetts, pizza shop owner Antonio Liquori participated in a city beautification project by using funds from his business to adopt and beautify a local traffic island, which included a sign clearly indicating the property was adopted by his business. Nevertheless, when the city found out that he chose to include a small statue of the Virgin Mary as part of his beautification efforts, the city forced him to remove it, embarrassing and upsetting Mr. Liquori. The mayor allowed Mr. Liquori to replace the statue while the city researched the law, but while Mr. Liquori was out of the country, a vandal smashed the statue.

Cross Atop Mt. Rubidoux in California Auctioned by Riverside City Council

http://blog.pe.com/riverside/2013/04/18/mount-rubidoux-cross-auction-outcome-satisfies-americans-united/

A cross has remained atop Mt. Rubidoux in Riverside, California, for more than a century. Americans United for Separation of Church and State sent a letter to the city urging it to remove the cross. The Riverside City Council responded by voting to auction off the property rather than face the threat of a lawsuit. A nonprofit group called Totally Mount Rubidoux purchased the 0.43 acres on which the cross sits.

Freedom From Religion Foundation Attacks North Dakota Town's Prayer Tradition
http://rapidcityjournal.com/news/council-votes-to-reject-prayer-policy/ article_48290210-053b-5a60-abd7-ee433a40b5c8.html
Rapid City, South Dakota, always opens its city council meetings with a prayer. The Freedom From Religion Foundation threatened to sue the city unless it ceases its invocation tradition. The city council unanimously rejected a proposed change in policy and still continues with prayer at the beginning of each meeting.

Christian Flower Shop Owner Attacked for Declining to Decorate Homosexual Wedding
http://christiannews.net/2013/04/22/christian-florist-slammed-with-second-lawsuit-for-declining-to-decorate-homosexual-wedding/
Baronelle Stutzman of Arlene's Flowers in Richland, Washington, had a long history of providing flowers to her homosexual customers . But when one of her long-time customers requested flowers to decorate his wedding with his male partner, she respectfully "took his hands and said, 'I'm sorry. I cannot do your wedding because of my relationship with Jesus Christ.'" For this, anti-Christian activists have threatened to burn down her shop and sent harassing hate mail. Additionally, both the State of Washington and the ACLU have filed lawsuits to force Ms. Stutzman to either participate in homosexual weddings that she strongly believes to be immoral or get out of the wedding business altogether and pay steep fines.

Logistics Corporation Fires Employee for Seeking Religious Accommodation
http://www.dispatch.com/content/stories/local/2013/04/11/suit-firing-based-on-religious-bias.html
When shipping corporation Excel hired Yusuf Sufi, a practicing Muslim, the company gave him permission to use his vacation time and other time-off hours to attend religious services required by the Muslim faith. However, after his local supervisors were replaced, his permissions were rescinded. Sufi told his supervisor that he would not be able to skip his mandatory services to work overtime and requested accommodation. Instead, Sufi was fired for his desire to honor his religious beliefs.

Company Fails to Reasonably Accommodate Muslim Employee

http://eeoc.gov/eeoc/newsroom/release/4-4-13.cfm

The Equal Employment Opportunity Commission (EEOC) sued Bo-Cherry, Inc., for refusing to accommodate the religious exercise of a Muslim employee. The restaurant required the man to shave his beard rather than permitting him to use a beard hair net.

Woman Thrown off Metro Rail for Singing Spiritual Hymns

http://www.wsvn.com/news/articles/local/21010031056296/elderly-woman-forced-off-metrorail-for-singing-hymns/

A security guard physically forced Emma Anderson—an eighty-two-year-old woman—off the Metrorail at the Brickwell Metrorail Station in Miami, Florida, for publicly singing spiritual hymns. According to the security guard, public singing, dancing, and playing music without a permit is against the Miami-Dade Transit rules. However, the security guard overreacted to Ms. Anderson's religious songs, using excessive and unnecessary physical force to remove her. Ms. Anderson filed a lawsuit to recover for battery, assault, and negligence, in addition to filing charges to protect the rights of future passengers.

Park Ranger Demands Vendor at Farmer's Market Remove Free Bibles from Her Table

http://www.lc.org/index.cfm?PID=14102&AlertID=1583

Shirley Elliot sold produce at Thibodaux Farmer's Market in Louisiana and provided free Bibles on her table to anyone that wanted one. When a park ranger discovered the Bibles, he demanded Ms. Elliott remove the Bibles from her table because "they were on federal property." After the superintendent of the nearby park was informed of the unconstitutional religious discrimination against Ms. Elliot, he put an end to the park ranger's discrimination and restored Ms. Elliot's right to freely display Bibles on her table.

Atheist Group Demands Vietnam Veterans Memorial Be Removed

http://blog.libertyinstitute.org/2013/04/freedom-from-religion-foundation.html

The Freedom From Religion Foundation sent a letter to Coos Bay, Oregon, demanding that the city remove its Vietnam veterans memorial because the memorial includes a cross. Liberty Institute is working with the city to preserve the veterans memorial. Since the FFRF sent its letter, the cross has been vandalized and a bomb was placed on the cross near a playground.

Freedom From Religion Foundation Demands Health Clinic Remove Religious Displays
http://ffrf.org/legal/other-legal-successes/item/17332-ffrf-removes-religious-postings-from-mo-health-clinic-march-10-2013
The Freedom From Religion Foundation sent a letter to Swope Health East in Kansas City, Kansas, demanding it remove any religious symbolism on its walls to create a "welcoming and respectful" environment. The health clinic complied with the demand and removed all displays relating to religion.

Social Justice Organization Issues Report Urging Attacks on Religious Liberty
http://www.politicalresearch.org/wp-content/uploads/downloads/2013/04/PRA_Redefining-Religious-Liberty_March2013_PUBLISH.pdf
A report issued by Political Research Associates, a self-proclaimed social justice organization, uses hyper-partisan political language to attack laws protecting the rights of individuals to live according to their religious beliefs and conscience. For example, the report describes laws protecting the rights of religious healthcare providers and employees to abstain from abortions, and litigation fighting to protect religious employees and small business owners from having to participate in homosexual commitment celebrations, as part of a "Christian right campaign to redefine 'religious liberty.'" It characterizes these protections as a nefarious conservative conspiracy to harm women and homosexuals. Instead, the report argues, "true religious freedom" is merely "one of many civil rights" competing for public favor. Thus its scope and existence is subject to a "whole host of rules" issued by the sovereign state, which can choose to entirely eliminate religious liberty in hospitals and businesses. The report calls on "social justice forces" to engage in a coordinated campaign to overturn existing religious protections by enshrining its state-centric view of religious liberty into law and culture.

Kentucky Governor and LGBT Groups Warn That Religious Believers Pose Public Threat
http://www.christianpost.com/news/ky-lawmakers-override-governors-veto-of-religious-liberties-bill-92857/
The Kentucky Legislature overwhelmingly voted to override the Governor's veto of a bill intended to protect sincere religious believers against government overreach and coercion. Opponents vilified religious believers by spreading offensive and invidious messages. A gay, lesbian, bi-sexual, and transgender advocacy group labeled religious protections an "endorsement of discrimination," placing "women, children, people of color, and all Kentuckians"

at risk. Similarly, the Governor publicly expressed worry that protecting religious believers from governmental coercion may "threaten public safety, health care, and individuals' civil rights."

Secularists Challenge National Motto "In God We Trust"

http://religionclause.blogspot.com/2013/03/suit-challenges-in-god-we-trust-on.html

Michael Newdow, Freedom From Religion Foundation, and New York City Atheists challenged the national motto on Establishment Clause grounds. A New York district court dismissed the lawsuit. In 2006 a similar challenge by Newdow failed in a California federal district court.

Anti-Prayer Groups Intimidate Small Wisconsin Town to Abandon City Council Prayer

http://lacrossetribune.com/news/local/onalaska-council-to-consider-meeting-prayer/article_859510b0-5ae5-11e2-9b20-001a4bcf887a.html

http://bloximages.chicago2.vip.townnews.com/lacrossetribune.com/content/tncms/assets/v3/editorial/c/af/caf05376-6f18-11e2-8ff4-001a4bcf887a/511033ec7fd27.pdf.pdf

Onalasaka, Wisconsin, was considering whether it should open its city council meeting in prayer. The council originally appeared open to the idea; however, the Freedom From Religion Foundation and a local Freethought Society strongly objected to prayer of any kind and scornfully referred to prayer as "coercive," "presumptive," and "unnecessary." The groups warned of expensive lawsuits to follow. Concerned about the vocal opposition and fearful of future lawsuits, the city council reluctantly chose not to open its meetings with a prayer, even though The League of Wisconsin Municipalities maintains its legality and a neighboring town, the state legislature, and Congress all open in prayer.

ACLU Abandons Five-Year Challenge to Ten Commandments

http://www.lc.org/media/9980/attachments/pr_11th_district_fl_dixie_cty_10_command_dismissal_021313.pdf

http://www.lc.org/index.cfm?PID=14100&PRID=1283

In 2008, the ACLU sued Dixie County, Florida, to tear down the Ten Commandments display at the county courthouse. The only plaintiff it could find was an anonymous ACLU member from North Carolina claiming an intention to someday purchase property in the county to "park a recreational vehicle." In 2012, the Eleventh Circuit remanded the case to fully investigate the plaintiff's standing and ordered the anonymous plaintiff's deposition.

In response to this, the ACLU filed a motion to dismiss its own suit in 2013, claiming that its anonymous plaintiff finally decided—six years after initiating the lawsuit—against purchasing property in the county.

Family-Owned Bakery Harassed for Owners' Religious Beliefs

http://www.huffingtonpost.com/2013/02/06/sweet-melissa-cakes-in-co_n_2632108.html

http://www.katu.com/news/local/Slew-of-online-hate-reviews-plague-Sweet-Cakes-190072751.html

http://abcnews.go.com/blogs/business/2013/02/bakery-denies-same-sex-couple-wedding-cake/

The Klein family regularly serves homosexuals at its bakery in Oregon; however, the family cannot participate in homosexual weddings by providing a celebratory wedding cake without violating sincerely held religious beliefs about marriage. The family explained this to the media and the customers whose order it could not complete. Nevertheless, hate-filled messages from around the world flooded social media outlets and review sites in an apparent attempt to ruin the family-owned business. There were even attacks against similarly named bakeries in different states. One such mistaken bakery owner complained that she was scared because of the threats made by angry anti-religious activists. The state formally investigated the Kleins, but no lawsuit has been filed.

Anti-Semitism Drives Lawsuits Against Proposed Jewish Eruvim in New York Town

http://www.nytimes.com/2013/02/05/nyregion/in-westhampton-beach-a-ritual-jewish-boundary-stirs-real-town-divisions.html?pagewanted=1

Lawsuits have been filed to stop narrow plastic strips from being placed on telephone poles in the town of Westhampton Beach, New York, creating a symbolic boundary called an "eruvim." Within an eruvim boundary, Orthodox Jews are permitted to carry items outside their homes on the Sabbath. The strips are painted to blend in and thus easily go unnoticed—much of Manhattan sits within an eruvim. Nevertheless, strong opposition has mounted against a proposed eruvim in Westhampton for fear that more Orthodox Jews will want to move into the city. Opponents filed three federal lawsuits, one of which was dismissed by a federal district court.

California Mall Threatens to Arrest Customer Peacefully Sharing His Faith with Shoppers

http://www.pacificjustice.org/1/post/2013/01/-visalia-mall-sued-after-threatening-arrest-for-religious-speech.html

John Vadanais would strike up peaceful conversations with mall visitors and discuss his faith in the common areas. The mall threatened to arrest him unless he ceased speaking about his faith in the mall. A lawsuit against the mall is pending.

Government Bans Prayer at Homeless Shelter in Illinois

http://www.tristatehomepage.com/story/feds-pull-plug-on-pre-meal-prayer-at-shelter/d/story/PjlU1TIktkaARlubgMguQA

The United Caring Shelter (UCS) in Evansville, Illinois, allowed anyone who wanted to pray before the free meal provided by the shelter to do so. The prayers were open to all and were not mandatory. The U.S. Department of Agriculture, however, demanded that UCS stop the prayers or stop accepting federal assistance to feed the homeless. The UCS now permits only a moment of silence before meals.

Steakhouse Threatened for "Church Member Appreciation Day"

http://ffrf.org/legal/other-legal-successes/item/15923-ffrf-stops-mississippi-restaurant%E2%80%99s-discriminatory-discount-sept-11-2012

The Western Sizzlin' Steakhouse in Wiggins, Mississippi, developed promotional offers to attract customers. One such offer was the "church member appreciation day," during which church members could get a discount at the steakhouse. The Freedom From Religion Foundation threatened the steakhouse for offering this discount, asserting that this promotion violated the Civil Rights Act. The restaurant responded by stating that it would "discontinue including churches in [its] discount promotions and programs moving forward and will only offer them to other local businesses and companies that are not religious in nature."

Freedom From Religion Foundation Fights Prayers Before County Commission Meetings

http://www.timesfreepress.com/news/2012/jun/16/chattanooga-citizens-sue-over-countyprayers/

After the Freedom From Religion Foundation (FFRF) sent a letter to Hamilton County Commissioners objecting to the practice of praying before County Commission meetings, the Commission continued the practice. The FFRF then filed suit, alleging the prayers violate the Establishment Clause.

Freedom From Religion Foundation Complains About Email Containing a Prayer

Religion Clause, "Group Says E-mail of Department Head's Prayer to Employees Violated Establishment Clause," available at http://religionclause.blogspot. com/2012/05/group-says-e-mail-of-department-heads.html (May 5, 2012)

The Freedom From Religion Foundation sent the governor of Florida a letter complaining about an email sent by the Secretary of the Department of Children and Families, David Wilkins. The email included a prayer that was read at the Florida National Day of Prayer ceremony. Wilkins claims that the email was merely a recap of a public appearance.

Massachusetts Town Attacked for Historic Cross Monument

http://www.bostonglobe.com/metro/regionals/south/2012/05/26/cross-traffic-island-middleborough-draws-complaint-sparks-constitutional-clash/aTbguKibe6mu86BrNCatdJ/story.html

http://www.tauntongazette.com/x574280362/Middleboro-could-face-lawsuit-over-cross-on-public/?tag=1

Over fifty years ago, the Kiwanis Club erected a twelve-foot cross on a traffic island in Middleborough, Massachusetts. Although considered a historic landmark, the town received a complaint about the constitutionality of the cross from a Boston attorney passing through the town. The Freedom From Religion Foundation (FFRF) and the American Civil Liberties Union (ACLU) then condemned the display once the complaint went public. City officials initially resisted any change to the cross, but eventually decided to transfer the property to private ownership in an attempt to ensure the cross's vitality and to avoid a constitutional lawsuit. Nevertheless, the FFRF and ACLU continue to call for the cross's demolition.

City Council Reacts to Atheist's Complaints About Opening Prayer

Religion Clause, "Move of Prayer to Precede City Council Meeting Draws Protest," available at http://religionclause.blogspot.com/2012/05/move-of-prayer-to-precede-citycouncil.html (May 21, 2012)

An atheist University of Ohio student complained that the usual opening prayer of the Mount Vernon, Ohio, city council did not reflect the diversity of the community. After the council president moved the prayer to two minutes before the meeting, in answer to the student's request, several council members protested the move in the prayer time.

Pro-Homosexual Organization Sues Christian-Owned T-Shirt Company for Refusing to Make Pride Shirts

http://religionclause.blogspot.com/2012/04/public-accommodations-complaint-filed.html

The Gay and Lesbian Services Organization sued a Christian-owned T-shirt making company called "Hands on Originals" for refusal to make homosexual-pride T-shirts. The company had bid on the order before it knew the message the shirts would carry or that they were for the Pride festival. The suit alleges discrimination based on sexual orientation in public accommodation.

Freedom From Religion Foundation Complains Florist Refuses to Deliver Their Flowers

http://www2.turnto10.com/news/2012/jan/19/10/florists-wont-make-delivery-prayerbanner-teen-ar-902053/

Freedom From Religion Foundation (FFRF) forced a Rhode Island school to remove a fifty-year-old school prayer banner from the auditorium, which contained a prayer for the academic success of the students, because it said "Our Heavenly Father" and "Amen." Following the removal of the banner, a florist refused to deliver flowers from the FFRF to their successful plaintiff. FFRF filed a formal complaint against the florist.

Jewish Police Officer Files Employment Discrimination Claim After Run-in with Mel Gibson

http://religionclause.blogspot.com/search?updated-max=2012-01-16T07:10:00-05:00&max-results=20&start=620&by-date=false

A Jewish police officer claims Mel Gibson verbally abused him because of his religion, and then the officer's superiors forced him to delete the anti-Semitic statements from his report. The officer claims he was later ostracized and denied promotion because of the incident.

City Threatened for Renting Amphitheater to Christian Musician

http://www.christianpost.com/news/michael-w-smith-says-atheist-lawsuit-threat-is-absurd-78569/

A resident of Draper, Utah, threatened to sue the city if it did not cancel a Michael W. Smith concert because the city rented the city's amphitheater to the Christian musician and facilitated ticket sales through the city's website. The city refused to cancel the concert and noted that it treated the Michael W. Smith concert in the same manner that it treats all groups that desire to perform at the amphitheater.

ACLU Silences Religious Prayer at City Council Meetings

http://pointpleasant.patch.com/articles/point-beach-to-settle-lawsuit-with-aclu-afterchanging-prayer

The city council of Point Pleasant Beach, New Jersey, was opening its meetings with prayer, but a resident objected to the Lord's Prayer because it was Christian. The ACLU filed a claim against the city, but dropped it after an agreement was reached that the city council would use general prayers, not specific to any religion. The council must now pay over $11,000 in attorney's fees to the ACLU.

Colorado Park and Recreation District Bans Menorah from Holiday Display

http://www.denverpost.com/news/ci_19527120

The Colorado Park and Recreation District has banned the Lake House in Evergreen, Colorado, from displaying a menorah in its holiday display because the menorah is a religious symbol. The Lake House is still permitted to display a Christmas tree.

Christian Baker Sued for Refusing to Create Wedding Cake for Homosexual Wedding

http://news.yahoo.com/colo-gay-discrimination-alleged-over-113354165.html
http://www.breitbart.com/Big-Government/2013/12/12/Christian-Baker-Willing-to-Go-to-Jail-for-Declining-Gay-Wedding-Cake

Jack Phillips, owner of the Masterpiece Cakeshop in Lakewood, Colorado, refuses to make cakes that would violate his religious convictions. In the past, this has included refusing to make a Halloween-themed wedding cake. Now, however, the ACLU and the Colorado Attorney General's office are suing Mr. Phillips for refusing to create a cake for a homosexual wedding. A Colorado administrative law judge ruled that Phillips violated Colorado's antidiscrimination law and would face fines and prison if he persisted in refusing to supply cakes for gay marriages in the future. Phillips plans on taking the case before the Colorado Court of Appeals.

City in Tennessee Sued for Having Crosses in Town

http://religionclause.blogspot.com/2011/12/suit-challenges-crosses-on-public.html

Freedom From Religion Foundation filed suit against the city of Whitesville, Tennessee, for having a cross on the water tower, in front of city hall, and on a city sidewalk.

Social Media Sites Censor Christian Views

Dave Bohan, "Study Shows Social Media Sites Censor Christian Views," The New American, available at http://www.thenewamerican.com/culture/faith-and-morals/item/997-study-shows-social-media-sites-censor-christian-views (Sept. 18, 2011)

Social media websites are censoring Christian viewpoints, according to a new study from the National Religious Broadcasters association. The NRB published a press release claiming a recent study conducted by the organization found that Apple, the iTunes App Store, Google, Facebook, MySpace, Twitter, AT&T, Comcast, and Verizon are potentially censoring Christian views from websites as part of a routine business practice.

Atheist Group Bullies City in California to Remove Historical Marker

http://ffrf.org/news/action/item/15057-help-remove-cross-in-santa-clara-park
http://santaclaraca.gov/index.aspx?page=1455#memorial

The Freedom From Religion Foundation demanded that Santa Clara, California, remove a granite cross from Memorial Cross Park. The Santa Clara Lions Club had donated the cross for the park as a historical marker to mark the location of a mission built in 1779.

NBC Removes "Under God" from Pledge of Allegiance

Huffington Post, *"NBC Apologizes For Omitting 'Under God' From Pledge Of Allegiance," available at http://www.huffingtonpost.com/2011/06/19/nbc-us-open-undergod_n_880114.html (June 19, 2011)*

NBC omitted the phrase "under God" from the Pledge of Allegiance during an opening segment of the U.S. Open. NBC later apologized for the omission and changed its policy to ensure that senior level approval accompanies each piece of a broadcast.

Cisco Employee Fired for Religious Views About Marriage

http://townhall.com/columnists/mikeadams/2011/06/16/the_cisco_kid/page/full/

Dr. Frank Turek, a Cisco employee, was fired for his religious view that marriage should be between a woman and a man. He had never expressed this view at work, but did express it through a book he authored. Cisco's leadership discovered on the Internet that he had authored the book. The employee was fired without having been addressed about the issue or given opportunity to speak and despite high regard from other employees and managers.

Prayer at North Carolina County Commissioner Meeting Under Attack

http://www.mountainx.com/article/26212/Buncombe-Commissioners-On-a-meeting-and-a-prayer

Following the outcome in *Joyney v. Forsyth County,* many other North Carolina counties that open their county commissioner meetings with prayer are under attack. After twenty years of opening with prayer, the Buncombe County, North Carolina, commissioner meeting's prayer is being challenged.

Virginia High School Bans Students from Posting the Ten Commandments on their Lockers

Liberty Counsel, "Ten Commandments Pulled Off Students' Lockers by Virginia School Administration," available at http://www.lc.org/index. cfm?PID=14102&AlertID=1244 (Feb. 28, 2011)

The Floyd County High School administration banned students from posting religious material. This censorship came about when students who are members of the Fellowship of Christian Athletes placed copies of the Ten Commandments on the fronts of their lockers. The administration removed the copy from each locker that displayed the Ten Commandments.

Freedom From Religion Foundation Fights Opening Meetings in Lodi, California, with Prayer

http://www.examiner.com/article/lodi-city-council-votes-to-keep-prayer-as-uncensored-invocation-local-reactions

http://www.lodinews.com/news/article_5aec0fac-b0a5-11e1-9ae5-001a4bcf887a.html

http://www.fox40.com/news/headlines/ktxl-news-lodiprayer,0,2350438.story

The Freedom From Religion Foundation threatened to file a lawsuit against the City of Lodi, California, unless it ended its tradition of opening meetings with an invocation. The City Council unanimously chose to continue its invitation to people of any faith or no faith to pray or offer a "call to civic responsibility" before its meetings. Opponents were still unhappy with the nonexclusion policy, claiming that those of minority religions or no religion would still feel excluded because Christianity was the majority religion.

Freedom From Religion Foundation Intimidates City Council into Banning "Jesus" from Prayers

http://www.tracypress.com/pages/full_story/push?article-Council+asks+pastors+to+leave+-Jesus-+out+of+prayers%20&id=3618283-Council+asks+pastors+to+leave+-Jesus-+out+of+prayers&instance=home_news_bullets

The Tracy, California, city council bowed to legal threats brought by the Freedom From Religion Foundation and instructed any person giving an opening prayer that it is illegal to mention Jesus Christ in the prayer.

Freedom From Religion Foundation Celebrates Making Ohio City "Less Holy"

http://ffrf.org/publications/freethought-today/articles/foundation-takes-on-prayer/

The city council of Toledo, Ohio, invited various religious organizations from the community to open its meetings in prayer. The Freedom From Religion Foundation (FFRF) threatened to sue the city for opening with prayer, urging the city to end the prayers completely. The city avoided litigation by prohibiting references to specific religions, prompting FFRF to announce that it made the city "a little less holy."

Atheist Group Requests to Display a Sign with an Atheistic Message Next to a Nativity Scene

http://www.cbs19.tv/story/16222265/nativity-controversy-in-east-texas-stirs-emotions

The Freedom From Religion Foundation has caused a controversy by requesting that a sign be put up next to the Nativity scene decoration in Athens, Texas, that says, "There are no gods, no devils, no angels, no heaven or hell."

Indiana Town Stands Up to Freedom From Religion Foundation over Nativity Scene

http://religionclause.blogspot.com/2010/12/indiana-county-will-not-remove-creche.html

Franklin County, Indiana, announced that it would refuse to remove a Nativity scene from the courthouse lawn unless a court orders it to do so. The Freedom From Religion Foundation wrote the county a letter complaining that the Nativity scene was too religious despite the presence of reindeer and a Christmas tree in the display. The county commissioner gave quite a feisty reply, saying that the people of Franklin County could fight and that the FFRF should be ready for it.

Sheriff's Personally-Funded Ad Draws Criticism from Atheist Organization

http://www.jdnews.com/articles/watchdog-97742-group-county.html

The sheriff of Onslow County, North Carolina, ran an ad in the local newspaper encouraging citizens to live by good values, which he claims in the ad line up with Christian values. The sheriff paid for the ad with his own money, although it did bear the image of his badge. The Freedom From Religion Foundation wrote a letter to the county claiming that the ad showed that the police supported Christianity. The sheriff denies the claims in FFRF's letter and says that he will continue to run the ad.

County in South Carolina Permits Political Signs but Bans Religious Signs

http://religionclause.blogspot.com/2010/10/suit-says-county-sign-control-ordinance.html

Berkeley County, South Carolina, requires its residents to obtain a permit to place signs in their yards. Political signs and for sale signs are deemed appropriate, but signs that carry a religious message are not. One resident, Moultrie, was cited for having signs with Bible verses on them. Moultrie filed suit against the county alleging violations of free expression, free exercise, and equal protection rights.

Suggested Ten Commandments Monument Sparks Tension in Marion, Illinois

http://religionclause.blogspot.com/2010/08/heated-debate-on-10-commandments.html

At a city council meeting in Marion, Illinois, a resident proposed that a Ten Commandments monument be put up on a church or other private property in town. An atheist activist named Rob Sherman, however, who had come from Chicago to attend the meeting, vehemently objected to the idea. Sherman's objection sparked anger among the Marion citizens, who swore to build the monument.

Owners of Vermont Inn Fined $30,000 for Refusing to Host Homosexual Wedding

http://www.christianpost.com/news/owners-of-vermonts-wildflower-inn-oppose-maines-same-sex-marriage-referndum-in-new-video-83747/

Jim and Mary O'Reilly own the Wildflower Inn in Vermont. Although the O'Reilly's open their inn to homosexuals, they could not, because of their Catholic faith, host a homosexual wedding at the inn. The ACLU then filed a lawsuit against the O'Reillys. They were forced to pay $30,000 to the homosexual couple and the Vermont Human Rights Commission.

Kentucky Rejects "In God We Trust" License Plate

http://www.foxnews.com/us/2010/10/07/kentucky-group-sues-rejection-god-trustlicense-plate/

A group that advocates against pornography, called ROCK, applied for a special license plate that had "In God We Trust" on it. Kentucky rejected the application, stating that the primary purpose of ROCK is to advance religion because there is one Bible verse on ROCK's website. The group filed suit against Kentucky, claiming a violation of its equal protection rights.

Evangelists Detained at the NCAA Final Four in Indianapolis

http://www.lc.org/index.cfm?PID=14102&AlertID=1179

A group of street evangelists called the Good Messengers distributed tracts on a public sidewalk outside Lucas Oil Stadium during an NCAA Final Four game. They were questioned by two police officers, and one of the evangelists was detained and accused of solicitation and trespass. As a result of this event, Indianapolis released a legal bulletin to local law enforcement officers clarifying that street evangelists are engaging in constitutionally protected activity.

Hawaii Citizens for Separation of Church and State Oppose Honolulu City Council Prayers

http://religionclause.blogspot.com/2010/04/prayers-at-honolulu-city-council.html

The Honolulu City Council opens its meetings with an "aloha message." Many people who deliver the message choose to do so with a prayer. The Hawaii Citizens for Separation of Church and State complained to the city council about the practice, saying it is unconstitutional. The council chairman, however, refused to stop the practice.

Man Challenges Use of Recycled Church Pews in Courtroom

http://www.commercialappeal.com/news/2010/feb/22/man-decries-courts-church-pews/

A Mississippi municipal courthouse recycled pews from a local church to save money. Carroll Roberson, after seeing the pews when at his hearing for disorderly conduct, decided to challenge their use on Establishment Clause grounds because the pews contained crosses on each end.

Ohio Town Removes Ten Commandments Sign to Avoid Litigation

http://www.upi.com/Top_News/US/2009/12/17/Village-to-remove-Ten-Commandmentssign/UPI-49941261096450/

A Lockland, Ohio, resident filed a federal lawsuit asking for removal of a

Ten Commandments sign outside the town hall and $500,000 in punitive damages. To avoid litigation, the town submitted to the resident's wishes and removed the sign.

Christmas Displays Banned from Washington State Capitol After Complaint
http://www.foxnews.com/politics/2009/11/27/washington-state-implement-rules-barring-holiday-displays-inside-capitol/
The state of Washington no longer permits any holiday display other than the "holiday tree" inside its capitol building, following a complaint from the Freedom From Religion Foundation.

Federal Reserve Board Demands Bank Remove Religious Christmas Decorations
http://www.koco.com/After-Outcry-Feds-Back-Down-Banks-Can-Display-Crosses/-/9844716/10744924/-/blj7m4/-/index.html
An Oklahoma bank was forced to remove Bible verses from its website, crosses from teller stations, and buttons that carried a Christian Christmas message for a day after a visit from Federal Reserve employees. The Federal Reserve Board ruled that banks may not make any religious statement as doing so might discourage people from applying for loans. The Federal Reserve employees checking the bank to make sure it complied with regulations cited the religious material and demanded its removal. After the president of the bank challenged the Federal Reserve, however, the religious items were restored while the Federal Reserve made a more thorough investigation of the issue.

Employee Fired for Religious Conviction Against Saying "Happy Holidays."
Liberty Counsel, "Employee Forced to Say "Happy Holidays" Was Fired After Objecting to the Greeting," available at http://www.lc.org/index. cfm?PID=14100&PRID=760 (Dec. 22, 2008)
An employee in Panama City, Florida, was fired after claiming religious convictions barred her from using the greeting "happy holidays." The employee was asked to leave immediately and verbally abused. The police were called and forced her to leave.

Governor of Washington Permits Anti-Faith Display in the Capitol
Liberty Counsel, "Washington Governor Approves Anti-Faith Sign," available at http://www.lc.org/index.cfm?PID=14100&PRID=757 (Dec. 10, 2008)
The governor of Washington allowed an anti-faith sign to be displayed in the state Capitol. The sign stated, "There are no gods, no devils, no angels, no heaven or hell. There is only our natural world. Religion is but myth and

superstition that hardens hearts and enslaves minds." The governor argued that she had no choice, as other symbols of faith were allowed to be displayed.

Freedom From Religion Foundation Challenges Nativity Scene in Green Bay, Wisconsin

Liberty Counsel, "City Receives Early Christmas Present in Legal Victory Over Anti-Religious Group," available at http://www.lc.org/index.cfm?PID=14100&PRID=737 (Oct. 8, 2008)

A federal judge dismissed a lawsuit from the Freedom from Religion Foundation challenging Green Bay, Wisconsin's display of a Nativity scene at city hall.

Street Preachers Threatened with Arrest in Canon City, Colorado

Liberty Counsel, "Police Back Away From Threats to Arrest Christians for Publicly Sharing Their Faith," available at http://www.lc.org/index. cfm?PID=14100&PRID=560 (Mar. 30, 2007)

Norman Robinovitz and Bill Phillips stood on public sidewalks talking to people about their Christian faith and handing out literature. One evening, after they shared their Christian faith with individuals outside of two local bars, someone called police to investigate their activities. The men were threatened with arrest for disorderly conduct and were told if they continued their activities they were "headed for jail time."

Employee Fired for Religious and Political Message Written on His Car

http://www.crosswalk.com/1441745

A Cargill Foods employee was fired over the display of a sign on his private vehicle. The sign said, "Please vote for marriage on Nov. 7." The statement reflected the employee's religious conviction that marriage should remain a union of one man and one woman. The company tried to force him to remove the hand-painted sign from his rear window after other employees claimed to be offended.

City Pressures Christmas Festival to Not Display Movie *The Nativity*

Letter from Jay Alan Sekulow to Mara S. Georges, available at http://www.aclj. org/media/pdf/ChicagoLetter.pdf (Nov. 28, 2006)

Christmas festival organizers were pressured by city officials to remove the movie "The Nativity" from the festivities. City officials feared that the movie would be offensive to non-Christians.

School Stops Third Grader from Handing Out Candy Canes with the Story of Jesus' Birth

Rob Phillips, "School quashes handing out Jesus candy canes," Northwest Herald, *available at http://aclj.org/aclj/northwest-herald---crystal-lake-il---school-quasheshanding-out-jesus-candy-canes (Jan. 14, 2005)*

Third grader Renee Crout was told by her teacher that she could not hand out candy canes with the story of the birth of Jesus attached. Renee's mother removed her from the school and sent her to a nearby private school.

Florida County Orders the Removal of All Christmas Trees from County Facilities

Letter from Francis J. Manion to John J. Gallagher, County Administrator, available at http://c0391070.cdn2.cloudfiles.rackspacecloud.com/pdf/041216_fl_christmas_tree_letter2.pdf (Dec. 16, 2004)

Pasco County, Florida, demanded that all county offices and facilities remove Christmas trees. The county claimed that displays of Christmas trees are a violation of the Constitution. The county rescinded its order two days after demanding the trees be removed.

Police Officer Banned from Posting About Prayer Meeting

Alliance Defense Fund, "Another Effort to Censor Religious Speech Halted...," available at http://oldsite.alliancedefensefund.org/userdocs/updates/2004_0810. html (Aug. 10, 2004)

The chief of the Janesville, Wisconsin, police department banned officer Sean Jauch from posting announcements for his prayer group on the police department's bulletin board after receiving a complaint that one of the posts was harassing and offensive because it quoted Hebrews 11:6. After Jauch sought legal assistance, the police chief relented.

Employee Fired for Wearing Ten Commandments Lapel Pin

Jeremy Gray, "Man Fired Over Lapel Pin Garners Support," Birmingham News *(June 27, 2004)*

The Hoover Chamber of Commerce fired employee Christopher Word because he wore a Ten Commandments lapel pin.

Los Angeles County Removes Cross from Seal After Threat from the ACLU

Sue Fox, "Facing Suit, County to Remove Seal's Cross," L.A. Times, *June 2, 2004, at B1*

Los Angeles County was threatened with a lawsuit if the county did not remove a cross from the county's seal. The county succumbed to the ACLU's pressure and decided to remove the cross. The cross had adorned the seal since 1957 along with a cow, a tuna fish, a Spanish galleon, the Hollywood Bowl, and the Goddess Pomono. The region was settled by Catholic missionaries and the cross memorialized that historical fact. In January of 2014, the Los Angeles Board of Supervisors approved the restoration of the cross to the seal.

ACLU Pressures Redlands, California, into Removing Cross from City Seal
Hugo Martin, "Facing ACLU Complaint, City to Drop Seal's Cross," L.A. Times, April 29, 2004, at B1
The City of Redlands was threatened with a lawsuit if the city did not remove a cross from the city's seal. The city decided to remove the cross rather than fight a legal battle against the ACLU, despite many protests from citizens who wanted the cross to stay on the city seal.

Vermont Couple Denied License Plates with Religious Message
FoxNews.com, "Tongue Tied: A Report From the Front Line of the Culture Wars," available at http://www.foxnews.com/story/0,2933,28025,00.html (June 27, 2001)
Robert and Nancy Zins attempted to purchase specialty plates in Vermont for herself and for her husband with the messages "ROMANS8" and "ROMANS5" on the plates, but her request was denied by the Vermont DMV, which claimed that the messages might be offensive. After first going through the Agency of Transportation, a lawsuit was filed to protect her free speech rights and her ability to select a message for her license plate, just as other, nonreligious citizens were free to do.

U.S. Capitol Visitor's Center Replaces "In God We Trust" with Erroneous National Motto
http://www.mcclatchydc.com/2008/12/02/56905/conservative-lawmakers-bring-god.html
When the $621 million U.S. Capitol Visitor's Center was opened, Senator DeMint pointed out that it incorrectly identified "E Pluribus Unum" as the national motto instead of the actual motto: "In God We Trust." The center also downplays the Founding Fathers' faith in God but prominently displays a quote from a Massachusetts lawyer from the 1830s: "We have built no temple but the Capitol. We consult no common oracle but the Constitution."

Jewish Prison Guard Refused Ability to Schedule Work Around the Sabbath
http://www.colorado.gov/cs/Satellite?blobcol=urldata&blobheader=application%2Fpdf&blobkey=id&blobtable=MungoBlobs&blobwhere=1251759857274&ssbinary=true
Schutte, a Jewish prison guard, sued the Department of Corrections in

Colorado for not allowing him to schedule his work around the Sabbath, which spans from Friday night to Saturday. As a Messianic Jew, Schutte does not believe in working on the Sabbath. An Administrative Law Judge found the Department of Correction's refusal to work to accommodate Schutte a violation of Title VII.

Tennessee Attorney General Finds "Jesus is Lord" License Plate Unconstitutional

http://religionclause.blogspot.com/2010/04/tennessee-ag-opinion-says-jesus-is-lord.html

The Tennessee Attorney General decided that a specialty license plate bearing the message, "Jesus is Lord" was unconstitutional. Tennessee refused to issue the plate.

ACLU Works to Stop Tourism Grant from Going to Christian Concert

http://www.tampabay.com/news/humaninterest/aclu-wants-to-ensure-freedom-fest-not-overtly-christian/912837

Hernando County, Florida, makes grants available for events that will bring tourists into the county in order to spur economic development and promote the county as a tourist destination. The Tourist Development Council approved a grant for the Freedom Fest, a Christian music festival held on the Fourth of July weekend. Despite the secular purpose of the grant and the neutral manner in which it is granted, the ACLU complained about the funds going to a religious festival. In response to the complaints, the festival was forced to change its name from the "God and Country" festival to the "Family, Freedom, and Country" festival, and the grant had to be given directly to vendors instead of the organization promoting the festival. The ACLU nevertheless warned that any "overt religious overtones" at the event would cause "trouble" for the county.

Voluntary After-Prison Rehab Center Closed Because of Its Faith-Based Technique

http://www.southcoasttoday.com/apps/pbcs.dll/article?AID=/20070510/NEWS/705100414

http://www.au.org/our-work/legal/successes/falls-river-ma

The Bristol County, Massachusetts, sheriff's department funded a rehabilitation program to help recently released prisoners reintegrate into society. The program was completely voluntary and boasted an 86% success rate at keeping participants from returning to jail versus a 7% success rate for secular programs. Despite the program's success, Americans United for

Separation of Church and State threatened legal action against the county for funding a faith-based organization. The sheriff gave in to the pressure and closed the program.

Girl Barred from Singing "Kum Ba Yah" at Boys & Girls Club Talent Show
http://articles.sun-sentinel.com/2000-08-16/news/0008160005_1_talent-show-girls-club-club-s-executive-director
Samantha Schulz, an eight-year-old girl from Port Charlotte, Florida, was barred from singing "Kum Ba Yah" at a Boys & Girls Club talent show because the song included the words "Oh, Lord." The club's director said, "You have to check your religion at the door." The executive director of the Sarasota County Boys & Girls Club apologized and invited Schulz to perform the song at another talent show.

Post Office Promotes Secularization of Christmas Season
Bill McAllister, "Gearing Up for Christmas," Washington Post, *Sept. 29, 1995, at N66*
The Post Office issued guidelines advising clerks to use words like "Happy Holidays" and to avoid any decorations with a religious theme.

Coach Banned from City Recreation Facility for Religious Speech
http://oldsite.alliancedefensefund.org/actions/victories/freedom.aspx?cid=3176#victory27
A swim coach in Northglenn, Colorado, shared his faith as he coached swimming in the city recreation facility. The city recreation facility's director sent the coach a letter informing him that he was no longer welcome on the premises of the city recreation facility. A concerned parent inquired to the city to find out why the coach had been banned and was told that the coach used offensive language, but upon further investigation the parent discovered that the coach's religious speech was the problem. A lawsuit was filed to protect the man's right to access the city recreation facility.

Freedom From Religion Foundation Threatens Commissioner for Having a Cross and Nativity Scene in His Personal Office
http://www.upnorthlive.com/news/story.aspx?id=584728
The Freedom From Religion Foundation sent a letter to Dennis Lennox, a county drain commissioner, threatening a lawsuit if he would not remove a cross and Nativity scene from his personal office. FFRF claimed the display is a violation of the Establishment Clause. Lennox commented, "This is my private office in my private area, I'm not trying to force my faith down anybody's throat[;] I'm just saying I celebrate Christmas."

High School Student Threatened with Suspension for Posting Flyers of the Ten Commandments

Nicole Buzzard, "A Youth with a Mission: A Santiago High School Junior Seeks to Post the Ten Commandments at Corona-Norco Campuses," The Press Enterprise Co. (Riverside, CA), June 30, 2004 at B01

High school junior Jason Farr wanted to post the Ten Commandments in his school and other schools in his district. He posted flyers of the Ten Commandments, which resulted in a threat of a five-day suspension. Additionally, Farr was informed that the Bible was not suitable material for the silent reading period, despite the fact that it fulfilled page and genre requirements.

Library Refuses to Include Christmas in Holiday Book Display

Terry Mattingly, "On Religion: Things Got Rough on Church-State Front This Holiday Season," Naples Daily News, Jan. 17, 2004

When a pastor in Chandler, Arizona, complained that a public library display excluded Christmas and only included Hanukkah and Kwanzaa, the library took down the entire display rather than add any information about Christmas.

Freedom From Religion Foundation Attacks Mother Teresa Stamp

http://www.foxnews.com/story/0,2933,584165,00.html

The United States Postal Service (USPS) honored Mother Teresa, a Noble Peace Prize recipient, with a memorial stamp for her humanitarian relief. The Freedom From Religion Foundation criticized the stamp as a violation of USPS regulations by honoring a religious figure and called on its members to boycott the stamp and begin a letter campaign to expose the "darker side" of Mother Teresa.

Historical Cross Attacked by ACLU and Cut Down by Vandals

http://www.kionrightnow.com/story/11277495/city-of-monterey-wants-to-restore-cross
http://www.au.org/church-state/april-2010-church-state/au-bulletin/beach-cross-movesto-church-land-in-california

A cross, erected in 1969 on Del Monte Beach in Monterey, California, to commemorate the bicentennial of Don Gaspar de Portol's raising a cross to signal a supply ship, was attacked by the ACLU as a violation of the Establishment Clause. During the dispute, vandals cut down the cross. The ACLU vigorously objected when the city council considered replacing the cross. Despite an initial unanimous decision to rebuild the cross, the city eventually relented to the legal threats and submitted to the ACLU's demands.

High School Student Threatened with Suspension for Posting Flyers of the Ten Commandments

Nicole Buzzard, "A youth with a Mission: A Santiago High School Junior Seeks to Post the Ten Commandments at Corona-Norco Campuses," The Press Enterprise Co. (Riverside, CA), June 30, 2004 at BO1

High school junior Jason Farr wanted to post the Ten Commandments in his school and other schools in his district. He posted flyers of the Ten Commandments, which resulted in a threat of a five-day suspension. Additionally, Farr was informed that the Bible was not suitable material for the silent reading period, despite the fact that it fulfilled page and genre requirements.

Freedom From Religion Foundation Scares Michigan Town into Abandoning "Christmas Break"

http://ffrf.org/uploads/legal/petoskeynews.pdf

The Petoskey, Michigan, School Board wanted to reinstate "Christmas Break" as a replacement for "Winter Holiday Break." The Freedom From Religion Foundation (FFRF) quickly responded with the threat of litigation unless "Christmas" was removed. The school avoided litigation by submitting to FFRF's requests.

Complaint Leads Tennessee Town to End Tradition of Reading from Luke at Christmas

http://www.knoxnews.com/news/2009/dec/07/biblical-reading-scratched-from-maryvilleyuletide/

For twenty-two years, the town of Maryville, Tennessee, had a local radio personality read from the Book of Luke during the Christmas tree lighting ceremony. Following a complaint, the town decided that it would no longer include the traditional reading during the ceremony.

Oregon Elementary School Bans Christmas Trees, Santa Claus, and Dreidels

http://www.mailtribune.com/apps/pbcs.dll/article?AID=/20091204/NEWS/912040329

An elementary school in Ashland, Oregon, banned Christmas trees, Santa Claus figures, and dreidels following a complaint from a parent. The school decided that the only acceptable decorations are wreaths, snowflakes, snowmen, candles, and candy canes. The school's Christmas tree, which had no religious decorations, was replaced with a large snowman.

Sonoma County Keeps Star and Angels on Christmas Tree

http://religionclause.blogspot.com/2009/12/county-reverses-order-on-removing-stars.html

An atheist activist pressured Sonoma County, California, administrator Chris Thomas into removing the star and angels off of the county's Christmas tree. The activist complained that the decorations were religious symbols. After further reflection, however, Thomas reinstated the star and angels because he found them to be generic Christmas decorations.

City in California Backs Down from Replacing Its "Christmas Parade" with a "Holiday Parade"

http://www.mercedsunstar.com/2009/12/01/1201213/christian-organization-sayschristmas.html

Merced, California, attempted to change the name of its annual parade from the "Christmas Parade" to the "Holiday Parade" to avoid lawsuits. The city officials quickly backed down, however, following a strong backlash from its citizens and changed the name back to the "Christmas Parade."

Town Bans All Holiday Decorations from Memorial Square

http://religionclause.blogspot.com/2009/11/town-decides-to-remove-creche-rather.html

The council of Chambersburg, Pennsylvania, decided that it would rather have no holiday decorations on its Memorial Square than have a variety of different religious decorations. This decision was prompted by a complaint from an atheist group that wanted to put up a sign on the square that said, "Celebrating Solstice. Honoring Atheist War Veterans." The only decorations now allowed on the square are flowers and American flags.

Freedom From Religion Foundation Threatens Technical Colleges in Wisconsin for Observing Good Friday Holiday

http://religionclause.blogspot.com/2009/01/good-friday-time-off-at-wisconsin-tech.html

The Freedom From Religion Foundation sent letters to technical colleges in Wisconsin threatening the colleges for having Good Friday as a holiday. Several technical colleges indicated that they would eliminate the holiday.

Garden City Long Island, New York, Schools Ban Teachers from Observing Religious Holidays

Teachers in Garden City Long Island, New York, wanted to use personal days to observe religious holidays, which is one of the listed permissible uses for a personal day. When some Catholic teachers requested to use a personal day for Holy Thursday and some Jewish teachers wanted to use a personal day during Passover, however, they were denied and were forced to use arbitration to prevent the religious discrimination.

Governor of Washington Allows Menorah and Christmas Tree but Not Creche at Christmas

Eugene Register-Guard, *"Menorah, not Nativity scene, finds place in state Capitol," Dec. 22, 2006, at D5.*
Governor Chris Gregoire lit a menorah in a celebration at the state Capitol, and accepted the gift of a menorah for her home. The menorah that was lit during the ceremony was displayed in the Capitol rotunda with a Christmas tree. However, when a local resident asked for a Nativity scene to be displayed with the menorah and the tree, the Governor refused.

Nativity Scene and Star of David Removed from Teacher's Holiday Decorations

Liberty Counsel, "'Twas Two Weeks Before Christmas, And All Through The Land...," available at http://www.lc.org/index.cfm?PID=14100&PRID=261 (Dec. 13, 2006)
McNair Middle School in Fayetteville, Arkansas, removed a Nativity scene and a Star of David from a teacher's holiday display, which also included secular holiday decorations. After being provided with a legal memorandum explaining that the display was constitutional, the school returned the decorations.

ACLU Threatens County for Allowing Nativity Scene to Be Displayed in Open Forum

Liberty Counsel, "'Twas Two Weeks Before Christmas, And All Through The Land...," available at http://www.lc.org/index.cfm?PID=14100&PRID=261 (Dec. 13, 2006)
The ACLU threatened Cumberland County, Tennessee, because a Nativity scene was placed in an open forum outside of the county courthouse.

"Cold in the Night" Replaces "Silent Night" in Wisconsin School

Liberty Counsel, "School Dumps 'Cold in the Night' and Returns to 'Silent Night,'" available at http://www.lc.org/index.cfm?PID=14102&AlertID=480 (Dec. 14, 2005)
Ridgeway Elementary School in Dodgeville, Wisconsin, planned to perform "Cold in the Night," a secularized version of "Silent Night," at its "winter party." The plan was abandoned after the school received large numbers of

phone calls and emails opposing the violation of this traditional and historic Christmas song.

Senior Citizens Banned from Singing Christmas Carols in Their Homes
Liberty Counsel, "Housing Authorities Tell Senior Citizens and Persons with Disabilities 'No Christmas this Year,'" available at http://www.lc.org/pressrelease/2005/nr121305b.htm (Dec. 13, 2005)
Senior citizens living in facilities owned by the Housing Resource Development Corporation were told they could not sing Christmas carols. Following an attorney's demand letter, the facility reversed its decision.

No Christmas Decorations at Senior Citizens' Home
Liberty Counsel, "Housing Authorities Tell Senior Citizens and Persons with Disabilities 'No Christmas this Year,'" available at http://www.lc.org/pressrelease/2005/nr121305b.htm (Dec. 13, 2005)
Residents at Bethany Towers, which provides housing for low-income senior citizens and persons with disabilities, were told that they could not display any religious decorations in any common area or on the exterior of their rooms. Management removed nativity scenes and other religious decorations set up by the seniors, even taking angels off of the Christmas tree.

NYC's Environmental Protection Agency Allows Hanukkah Banners, Bans Christmas Banners
Liberty Counsel, "Christmas 'Grinches' Are On The Run," available at http://www.lc.org/index.cfm?PID=14100&PRID=536 (Dec. 13, 2005)
The NYC Environmental Protection Agency allowed its employees to have Hanukkah banners and, in the past, allowed employees to celebrate the Indian festival of Diwali. The agency banned Christmas banners, however, along with red and green decorations and even removed the "holiday trees." Following a staff petition, the agency allowed the Christmas decorations and issued an apology to employees.

Indiana State Department of Health Requires "Holiday," Not "Christmas," Parties
Liberty Counsel, "Christmas 'Grinches' Are On The Run," available at http://www.lc.org/index.cfm?PID=14100&PRID=536 (Dec. 13, 2005)
The Indiana State Department of Health told its employees that they could not have Christmas parties during lunch hours. The parties had to be "holiday" rather than "Christmas" parties, and the employee-initiated parties could have no religious content. Following a demand letter, the department allowed employees to have their own Christmas parties with religious content.

Florida Elementary Schools Bans "Merry Christmas"

Liberty Counsel, "Christmas 'Grinches' Are On The Run," available at http://www.lc.org/index.cfm?PID=14100&PRID=536 (Dec. 13, 2005)

Teachers and students at Boulevard Heights Elementary School in Fort Lauderdale, Florida, were told that they may not say, "Merry Christmas." The school recommended "Happy Holidays" as an alternative.

School Door Decorating Contest Bans Religious Content

Liberty Counsel, "Christmas Themes Once Banned From Student Door Decorating Competition Will Now Be Allowed," available at http://www.lc.org/index.cfm?PID=14102&AlertID=475 (Dec. 9, 2005)

D.C. Everest Senior High School announced a "Winter Spirit Week Door Decorating Contest." The rules stated that doors could be decorated to depict "[a]ny winter scene," so long as there were "[n]o religious ties." The principal said that any doors with religious themes would be disqualified. After receiving more than 200 student petitions and a demand letter, as well as legal advice of their own, the school changed the rules to allow religious depictions.

Freedom From Religion Foundation Attempts to Eliminate Good Friday As Government Holiday

http://www.jsonline.com/blogs/news/90885039.html#!page=10&pageSize=10&sort=newestfirst

The Freedom From Religion Foundation wrote a letter of complaint to the city of Milwaukee to end its Good Friday Holiday. It cited a 1996 federal district court case declaring the holiday unconstitutional.

Firefighters Remove Christmas Lights After Neighbors Complain of Being Offended

Terry Mattingly, "On Religion: Things Got Rough on Church-State Front This Holiday Season," Naples Daily News, Jan. 17, 2004

Firefighters in Glenview, Illinois, were forced to take down their station's Christmas lights after neighbors complained of being offended.

Florida City Council Suggests Limiting Religious Holidays

http://www.onenewsnow.com/Culture/Default.aspx?id=950434

The multicultural committee for North Miami Beach, Florida, recommended that city council limit each "legal" religion to one religious holiday proclamation. Not only does this require the city to choose which religions are acceptable, but it forces Christians to choose between Easter and Christmas.

Post Office Replaces Madonna and Child Stamp

McAllister, Bill "Postal Service Ends Christ Camp Stamp Series", Washington Post, Nov. 19, 1994 at Fl.

The Post Office replaced its Madonna and Child stamp in the holiday stamp collection with an angel stamp after using the Madonna and Child for 28 years. The Post Office resumed the stamp after there was a public outcry.

ATTACKS IN THE SCHOOLHOUSE

Supreme Court Upholds Indirect School Tax Credits
Arizona Christian School Tuition Organization v. Winn, 131 S. Ct. 1436 (2011)
Arizona provides tax credits for donations to school tuition organizations that fund scholarships to Arizona private schools. A group of taxpayers sued the state, arguing the law violated the Establishment Clause because program funds were allotted to religious schools. The Supreme Court held that because the system was based on individual tax credits and only affected those directly participating in the program, the taxpayers had no grounds on which to sue the state. As a result, Arizona citizens' right to choose where to use their scholarship funds was upheld.

Christian Legal Society Denied Recognition at Hastings College of Law
Christian Legal Society Chapter of the University of California, Hastings College of the Law v. Martinez, 130 S. Ct. 2971 (2010)
In 2004, the Christian Legal Society (CLS) filed a lawsuit against Hastings College of the Law in San Francisco for not giving the CLS chapter at Hastings College official recognition due to the CLS's refusal to comply with the school's nondiscrimination policy. A district court ruled in favor of Hastings College. The Ninth Circuit Court of Appeals upheld their ruling. In January of 2010, the Supreme Court agreed to intervene in the case. About eighteen organizations petitioned the Supreme Court to encourage them to uphold the right of religious organizations to determine the requirements for their own membership. The Supreme Court, however, affirmed the decisions of the lower courts.

Public School Bans Bible Club in Name of Nondiscrimination
Truth v. Kent School District, 129 S. Ct. 2889 (2009)
A public school prevented students from forming a Bible club, stating that the club's requirement that club members possess a true desire to grow in a relationship with Jesus Christ would exclude non-Christians and violate the school's nondiscrimination policy.

Scholarship Awarded for Any Career but Pastor
Locke v. Davey, 540 U.S. 712 (2004)
Josh Davey received a Promise Scholarship, which was awarded to academically gifted students with postsecondary education expenses to use at any college in the state. He decided to pursue a double major in pastoral ministries and business management and administration. Davey was told that he could use the scholarship for any major unless he was devoted to

becoming a pastor. The U.S. Supreme Court ruled his scholarship could be withdrawn.

Lawsuits Challenge Voucher Program

Zelman v. Simmons-Harris, 536 U.S. 639 (2002)

An Ohio voucher program was enacted because the public school system was in a "crisis of magnitude," and families were given voucher funds to use toward a school of their choice. Many families elected to use their vouchers for religious schools. As a result, a lawsuit was filed to challenge the program, claiming it was unconstitutional because parents are allowed to choose religious or secular schools. The Supreme Court held that the program was neutral and thus not a violation of the Establishment Clause.

Religious After-School Club Sues for Equal Treatment

Good News Club v. Milford Central School, 533 U.S. 98 (2001)

Milford Central School denied the Good News Club use of the school's facilities after school. A lawsuit was filed to protect the religious group's right to use the school's facilities, as other organizations were permitted to do, without being discriminated against. A federal district court and the Second Circuit Court of Appeals both upheld the discrimination, but the Supreme Court reversed.

Lawsuit Attacks Prayer Before High School Football Games

Santa Fe I.S.D. v. Doe, 530 U.S. 290 (2000)

A lawsuit was filed to challenge a school district policy permitting student-led prayer prior to football games. The court struck down the policy, determining that it violated the Establishment Clause. In the lower court in this same case, the judge ordered students not to pray in Jesus' name and told them that federal marshals would be on hand to take students to the county jail, saying, "Anyone who violates these orders, no kidding, is going to wish that he or she had died as a child when this court gets through with it."

Lawsuit Attacks Public Support for Materials and Equipment for Public and Private Schools

Mitchell v. Helms, 530 U.S. 793 (2000)

Under the Education Consolidation and Improvement Act of 1981, government aid for materials and equipment was provided to public as well as private schools. A lawsuit was filed against the Act because it would allow private schools, which are religious schools, to receive a benefit. The Supreme Court held that this funding did not violate the Establishment Clause.

University of Virginia Discriminates Against Religious Journal

Rosenberger v. Rector & Visitors of University of Virginia, 515 U.S. 819 (1995)
The University of Virginia refused to provide funds to print a journal because of the journal's religious viewpoint. The student filed a lawsuit to challenge the fund's disbursement guidelines that discriminated against religious viewpoints. The Supreme Court held that providing funds to publish the journal would not violate the Establishment Clause so the school could not discriminate against the journal because of its religious viewpoint.

School District Denies Sign-Language Interpreter to Deaf Student Who Attends Catholic School

Zobrest v. Catalina Foothills Sch. Dist., 509 U.S. 1 (1993)
Through the Individuals with Disabilities Education Act (IDEA), a deaf student was entitled to assistance from a sign language interpreter during the school day, and the student asked the Catalina Foothills School District to provide such an interpreter. However, the student attended Catholic school, and the district refused to provide an interpreter. A lawsuit had to be filed to uphold this religious student's rights.

New York School District Discriminates Against Religious Use of Its Facilities

Lamb's Chapel v. Center Moriches Union Free School District, 508 U.S. 384 (1993)
A New York school board denied a church after-hours access to a school to exhibit a film series about Christian family values because of a policy prohibiting use by any group for religious purposes. A lawsuit was filed to protect the church's right to have equal access to the school premises.

Prayer Prohibited at Middle School Graduation

Lee v. Weisman, 505 U.S. 577 (1992)
In Providence, Rhode Island, principals of a public school were permitted to ask clergy to give invocations and benedictions at graduation exercises, but when a middle school principal invited a rabbi to give a "nonsectarian" prayer, a student's parent got a temporary restraining order to prevent the prayer and sought a permanent injunction to prevent the practice of inviting clergy to perform prayers. The U.S. Supreme Court prohibited the prayer but noted that it was wrong of the school officials to attempt to censor the rabbi by requiring that a given prayer be "nonsectarian."

School Board Bans Students from Forming Religious Extracurricular Clubs
Board of Education of the Westside Community Schools v. Mergens, 496 U.S. 226 (1990)
A school board refused to allow students to form an extracurricular Christian club, claiming such a club would violate the Establishment Clause. A lawsuit had to be filed to protect the Christian group from being unlawfully discriminated against by the school board.

Act Seeking to Ensure Both Sides of Origins Debate Are Taught Declared Unconstitutional
Edwards v. Aguillard, 482 U.S. 578 (1987)
A suit was filed to challenge Louisiana's Creationism Act. The Creationism Act provided that if evolution is taught in public schools, creation science must also be taught; and if creation science is taught, then evolution must also be taught. The suit sought to strike down the act as a violation of the Establishment Clause. The Supreme Court obliged, striking down the law.

Time Set Aside for Voluntary Prayer Challenged
Wallace v. Jaffree, 472 U.S. 38 (1985)
A resident brought suit to challenge the practice of having a period of meditation and voluntary prayer in schools in Alabama and won.

University Discriminates Against Religious Student Groups
Widmar v. Vincent, 454 U.S. 263 (1981)
The University of Missouri at Kansas City refused to allow a religious student group equal access to university facilities like other student groups. The students were forced to file a lawsuit in order to protect their rights to equal access and to stop the religious discrimination.

Humanist Group Attacks Public School Graduation Ceremony Held at Religious College
Am. Humanist Ass'n v. Greenville County Sch. Dist., No. 13-2502, 2014 WL 1979305 (4th Cir. 2014)
Mountain View Elementary School in Taylors, South Carolina, held its graduation at North Greenville University, a local Christian college. When the American Humanist Association (AHA) heard about the location and discovered that several of the students had led prayer as part of the graduation ceremony, they sent a demand letter to the elementary school superintendent and principal that called for the elimination of the prayers and a change in venue. The school responded that no changes would be forthcoming. Consequently, the AHA sued the school. A South Carolina

district court found in favor of the school, but the Fourth Circuit Court of Appeals vacated the decision and remanded it for reconsideration.

Eighth-Grade Class President Banned from Quoting Sentence from Old Testament

A.M. v. Taconic Hills Cent. Sch. Dist., 510 Fed. Appx. 3 (2d Cir. 2013)

An eighth-grade student, the president of her class, wanted to include a sentence from the Old Testament in her graduation speech. The school told the student that she could not include the sentence because it was "too religious." The Second Circuit upheld the school's censorship, stating that a reasonable observer might perceive the student's message as having been endorsed by the school. The Supreme Court refused to review the decision.

Public School Discriminates Against Invitations to Religious Parties

K.A. ex rel. Ayers v. Pocono Mountain Sch. Dist., 710 F.3d 99 (3rd Cir. 2013)

A Pennsylvania public school prohibited a fifth-grade student from handing out invitations to a Christmas party at her church, even though the school permitted students to hand out invitations to other private parties. The Third Circuit upheld the student's right to hand out invitations to a Christmas party at her church and granted a preliminary injunction against the school's policy.

Evangelist Prohibited from Preaching on Campus by Unconstitutional Restrictions

McGlone v. Cheek, 534 Fed. Appx. 293 (6th Cir. 2013)

John McGlone, wanting to preach on campus, was denied access to the University of Tennessee's campus because student groups would not sponsor his message. A Tennessee federal district court held that the school policy requiring outside speakers to obtain an invitation from student, faculty, or staff before speaking on campus was constitutional. The U.S. Court of Appeals for the Sixth Circuit reversed, holding that the requirement was unconstitutionally vague and stopped its enforcement.

Parents Sue to Stop Other Parents from Allowing Their Children to Be Released for Religious Instruction

Moss v. Spartanburg County Sch. Dist. Seven, 683 F.3d 599 (4th Cir. 2012)

Parents of two Spartanburg County High School students sued Spartanburg County School District claiming that the school's release time program, which permits students to take religious instruction offered by private educators and receive up to two academic credits, violated the Establishment Clause. After the district court granted summary judgment to the school district, the parents appealed, and the Fourth Circuit held that the school's program is constitutional.

Professor Fired for Voicing Religious Views in a Newspaper Editorial
Dixon v. University of Toledo, 702 F.3d 269 (6th Cir. 2012)
University of Toledo professor Crystal Dixon was fired for writing a newspaper editorial about her religious views opposing homosexuality. The district court and the U.S. Court of Appeals for the Sixth Circuit held that Dixon's speech was not protected.

University Student Expelled from Counseling Program for Refusing to Affirm Sexual Conduct Outside of Marriage
Ward v. Polite, 667 F.3d 727 (6th Cir. 2012)
Julea Ward was expelled from Eastern Michigan University's (EMU) graduate counseling program because she would not affirm homosexual conduct or heterosexual conduct outside of marriage to clients that she saw during the clinical portion of her program, instead referring these clients to another counselor. A federal district judge ruled against Ms. Ward, but the Sixth Circuit Court of Appeals reversed. Following the Sixth Circuit's ruling in Ward's favor, the case settled with EMU reinstating Ms. Ward and providing financial compensation to her.

Tennessee Public School Bans Fourth-Grade Student from Having Bible Studies with Peers
Whitson v. Knox County Board of Education, 468 Fed. Appx. 532 (6th Cir. 2012)
L.W., a fourth-grade student at Karns Elementary School in Tennessee, was stopped by school officials from holding Bible studies with his peers during recess. A jury found for the school, and the Sixth Circuit affirmed.

Evangelist Sues for Right to Share the Gospel and Distribute Religious Tracts at University
McGlone v. Bell, 681 F.3d 718 (6th Cir. 2012)
John McGlone wanted to share the Gospel and distribute religious tracts in the public areas of the Tennessee Technological University. The university demanded that McGlone first receive a permit to share the gospel and distribute the tracts. A district court ruled in the university's favor, but the Sixth Circuit overturned the district court, holding that the university's requirement was unreasonable.

Lawsuit Stops Public School from Using Church for Graduation Ceremony

John Doe, 3 v. Elmbrook School District, No. 10-2922 (7th Cir. 2012) (en banc)

Plaintiffs sued the Elmbrook School District in Wisconsin, claiming its practice of using a Christian church as the locale for the high school's annual graduation ceremony violated the Establishment Clause of the First Amendment. The district court granted the school district's motion for summary judgment. The plaintiffs appealed to the Seventh Circuit, which held that the practice of holding the ceremony in a church "did not constitute governmentally coerced participation in religion," did not qualify as an endorsement of religious practices or beliefs, and did not entangle the state with religion. The Seventh Circuit then granted en banc review, however, and reversed the lower decisions, holding that holding graduation in a church violates the Establishment Clause.

Ex-Teacher Sues Private School for Discrimination After She Is Fired for Having Pre-Marital Sex

Hamilton v. Southland Christian Sch., Inc., 680 F.3d 1361 (11th Cir. 2012)

A teacher was fired from a Christian school because she engaged in pre-marital sex. The teacher sued the school under Title VII, claiming that she was fired because she was pregnant. The district court dismissed the case, but the Eleventh Circuit reversed, holding that the teacher may sue the school. The Eleventh Circuit acknowledged *Hosanna-Tabor* and the ministerial exception but noted that the school did not raise the ministerial exception until the appellate level, which was too late.

Lawsuit Bans School Board from Opening Meetings with Prayer

Doe v. Indian River School District, 653 F.3d 256 (3d Cir. 2011)

Since 1969, the School Board of the Indian River School District had a practice of opening their public meetings with a moment of prayer. Until 2004, the president of the board would designate one person at each meeting to give the prayer. After 2004, the Board adopted a policy that created a rotating basis that allows one member of the board to offer a prayer or request a moment of silence. No one was required to participate in the prayer, and no school employee could be involved in the prayer. Mona and Marco Dobrich filed a suit individually and as the parents of their two children to challenge this practice. The court of appeals held that because students regularly attended school board meetings, the opening prayer violated the Establishment Clause.

University Professor Denied Promotion Because of His Religious Beliefs

Adams v. The Trustees of the University of North Carolina-Wilmington, 640 F.3d 550 (4th Cir. 2011)

A professor at the University of North Carolina-Wilmington was denied a promotion based on the religious and political views he expressed in his columns and speeches. The Fourth Circuit overturned the lower court by holding that the professor's speech was constitutionally protected private speech.

Public School Prohibits Third Grader from Sharing Goodie Bags with Religious Content

Morgan v. Swanson, 659 F.3d 359 (5th Cir. 2011) (en banc)

Jonathan Morgan, a third-grader in Plano, Texas, was told that he could not include a religious message in the goodie bags that he was bringing to the "Winter Party" to share with his classmates. Other children at the school were prohibited from distributing pencils that stated "Jesus is the Reason for the Season" and "Jesus Loves me this I know for the Bible tells me so." Another student was ordered by a school official to discontinue distributing tickets to a Christian drama and to discard the remaining tickets. In a fractured en banc opinion, the Fifth Circuit stated that the students are protected by the First Amendment but that their protection was not clearly enough established to award damages against the school officials involved.

High School Valedictorian Sues for Freedom to Express Her Faith in Valedictorian Address

Schultz v. Medina Valley I.S.D., No. 11-50486 (5th Cir. 2011)

Angela Hildenbrand, the valedictorian of her class, wanted to say a prayer during her graduation ceremony from Medina Valley High. A fellow student from an agnostic family filed a suit to prevent Hildenbrand from praying. The federal district court judge issued an order prohibiting Hildenbrand from using words like "Lord," "in Jesus' name," and "amen." The Fifth Circuit Court of Appeals reversed the ruling and allowed the prayer. On June 6, 2011, Hildenbrand gave her speech, which included a prayer.

Athletic Association Rules Single Out Catholic Schools for Additional Restrictions

Seger v. Kentucky High School Athletic Association, 453 Fed. Appx. 630 (6th Cir. 2011)

The Sixth Circuit Court of Appeals upheld a bylaw of the Kentucky High School Athletic Association that said Catholic schools could not offer students more than a twenty-five percent scholarship for athletics. Parents filed suit claiming that the bylaw was discriminatory based on religion because the rule grouped Catholic schools together. The court rejected this argument and found that the bylaw merely grouped the schools together because they were similar for reasons other than religion.

Students Forced to Sue for Right to Wear Shirts Opposing Day of Silence
Zamecnik v. Indian Prairie School District #204, 636 F.3d 874 (7th Cir. 2011)
A school prohibited two students in Naperville, Illinois, from wearing T-shirts that stated, "Be Happy, Not Gay," to protest the Day of Silence, a day intended to draw attention to discrimination faced by homosexual students. The two students wished to wear the shirts to show their religious beliefs. The Seventh Circuit held that the school could not prohibit the students from wearing the T-shirt because of the potential for "hurt feelings."

Lawsuit Blocks Charter School from Including Religious Texts in Curriculum
Nampa Classical Academy v. Goesling, 447 Fed. Appx. 776 (9th Cir. 2011)
The U.S. Court of Appeals for the Ninth Circuit affirmed a district court's holding that Nampa Classical Academy, a charter school in Idaho, could not use religious texts as part of its curriculum because the school is technically classified as a governmental entity. The plaintiffs, Nampa Classical Academy; Isaac Moffett, a minor; and Maria Kosmann sued the Idaho Public Charter School Commission on the grounds that its decision to prohibit the use of sectarian or denominational texts in public schools violated the First and Fourteenth Amendments of the U.S. Constitution. The Ninth Circuit held "[b]ecause Idaho charter schools are governmental entities, the curriculum presented in such a school is not the speech of teachers, parents, or students, but that of the Idaho government."

Public School District Orders Teacher to Remove Classroom Decorations Mentioning God
Johnson v. Poway Unified School District, 658 F.3d 954 (9th Cir. 2011)
Bradley Johnson, a public school teacher, sued the Poway Unified School District in San Diego, claiming the district violated his right to free speech, the Establishment Clause, and his right to Equal Protection under the law when the district forced him to remove banners referring to God from his classroom. The case made it to the Ninth Circuit Court of Appeals, which held that the Poway Unified School District's decision to force the removal of the materials did not violate any of the constitutional rights asserted by Johnson.

History Teacher Allowed to Make Derogatory Remarks About Religious Beliefs

Farnan v. Capistrano Unified School District, 654 F.3d 975 (9th Cir. 2011)

History teacher James Corbett of Mission Viejo, California, was accused of violating the Establishment Clause by making derogatory comments about religious faith in the classroom. The dispute arose after he called creationism "superstitious nonsense." The Ninth Circuit held that Corbett was entitled to qualified immunity because whether such comments violate the Establishment Clause is not clearly established. The Ninth Circuit refused to decide that issue.

Counseling Student Threatened with Expulsion for Biblical Beliefs

Keeton v. Anderson-Wiley, 664 F.3d 865 (11th Cir. 2011)

Jennifer Keeton, a graduate student in counseling at Augusta State University, was asked to complete a remediation plan that included diversity training and a recommendation to attend the Augusta Gay Pride Parade. According to the university, Ms. Keeton's Christian beliefs did not align with the department's professional guidelines. As a result, Ms. Keeton faced the remediation plan or expulsion from the program. Ms. Keeton sued the university to protect her religious freedom but lost in court.

University Forced to Treat Catholic Group Equally with Other Student Groups

Badger Catholic, Inc. v. Walsh, 620 F. 3d 775 (7th Cir. 2010)

Badger Catholic, a student organization at the University of Wisconsin-Madison, was denied reimbursement for religious events. Badger Catholic filed a lawsuit. The Seventh Circuit held that the University of Wisconsin-Madison was engaging in viewpoint discrimination and must allow reimbursements for religious events as well as secular.

Lawsuit Opposes Mandatory Period of Silence in Illinois Schools Because It Could Be Used for Prayer or Meditation

Sherman v. Koch, 623 F.3d 501 (7th Cir. 2010)

Illinois passed a statute mandating a period of silence in public schools. The period of silence could be used for meditation, prayer, or silent reflections on the day's activities. Students filed a suit claiming that the statute violated the establishment of church and state. The district court held that the statute was unconstitutional, but the United States Court of Appeals for the Seventh Circuit held that the statute did not violate the constitution.

Professor Threatens Student for Speech About Faith and Marriage

Lopez v. Candaele, 630 F.3d 775 (9th Cir. 2010)

Jonathan Lopez, a student at Los Angeles City College, gave a speech about his faith and his traditional view of marriage. Lopez's professor stopped the speech, refused to grade it, and threatened to have Lopez expelled. Lopez sued the professor, a dean of the school, and the school for violating his First Amendment rights. The district court sided with Lopez, but the Ninth Circuit Court of Appeals held that Lopez did not have standing to sue because the teacher's statements are not a credible threat of harm.

University Rejects Class Credit for Religiously Motivated Classes

Association of Christian Schools International v. Stearns, 362 F. Appx. 640 (9th Cir. 2010)

The University of California's admissions policy does not accept high school courses that focus on one religion's viewpoint. The Ninth Circuit upheld the policy, rejecting First Amendment and Equal Protection claims.

School Covers Religious Content in Kindergarten Student's Work

Peck v. Baldwinsville School District, 351 Fed. Appx. 477 (2nd Cir. 2009)

Antonio Peck's kindergarten teacher instructed her class to draw a poster about how to save the environment. Antonio's first poster contained several religious figures and the statement: "The only way to save the world." The poster was rejected. Antonio's second poster included cutout figures of children holding hands around the world, people recycling trash, and children picking up garbage. On the left side of the poster was a picture of Jesus kneeling, with his hands stretched toward the sky. The poster was displayed along with eighty other student posters; but, unlike the other posters, school officials folded Antonio's poster in half so that the figure of Jesus could not be seen.

School Rejects Student's Selection of the Bible to Have Read to Class

Busch v. Marple Newtown School District, 567 F.3d 89 (3d Cir. 2009)

Elementary school students in the Marple Newtown School District were asked to select their favorite book, which their parents would then read to the class. Donna Busch's son chose the Bible. Busch selected a few verses that she often read with her son, being careful to select a Psalm because it omitted references to Jesus Christ. The school's principal refused to allow Busch's son to fully participate because "reading the Bible to the class would be against the law" by "promoting religion," despite numerous other presentations about

Hanukkah, Passover, Christmas, and Easter being permitted in the classroom. The Third Circuit Court of Appeals upheld the restriction.

New Jersey School District Bans Religious Holiday Music
Stratechuk v. Board of Education, S. Orange-Maplewood School District, 587 F.3d 597 (3d Cir. 2009)
A New Jersey School District prohibited celebratory religious music at school holiday events. The Third Circuit Court of Appeals upheld the school district's policy as constitutional, rejecting claims that it violated the First Amendment.

Lawsuit Attacks Minute of Silence in Texas Schools
Croft v. Governor of Texas, 562 F.3d 735 (5th Cir. 2009)
An atheist sued the State of Texas because of a Texas statute that allows a minute of silence for students to pray, meditate, or reflect. The statute was upheld by the Fifth Circuit Court of Appeals.

Lawsuit Stops Thirty-Year Tradition of Gideons Distributing Bibles to Students
Roark v. South Iron R-1 School District, 573 F.3d 556 (8th Cir. 2009)
For thirty years, South Iron Elementary School had permitted the Gideons to distribute Bibles to the students. A student sued, claiming that the distribution of Bibles in school violated the Establishment Clause. The district court prohibited the distribution, and the court of appeals affirmed.

School District Censors Valedictorian's Address
McComb v. Crehan, 320 Fed. Appx. 507 (9th Cir. 2009)
School officials at Foothill High School in Las Vegas, Nevada, told valedictorian Brittany McComb that she could not mention God or Jesus in her valedictorian address. When McComb did so anyway, the school officials turned off her microphone. McComb sued the school for violating her free speech rights, but the Ninth Circuit Court of Appeals found that the school district did not violate her constitutional rights.

School Bans Instrumental Music Associated with a Religious Song
Nurre v. Whitehead, 580 F.3d 1087 (9th Cir. 2009)
A California high school banned a student from playing an instrumental version of a religious song at its graduation ceremony. The Ninth Circuit held that this prohibition did not violate the student's free speech rights.

Valedictorian Told She Would Not Receive Diploma Until She Apologized for Her Religious Speech

Corder v. Lewis Palmer Sch. Dist. No 38, 566 F.3d 1219 (10th Cir. 2009)
Erica Corder, class valedictorian, made a short speech during her graduation in 2006. The official policy of the school for school speeches did not mention religion but prohibited speech that "tends to create hostility or otherwise disrupt the orderly operation of the educational process." Corder gave a speech that referenced her personal faith. At the conclusion of the ceremony, a teacher escorted Corder to speak with a school official. The official informed Corder that she would not receive her diploma until she made a public apology for her speech. A federal district court found for the school district because Corder did not submit her speech for pre-approval as she had been instructed, and the Tenth Circuit Court of Appeals affirmed.

Christian Fraternity Refused Recognition for Limiting Admission to Christian Men

Beta Upsilon Chi Upsilon Chapter at the University of Florida v. Machen, 586 F.3d 908 (11th Cir. 2009)
Beta Upsilon Chi, a Christian fraternity whose members and officers profess faith in Jesus Christ and adhere to a Code of Conduct, was denied official recognition by the University of Florida. The university rejected the fraternity's application because the group allowed only males to join and restricted membership based on religious belief. After being sued, the university modified its policy to allow an exception for religious organizations, and Beta Upsilon Chi was recognized as an official student organization.

Lexington School District Teaches Students About Sexual Orientation Without Notifying Parents

Parker v. Hurley, 514 F.3d 87 (1st Cir. 2008)
Two sets of parents from Lexington, Massachusetts, sued after the school district refused to provide the parents with prior notice that their children would undergo instruction recognizing differences in sexual orientation. The parents argued that forcing their children to undergo the education violated due process and free exercise of religion. On January 31, 2008, the court found that the due process clause was not implicated, and the instruction did not infringe on either the parents or children's free exercise of religion.

Parents Challenge Restrictive Pennsylvania Homeschool Law

Combs v. Homer-Center School District, 540 F.3d 231 (3d Cir. 2008)
Pennsylvania passed the Pennsylvania Home Education Law in 1988. It is

the most restrictive homeschooling law in the United States, requiring that families submit a teaching log, submit a portfolio of the child's work for review, and meet the requirements for the minimum number of days and hours in certain subjects. Six homeschool families sued to protect their right to educate their children after being subjected to truancy proceedings and social service investigations. The court ruled that the law did not substantially burden the parents.

Football Coach Seeks Declaration That His Silent Prayer Is Permissible
Borden v. School District of the Township of East Brunswick, 523 F.3d 153 (3d Cir. 2008)
Marcus Borden, the head football coach at East Brunswick High School, often engaged in silent acts of prayer such as bowing his head to say grace prior to eating or taking a knee with his team during a locker-room prayer. He filed a suit to declare that he was allowed to engage in the silent behavior despite the East Brunswick School District's policy prohibiting faculty participation in student-initiated prayer. The district court found that Borden's acts did not violate the Establishment Clause, but the Third Circuit found that Borden's activities would lead a reasonable observer to conclude that Borden was endorsing religion.

Teacher Forced to Remove Religious Decorations and Material from Classroom
Lee v. York County School Division, 484 F.3d 687 (4th Cir. 2007)
A teacher was made to remove religious materials from his classroom including a picture of George Washington praying, an article showing religious differences of political candidates, and an article dealing with missionary activities of a student. The district court awarded summary judgment to the school district. The appellate court ruled that the teacher was not protected by the First Amendment and affirmed the district court's ruling.

ACLU Sues to Stop Prayers Before School Board Meetings
Doe v. Tangipahoa Parish School Board, 494 F.3d 494 (5th Cir. 2007) (en banc)
The ACLU sued a Louisiana school board for allowing prayers before school board meetings. The Fifth Circuit Court of Appeals, en banc, found that the plaintiffs did not have standing to challenge the school board prayers.

Ex-Teacher Sues Catholic School for Firing Her After She Publicly Supports Abortion
Curay-Cramer v. The Ursuline Academy of Wilmington, Delaware, Inc., 450 F.3d 130 (3d Cir. 2006)
Michele Curay-Cramer, a teacher at Ursuline Academy, was fired from her position at the Catholic school after she signed her name to a pro-choice ad in a local newspaper. School officials asked Ms. Curay-Cramer to withdraw her support for the pro-abortion position (one that was in direct opposition to Catholic teaching) or lose her job. Ms. Curay-Cramer refused and instead took the school to court. The courts ruled in favor of the Academy, however, and affirmed the school's First Amendment rights.

School District Attempts to Charge Religious Club Extra Fee to Use Facilities
Child Evangelism Fellowship of South Carolina v. Anderson School District Five, 470 F.3d 1062 (4th Cir. 2006)
Child Evangelism Fellowship was charged a fee to use school facilities, although the district waived fees whenever deemed "in the best interest of the district." After filing suit, the district changed its policy and sought to "grandfather" free use to the previously authorized groups.

Lawsuit Attacks Christian Prayer Before the Indiana House of Representatives
Hinrichs v. Bosma, 440 F.3d 393 (7th Cir. 2006)
Four taxpayers brought suit seeking an injunction to prohibit opening the Indiana House of Representatives with Christian prayer by saying it violated the Establishment Clause of the First Amendment. The district court ruled that the historical opening prayer at the House was unconstitutional because of its sectarian nature and enjoined further sectarian prayer (e.g. praying in Jesus' name). The appellate court denied a stay.

Cosmetology Instructor Accused of Sexual Harassment for Distributing Religious Material
Piggee v. Carl Sandburg College, 464 F.3d 667 (7th Cir. 2006)
A student at Carl Sandburg College complained when cosmetology teacher Martha Louise Piggee gave him tracts that called homosexuality a sin and called for people to read the Bible and be baptized. Piggee was told she could not hand out the material and that her action qualified as sexual harassment. Piggee went to court against the college, the board of trustees, and five college administrators for violating her due process rights and her constitutional rights to free speech. The suit said that the college's sexual

harassment policy was not clear. A lower court ruled against her, and the case was appealed to the Seventh Circuit. The appellate court ruled that the college had a right to insist Piggee refrain from proselytizing while serving as an instructor because her expression of religious beliefs was unrelated to her job of teaching cosmetology.

Christian Legal Society at Southern Illinois University Revoked as an Official Student Group
Christian Legal Society v. Walker, 453 F.3d 853 (7th Cir. 2006)
Southern Illinois University revoked the Christian Legal Society (CLS) student chapter's registration and all of the associated benefits because the group's "Statement of Faith" and sexual morality policy for its voting members and leaders violated the university's policy prohibiting discrimination on the basis of religion or "sexual orientation." A lawsuit was filed to reestablish CLS's official recognition.

Public School Student Banned from Expressing Opposition to Homosexuality
Harper v. Poway Unified School District, 445 F.3d 1166 (9th Cir. 2006)
Poway High School had a special day to celebrate homosexuality. A Christian student who wore a T-shirt that had an opposing view and that mentioned God was banned from wearing the shirt. The district court ruled that the student's speech was not protected because it offended the "identity" of another person. The Ninth Circuit affirmed.

County Employee Banned from Expressing His Religious Beliefs at Work
Berry v. Department of Social Services, 447 F.3d 642 (9th Cir. 2006)
A county social services employee was prohibited from discussing religion with clients, displaying religious items in his cubicle, and using the conference room for voluntary employee-only prayer meetings. The district court ruled that since he was an employee of a public entity, the employer could restrict his exercise of religion so the employer would not appear to endorse religion and thus violate the Establishment Clause. The appellate court affirmed.

Religious Employee of the Police Department Singled Out for Discriminatory Treatment
Shrum v. City of Coweta, 449 F.3d 1132 (10th Cir. 2006)
An employee of the police department was scheduled to work on Sunday because the police chief knew that it conflicted with the employee's religious convictions and the chief wanted the employee to resign. The district court ruled that the mere refusal to accommodate the employee's religious scheduling needs did not establish a constitutional violation. The court did

rule in favor of the employee since the police chief's decision was not neutral but singled out the employee. The appellate court affirmed the district court ruling in this regard.

Parents File Lawsuit Challenging Sticker on Textbooks Stating That Evolution Is a Theory

Selman v. Cobb County Sch. Dist., 449 F.3d 1320 (11th Cir. 2006)

A Georgia school district decided to place a sticker in new science textbooks explaining that evolution is theory rather than fact and encouraging students to study with open minds and critical thinking skills. A handful of parents complained that the sticker restricted teaching evolution and promoted creationism and filed a lawsuit claiming that the sticker violated the Establishment Clause.

Speaker Banned from Speaking at Middle School Solely Because of His Affiliation with a Religious Organization

Carpenter v. Dillon Elementary School District 10, 149 Fed. Appx. 645 (9th Cir. 2005)

Jaroy Carpenter, a motivational speaker, was prevented from speaking at an assembly in the Dillon Middle School because he was affiliated with a Christian organization, despite the fact that he had previously spoken in over 200 secular schools and that he agreed to omit discussions of his religious faith and references to a youth rally being held nearby. The district court held that Carpenter was not harmed, thus there was no First Amendment violation. The court of appeals affirmed.

Religious Student Club Forced to File a Lawsuit for Equal Treatment with Other Clubs

Child Evangelism Fellowship of New Jersey, Inc. v. Stafford Township School District, 386 F.3d 514 (3d Cir. 2004)

Child Evangelism Fellowship (CEF) was denied permission to post flyers, pass out flyers, staff tables at the back-to-school-night event, or allow students to pass materials to other students about a religious club forming in schools. A lawsuit was filed to protect the right of CEF to utilize the same forums that were afforded to other groups and to prevent viewpoint discrimination.

Maryland School District Limits Religious Student Club's Access to Forum

Child Evangelism Fellowship of Maryland, Inc. v. Montgomery County Public Schools, 373 F.3d 589 (4th Cir. 2004)

The Montgomery County Public Schools refused to allow Child Evangelism Fellowship (CEF) to participate in the district's take-home flyer forum to distribute flyers about the Good News Club, citing fears about the separation of church and state. A lawsuit had to be filed to end the religious discrimination.

School District Bans Teacher from Participating in After-School Religious Club
Wigg v. Sioux Falls School District 49–5, 382 F.3d 807 (8th Cir. 2004)
A school district refused to allow a teacher to participate in a Good News Club meeting at the school after school hours, so the teacher filed a lawsuit to protect her right of assembly with the religious group. The Eighth Circuit Court of Appeals held that the school district violated the teacher's free speech rights by prohibiting her from attending the Good News Club meetings at her school.

Acting Student Forced to Withdraw from Program to Avoid Violating Religious Beliefs
Axson-Flynn v. Johnson, 356 F.3d 1277 (10th Cir. 2004)
University of Utah acting student Christina Axson-Flynn had to withdraw from the acting program and leave the university after her instructors heavily pressured her to perform scenes that required her to say profane words. Axson-Flynn, a Mormon, had informed the instructors of her religious objections to profane phrases during her audition for acceptance to the acting program, but her objections were ignored.

Church Seeks Equal Treatment with New York Public Schools
Bronx Household of Faith v. Bd. of Educ. of the City of New York, 331 F.3d 342 (2d Cir. 2003)
The Bronx Household of Faith filed suit to prevent New York's public schools from discriminating against churches. The public schools refused to allow churches to use school facilities, but permitted other community groups to have access. Several years and court decisions later, the church's constitutional rights to use school facilities were upheld. However, in *Bronx Household of Faith v. Bd. of Educ. of City of New York,* No. 12-2730, 2014 WL 1316301 (2d Cir. Apr. 3, 2014), the Second Circuit Court of Appeals decided that the school's policy of barring the use of school facilities by churches for religious worship services did not violate the Constitution. The church has filed a petition for a rehearing *en banc.*

Father Sues to Direct Education of His Son According to His Religious Beliefs
Leebaert v. Harrington, 332 F.3d 134 (2nd Cir. 2003)
Turk Leebaert, the father of his son, Corky Leebaert, sued to protect his right

to direct the upbringing and education of his child. Leebaert, a resident of Fairfield, Connecticut, requested to excuse his son from a health education program describing health, sex, and character development. The principal responded that the health curriculum was mandatory but that Leebaert could opt out of the six classes related to family-life instruction. Leebaert filed suit to protect his rights, but the district court found that the curriculum did not infringe upon Leebaert's constitutional rights. The Second Circuit affirmed.

Young Students Prohibited from Sharing Their Faith Through Gifts
Walz v. Egg Harbor Township, 342 F.3d 271 (3d Cir. 2003)
A pre-kindergarten student, Daniel Walz, was prevented from giving out pencils with the message "Jesus Loves the Little Children" engraved on them and later, as a first-grader, was prevented from distributing candy canes with "The Candy Maker's Witness" attached to the candy. A lawsuit was filed to protect Daniel's rights to give gifts at school just like other children could, but the Third Circuit Court of Appeals held that the school could prohibit proselytizing speech.

Parent of Students at Christian School Denied Position at Public School
Barrow v. Greenville I.S.D., 332 F.3d 844 (5th Cir. 2003)
Karen Jo Barrow was denied an assistant principal position because she refused to remove her children from a private Christian school. The U.S. District Court in Dallas ruled against Ms. Barrow, arguing that the right of parents to choose private education was not a fundamental right. The Fifth Circuit Court of Appeals, however, found that the superintendent had violated Ms. Barrow's constitutional parental rights and awarded Ms. Barrow lost wages and punitive damages.

Student Sues School District After Board Member Says a Prayer
Doe v. School District of the City of Norfolk, 340 F.3d 605 (8th Cir. 2003)
A student filed a lawsuit after a school board member said a prayer during a graduation. The Eighth Circuit held that, because the prayer was part of the board member's address and not sponsored by the school district, the prayer was private speech and dismissed the lawsuit.

Columbine High School Censors Religious Expression Following Shooting
Fleming v. Jefferson County School District R-1, 298 F.3d 918 (10th Cir. 2002)
Columbine High School hosted a tile-painting project so students could express themselves following the school's tragedy. Some students expressed themselves with religious symbols, including a victim's sister who incorporated a small yellow cross in her tile design. After the tiles were posted, the school

officials eradicated the religious symbols from the tile display. A lawsuit was filed to prevent the school officials from censoring the religious expression of the students. Unfortunately, the court chose not to uphold the students' expression rights, and instead validated the school's censorship.

Lawsuit Attempts to Stop Election of Graduation Speakers to Prevent Religious Expression

Adler v. Duval County School Board, 250 F.3d 1330 (11th Cir. 2001)
A lawsuit was filed to challenge a school policy permitting high school seniors to use a popular vote to select a graduation speaker who could deliver a message of their choosing, without approval by school officials. The lawsuit sought to ban the students because some students might use their speech to express religious thoughts.

Student Banned from Reading a Story from His Bible to the Class

C.H. v. Oliva, 226 F. 3d 198 (3rd. Cir. 2000)
Zachary Hood brought his Beginner's Bible to school to share a story about Jacob and Esau called "A Big Family" as part of class activities, but Zachary's teacher refused to allow the story to be read because it was religious. Zachary's mother had to file a lawsuit to allow Zachary to share his story, just as the other students were permitted to share theirs.

Public School Officials Censor Student's Graduation Prayer

Furley v. Aledo I.S.D., 218 F.3d 743 (5th Cir. 2000)
Katherine Furley was elected to give the invocation at her graduation ceremony and was ordered to submit any prayer to officials. School officials then proceeded to edit, word by word, which words she could and could not pray. A lawsuit was filed to protect Katherine's right to pray without being edited by the government. The Court ruled against her right to pray without government editing.

Muslim Police Officers Told They Must Shave Their Beards

Fraternal Order of Police Newark Lodge No. 12 v. City of Newark, 170 F.3d 359 (3d Cir. 1999)
Two Muslim police officers in Newark were required to shave their beards after the city issued an order requiring all police officers to be clean-shaven. The order permitted a medical exemption, but not a religious exemption. The officers had to file a lawsuit to protect their constitutional right to freely exercise their religion.

Lawsuit Challenges Distribution of Religious Materials to Students
Peck v. Upshur County Board of Education, 155 F.3d 274 (4th Cir. 1998)
A school board policy permitted religious groups to provide religious materials and Bibles to students on one designated day each school year. A lawsuit was filed to strike down the policy.

School District in San Diego Discriminates Against Religious Club
Ceniceros v. Board of Trustees of the San Diego Unified School District, 106 F.3d 878 (9th Cir. 1997)
San Diego Unified School District refused a religious club the opportunity to meet during lunchtime, though other groups were permitted to meet. A lawsuit was filed on behalf of the students to prevent the district's unlawful discrimination and to uphold the students' rights under the Equal Access Act.

Lawsuit Attempts to Ban Choir from Singing Christian Music
Bauchman v. West High School, 132 F.3d 542 (10th Cir. 1997)
A school choir's repertoire included Christian music; and, on occasion, the group sang at a church. A Jewish choir student's family filed a lawsuit, essentially asking the court to censor the choir from singing any religious music. The case had to be fought all the way to the Tenth Circuit to prevent unlawful religious censorship.

Students File Lawsuit to Get Recognition for Their Bible Study Club
Hsu v. Roslyn Union Free School District, 85 F.3d 839 (2nd Cir. 1996)
Students Emily and Timothy Hsu wanted to form a student Bible club at school, but were denied club recognition because the students insisted on a policy permitting only Christians to serve as officers. A lawsuit was filed to protect the club's right to pick leaders in accordance with their faith.

ACLU Stops Vote to Determine Whether to Have Student-Led Prayer at Graduation
ACLU of New Jersey v. Black Horse Pike Regional Board of Education, 84 F.3d 1471 (3rd Cir. 1996)
A lawsuit was filed challenging a school policy that permitted the graduating class a vote to determine if there would be student-led prayer during graduation ceremonies. The court struck down the policy, determining it violated the Constitution and ordered the school to forbid the prayer.

Student Sues to Limit Religious Participation from School Employees and School Choir

Doe v. Duncanville I.S.D., 70 F.3d 402 (5th Cir. 1995)

A student and her father filed a lawsuit because the school permitted employees to be involved with student prayer after basketball games, permitted the choir to use a Christian song as its "theme song," and permitted the distribution of Gideon Bibles to fifth-grade classes. The court upheld the right of the choir to sing the religious song but struck down the employees' involvement with prayer, determining that such an exercise violated the Establishment Clause.

Teacher Gives Student a Zero for Paper About Jesus

Settle v. Dickson County School Board, 53 F.3d 152 (6th Cir. 1995)

Ninth-grader Brittney Settle selected Jesus Christ as the topic for her open research project, but her teacher refused to approve the subject, gave Brittney a zero for her grade, and did not permit her to submit another project. A lawsuit was filed to protect Brittney's free expression rights, but the court refused to uphold Brittney's rights and ruled in favor of the school.

Lawsuit Attacks School District for Students' Recitation of the Lord's Prayer Before Graduation

Goluba v. The School District of Ripon, 45 F.3d 1035 (7th Cir. 1995)

After students recited the Lord's Prayer on their own accord before the opening of graduation ceremonies, student Nikki Goulba filed a civil contempt motion against the school district of Ripon and the Ripon High School principal. The motion claimed the officials violated a permanent injunction that prevented them from allowing prayer during school graduations by allowing the students to recite the prayer.

Portrait of Jesus That Hung with Other Portraits Ordered Removed

Washegesic v. Bloomingdale Public Schools, 33 F.3d 679 (6th Cir. 1994)

A portrait of Jesus Christ hung in a hallway of a school along with other portraits of famous individuals, and a former student filed suit against the school, asserting that the portrait was an Establishment Clause violation. The court agreed and ordered the picture removed.

Teacher Banned from Discussing Religion with Students, Even Outside of Class

Peloza v. Capistrano Unified School District, 37 F.3d 517 (9th Cir. 1994)

A biology teacher was forbidden from discussing religious matters with students while on the school campus, even if the discussion occurred outside of class time and was student-initiated. A lawsuit was filed to protect his constitutionally protected free speech and equal protection rights, but the court dismissed the complaint finding that the school district's interest in avoiding an unlikely constitutional violation trumped the teacher's rights.

School Censors Student's Video of Herself Singing a Solo at Church
Denooyer v. Merinelli, No. 92-2080, 1993 U.S. App. LEXIS 20606 (6th Cir. 1993)
When Kelly Denooyer was selected as her class's "VIP of the Week," she brought a video of herself singing a solo at church to share with her class, but the teacher refused to play the tape for a variety of reasons, including concern about the videotape's religious message. A lawsuit was filed to protect Kelly's rights, but the court upheld the censorship of the video.

Parent Sues to Stop Graduation Prayers
Jones v. Clear Creek I.S.D., 977 F.2d 963 (5th Cir. 1992)
A Clear Creek I.S.D. parent filed suit to stop a policy permitting high school seniors to select student volunteers to give nonsectarian, non-proselytizing invocations at graduation ceremonies.

Teacher Banned from Reading Bible or Having Christian Books in His Classroom Library
Roberts v. Madigan, 921 F.2d 1047 (10th Cir. 1990)
Mr. Roberts's class had a silent reading period daily, and Mr. Roberts had a library of 239 books, two of which dealt with Christianity, from which the students could select reading material. Mr. Roberts participated in the reading period, often choosing to read his Bible, and he kept the Bible on his desk during the school day. The school principal censored Mr. Roberts, forbade him from placing his Bible on his desk during the school day and from reading it during the school day, and forbade him from keeping the two Christian books in the library. A lawsuit was filed to end the religious bigotry against Mr. Roberts, but the court upheld the school's action and even awarded the school district court costs.

Court Holds Ten Commandments Monument Unconstitutional
Freedom From Religion Found., Inc. v. Connellsville Area Sch. Dist., No. 2:12-cv-1406-TFM (W.D. Penn. Aug. 28, 2015)
A granite monument of the Ten Commandments was donated to a junior high school in the Connellsville Area School District in 1956. The Star of David, the Greek letters chi and rho, and an eagle grasping an American flag are also inscribed on the monument. A court found the monument to

be unconstitutional, but declined to order the monument removed at this time because the complaining student has graduated.

Church Barred from Using Public School Building on Sunday
Basevitz v. Freemont RE-2 Sch. Dist., No. 15-cv-01095-RBJ (D. Colo. July 28, 2015)
A lawsuit was filed against Florence High School, a public high school in Colorado, complaining about the students' morning prayer circles around the flagpole and the use of the school's facilities by a local church. As a result of a settlement, the Cowboy Church at the Crossroads will no longer be meeting on Sundays in the school's building. The settlement also stipulates that non-school people, such as pastors, may not lead or attend the prayer meetings in the mornings, and teachers may only be present as observers to ensure the rules are not broken.

School District Defies Court by Offering Prayer Before Awards Ceremony
M.B. v. Rankin Cty. Sch. Dist., No. 3:13-cv-00241-CWR-FKB (S.D. Miss. July 10, 2015)
A student has sued the Rankin County School District in Mississippi for hosting an awards ceremony that began with a prayer. The school district had previously gone before the court for a similar incident. For the second time, the court sided against the school district. The judge wrote that the student should have been able to receive her award without being "subjected to the deeply religious prayers." The court also found the district in contempt for allowing the Gideons to pass out Bibles to students. The judge ordered fines for past and future violations.

Students Denied Admission Were Told Medical Field Is "No Place for Religion"
Buxton v. Kurtinitis, No. ELH-14-2836, 2015 U.S. Dist. LEXIS 83053 (D. Md. June 25, 2015)
Jenkins v. Kurtinitis, No. ELH-14-01346, 2015 U.S. Dist. LEXIS 34772 (D. Md. Mar. 20, 2015).
Brandon Jenkins and Dustin Buxton were denied admission to the Radiation Therapy Program at the Community College of Baltimore County, Maryland, for talking about their faith during the admissions interview. After Jenkins was denied admission, he wrote to the school to ask why. One of the interviewers, Adrienne Dougherty, responded that "this field is not the place for religion" and "[i]f you interview in the future, you may want to leave your thoughts and beliefs out of the interview process."

Washington High School Suspends Student for Passing Out Gospel Tracts

Leal v. Everett Public Schools, No. C14-1762 TSZ (W.D. Wash., May 29, 2015)
Cascade High School in Everett, Washington, suspended and threatened with
expulsion high school senior Michael Leal for distributing Gospel tracts to his
peers on school property. Leal filed a lawsuit against the school district, and
a federal district court judge declared the school's policy unconstitutional
and removed the suspensions from Leal's record.

American Humanist Association Sues School Officials for Field Trip to Sports Complex

Doe v. Huff, No. 3:15-CV-5052 (W.D. Mo., filed May 27, 2015)
The American Humanist Association (AHA) sued a Joplin, Missouri, middle
school principal and superintendent after the school went on a field trip to a
Christian sports complex that contains a café, video games, a gym and fitness
center, athletic courts, a rock climbing wall, and a batting cage. The students
selected the venue, and the field trip was secular. Although no proselytizing
took place at the sports complex, the AHA argued that exposing the students
to the facility violated the Constitution.

Student Sues for Freedom to Pass Out Religious Flyers

Harper v. McArthur, No. 14-495 (W.D. Ok. filed May 14, 2014)
http://religionclause.blogspot.com/2014/05/christian-student-challenges.html
http://www.washingtonpost.com/news/volokh-conspiracy/wp/2014/05/22/
public-university-forbids-criticizing-religious-group-as-a-cult/
http://www.adfmedia.org/files/HarperComplaint.pdf
Cameron University student Daniel Harper filed a lawsuit after he was told
that he could not hand out flyers presenting his religious belief that a group
on campus was a cult. Harper, an evangelical honor student, handed out
flyers with reasons of why he disagreed with the World Mission Society.
The suit claims that the speech codes that prohibited Harper from handing
out his flyers violate the First Amendment.

Ohio City Prevents Christian School from Expanding Its Facilities

Tree of Life Christian Sch. v. City of Upper Arlington, No. 2:11-CV-009, 2014 WL
1576873 (S.D. Ohio Apr. 18, 2014)
Tree of Life Christian School (ToL) in Columbus, Ohio, ran out of room in its
existing facilities due to exponential growth. After locating a site in downtown
Upper Arlington, Ohio, ToL requested a zoning amendment to allow the
school to use the building, but the city argued that ToL was not a church as
required by the zoning ordinance and consequently denied ToL's requests.

ToL finally filed a lawsuit against the city, but an Ohio federal district court ruled in favor of the city.

Diversity Officer at Gallaudet University Fired for Supporting Traditional Marriage

McCaskill v. Gallaudet Univ., No. 13-cv-1498, 2014 WL 1443472 (D.D.C. Apr. 14, 2014)

Angela McCaskill, Chief Diversity Officer and the first deaf black woman to earn a Ph.D. at Gallaudet University, was placed on administrative leave and ultimately demoted after she signed a petition supporting traditional marriage in Maryland that circulated at her church. Mrs. McCaskill brought a lawsuit against the university for its discrimination, but a federal district court dismissed her claims.

Former Employee Sues InterVarsity Christian Fellowship for Firing Her Because of Her Divorce

Conlon v. InterVarsity Christian Fellowship/USA, No. 1:13-cv-1111, 2014 WL 1340752 (W.D. Mich. Apr. 3, 2014)

InterVarsity Christian Fellowship (IVCF), a Christian ministry for college students, employed Alyce Conlon as a spiritual director. However, Conlon decided to consider a divorce from her husband, which was against IVCF's religiously motivated conduct policies for staff. IVCF gave Conlon time off to work on her marriage and seek counseling but was ultimately forced to terminate Conlon when she did not reconcile her marriage. Conlon sued IVCF, but a Michigan federal district court protected IVCF's right as an employer to use biblical principals when making employment decisions.

Lubbock School District Discriminates Against Religious Organization in Use of Jumbotron

Little Pencil, LLC v. Lubbock Indep. Sch. Dist., No. 5:14-cv-00014 (N.D. Tex. filed Jan. 28, 2014)

Little Pencil, LLC filed a viewpoint discrimination complaint against the Lubbock Independent School District because the district refused Little Pencil the use of the district's jumbotron during high school football games to advertise "Jesus Tattoo." While the school permits other non-school-related advertisements, including other religious organizations, to use the jumbotron, the district denied access to Little Pencil because of this ad's particular religious message.

Teachers Sue to Stop Religious Private School from Operating Alternative School System

Kucera v. Jefferson County Bd. of Sch. Com'rs, 956 F. Supp. 2d 842 (E.D. Tenn. July 9, 2013)

A public school in Tennessee decided to contract with a religious private school to run its alternative school system. Even though the decision was made for financial reasons and the private school did not mandate religious instruction, several teachers filed a lawsuit alleging that the contract violated the Establishment Clause of the First Amendment. The Eastern District Court of Tennessee held that the contract was unconstitutional. The ruling is now on appeal.

Student Sues Schools After Being Punished for Speaking Out Against Homosexuality

Glowacki ex rel. D.K.G. v. Howell Pub. Sch. Dist., No. 2:11-cv-15481, 2013 WL 3148272 (E.D. Mich. June 19, 2013)

A teacher in a Howell, Michigan, public school kicked a Catholic student out of class for speaking out against homosexuality. The student commented about the homosexual-pride flags being offensive and then told her that his religion taught that homosexuality is wrong. The Thomas More Law Center filed suit on behalf of the student against the school. A federal district court held that the school violated the student's constitutional rights.

School Stops Sixth-Grade Student from Distributing Pro-Life Flyers

A.Z. v. Nova Classical Academy, No. 0:13-cv-975 (D. Minn. filed Apr. 25, 2013)

A Minnesota public charter school banned a sixth-grade student from peacefully distributing pro-life flyers to her classmates during lunch, even though she was motivated by religious convictions to save unborn children. The school asserted that it can censor student religious and political speech prior to high school. After a lawsuit was filed, the school agreed to enforce a new policy that forbid viewpoint discrimination and restored younger students' freedom of speech.

Community College Officials Banned Student from Speaking About His Religious Views in Outdoor Common Areas

Parks v. Members of the State Bd. of the Va. Community Col. Sys., No. 4:14-cv-30 (E.D. Va. filed Mar. 13, 2014)

http://www.alliancealert.org/2014/06/09/va-christian-student-wins-free-speech-lawsuit-23-college-campuses-agree-to-change-policy/

School officials at Thomas Nelson Community College told student

Christian Parks that he could not preach or discuss his religious views in an outside common area. Parks was ordered to stop preaching while giving a presentation because the school thought other students may find his viewpoints offensive. He was also told that he could not preach because he did not notify a school official four days prior to his presentation. Parks filed a lawsuit against the school for violating his freedom of speech and freedom of religion. A federal district court held that the school's policies on student speech were unconstitutional.

New York School District Bans All Religious Content from Classrooms

Silver v. Cheektowaga Cent. Sch. Dist., No. 1:13-31 (W.D.N.Y., filed Jan. 10, 2013)
Cheektowaga Central School District in New York permits teachers to display personal messages, including inspirational messages, in their classrooms—so long as those messages have no religious content. Joelle Silver, a high school science teacher, was given a "counseling letter" and forced to remove any posters with religious messages from her classroom as well as sticky notes on her desk with religious verses and the Bible Study Club's prayer request box that was in her room. As a result of the school's actions against Ms. Silver, she filed a lawsuit against the school district to protect her freedoms of speech and religion.

Jewish High School Student in New York Sues to Stop Harassment and Bullying

G.D.S. v. Northport-East Northport Union Free Sch. Dist., 2012 U.S. Dist. LEXIS 182976 (E.D.N.Y. Dec. 22, 2012)
A Jewish high school student filed a federal equal protection complaint and a state discrimination complaint after his New York high school ignored anti-Semitic bullying by other students. The student gave the school names of the abusive students and details of the bullying, which included mocking references to the Holocaust. Nevertheless, school officials took no action. A federal judge held that the student stated a valid claim under both complaints.

California School District Refuses to Treat Religious After-School Clubs Equally

Child Evangelism Fellowship, Inc. v. Buena Park Sch. Dist., No. 12-2012 (C.D. Cal., filed Nov. 19, 2012)
Buena Park School District in Orange County, California, rejected a Christian after-school club's request to meet in the school's facilities on equal terms with similar but nonreligious organizations. The Christian club filed a lawsuit

against the school district to be given equal access to the school district's facilities.

Utah College Bans Religious Club from Participating in Homecoming Decorations

Solid Rock Christian Club v. Wyatt, No. 2:12-978 (D. Ut., filed Oct. 22, 2012)
Snow College in Utah has an annual homecoming tradition called "Paint the Town" in which student groups decorate the windows of participating businesses. The Solid Rock Christian Club had participated in the past; but, in 2012, Snow College changed their policies and refused to permit the Solid Rock Christian Club to fully participate because of the club's religious affiliation. Snow College forced the Solid Rock Christian Club to wash away their displays, and the college itself washed away a display on private property whose owner had personally invited the Solid Rock Christian Club to create. The Solid Rock Christian Club filed a lawsuit against Snow College because of the college's discriminatory conduct.

Assistant Principal Sues Principal for Including Religious Statements in Emails

Capriola v. Clay County Sch. Dist., No. 3:11-cv-1152 (M.D. Fla. Oct. 11, 2012)
The assistant principal of a Clay County, Florida, public school sued his boss, the principal, for including religious statements in emails. The assistant principal sought an injunction against further religious or political emails based on the Establishment Clause and the Free Exercise Clause. The case settled.

FFRF Challenges Election of Graduation Prayer

Nielson and the Freedom From Religion Foundation v. School District Five of Lexington & Richland Counties, No. 3:12-cv-01427 (D.S.C., filed May 29, 2012)
Irmo High School in South Carolina permits students to vote each year on whether to have prayer at its graduation ceremony. The Freedom From Religion Foundation filed a complaint alleging such a vote and the resulting prayer in the graduation ceremony violates the Establishment Clause of the First Amendment.

Science Professor Sues College for Anti-Christian Remarks and Termination for Religious Beliefs

Baiyasi v. Delta College, U.S. Dist. LEXIS 65715 (E.D. Mich. May 10, 2012)
A science professor at Delta College filed suit against the university under Title VII claiming that the chair of her department made anti-Christian remarks. Though the district court threw out Baiyasi's hostile work environment claims,

it did allow her to pursue her claims that she was denied promotion and subsequently fired because of her religious beliefs, and also that the denial of her promotion was in retaliation for her filing complaints against her department chair.

Lawsuits Seeks to Stop Private Schools from Using City Athletic Fields

Rogers v. Mulholland, 2012 WL 1565091 (D. R.I. May 4, 2012)

A federal district court in Rhode Island decided that the use of city athletic fields by private schools did not violate the Establishment Clause because the fields were being used in a secular way. An objective observer would not view the use by private schools as a sign that the city favored a certain religious view.

Florida Withheld Grant Money from Students Attending Florida Christian College

Florida Christian College v. Shanahan, No. 4:12-109 (N.D. Fla., filed Mar. 8, 2012)

The State of Florida withheld grant money from students attending Florida Christian College because the college did not satisfy the state's "secularity checklist." Florida Christian College and three of its students whose grant money was withheld filed a lawsuit against the Florida Board of Education to stop the state's religious discrimination. The case settled, and the Board of Education agreed to allow grant money to be distributed to students at Florida Christian College.

School District Prohibits Distribution of Religious Literature in Its Schools

Child Evangelism Fellowship Phoenix v. Dysart Unified Sch. Dist., No. 2:12-123 (D. Ariz. Jan. 19, 2012)

The Dysart Unified School District prohibited the distribution of religious literature in its schools. After a suit was filed, the school district reversed its policy and allowed the Good News Club to distribute flyers at school.

ACLU and Atheist Attack Decades-Old School Mural

Ahlquist v. City of Cranston, No. 11-138L, 2012 U.S. Dist. LEXIS 3348 (D. R.I. Jan. 11, 2012)

After an atheist student complained about a decades-old school mural in Cranston, Rhode Island, containing a prayer and the words "Heavenly Father," the ACLU stepped in to sue on her behalf. A federal district court held that the mural violated the Establishment Clause and must be removed.

School Rejects Volunteer Service Hours for Religious Purpose
Stites v. Fairfax County School Board, No. ____ (E.D. Va. 2012)
Membership in Thomas Jefferson High School for Science and Technology's National Honor Society chapter requires twelve volunteer service hours each year. Sarah Stites performed forty-six hours of service for her church, but the school refused to count those hours because they did not have a "secular purpose." Stites is suing the school board to have her service hours credited.

Principal Fired for Promoting Prayer Breakfast Honoring Teachers
Richter v. Goleta Union School District, No. 10-7609 (C.D. Cal., Oct. 12, 2011)
Craig Richter, a principal in the Goleta Union School District in Santa Barbara, California, participated in a video made to promote a community prayer breakfast that honored teachers. The school district fired the principal on the grounds that his participation in the video implied that the school supported Christian values as well. Richter sued under Title VII, but the district court granted summary judgment in favor of Goleta Union School District.

Minnesota School District Bans Religious Club from After-School Program
Child Evangelism Fellowship of Minnesota v. Minneapolis Special School District No. 1., 822 F. Supp. 2d 878 (D. Minn. Sept. 30, 2011)
The Child Evangelism Fellowship of Minnesota filed suit against the Minneapolis Special School District No. 1, claiming the district violated the Christian organization's freedom of speech and religion by banning them from partaking in an after-school program. The group's participation was banned specifically for engaging in religious activity. The Child Evangelism Fellowship of Minnesota filed suit in a United States District Court in Minnesota, citing various constitutional violations. The Court denied the group's preliminary injunction on the grounds that it is unlikely to obtain permanent injunction.

Arkansas School Bans Flyers Advertising Religious Activities
Wright ex rel. A.W. v. Pulaski County Special Sch. Dist., 803 F. Supp. 2d 980 (E.D. Ark. Mar. 25, 2011)
An Arkansas school banned flyers advertising religious activities, but allowed students to distribute flyers for other activities. After a federal district court granted a preliminary injunction stopping the policy, the school settled the case, agreeing to treat religious flyers and nonreligious flyers equally.

Community College Bans Student from Preaching or Distributing Religious Literature
Dew v. Ashford, No. 03:11-00262 (E.D. Tenn. 2011)
Mark Dew, a student at Pellissippi State Community College, was told by

school officials that he could not hand out Christian literature or preach on campus. The officials claimed these actions are solicitation and therefore against college rules. The school offered him the option to speak once a week on campus as a guest of a student group or to pay a fee as a nonstudent speaker. Dew filed a lawsuit against the school to defend his right to free speech.

Police Captain Disciplined for Refusing to "Voluntarily" Attend Muslim Lecture
Fields v. City of Tulsa, No. 4:11-00115 (N.D. Okla. 2011)
Paul Fields, a police captain, was stripped of his command and is in the midst of an internal investigation because he declined to attend or force his officers to attend a lecture by Imam Siraj Wahhaj, a Sharia Muslim who promotes the destruction of Western civilization, put on by a mosque in Tulsa, Oklahoma. The mosque's event was in no way connected with Field's work as a police officer and was voluntary in nature.

Court Holds Teacher May Ask Student About God
Sabol v. Walter Payton Coll. Preparatory High School, 804 F. Supp. 2d 747, 751 (N.D. Ill. 2011)
A U.S. District Court for the Northern District of Illinois held that a teacher's asking a student if he or she believed in God and making other comments about God, when questioning the student about an infraction, does not violate the Establishment Clause.

Former Teacher Sues Catholic School for Religious Discrimination
Braun v. St. Pius X Parish, 827 F. Supp. 2d 1312 (N.D. Okla. 2011)
A former teacher sued a Catholic school for religion and age discrimination. A U.S. District Court for the Northern District of Oklahoma granted summary judgment for the school because Title VII of the 1964 Civil Rights Act permits religious institutions to make employment decisions based on religion and there was no evidence of age discrimination.

School Suspends Student for Wearing Rosary Beads
R.H. v. Schenectady City Sch. Dist., No. 1:10-cv-640 (N.D.N.Y. Nov. 3, 2010)
Raymond Hosier, a seventh-grader from Schenectady, New York, was suspended from school for wearing rosary beads around his neck. The school had adopted a policy prohibiting rosary beads because they are sometimes used as a gang symbol. Hosier sued the school district for the right to wear the rosary beads. The case settled, and the court ordered the school to clear Hosier's record.

School Board Prevents Christian Organization from Placing Bibles on a Distribution Table

World Changers of Florida, Inc. v. District School Board of Collier County, Florida, No. 2:10-00419 (M.D. Fla. Nov. 2, 2010)

For several years, World Changers had been allowed to place free Bibles on tables in Collier County schools where the Bibles could be voluntarily taken. On Religious Freedom Day 2009, however, the school board stopped the tradition. World Changers filed a lawsuit, which settled favorably, ensuring that World Changers may continue to provide free Bibles to students who want them.

Holly, Michigan, Schools Prohibit Student from Distributing Flyers for Church Summer Camp

J.S. ex rel Smith v. Holly Area Schools, 749 F.Supp.2d 614 (E.D. Mich. Oct. 26, 2010)

A Christian student and his mother sued Holly, Michigan, schools for stopping the child from distributing flyers for summer camp at Cornerstone Church. The teacher told the student to put the flyers in his backpack so that there would not be a violation of separation of church and state. The district court that heard the case granted the Smiths a preliminary injunction, allowing him to distribute the flyers to his classmates.

School District Bans Religious Valentine's Day Card and Christmas Items

Pounds et al. v. Katy I.S.D., 730 F.Supp.2d 636 (S.D. Tex. July 30, 2010)

A Houston-area school district put in writing that it would allow no religious items at Christmas and banned certain Valentine's Day cards at school, simply because they were religious. The school district has a long history of anti-religious actions, telling one student she could not say the word "Jesus" when asked what Easter meant to her. A federal district court held that Katy I.S.D. violated the students' constitutional rights.

Counseling Student Expelled for Referring a Homosexual Client to Another Counselor

Ward v. Wilbanks, 2010 U.S. Dist. LEXIS 127038 (E.D. Mich. Jul. 26, 2010)

Julea Ward, a graduate student in counseling at Eastern Michigan State University, was dismissed from the program after she referred a homosexual client to another counselor during the clinical portion of her degree. Ward's supervisor stated that her refusal to see a client presenting concerns about a gay relationship signified an inability on Ward's part to meet the required expectation of ethical standards supplied by the American Counseling

Association. Being faced with the options of completing a "remediation program," voluntarily leaving the program, or a formal hearing, Ward chose to have a formal hearing. After the hearing, Ward was dismissed because she had violated the American Counseling Association's code of ethics. Both the Dean of the EMU College of Education and the federal district court affirmed the decision of the hearing.

Lawsuit Stops Voted-For Prayer at Graduation
Workman v. Greenwood Community School Corp., No. 1:10-0293, 2010 U.S. Dist. LEXIS 42813 (S.D. Ind. Apr. 30, 2010)
Greenwood Community School had a tradition of allowing a nondenominational prayer during graduation ceremonies if the senior class voted to approve such a measure. In September of 2009, the senior class voted to allow a prayer. Eric Workman, a student at Greenwood, filed a suit to challenge the constitutionality of the electoral process, allowing the prayer. The court issued a preliminary injunction stopping prayer.

Student Sues for Freedom to Protest Abortion on Pro-Life Day of Silent Solidarity
C.H. v. Bridgeton Board of Education, No. 09-5815, 2010 U.S. Dist. LEXIS 40038 (D.N.J. Apr. 22, 2010)
C.H., a student at Bridgeton High School, wanted to wear a piece of red duct tape around her arm as a part of the Pro-Life Day of Silent Solidarity. The tape was meant to draw attention to pro-life issues. C.H. also desired to distribute pro-life flyers and remain silent during the Day of Silent Solidarity. School officials told C.H. that she could not wear the armband or distribute literature because of the controversial nature of its topic. They informed C.H. that she could remain silent, but her participation grade would suffer as a result. C.H. filed a suit to determine her rights. On April 22, 2010, the court enjoined the school from enforcing their policies, allowing C.H. to fully participate in the Pro-Life Day of Silent Solidarity.

Lawsuit Attempts to Stop Church from Meeting in School District's Building
Henley v. Cleveland Board of Education, No. 1:10-431, 2010 WL 796835 (N.D. Ohio Mar. 3, 2010)
The U.S. District Court for the Northern District of Ohio dismissed for lack of standing a taxpayer's First Amendment claim against a school district for allowing a local church to use the district's building for weekly worship services.

School Prohibits Teachers from Replying to Parent Emails Saying, "God Bless You" or from Attending Non-School-Related, Off-Campus Religious Events

Minor I Doe ex rel. Parent I Doe v. School Board for Santa Rosa County, Florida, 264 F.R.D. 670 (N.D. Fla. Feb. 19, 2010)

The Santa Rosa County School District entered into a consent decree drafted by the ACLU that prohibited students from saying "God Bless" and teachers from replying to parents' emails if they said "God Bless" in the email. School district employees were even prohibited from participating in non-school-related, privately sponsored, off-campus religious events. Faculty and staff were also told to stop praying at privately sponsored after-school clubs. The school has now modified and clarified the decree to protect the religious liberties of its faculty and students.

Religious Club Sues to End Discriminatory Treatment by School District

Child Evangelism Fellowship of Greater San Diego v. Acle, No. 05-1166, 2008 U.S. Dist. LEXIS 97257 (S.D. Cal. Dec. 1, 2009)

Child Evangelism Fellowship of Greater San Diego (CEF) requested to use school facilities to hold Good News Clubs after school hours. From 1999 until the 2004–05 school year, CEF had been charged fees to use the school facilities when other similar secular groups had not been charged. Each year the district increased the cost of the fees, and the fees became so large that CEF was forced to discontinue the Good News Clubs. District employees and parents pleaded for the Good News Clubs to return, but the increased usage costs prohibited the meetings. CEF filed a lawsuit to be treated the same as other similarly-situated groups, which did not have to pay the large fees.

ACLU Sues to Defund Religious Abstinence Education

Robinson v. Thompson, No. 3:09-537 (S.D. Miss., filed Sept. 9, 2009)

A Mississippi teen summit promoting National Teen Pregnancy Prevention Month incorporated religious language in its abstinence education. The ACLU sued the state to remove the religious language or end its funding of the program.

University of Montana School of Law Derecognizes Christian Legal Society

Christian Legal Society v. Eck, 625 F. Supp. 2d 1026 (D. Mont. May 19, 2009)

The University of Montana School of Law derecognized the school's chapter of the Christian Legal Society (CLS), because CLS requires voting members and officers to adhere to a statement of faith. CLS sued to gain official recognition and access to funds, but the court held that CLS's policy on sex being reserved for marriage violated the law school's diversity statement, allowing the school to freely discriminate against CLS.

City College of San Francisco Bans Jews for Jesus from Evangelizing or Distributing Flyers

Jews for Jesus, Inc. v. City College of San Francisco, 2009 WL 86703 (N.D. Cal. April 15, 2009)
City College of San Francisco refused to allow Jews for Jesus to evangelize or distribute religious literature on its campus. After Jews for Jesus filed a lawsuit against the college, the college agreed to allow Jews for Jesus to distribute its flyers on campus so long as Jews for Jesus notified the school ahead of time.

College of Alameda Suspends Students for Praying

Kyriacou v. Peralta Community College District, 2009 U.S. Dist. LEXIS 32464 (N.D. Cal. Mar. 31, 2009)
Kandy Kyriacou and Ojoma Omaga were students at the College of Alameda. Both are Christians and would pray together on the balcony outside of class. On November 1, 2001, Kyriacou went to speak with her instructor. After the conversation turned to personal matters, Bell consented, and Kyriacou prayed for Bell. Kyriacou offered to pray for Bell on a separate instance when Derek Piazza, another instructor, interrupted and ordered Kyriacou to stop praying in the office. Kyriacou and Omaga received letters from the Vice President of Student Services at the College stating that they had engaged in disruptive behavior and were suspended from class. Kyricaou and Omaga filed suit to challenge the suspension. The case settled after two years of legal battles with an acknowledgement that prayer on campus is permitted.

Parent Sues School to Stop Religious Instruction in School Parking Lot

H.S. v. Huntington County Community School Corporation, 616 F.Supp.2d 863 (N.D. Ind. Mar. 19, 2009)
An elementary school in Huntington County, Indiana, allowed students to be released to religious instruction time for thirty minutes each week if their parents signed a permission slip. A local church that conducted the religious instruction parked a trailer in the school parking lot during the instruction time. A parent of a student complained that the school should not allow the instruction to occur on school property. A federal district court agreed with the parent and issued an injunction against religious instruction occurring on school property.

Art Teacher Sued to Stop Her Coworkers from Voluntarily Praying

Eder v. City of New York, 2009 U.S. Dist. LEXIS 11501 (S.D.N.Y. Feb. 12, 2009)
Melissa Eder, an art teacher at the East New York Family Academy, filed a suit claiming discrimination and retaliation. Eder, who is Jewish, asserted that her coworkers' practice of voluntarily forming prayer circles before meetings was unconstitutional. She claimed that this practice, as well as prayer offered before a holiday party, was unconstitutional violations of her rights. The court held that the faculty members' voluntary decision to engage in prayer before meetings and at the holiday party were not a violation of Eder's rights.

Student Sues School to Stop Discrimination Against Bible Club

A.Q. v. Board of Education of Lindenhurst Union Free School District, No. ____ (E.D.N.Y., filed Jan. 30, 2009)
A.Q., a student at Lindenhurst High School in Lindenhurst, New York, wanted to have Bible Club at the school. The school repeatedly refused to recognize Bible Club as an official club because the board claimed it would violate the Establishment Clause. A lawsuit was filed against the school district for violating the student's rights to free speech, religion, equal protection, and due process. After the suit was filed, the school agreed to recognize the club and give it the full rights afforded to other clubs.

Student Sued to Stop Singing of Patriotic Song Referencing God

S.D. v. St. Johns County School District, 632 F.Supp.2d 1085 (M.D. Fla. 2009)
Students at St. John's elementary school were planning to sing a country song called "In God We Still Trust" for the third grade end-of-year performance. The song made references to the Pledge of Allegiance and the nation's still trusting in God. A student and her parents filed suit against the school arguing that it was in violation of the Establishment Clause. A federal district court agreed with the plaintiff and granted a temporary injunction against the singing of the song.

Federal Employee Banned from Warning About Charitable Contributions

Lister v. Defense Logistics Agency, No. 2:05-CV-495, 2009 U.S. Dist. LEXIS 7414 (S.D. Ohio 2009)
A federal employee was denied a request to post a flyer warning that donations made to a federal charitable contribution program may be used to support abortion, sexual promiscuity, the homosexual agenda, and New Age mysticism. Agency policy prohibited "items of religious preference" from being posted on employee bulletin boards.

Religious After-School Club Sues for Equal Treatment

Child Evangelism Fellowship of Virginia v. Williamsburg-James City County School Board, No. 4:08-cv-4, 2008 U.S. Dist. LEXIS 61392 (E.D. Va. Aug. 8, 2008)
A school board in Williamsburg, Virginia, allowed several nonprofit after-school programs for students to use school facilities for free. The board required that Child Evangelism Fellowship (CEF), a religious organization, pay to use school facilities. CEF sued the school board, challenging the discrimination. A federal district court held that charging CEF to use school facilities while providing facilities for free to other organizations is unconstitutional.

Boise State University Funds Atheist Group but Not Christian Legal Society

Cordova v. Laliberte, No. 1:08-00543 (D. Idaho 2008)
Boise State University (BSU) denied the Christian Legal Society (CLS) funding from student activity fees. BSU already funded other student groups, including an atheist society. After facing a lawsuit from the CLS, BSU rewrote its policies for student activity fee distribution to provide protection for all students. The school also amended its policies to allow student groups to limit their leadership to those who share the group's beliefs and conduct themselves according to those beliefs.

University of South Carolina Denies Funding to Religious Clubs

Christian Legal Society v. Sorenson, No. 3:08-99999 (D.S.C. 2008)
The Christian Legal Society (CLS) chapter at the University of South Carolina was denied funding on the basis that it was a religious organization. The university barred religious organizations from receiving funding, while all other student groups were permitted to receive funding. The CLS chapter sued, and they reached a settlement with the university allowing for equal funding of all student organizations.

Shippensburg University Speech Codes Attempt to Regulate Student "Attitudes and Behaviors"

Christian Fellowship of Shippensburg University et al. v. Ruud et al., No. 4:08-898 (M.D. Pa. 2008)
Members of the Christian Fellowship of Shippensburg University felt their right to free speech was violated by the university's policies and speech codes, which require that students reflect the university's official views in their "attitudes and behaviors." The group feared engaging in discussions from a religious point of view. Following the filing of a lawsuit, Shippensburg

University changed its speech codes so as not to violate the members' First Amendment rights.

Wayne State University Refuses to Fund Pro-Life Event
Wayne State University Students for Life v. Driker, No. 2:08-13181 (E.D. Mich. 2008)
Wayne State University requires all students to pay a student activities fee, a portion of which supports student organizations on campus. When the Wayne State University Students for Life requested funding for its Pro-Life Week 2008, the university refused because the event included "spiritual and religious references." After Students for Life eliminated these elements, the university still refused to release funds because they deemed the event "offensive" to women. Not until Students for Life filed suit did Wayne State officials finally reverse their position.

High School in Michigan Discriminates Against Religious Student Club
ALIVE v. Farmington Public Schools, No. 07-12116, 2007 U.S. Dist. LEXIS 65326 (E.D. Mich. Sept. 5, 2007)
A high school in Farmington, Michigan, refused to recognize the ALIVE Bible club as a student club. Without recognition, ALIVE could not advertise over the school's PA system, use the school's bulletin board, or appear in the school's yearbook. A federal district judge granted a permanent injunction allowing the group to have equal opportunities as other student groups.

School Prohibits Fourth-Grade Student from Distributing Flyers About Her Faith
M.B. v. Liverpool Central School District., No. 5:04-CV-1255 (S.D.N.Y. 2007)
Michaela Bloodgood, a fourth-grader at Nate Perry Elementary School in Liverpool, New York, wished to share homemade flyers with other students that explained what Jesus Christ had done in her life. Although Michaela would only hand out the flyers during noninstructional time, school officials stated that there was a "substantial probability" that the school would be seen as endorsing the statements in the flyers, and refused to allow her to hand them out. A lawsuit was filed on Michaela's behalf, and a federal district judge ruled that the school had violated Michaela's rights.

ACLU Sues to Stop Class on the Bible's Influence in History and Literature
Moreno v. Ector County I.S.D., No. 7:07-0039 (W.D. Tex. 2007)
The ACLU and People for the American Way Foundation filed suit in federal court against the Ector County I.S.D. in Odessa, Texas, to stop a course taught

on the Bible's influence in our history and literature as an elective in two of
the district's high schools.

Minnesota School District Prohibits Religious Flyers While Allowing Others
Greater St. Paul Area Evangelicals, Inc. v. Independent School District No. 625,
No. 0:07-01841 (D. Minn. 2007)
A Minnesota school district refused to allow a group to distribute flyers
containing religious content, even though other groups were permitted to do
so. The school district's policy specifically prohibited materials of a "sectarian
nature" for distribution.

**InterVarsity Christian Fellowship Sues for Equal Treatment at Wisconsin
University**
InterVarsity Christian Fellowship-UW Superior v. Walsh, No. 06-0562 (W.D.
Wis. 2007)
The University of Wisconsin-Superior refused to recognize the InterVarsity
Christian Fellowship chapter at the school. Only after a lawsuit was filed did
the University agree to officially recognize the chapter.

**School Bans Elementary Student from Singing Religious Song in Talent
Show**
Turton v. Frenchtown Elementary Sch. Dist. Bd. of Educ., 465 F.Supp.2d 369
(D.N.J. Dec. 11, 2006)
An elementary student was told by her school that she could not sing
"Awesome God" in a school talent show. The district court held that the
school had violated the student's constitutional rights.

Judge Issues Emergency Order Banning Prayer at High School Graduation
Doe v. Gossage, No. 1:06-cv-070, 2006 U.S. Dist. LEXIS 34613 (W.D. Ky. May
24, 2006)
Judge Joseph McKinley entered an emergency order restraining the principal
of Russell County High School from allowing prayer at the graduation
ceremony. Despite the judge's order barring the valedictorian from including
prayer at the graduation ceremony, the senior class spontaneously stood
during the opening remarks of the principal and recited the Lord's Prayer.

Christian Fraternity Sues UNC for Official Recognition
Alpha Iota Omega Christian Fraternity v. Moeser, No. 1:04-00765, 2006 U.S.
Dist. LEXIS 28065 (M.D.N.C. May 4, 2006)
The Alpha Iota Omega (AIO) fraternity sued the University of North Carolina
after being denied official recognition and funding because the organization

limited its membership to those of the Christian faith. A federal lawsuit was filed in AIO's behalf and the University changed its policy and reinstated funding and official recognition status to the fraternity.

High School Removes Bricks Inscribed with Religious Messages
Kiesinger v. Mexico Academy & Central School, 427 F. Supp. 2d 182 (N.D.N.Y. Mar. 31, 2006)
The Mexico Academy High School decided to remove bricks that had been purchased and inscribed as part of a school fundraiser if the brick contained a Christian message. The district court held that removing the bricks with Christian messages violated the First Amendment.

Christian Legal Society Sues ASU for Official Recognition
Christian Legal Society Chapter at Arizona State University College of Law v. Crow, No. cv 04-2572, 2006 U.S. Dist. LEXIS 25579 (D. Ariz. 2006)
The Christian Legal Society (CLS) requires its members to agree with CLS's statement of faith. Arizona State University denied its CLS chapter from becoming an official student organization because requiring agreement with a statement of faith did not comply with the university's religious nondiscrimination policy. CLS filed a lawsuit and received a favorable settlement. Arizona State University now allows religious student groups to limit membership to those who share their religious beliefs.

Christian Student Organization Sues to Be Listed with Other Student Organizations
SWAT et al. v. Plano I.S.D., No. 4:06-0119 (E.D. Tex. 2006)
SWAT, a Christian student organization, was prevented from being listed on Plano I.S.D.'s website because SWAT is a religious organization. A federal district court judge held that the school district violated SWAT's constitutional rights.

Missouri State University Professor Mandates Support for Same-Sex Adoption
Brooker v. Franks et al., No. 6:06-03432 (W.D. Mo. 2006)
A class assignment at Missouri State University required Emily Brooker to draft and sign a letter in support of same-sex adoptions that would be sent to state legislators. When she refused because of her Christian beliefs, Ms. Brooker was forced to sign a contract stating she would alter her beliefs to align with the social work department's ideological standards. After Ms. Brooker filed suit, the university cleared her record and revoked teaching privileges from the professor who had given the discriminatory assignment.

Seventh-Grade Student Sues for Freedom to Distribute Pro-Life Literature
Heinkel v. School Board of Lee County, Florida, No. 05-13813 (M.D. Fla. 2006)
Michelle Heinkel, a seventh-grade student at Cypress Lake Middle School, wished to distribute religious and pro-life literature about the "Day of Remembrance," an event to remember unborn children who lost their lives through abortion. The superintendent stated that Heinkel's handing out the literature was not allowed due to the school board's policy prohibiting the distribution of literature that is political, religious, or proselytizing. Through a lawsuit filed on Michelle's behalf, a federal court of appeals ruled that the school district's policy was unconstitutional.

Student Suspended for Wearing Religious T-Shirt
Arthurs v. Sampson County Board of Education, No. 7:06-0066 (E.D.N.C. 2006)
The annual "Day of Truth" event is a response to the annual "Day of Silence," which supports the homosexual agenda. During the Day of Truth in Wilmington, North Carolina, Benjamin Arthurs was suspended for wearing a religious shirt and handing out information. The Sampson County Board of Education Superintendent stated that Arthurs would be "pushing his religion on others" and that "religion is not allowed in school."

Christian Legal Society Threatened for Including Religious References in Constitution
Christian Legal Society Chapter of the University of Toledo v. Johnson, No. 05-7126 (N.D. Ohio Jun. 16, 2005)
In 2005, the Christian Legal Society (CLS) national office redrafted its constitution. The University of Toledo CLS chapter submitted the new constitution to the Office of Student Activities. The assistant director of Student Activities told the chapter that he would not approve the new constitution unless they removed scriptural references and added antidiscrimination language. He threatened that the group would lose recognition unless they did what he asked. CLS filed a lawsuit. The University of Toledo agreed to a settlement and, as a result, allowed the CLS chapter to keep the new constitution. The university also agreed to allow other student clubs to make references to religious texts in their constitution.

Christian Club Sues Penn State for Freedom to Select Christian Officers
DiscipleMakers, Inc. v. Spanier, No. 4:04-02229 (M.D. Penn. 2005)
DiscipleMakers Christian Fellowship challenged a Pennsylvania State University policy that banned student organizations from taking into account the religious views or sexual orientation of those seeking to become an officer

in the club. After the lawsuit was filed, the case settled and the university agreed to change its policies to allow student organizations to create their own guidelines for selecting officers.

Christian Student Club Sues for Equal Treatment

Child Evangelism Fellowship, Butte-Tehama-Glenn Chapter v. Brown, No. 2:05-0939 (E.D. Cal. 2005)

In November 2004, Child Evangelism Fellowship (CEF) of Butte-Tehama-Glenn requested to use school facilities to hold a Good News Club. The district informed CEF that they would have to pay higher usage fees than secular groups would. Under protest, CEF paid the fees. Because the local CEF operated on a limited budget, however, it had to discontinue the Good News Club meetings in several schools. Although the local CEF chapter advised the school district of legal cases recognizing the equal access rights of Good News Clubs, district officials refused to listen and CEF was forced to file a lawsuit.

Students Sue for Free Speech Rights at Texas Tech University

Roberts v. Haragan, 346 F.Supp.2d 853 (N.D. Tex. Sept. 30, 2004)

The Texas Tech University speech code denied all students the right to free speech except in a small gazebo area in one spot on the campus. The code also stated that students could not speak in a way that caused shame or humiliation to another student. Any speech outside the designated area required advance permission. A lawsuit was filed to force the school to change its policy.

Family Denied Funding for Religious High School Tuition

Eulitt v. Maine Department of Education, 307 F. Supp. 2d 158 (D. Me. Mar. 9, 2004)

Though Maine state law required free public education for children through the twelfth grade, the town of Minot only had schooling through the eighth grade and either contracted to send its students elsewhere for high school or provided the parents with funding for school. A Minot family was denied access to public funding for their child's tuition to a Catholic high school, despite the fact that the state had the authority to approve payments to alternative schools. The court held that the state does not have to provide tuition for religious sectarian education.

Arizona School Bans Religious Messages from Hallway of Tiles

Seidman v. Paradise Valley Unified Sch. Dist. No. 69, 327 F. Supp. 2d 1098 (D. Ariz. 2004)

Paul and Ann Seidman of Scottsdale, Arizona, wanted to purchase tiles encouraging their children in the hallway of their local elementary school. They wanted the tiles to say "God bless Quinn. We love you Mom & Dad" and "God bless Haley. We love you Mom & Dad." However, the mention of the word "God" caused the Pinnacle Peak School District to reject the tiles' messages. Other tiles were accepted, and in the federal judge's words, "some nearly identical to the Seidmans' messages only from a secular viewpoint." The school refused to change their position, despite this being a clear case of viewpoint discrimination. After two years, the Seidmans received a court ruling in their favor.

Christian Student Newspaper Provided Fraction of Funds that Secular Newspapers Provided

Thomas v. Boren (W.D. Okla. 2004)

Rick Thomas, editor of a Christian student newspaper at the University of Oklahoma, applied for funds to cover printing costs. Thomas was awarded only $150, while similar newspapers were awarded in excess of $4,000. The student committee responsible for the allocation of funds claimed that they could not award the newspaper with more money because they were prohibited from using student funds for religious services. After Thomas sued, the university settled and provided sufficient funds to print the newspaper.

Library Employee Fired for Wearing Cross

Draper v. Logan County Public Library, 403 F. Supp. 2d 608 (W.D. Ky. Sept. 2, 2003)

The Logan County Public Library in Kentucky banned its employees from wearing "clothing depicting religious ... decoration." An employee was fired for wearing a cross. A lawsuit was filed to protect the employee's right to free speech and religious freedom.

School District Removes Crosses from Inscribed Bricks

Demmon v. Loudoun County Public Schools, 279 F. Supp. 2d 689 (E.D. Va. Aug. 28, 2003)

For a school fundraiser, people could purchase bricks and have text and symbols inscribed on them to be used in a sidewalk surrounding the school's flagpole. Some purchasers elected to have a Latin cross inscribed. A parent complained, so the school district removed all the crosses. A lawsuit was filed to protect this religious expression from censorship.

Teaching Assistant Suspended for Wearing Cross Necklace
Nichol v. ARIN Intermediate Unit 28, 268 F. Supp. 2d 536 (W.D. Pa. June 25, 2003)
A school district suspended an elementary school instructional assistant for wearing a cross necklace, finding her in violation of a Pennsylvania statute that prohibited teachers and other public school employees from wearing religious emblems or insignia. The assistant filed a lawsuit against the school district challenging the statute, which was overtly and openly hostile to religion, and to prevent the district from forbidding symbolic speech by employees from a religious viewpoint. After the district court granted a preliminary injunction stopping enforcement of the statute, the case settled.

School Suspends Students for Distributing Candy Canes with Religious Messages
Westfield High School L.I.F.E. Club v. City of Westfield, 249 F.Supp.2d 98 (D. Mass. 2003)
Students started a religious club and wanted to hand out candy canes with a religious message at school. The school denied the students permission and suspended the students for distributing their candy canes. The students were forced to file suit in federal court to protect their rights without facing suspension.

High School Censors Christian Student Group
Friesner v. Ogg, No. 0:03-00893 (D. Minn 2003)
The Crosby-Ironton High School censored the "Lunch Bunch," a Christian group, from using flyers to describe their group or to promote the "See You at the Pole" event. A lawsuit had to be filed to protect the students' rights.

Honolulu Bans Religious Postings on Employee Bulletin Boards
Jenkins v. Honolulu, No. 1:03-00159 (D. Haw. 2003)
Honolulu city employee Kelly Jenkins was prohibited from posting religious literature, like an invitation to his church, in common areas of the employee break room and employee bulletin boards because of "separation of church and state" concerns. After Jenkins filed a lawsuit, Honolulu reversed its policy.

Parent Sues to Ban Religious Groups from Putting Flyers in Students' Mailboxes

Rusk v. Crestview Local Schools, 220 F. Supp. 2d 854 (N.D. Ohio Aug. 7, 2002)

A school permitted nonprofits, including religious nonprofits, to submit flyers to the school for distribution to the students' mailboxes. A parent filed a lawsuit, objecting to the religious groups being able to submit flyers, even though the flyers did not advocate religion and were not proselytizing. The court halfheartedly upheld the religious groups' rights to utilize the mailbox distribution, but only permitted the groups to distribute certain messages and censored information relating to a religious or sectarian event.

Christian Student Club Forced to Sue School for Access to Facilities

Child Evangelism Fellowship, Inc., San Fernando Valley Chapter v. Los Angeles Unified School District, No. 02-1329 (C.D. Cal. 2002)

The Child Evangelism Fellowship (CEF) applied to the Los Angeles Unified School District to use an elementary school to host a Good News Club. The school policy permitted use by civic and community groups, but prohibited use by "sectarian or denominational religious exercises or activities." In response, CEF applied through the real estate branch and was willing to pay application and rental fees, which are not required of any other groups, but CEF was still denied. A lawsuit had to be filed to gain equal access for the religious group and to prevent the school district's religious discrimination.

Parents Sue Charter School to Stop Neutral Treatment of Religion

Daugherty v. Vanguard Charter School Academy, 116 F. Supp. 2d 897 (W.D. Mich. Sept. 25, 2000)

Parents of children attending the academy claimed that the school violated the Establishment Clause because a moms' prayer group met in the parent room, teachers and staff prayed on their own accord on school property, religious materials were distributed in students' folders, a content-neutral forum, and the school taught morality. These parents filed a lawsuit to prevent the school from permitting the religious activity at the school.

Student Bible Club Prohibited from Meeting When Other Student Clubs Meet

Pearce v. Northville Public Schools, No. 00-CV-75174 (E.D. Mich. 2000)

A Bible club was told it would have to meet before or after school and not during seminar periods as other groups were permitted to do because the group was religious. Bible club members filed suit to protect their right to meet without being discriminated against on the grounds of religion.

New York High School Discriminates Against Religious Community Groups
Liberty Christian Center v. Board of Education of the City School District of Watertown, 8 F. Supp. 2d 176 (N.D.N.Y Jun. 10, 1998)
The Board of Education of Watertown, New York, denied the Liberty Christian Center access to the Watertown High School Cafeteria during nonschool hours. The school permitted other groups to use the cafeteria during nonschool hours, but rejected the Liberty Christian Center because of the center's religious affiliation. A lawsuit was filed to prevent the school board from discriminating against a religious group and denying the group's rights to equal access.

Court Bans School from Accommodating Religion
Chandler v. James, 985 F. Supp. 1068 (M.D. Ala. Nov. 12, 1997)
Civil liberties activists filed a lawsuit because school officials permitted prayer at school functions, excused students from school for baccalaureate services, and permitted religious study with non-school persons during school hours. The court determined that this behavior violated the Establishment Clause and permanently enjoined the school board and public officials from accommodating religious activity in schools.

Court Orders School to Ban Prayer from Graduation Ceremonies
Gearon v. Loudoun County School Board, 844 F. Supp. 1097 (E.D. Va. Dec. 22, 1993)
Parents and students filed a lawsuit challenging prayer at a high school graduation, and the court permanently enjoined the school from permitting prayer at graduation ceremonies.

Fifth-Grade Student Stopped from Completing Independent Study Project on the Power of God
Duran v. Nitsche, 780 F. Supp. 1048 (E.D. Pa. 1991)
Diana Duran, a fifth-grader and member of the Academically Talented Program, was assigned an independent study project, which she completed on "the power of God," a topic originally approved by her teacher. Her research included a survey of her classmates' religious beliefs, and the assignment included presenting her project to the class. However, school officials intervened and prevented Diana from successfully completing the project. A lawsuit was filed to protect her First Amendment freedoms, but the court held that she had no such rights in the classroom.

Court Bans School from Allowing Religious Groups Access Before or After School

Ford v. Manuel, 629 F. Supp. 771 (N.D. Ohio Aug. 8, 1985)
The Findlay Board of Education permitted the Findlay Weekday Religious Education Council to operate before and after school hours in the public schools in accordance with "Community Use of School Facilities." Parent-taxpayers complained about the program because of concerns regarding the Establishment Clause and filed a lawsuit to strike down the program. A federal district court held that the school district's allowing the before-school and after-school religious group to meet violated the Establishment Clause.

New Jersey Sued for Treating Jewish and Christian Schools the Same as Secular Schools

ACLU of N.J. v. Hendricks, No. A-004399-13 (Super. Ct. N.J. 2013)
As part of a construction project to improve the facilities of universities throughout the state, New Jersey has awarded 176 grants worth $1.3 billion. Only two of the schools receiving grants are religious, Lakewood Yeshiva Beth Medrash Gohova and the Princeton Theological Seminary. They will use the funds for the secular purpose of improving their classrooms and libraries. Although the grants will not go toward furthering the religious teachings at either school, the American Civil Liberties Union has brought a lawsuit against New Jersey, arguing that the state should have discriminated against religious schools.

American Humanist Association Sues School District Over "Under God" in Pledge

American Humanist Association v. Matawan-Aberdeen Regional Sch. Dist. and The American Legion, No. MON-L-1317-14 (Super. Ct. N.J., Feb. 4, 2015)
Court have long recognized that the phrase, "Under God," in the Pledge of Allegiance is constitutional. Nevertheless, in March of 2014, the American Humanist Association filed a lawsuit against a New Jersey school district to stop the district from including "Under God" in the pledge. Liberty Institute represented The American Legion in defending the constitutionality of the Pledge of Allegiance. A New Jersey superior court judge agreed with The American Legion and Liberty Institute that the Pledge of Allegiance is constitutional and dismissed the American Humanist Association's lawsuit.

School District Bans Students from Bringing Signs with Religious Messages to Sporting Events

Kountze Indep. Sch. Dist. v. Matthews, No. 09-13-00251 (Tex. App.—Beaumont 2014)

The Kountze High School (KHS) cheerleaders wanted to display encouraging messages to the football players of both KHS's team and the opposing teams. The cheerleaders decided that the best way to encourage the players was to write Bible verses on the "run-through" banners that the football players run through at the beginning of each game. The Freedom From Religion Foundation discovered that the cheerleaders were writing Bible verses and sent a letter to Kountze I.S.D. demanding that the school district stop the cheerleaders. The superintendent of Kountze I.S.D. then banned any student group, including the cheerleaders, from bringing signs with religious messages to sporting events. The cheerleaders sued the school district to protect their free speech and religious liberty rights. A state district court judge held that the cheerleaders' speech is protected and may not be censored by the school district. A state appellate court held that the parents' claims were mooted but that the parents of the cheerleaders may still recover attorney's fees because the parents' lawsuit caused the school district to change its unconstitutional policies.

Phrase "Under God" in Pledge of Allegiance Attacked

Doe v. Acton-Boxborough Regional Sch. Dist., No. SJC-11317 (Mass. 2014)

Atheist parents filed a lawsuit challenging the use of the phrase "Under God" in the Pledge of Allegiance. The Massachusetts Supreme Court held that "under God" can be said when students recite the Pledge of Allegiance. The court held that the phrase neither violates the Massachusetts Constitution nor infringes upon atheists' rights because reciting the pledge is fundamentally a patriotic exercise.

ACLU and AUSCS Sue to Stop Tax Credits for Scholarship Programs

Duncan v. State of New Hampshire, No. _____ (Sup. Ct., Strafford County, N.H., Jun. 17, 2013)

New Hampshire implemented a program to encourage private donations to scholarship organizations by granting an up-to-eighty-five percent tax credit for such donations. The ACLU and Americans United for Separation of Church and State, however, opposed the program because the state did not require the scholarship organizations to discriminate against students who attend religious schools. A court struck down the program under the New Hampshire Constitution.

Science Teacher Fired for Presenting Both Sides of Evolution Debate
Freshwater v. Mount Vernon City Sch. Dist. Bd. of Educ., 137 Ohio St. 3d 469 (Ohio 2013)
John Freshwater, a science teacher of twenty-one years and praised by his own school as one of the better teachers and effective at teaching evolution as evidenced by Ohio Achievement Test results, was fired because his comprehensive coverage of evolution included evidence of unaccounted for gaps in the evolutionary fossil record. The school derisively equated this to creationism and denounced it as pushing religious doctrine; however, there was never a finding that he was teaching any form of creationism and the evidence presented to students never mentioned God or religion. A referee determined that Mr. Freshwater violated the Establishment Clause, and thus the school board terminated his employment after twenty-one years of faithful and effective service. A state appeals court and the Ohio Supreme Court upheld his termination.

Lawsuit Attempts to Block Low-Income Families from Access to Religious Schools
Meredith v. Pence, 984 N.E. 2d 1213 (Ind. 2013)
Indiana increased the opportunity for low-income families to choose the best schools for their children's education through its innovative Choice Scholarship Program. Qualifying children receive scholarships to apply towards their primary education at schools of their choice. Opponents attacked the program in state court because it failed to ban qualifying children from attending religiously affiliated schools. The Indiana Supreme Court rejected hostile attempts to eliminate the program at the expense of low-income communities, and it upheld the freedom of families to choose the best schools for their children—regardless of creed or belief.

Lawsuit Attacks Colorado Voucher Program
Larue v. Colorado Board of Education, No. 11-4424 (Colo. Dist. Ct., Aug. 12, 2011)
A Colorado state court permanently enjoined the Douglas County, Colorado, Board of Education's voucher program that allowed students enrolled in the county's public schools to use seventy-five percent of per-student funding to attend private schools, including religiously affiliated schools. The court held that the program violated many of the religious provisions of the Colorado Constitution, which it recognized as more restrictive than the religion clauses in the U.S. Constitution.

Valedictorian Banned from Giving Speech Because of Her Desire to Include a Religious Message

Griffith v. Butte School District No. 1, 244 P.3d 321 (Mont. 2010)

Renee Griffith, the class valedictorian at Butte High School, was selected to give a speech at her graduation ceremony. There were no written guidelines for student speakers, but they were told that the remarks had to be, "appropriate, in good taste and grammar, and should be relevant to the closing of [their] high school years." After meeting with speech coach, Griffith was told that she needed to change her speech to omit any reference to "God" or "Christ" to be allowed to speak. Griffith refused to change her original remarks and was not allowed to speak. Griffith complained to the Human Rights Bureau, but was given a notice of dismissal. The district court found in favor of the school, but the Supreme Court of Montana found that the school had violated Griffith's right to free speech but not her right to free exercise of religion.

Education Students Sue for Freedom to Complete Student Teaching at Religious Schools

Harrison v. Gregoire, No. 02-2-01831-3 (Super. Ct. Wash. 2002)

The University of Washington and Eastern Washington University both enforced policies that barred student teaching at religious schools. The universities cited the "Blaine Amendment," which called for a strict "separation of church and state." Carolyn Harrison and Rene Penhallurick, teaching students at the universities, hoped to complete their student teaching at religious schools but were denied the opportunity. The students sued. As a result of the lawsuit, the State of Washington's policy now requires that universities either allow or deny student teaching at private schools regardless of religious status. The University of Washington changed its policies, allowing Harrison to teach at a Jesuit school. Eastern Washington University decided to prohibit student teaching at any private school.

Lawsuit Challenges Boy Scouts' Presentation of Information to Students

Powell v. Bunn, 59 P.3d 559 (Or. Ct. App. Dec. 11, 2002)

An Oregon school district allowed the Boy Scouts to present information on membership to students. A parent filed suit, claiming the policy violated the Establishment Clause.

School Board Derecognizes Fellowship of Christian Athletes

McKee v. City of Pleasanton, 750 P.2d 1007 (Kan. 1988)

Students in Pleasanton, Kansas, formed a Fellowship of Christian Athletes (FCA) chapter on their school campus and were recognized as an official student club on campus. A new superintendent and school board, however, stripped FCA of their official status and refused to recognize them as a school club. A lawsuit was filed to restore the group's recognition as an official student club.

ACLU Challenges Principal for Writing "God Bless You"

http://www.foxnews.com/us/2015/09/27/god-bless-greeting-lands-louisiana-school-in-hot-water-with-aclu/

The American Civil Liberties Union of Louisiana has accused Airline High School of promoting Christianity because the school allowed a student group to hang prayer boxes and the principal ended a letter with "May God Bless You All." The school board has placed the issue on its agenda for discussion. Louisiana State Representative Mike Johnson has offered free legal services to the school.

Coach Kennedy Suspended for Praying Silently After Games

http://www.seattletimes.com/sports/high-school/why-bremerton-coach-joe-kennedys-stance-on-postgame-prayer-is-admirable/

Bremerton High School in Washington State ordered football Coach Joe Kennedy to stop his seven-year practice of praying at the 50-yard line after every game. In October of 2015, the school district suspended Coach Kennedy over his silent, 30-second prayer, stripping Coach Kennedy of his right to free religious expression—a right protected by the First Amendment, federal law, and extensive case law precedent. Liberty Institute, on behalf of Coach Kennedy, filed an Equal Employment Opportunity Commission complaint for religious discrimination.

School Board Prayer Criticized

http://www.norwalkreflector.com/Local/2015/09/09/Should-Norwalk-school-board-have-right-to-pray-at-meetings.html

The Board of Education for Norwalk City Schools generally began monthly meetings with prayer, prompting the Freedom From Religion Foundation to send a demand letter to the board's president. Lutheran pastor Amy Little, who is also a district parent, commented that it is sad that the organization is attempting to "rob us of our faith." The board intends to research the legal issues before responding to the letter.

FFRF Calls to Abolish the Auburn Tigers' Volunteer Chaplain

http://www.foxsports.com/college-football/outkick-the-coverage/auburn-tigers-sec-freedom-from-religion-foundation-team-chaplain-chette-williams-082015

Chette Williams is a former college football player and current volunteer chaplain with Auburn University. In response to FFRF's letter calling Auburn to "abolish the chaplaincy," Auburn released a statement noting that participation in chaplain-led events is voluntary and chaplains are common in many public institutions, including the United States Congress.

MRFF Sues University Over 9/11 Memorial Service
http://campusreform.org/?ID=6019
The Military Religious Freedom Foundation (MRFF) threatened legal action against the University of North Georgia for allegedly requiring cadets to attend a 9/11 commencement service at which students prayed to the "Christian God." University officials dispute such allegations and claim the memorial service was not mandatory for cadets, nor were they required to be present in formation. Further, UNG President Bonita Jacobs and administrators are confident in their defense against MRFF's accusations, as the university did not plan the event or schedule the Corps Chaplain to conduct the prayer. Instead, UNG says the Student Government Association was responsible for planning the invocation, benediction, and for selecting the featured speakers. "Genuinely student initiated religious speech at events organized by student organizations on campus implicates both of our constitutional obligations," wrote Jacobs in a formal response to MRFF.

High School Band's Performance Cancelled Due to Religious Song
http://christiannews.net/2015/08/23/high-school-band-nixed-from-halftime-show-over-how-great-thou-art-performance/
Brandon High School's band was set to perform the hymn "How Great Thou Art" during a football game's halftime show. After a court sided with the American Humanist Association against the school district, the Rankin County School Board stopped the performance to avoid possible additional litigation. The district expressed its regret to the students who had spent the summer working on the piece.

ACLU Threatens Public School Districts for Prayer Before Sporting Events
http://www.delaware1059.com/story.php?id=12850
The American Civil Liberties Union of Delaware sent threatening letters to the superintendents of eighteen Delaware public school districts warning them not to allow coaches to participate in team prayers.

FFRF Stops University of Toledo Coach from Giving the Lord's Prayer
http://www.usatoday.com/story/sports/ncaaf/2015/06/12/toledo-football-coach-will-no-longer-lead-team-prayers/71141726/
The University of Toledo's head football coach used to lead his team in the

Lord's Prayer before football games, but will no longer do so following a letter from the Freedom From Religion Foundation (FFRF).

FFRF Demands That Coaches Not Participate in Student-Led Prayer∫

http://www.tampabay.com/blogs/gradebook/organization-complains-about-prayer-at-pasco-county-high-school-football/2232905

The Freedom From Religion Foundation (FFRF) sent a letter to the superintendent of the Pasco County, Florida, school district demanding that the district ban coaches from participating in student-led prayers. The school district responded that the coaches are merely present during student-led prayers and are not leading prayers themselves.

FFRF Sends Complaint Letter to the Levy County School Board in Florida

http://www.gainesville.com/article/20150608/ARTICLES/150609700?p=1&tc=pg

The Freedom From Religion Foundation (FFRF) sent a letter to the Levy County, Florida, school board complaining that the school board meetings begin with a prayer, that teachers participate in religious activities, that the school advertised a baccalaureate service on its website, and that signs in a school mention God. While none of these complaints are necessarily constitutional violations, the school board is investigating the FFRF's letter.

Sixth-Grade Student Prohibited from Mentioning Her Faith in "All About Me" Presentation

https://www.libertyinstitute.org/Fraiser

Mackenzie Fraiser, a sixth-grade student at Somerset Academy in Las Vegas, Nevada, was assigned to create a slideshow called "All About Me." The slideshow was to include an inspirational quote that represents the student. Because Mackenzie Fraiser is a Christian, she wanted to include John 3:16— her favorite Bible verse—as her inspirational quote. Mackenzie's teacher, however, stated that Bible verses and quotes from the Book of Mormon were prohibited from the slideshow. First Liberty Institute sent a letter to Somerset Academy explaining Mackenzie's religious liberty rights, and the school apologized to Mackenzie. Mackenzie was allowed to resubmit her original project with the Bible verse.

ACLU of Indiana Sues School to Stop Prayers at School Board Meetings, Graduations, and Sporting Events

http://www.nwitimes.com/news/local/lake/river-forest-school-prayers-critics-didn-t-follow-procedures/article_e076fa90-b3d7-5c5d-a52e-8354e479f38e.html

The American Civil Liberties Union (ACLU) of Indiana sued the River Forest

Community School Corporation (RFCSC) to stop prayers at school board meetings, graduations, and sporting events. RFCSC said that the prayers did not violate the First Amendment.

California School District Bans Native American from Wearing Eagle Feather to Graduation

http://www.csmonitor.com/USA/Education/2015/0603/Religious-freedom-Eagle-feather-allowed-in-California-graduation

Christian Titman, a graduating senior at Clovis High School and a Native American, wanted to wear an eagle feather for its religious significance to his graduation. The school district initially refused to allow Titman to wear the feather, but relented after Titman filed a lawsuit against the district.

FFRF Complains About School's Selected Quotations

http://www.kltv.com/story/29697983/ffrf-asks-mt-vernon-isd-to-remove-religious-quotes-from-buildings

Mount Vernon Independent School District in Texas has decorated its walls with over 130 inspirational quotes from a variety of sources. The Freedom From Religion Foundation (FFRF) has complained that seven of the quotes are Bible verses or religious in nature. The anti-religious organization has called on the school to censor religious perspectives.

Americans United for Separation of Church and State Threatens School for Field Trip to Dinosaur Museum

http://www.christianpost.com/news/children-have-constitutional-right-to-go-on-dinosaur-museum-field-trip-without-fearing-threats-from-anti-creationists-139814/

Americans United for Separation of Church and State sent a letter to the Glendive School District threatening a lawsuit if the district permitted a field trip to the Glendive Dinosaur & Fossil Museum—the second-largest dinosaur museum in Montana—because the museum has a religious viewpoint. Following receipt of the letter, the school district cancelled its planned field trip. A religious liberties organization then sent a letter to the school district explaining that the field trip would have been constitutional so long as the school did not select the museum for its religious viewpoint.

FFRF Attacks Middle School Memorial for Deceased Teacher

https://www.opposingviews.com/i/religion/first-amendment-group-calls-removal-memorial-wv-middle-school

Freedom From Religious Foundation sent a hostile letter to a middle school about religious images used in a memorial commemorating a teacher who passed away. A teacher taught at the school for over twenty-five years before tragically passing in an accident. The school dedicated an area in the school's garden with a display of crosses, Bible verses, and angels in honor of the late teacher. The school board was forced to remove the cross, but kept some of the angels, which the late teacher collected.

College Is Persecuted for Believing in Traditional Marriage

http://www.nationalreview.com/article/397905/standing-gordon-editors
Gordon College is a nationally ranked liberal arts institution located in the Boston area, with deep roots in the Christian faith and missionary training. In July 2014, when President Obama signed an order prohibiting the federal government and federal contractors from discriminating in hiring based on "sexual orientation" and "gender identity," it offered no exemption to religious organizations like Gordon College, who have faith-based objections to same-sex marriage. Michael Lindsay, president of Gordon College, signed, as an individual, not as a representative of Gordon College, an open letter to the President requesting the inclusion of a religious exemption. After Lindsay's letter to the President, the discovery that, like almost every other Christian school and church, the school had a policy that required students and employees to limit sexual activity to marriage, the school endured a stream of attacks. Salem Mayor Kimberly Driscoll suspended a long-term contract with Gordon College which then prohibited them from using Salem's historic Old Town Hall; nearby Lynn Public School board ended an eleven-year relationship with Gordon College and refused to accept their students in their student-teacher program; and Gordon's accrediting body gave a subtle threat that the school could lose their accreditation if they do not change their policies in one year.

FFRF Forces Alabama School to Change Policies

http://www.al.com/news/birmingham/index.ssf/2015/02/homewood_city_school_accused_0.html
It was a tradition at Alabama's Homewood Middle School to have a "team chaplain" pray and deliver a sermon for the football team during its weekly team pizza meal. Freedom From Religion Foundation (FFRF) forced the district to change the position of the football team chaplains to "team sponsors" who are "to deliver encouraging messages to the players regarding morals and character, not sermons," the school attorney said when responding to FFRF complaints. FFRF also took issue with the school's First Priority Club, which met in the gym before school started. A local youth pastor led a worship service for all those who wanted to attend. FFRF claimed a teacher

organized the club, so First Priority Club subsequently was forced to move their meetings into a private classroom with a faculty monitor present who is prohibited from participating in any form. The middle school previously allowed local churches to set up tables with brochures during lunchtime for any interested students. After FFRF's complaints, all lunchtime visitors are prohibited from proselytizing.

FFRF Demands University of Florida Remove Inscription from Building

http://www.christianexaminer.com/article/university.of.florida.under.fire.
by.atheists.for.bible.verse.inscription/49005.htm

The Freedom From Religion Foundation (FFRF) is demanding that the University of Florida remove an inscription from a university building. The university's College of Business Administration building has Micah 6:8 inscribed over an archway. While Micah 6:8 is respected by numerous religions, FFRF has declared that the existence of the quote on a building is an endorsement of Christianity.

Americans United for Separation of Church and State Threatens School over Religious Opera

*http://www.cleveland.com/opinion/index.ssf/2015/05/religious_opera_wont_*
be_perfor.html

Americans United for Separation of Church and State opposed Willoughby South High School's performance of an opera, "I am Martol," based on the music of Norwegian composer Ola Gjeilo, because the opera contains religious themes. The students were forced to perform the opera off school property and without the assistance of their choir director.

Students Protest After ACLU Forces Removal of National Motto from Sign

https://www.yahoo.com/parenting/middle-schoolers-rally-to-get-religious-
message-117531644637.html

Ridgewood Middle School in Shreveport, Louisiana, displayed the national motto, "In God We Trust," on its sign. The American Civil Liberties Union (ACLU) of Louisiana sent a letter to the Caddo Parish school district demanding that all religious references be removed from all schools in the district. In response to the letter, Ridgewood Middle School officials removed the motto from the sign. The students of Ridgewood Middle School, however, protested the removal of the national motto and held a lunchtime rally. Following the student rally, the school restored the national motto.

FFRF Opposes University Athletics Department Chaplains

http://www.opposingviews.com/i/religion/freedom-religion-foundation-sends-records-requests-five-collegiate-athletic-departments

The Freedom From Religion Foundation (FFRF) filed records requests on five universities in an effort to stop them from using chaplains in their athletics department.

Cranston Schools Prohibit Teachers from Taking Off Good Friday

http://www.providencejournal.com/article/20150330/NEWS/150339965/-1/breaking_ajax/?Start=1

After twenty-five years of having no school on Good Friday, Yom Kippur, and Rosh Hashanah, the Cranston School Committee in Cranston, Rhode Island, changed its academic calendar to hold classes on each of those days. While the Cranston School Committee's contract with the teacher's union permitted each teacher to take off up to two religious days, Cranston Public Schools denied teachers' requests to take off Good Friday. The union filed a lawsuit against the Cranston Public Schools, and a judge prohibited the school district from denying leave requests for Good Friday.

West Virginia School Board Bans All Student Prayer

http://www.inquisitr.com/1927547/school-board-bans-prayer-in-school-for-students-and-staff-in-west-virginia-district/

The Harrison County School Board in West Virginia imposed a complete ban on all student prayer at school and at any school events. Following receipt of a letter from the Freedom From Religion Foundation, Assistant Superintendent Anthony Fratto authored a memo requiring all teachers, coaches, and staff to stop any form of student prayer that they see. All staff were required to sign off on the memo.

American Humanist Association Threatens School for Student's Saying, "God Bless America"

http://www.onenewsnow.com/education/2015/03/06/fl-student-allowed-to-utter-three-word-phrase-over-atheists-objections

A student at Yulee High School in Nassau County, Florida, gave the announcements over the school's public address system but added the words "God bless America." Two atheist students who felt "uncomfortable" with the addition of the phrase "God bless America" contacted the American Humanist Association, who threatened legal action against the school if the student were allowed to utter the words again. A religious liberty organization contacted the school and explained the students' free speech and religious liberty rights, and the school has agreed that students may say "God bless America."

Student Bible Study Banned from Hudsonville, Michigan, School Grounds

http://www.wnd.com/2015/02/local-schools-evict-bible-study-from-grounds/

For years, Bible Club Ministries International—Western Michigan provided Bible instruction for Hudsonville, Michigan, students who wanted to attend the studies during lunch breaks or recess and who had parental permission. Following a complaint from the Michigan Association of Civil Rights Activists (MACRS), however, Hudsonville banned the ministry from meeting on property owned by the school district. According to the Detroit News, Mitch Kahle, the "force behind MACRS," "blame[s] religion for most of the world's problems" and equates it with "racism and child abuse."

Virginia School District Interrogates Homeschooled Students to Determine Their Religious Beliefs

http://www.foxnews.com/opinion/2015/01/15/school-district-to-stop-interrogating-christian-homeschool-kids.html?intcmp=latestnews

A school board in Goochland County, Virginia, enacted a new policy of interrogating homeschooled students aged fourteen years or older and quizzing them about their religious beliefs. Following huge opposition to the new policy by parents, the Goochland School Board repealed the policy.

Long Island School District Denies Access to Religious Student Club

http://www.christiantoday.com/article/school.recognises.christian.club.after.15.year.old.students.bold.stand/43577.htm

Liz Loverde, a fifteen-year-old student at Wantagh High School in Long Island, New York, wanted to start a Christian afterschool club called "Dare to Believe." While Wantagh High School permitted many afterschool clubs, it refused to accept Loverde's group because Dare to Believe is faith-based. First Liberty Institute represented Loverde and explained to Wantagh High School that engaging in religious discrimination against religious afterschool clubs can threaten the school's federal funding. The school reversed its position and permitted the Dare to Believe afterschool club.

American Humanist Association Threatens Lawsuit to Stop Students from Supporting Church's Food Pantry

http://www.ijreview.com/2014/12/209981-group-trying-stop-elementary-schools-thanksgiving-gift-definitely-feeling-holiday-spirit/

In an effort to teach its students gratitude and to help feed the poor, Oakbrook Elementary sold "Turkey Grams," messages of gratitude that could be sent to friends or teachers. The proceeds from the Turkey Grams were to be used to purchase canned goods that would be given to a local food pantry. When the American Humanist Association learned that the local food pantry was operated by a church, however, it threatened to sue the school for "assisting church-led projects." The school's student council chose the church's food pantry because it was the closest pantry to the school.

High School Salutatorian Mentions God in Speech Despite School Censorship

http://libertyinstitute.org/hamby

Brawley Union School District graduate Brooks Hamby mentioned God in his speech despite receiving threats from school officials that they would mute his microphone if he mentioned God. Hamby sent three versions of his speech to school officials before giving his speech at the ceremony. School officials rejected all three versions of the speech and censored all references to God and the Bible. Liberty Institute is assisting Brooks Hamby in pursuing an apology for censoring the student's speech.

American Humanist Association Sues South Carolina School for Hosting Graduation Ceremony in Chapel

http://www.christianpost.com/news/atheist-suit-against-sc-school-for-hosting-graduation-in-christian-chapel-to-be-reheard-in-district-court-129832/

A school in South Carolina reached capacity in their auditorium to host the graduation ceremony. Students would be limited to three family members each if the ceremony were held in the school. The school decided the most convenient alternative was a chapel that offered stadium seating and allowed as many family members as wanted to attend. The school even went to such lengths as to remove all Christian iconography, such as crosses and Bibles that were in the chapel. However, the school was still attacked for allegedly "proselytizing Christianity," when students led the graduation ceremony in prayer. A U.S. District Judge enjoined school-sponsored student prayers, which were held as a formal part of graduations in the school district from 1951 to 2013, but the judge upheld spontaneous student prayer. The district was forced to take steps to prevent official, school-sponsored prayers but said it would not prohibit prayer at graduations so long as it is student-led and initiated and doesn't create a disturbance.

School Forced to Stop Charitable Fundraiser

http://americanhumanist.org/news/details/2014-11-public-elementary-school-cant-fundraise-for-church-s

A South Carolina elementary school's student council organized a fundraiser and food drive to benefit a local church's mission trip. The American Humanist Association sent a threatening letter to the school, demanding that the school stop its fundraising effort.

School Choir Banned from Singing Christian Songs While Honoring Veterans

http://americanhumanist.org/news/details/2014-11-humanist-group-pleased-that-public-school-ceases-chr

During a school assembly, which honored veterans for their sacrifice and service in our military, a Kansas school choir chose two fitting songs for the program. These songs included references to "Jesus" and the school was immediately threatened for including religious references in their school programs. The school district was forced to announce that it would only use secular music in its future assemblies honoring veterans.

FFRF Sought to Prevent School's Beneficial, Non-Religious Assembly

http://wisconsindailyindependent.com/ohio-school-district-stands-up-to-atheist-groups-unfounded-threats/

Freedom From Religion Foundation (FFRF) threatened a school district in Ohio after the district supported a non-religious assembly based on promoting character development for students. Licking Valley Intermediate School hosted a "character education" assembly entitled "Be All You Can Be" for grades three through five. None of the information in the presentation was religious in nature and the program's content was consistent with the school's curriculum. The school principal said the assembly "was all based on goal setting, being a leader, making good choices, because other people are following your lead; how to persevere when you don't reach your goal the first time; how to try again." FFRF objected to the program simply because the presenters adhered to the Christian faith. Even though the group leading the assembly, Jubilee Gang, is a Christian group, they did not reference their Christian affiliation throughout the assembly. The school had "no intent to bring religion into the school, and there was absolutely no religious basis to the assembly," said the school principal. A religious liberties organization sent Licking Valley School District a letter in support of their decision to allow the assembly to continue, stating "Public schools should be commended when they decline to give in to unfounded threats by those who misunderstand the First Amendment," and "This is not neutrality but targeted religious discrimination that the First Amendment forbids."

FFRF Sues School Boards for Prayer in Meetings Despite Overwhelming Support
http://www.dailybulletin.com/general-news/20141121/chino-valley-unified-board-mulls-response-to-prayer-lawsuit
The Freedom From Religion Foundation filed suit against the Chino Valley Unified school board, alleging that the board members violated the Constitution by praying, reading Bible verses, and proselytizing at their meetings. At the recent school board gathering in support of prayer, the meeting began with an invocation, which included petitions for guidance and unity, but there were no references to Jesus or the Holy Spirit. There were no explicit calls to faith.

FFRF Condemns Virginia Professor's "Introduction to Islam" Course
http://ffrf.org/news/news-releases/item/21792-ffrf-objects-to-va-professor-s-promotion-of-islam-in-classroom
The Freedom From Religion Foundation (FFRF) sent a threatening letter to a college professor for his "Introduction to Islam" course at Northern Virginia Community College in Annandale, Virginia. The course is described as an objective investigation of Islam "in its historical, religious, and political dimensions," but FFRF claims the class is "a one-sided monologue by a government-paid employee whose agenda is to show the truth of religion—namely, the existence of a god." An attorney for the Virginia Community College System responded, informing FFRF that it was in the process of conducting a review.

Private School Prohibited from Hosting Sports Tournament Over Prayer
http://www.npr.org/sections/thetwo-way/2014/11/11/363309020/asked-to-stop-praying-alaska-school-won-t-host-state-tournament?utm_medium=RSS&utm_campaign=us
After seven years of hosting Alaska's wrestling tournament, Anchorage Christian School was given an ultimatum: either stop praying before the tournament or forfeit its right to host the tournament. An anonymous complaint about the tournament's introductory prayer led to a request to stop the practice, and Anchorage Christian School refused. "We do the Pledge of Allegiance, the flag is displayed, we sing the national anthem, say a prayer and then we wrestle," School Administrator Tom Cobaugh stated. Not praying is "a show stopper for us," he continued. "It was a basic prayer

for protection of the student athletes, that all would compete well, have good sportsmanship," said Cobaugh. But sadly, the Americans United for Separation of Church and State put an end to the tradition.

High School Prohibits Students from Praying, Singing, or Discussing Religious Topics

http://www.onenewsnow.com/legal-courts/2014/11/13/school-says-religion-must-stay-outside-perimeters-of-school-day#.VGUyoYflfk8

Pine Creek High School in Colorado Springs, Colorado, told a group of students they can no longer informally gather to pray, sing religious songs, or even discuss religious topics at school, even though they have been doing so for the past three years. Chase Windebank, the student who founded the group three years ago, was summoned to the assistant principal's office and told "he could no longer pray with his fellow students during free time because of the separation of church and state." Windebank was told they could only meet during the school day if their meetings did not include religious content. Since religious discussion was the purpose of the group, they have been forced to meet in the mornings, and the number of participants has drastically decreased—from 90 to around 12 students.

High School Terminates Graduate Intern Based on Religious Beliefs

http://www.oregonlive.com/faith/2014/11/devout_christian_claims_portla.html

A graduate student from Lewis & Clark College, interning at Madison High School in Portland, Oregon, was terminated shortly after privately asking her supervisor about the age-appropriateness of the high school's sex education curriculum. The intern was a devout Christian and simply asked whether there was any room for her own beliefs, after feeling the high school placed a disproportionate emphasis on sexual identity and school activities for LGBT students. After the graduate intern asked, her supervisor "immediately became combative" and accused her and Christians of being judgmental and terminated her a few days later. Her graduate school then forced her to change her major and subsequently she graduated without a license to work as a school counselor, and is $100,000 in debt in student loans for a degree that she is unable to obtain now. The graduate student filed suit for civil rights violations and employment discrimination.

MRFF Criticizes Wheaton College for Christian ROTC Officer Requirement

http://www.foxnews.com/opinion/2014/11/11/christian-schools-rotc-under-attack.html

Wheaton College is one of the nation's most prominent Christian schools, and the ROTC program has a long and storied history that is steeped in the school's Christian tradition. The ROTC program listed a position for an assistant professor of military science at Wheaton College, who "must be of Christian faith." The Military Religious Freedom Foundation (MRFF) immediately raised concerns about the ROTC, and demanded those involved be "visibly and meaningfully punished," MRFF founder Mikey Weinstein wrote. The U.S. Army responded and announced they have launched a review of ROTC policies nationwide, but denied the investigation had anything to do with Weinstein's threats. Wheaton Provost Stanton Jones believes the school is on solid constitutional ground, stating, "The constitutional requirement for no establishment does not mean we are all non-religious. It means the U.S. government supports a multiplicity of religions." Jones defended the religious requirement of the ROTC leadership saying, "Wheaton students come here because of the religious distinctive of the school. We feel that the resonance of the lead military officer with that religious identity helps that person bridge the gap with students."

FFRF Tries to Stop an Afterschool Club from Meeting On-Campus
http://www.centralmaine.com/2014/11/07/good-news-club-seeks-to-evangelize-boys-and-girls/
When the Good News Club, a religious afterschool program, distributed fliers to elementary school students in Skowhegan, Maine, the Freedom From Religion Foundation (FFRF) sought to abolish the club's activities. The club's goal was to teach Bible-centered character and moral education to students who wished to attend their program. FFRF campaigned for the Skowhegan school district to only allow school-sponsored groups to use the school's facilities. "Teaching young children to be preoccupied with fear, sin, retribution and salvation will destroy their innocent childhood and turn them into adults who lack critical thinking skills," FFRF posted to encourage parents to complain to the district superintendent.

New York School Sued for Anti-Semitism
http://www.courthousenews.com/2014/11/05/anti-semitism-may-nail-upstate-n-y-school.htm
A New York school district faced a federal trial for allegedly tolerating white power chants, swastika carvings and anti-Jewish harassment targeting Jewish students. The children endured bus rides during which other students sang songs about killing black and Jewish students. Students also reported that they were taunted with swastikas, "Hitler salutes," and crematoria imagery.

On a bus ride to school, another student reported seeing a student drawing a picture and saying "it is a Hasidic Jew, so let's shove pennies in his mouth."

Humanist Group Attacks Veterans Day Assembly Opening Prayer

http://americanhumanist.org/news/details/2014-11-public-high-school-veterans-day-assembly-cant-includ

A Louisiana high school hosted an assembly honoring veterans. The ceremony opened with a prayer remembering their sacrifice and paying tribute to their legacy. The prayer was attacked by the American Humanist Association as forcing religious beliefs on students.

Pickens School Board Debates Prayer

http://www.greenvilleonline.com/story/news/local/pickens-county/2014/06/24/pickens-school-board-prayer-issue-resurrected/11319767/

The Pickens School Board in South Carolina is currently debating their prayer policy in light of the *Town of Greece v. Galloway* decision from the U.S. Supreme Court. The school was threatened by the FFRF for allowing students to pray according to their consciences at board meetings. After the FFRF's letter, the school board changed its policy to require nonsectarian prayers offered by school board members in 2013. The school board is currently discussing the constitutionality of having clergy offer prayers at meetings.

Humanist Group Attacks School District for Supporting Students' Trip to Guatemala

http://americanhumanist.org/news/details/2014-06-humanist-group-calls-on-colorado-public-school-to-ce

http://www.denverpost.com/news/ci_26020470/group-claims-dougco-schools-violated-constitution-mission-trip

The Appigani Humanist Legal Center sent a letter accusing the Douglas County School District of Colorado of proselytizing for supporting a trip sponsored by the Fellowship of Christian Athletes. The Fellowship of Christian Athletes and Adventures in Missions asked the school for donations for their trip to Guatemala. The humanist group says that their fundraising efforts should not involve the entire school or be associated with the school's name and that supporting the trip violates the First Amendment.

Christian Club Risks Being Kicked Off Campus Because It Wants Christian Leaders

http://www.campusreform.org/?ID=5685

California Sate University officials told InterVarsity Christian Fellowship that requiring officers of the group to sign a statement of faith is considered a violation of a 2011 Executive Order forbidding discrimination. The group's leader explained that having Christian leaders is important for the function of the organization, as the leaders are not merely treasurers or secretaries. The group hopes to receive an exemption.

New York Mayor Introduces Program That Limits Participating Schools' Religious Freedom

http://religionclause.blogspot.com/2014/06/de-blasios-universal-kindergarten.html

New York Mayo Bill DeBlasio created a free full-day kindergarten program that included the participation of Orthodox Jewish Schools. However, DeBlasio's program bans staff from leading prayers and shortens the school day so that there is no time for religious instruction. The private Orthodox schools are considering a different program that does not require the restrictions that are in DeBlasio's plan.

School Bows to Humanist Group and Bans Faculty from Attending Baccalaureate Services

http://americanhumanist.org/news/details/2014-06-humanist-group-works-with-birdville-independent-scho

American Humanist Association sent a letter to Birdville I.S.D. in Haltom City, Texas. A student informed AHA that his school had religious Baccalaureate ceremonies, overnight retreats at a local church, and Christian iconography in public classrooms. The school responded to the grievances by removing faculty from the Baccalaureate services, religious items from classrooms, and retreats from the church to a community center.

Missouri School Settles with Humanist Organization

http://americanhumanist.org/news/details/2014-06-american-humanist-association-successfully-settles-l

http://religionclause.blogspot.com/2014/06/consent-decree-entered-in-suit-over.html

The Fayette R III School District settled with the American Humanist Association (AHA) on a suit AHA brought against the school district in November. AHA claimed that the school district showed unconstitutional favoritism toward Christianity. The school projected prayer over the intercom and allowed religious groups to meet before school. The settlement requires that the school not promote prayer or religious activities.

School Districts Change Graduation Locations Because of Threats from FFRF

http://www.cantonrep.com/article/20140601/NEWS/140609984

Two Ohio school districts were forced to find new venues for their gradation ceremonies after the Freedom From Religion Foundation (FFRF) sent them a letter of complaint. The Northwest Local School District and Canton Local School District planned to host graduation ceremonies in local churches. FFRF told the school officials that holding the ceremonies in churches would endorse religion.

Atheist College Professor Attacks Principal for Praying Silently

http://www.rawstory.com/rs/2014/06/02/atheists-attack-public-high-school-principal-for-praying-to-god-during-graduation-ceremony/

http://www.theblaze.com/stories/2014/06/02/high-school-principals-bold-graduation-speech-invokes-god-prayer-and-national-tradition/

An atheist college professor is upset with high school principal Kevin Lowrey after the principal offered a moment of silence at a graduation ceremony. The principal asked the audience to join him in a moment of silence, but told students that he would pray silently during that time. After the moment of silence ended, the principal told the audience that he asked God to bless the graduating class during the moment of silence.

Teacher Confiscates Student's Bible and Calls Parents in Front of Class

http://www.foxnews.com/opinion/2014/05/05/teacher-tells-student-cant-read-bible-in-my-classroom/

A Florida fifth grader had his Bible confiscated during free reading time. After the teacher took the Bible, she called the student's parents in front of the class to tell them that the student was not allowed to read religious books in her classroom. After the Liberty Institute confronted the school with evidence that they violated their own policies, the school apologized to the boy.

School Condemned for Praying for Veterans

http://christiannews.net/2014/05/30/nc-school-district-condemns-christian-prayers-at-vet-event-as-violation-of-policy/

A North Bunacombe High School booster club held a flag ceremony to honor veterans. Parents and other attendees opposed the opening and closing prayers offered by a local pastor. The district said that the prayers at the ceremony were unconstitutional because they mentioned Jesus.

Ex-Vice Principal Sues Catholic School After Marrying Same-Sex Partner

http://religionclause.blogspot.com/2014/05/court-lets-fired-catholic-school.html
Vice Principal Mark Zmuda sued Seattle Eastside Catholic High School for firing him because he broke his employee contract by marrying his same-sex partner. The school argued that the case should be dismissed because Zmuda breached the morality clause of his employee contract that requires him to uphold teachings of the Catholic faith. A Washington state trial court judge has decided not to dismiss the suit.

Teacher Bans Fifth Grader from Reading His Bible During "Free-Reading" Time

http://www.libertyinstitute.org/rubeo?
Giovanni Rubeo, a fifth-grade student at Park Lakes Elementary School in Ft. Lauderdale, Florida, wanted to read the Bible during his class's "free-reading" time. When Giovanni's teacher saw him reading the Bible, however, she ordered him to stop reading. Giovanni's teacher then left a voicemail for Giovanni's father stating, "I noticed [Giovanni] had a book, a religious book, in the classroom. He's not permitted to read those books in my classroom." After attorneys from Liberty Institute sent a letter to the school explaining Giovanni's religious liberty rights, the school apologized to Giovanni and agreed that he is permitted to read his Bible during free-reading time.

Activists Demand Phone Records and Emails from UVA Law Professor

http://www.slate.com/articles/news_and_politics/jurisprudence/2014/05/douglas_laycock_gets_smeared_lgbtq_groups_attack_on_the_university_of_virginia.html
GetEqual activists told University of Virginia law professor Douglas Laycock that his involvement in religious liberty cases has consequences. Laycock, who has argued both liberal and conservative ideals, argued in favor of the Hobby Lobby HHS Mandate case and the case involving a prisoner's right to express his religion. The LGBT activists filed Freedom of Information Act requests for Laycock's email and phone records to track any communication the professor had with religious rights groups.

FFRF Complains to College After Commencement Speaker Says "God" and "Godspeed"

http://ffrf.org/news/news-releases/item/20743-wisconsin-public-college-grads-told-to-rely-on-god
The chancellor at the University of Wisconsin at Stevens Point told students to rely on faith in God and wished them Godspeed in his commencement

address. A family member of one of the graduates contacted Freedom From Religion Foundation (FFRF). FFRF sent a letter to the chancellor telling him that he cannot mention religion at graduation ceremonies.

College Students Banned from Thanking God at East Carolina University

http://www.campusreform.org/?ID=5598

A professor at a public university told students that they could not thank God in their personal statements that were to be delivered at the departmental graduation ceremony. The professor complained that too many students thanked religious figures in the past. The provost sent a letter to students telling them to disregard the professor's instructions. Students were allowed to say anything permissible under the First Amendment.

ACLU and FFRF Protest Bible-Based Curriculum

http://www.rockymounttelegram.com/features/religion/groups-challenge-bible-based-program-2465495

The American Civil Liberties Union and Freedom From Religion Foundation (FFRF) protested a Mustang, Oklahoma, high school for adding a Bible course to its curriculum. The purpose of the course is to enhance students' understanding of archaeology, history, and the arts. FFRF sent a letter to the high school explaining that the course would be biased because it would not include "negative aspects" of God.

Student Told Bibles Not Allowed at School

http://aclj.org/school-prayer/justice-restored-after-little-girl-bible-banned-from-school

When a girl from Tucson, Arizona, started bringing her Bible to school to read and discuss with fellow students during free time, school administrators told her that she could no longer bring her Bible. With the help of a religious liberties group, the girl's mother confronted the school's principal about the violation of her daughter's religious rights, and the principal agreed to allow the girl to continue bringing her Bible to school.

Student Denied Use of School Facilities for Bible Study Club

http://aclj.org/school-prayer/victory-for-bible-club-in-ny

A student at a high school in Amsterdam, New York, requested permission to use school facilities for an after-school, student-led Bible study club. The school informed the student that he needed an insurance policy to use school facilities after hours, and denied the student's request, even though the school imposed no such mandate on other after-school clubs. A religious liberties group wrote a letter to the school on behalf of the student addressing the discriminatory policy, and the school subsequently allowed the student to start her club.

Freedom From Religion Foundation Pressures School into Eliminating Religious References

http://ffrf.org/legal/other-legal-successes/item/20640-ffrf-halts-inappropriate-thanksgiving-program-religious-icons-bibles-removed-from-elementary-school-april-15-2014

The Freedom From Religion Foundation (FFRF) complained that one of the teachers at Oakwood Elementary School in Peoria, Arizona, extended open invitations to her church, kept a Bible and coffee mugs decorated with Bible verses on her desk, and gave religious bookmarks to students. Additionally, the FFRF protested the school's Thanksgiving skit due to religious content regarding the Pilgrims. In response, the school informed the FFRF that the teacher's religious activities were curtailed and that the Thanksgiving program would be reviewed.

Antireligion Organization Kills Bible Distribution

http://ffrf.org/legal/other-legal-successes/item/20477-ffrf-stops-bible-distribution-in-elementary-school-april-9-2014

When the Freedom From Religion Foundation heard that Lincoln Elementary School in Pryor, Oklahoma, allowed Gideons International to distribute Bibles to students in the school cafeteria, it demanded that the school ban Bibles and Gideons International from campus. The school confirmed that all religious materials would be forbidden moving forward.

School Tells Elementary Student, "No Bibles Allowed"

http://blog.libertyinstitute.org/2014/04/liberty-institute-commends-cy-fair-isds.html

A second-grade student at Hamilton Elementary School in Houston, Texas, pulled out her Bible during the school's "Read to Myself" time. However, a teacher prohibited the student from reading her Bible, and told the student not to bring the Bible back to school again because it constituted inappropriate reading material. Liberty Institute sent a letter to the Cypress Fairbanks I.S.D. explaining the student's constitutionally protected right to read her Bible. The district responded by assuring Liberty Institute and the student that it is committed to religious freedom in its schools.

Renowned High School Baseball Coach Criticized for Pregame Prayers

http://christiannews.net/2014/04/30/acclaimed-baseball-coach-under-fire-from-atheists-for-pre-game-prayers/

Owasso High School Baseball Coach Larry Turner has been recognized as the best high school baseball coach in the United States, receiving awards such as the 2013 National Baseball Coach of the Year. Coach Turner is also a Christian and leads his team in community service as well as pregame prayers. The Freedom From Religion Foundation discovered Coach Turner's practice of prayer and sent a letter to the school condemning the practice and demanding an investigation.

Teacher Reprimanded for Showing "The Bible" Episodes in Class

http://ffrf.org/legal/other-legal-successes/item/20648-ffrf-halts-teacher-from-showing-%E2%80%9Cthe-bible%E2%80%9D-in-class-april-28-2014

The Freedom From Religion Foundation sent a letter to the superintendent over Atlanta High School in Atlanta, Texas, complaining that a teacher showed episodes from the TV show, "The Bible" in class. The superintendent confirmed that the teacher had "been instructed to align his instruction" with current law.

Atheist Organization Seeks to Eliminate High School Wrestling Team's Bible-Based Motto

http://www.thenewscenter.tv/news/headlines/Parkersburg-South-Wrestling-T-Shirts-Draw-Attention-255706021.html

The wrestling team at Parkersburg South High School in Parkersburg, West Virginia, chose Philippians 4:13 as its team motto, inscribing it on team T-shirts, the school website, and the wall of the gym. When the Freedom From Religion Foundation heard about the motto, it wrote a letter to the school superintendent complaining about the motto's religious nature. The team members hired an attorney and fought to keep their constitutional freedoms. The school allowed the students to keep the T-shirts, but removed the verse from the school website and the gymnasium wall.

High School Football Coach Told to Stop Praying and Witnessing

http://ffrf.org/legal/other-legal-successes/item/20647-ffrf-ensures-prayer-is-not-a-part-of-middletown-high-school-football-april-25-2014

The Freedom From Religion Foundation wrote a letter to the superintendent over Middletown High School in Ohio demanding that the school prohibit Coach Chris Wells from sharing his faith with his players and blessing post-practice meals. The district confirmed that Coach Wells had been reprimanded.

School Tightens Restraints on Religious Liberty Under Pressure from Atheist Group

http://ffrf.org/legal/other-legal-successes/item/20683-prep-school-adopts-religion-free-event-policy-april-23-2014

The Freedom From Religion Foundation criticized Tempe Preparatory Academy in Phoenix, Arizona, for a teacher's attempt to balance the presentation of scientific theories through the distribution of religious science materials after watching an atheistic science documentary, and for the holding of graduation ceremonies at a local church. The school subsequently decided to remove all religious items from the church prior to graduations. Additionally, they disciplined the teacher and fired him from his position as head of his department.

Teacher Criticized for Easter Message

http://losangeles.cbslocal.com/2014/04/21/teacher-questioned-after-putting-religious-message-on-public-school-marquee/

A teacher at Darby Elementary School in Northridge, California, posted the message "Rest, Rest, Go To Church He is Risen" on the school marquee over Easter weekend. The school principal received numerous complaints and confirmed that the teacher would be questioned.

FFRF Condemns High School Football Coach's Prayers

http://ffrf.org/legal/other-legal-successes/item/20650-ffrf-stops-georgia-coach-from-leading-students-in-prayer-april-19-2014

When the Freedom From Religion Foundation (FFRF) heard that a football coach at Thomas County Central High School in Thomasville, Georgia, led prayer before practices, it demanded that the school prohibit the prayers. The school superintendent informed the FFRF that it would address coach-led prayer, but would protect the First Amendment rights of both faculty and students.

School District Undergoes Hostile Examination Due to Bible Class

http://www.christianpost.com/news/atheist-group-vows-to-scrutinize-hobby-lobby-presidents-public-school-bible-class-118253/

http://ffrf.org/news/news-releases/item/20500-ffrf-blasts-hobby-lobby-bible-curriculum

When the Mustang Public School District in Oklahoma approved the implementation of a Bible class elective championed by Hobby Lobby

President Steve Green, the Freedom From Religion Foundation sent a letter to the district superintendent laying out its intent to scrutinize the class's religious content in search of constitutional violations that could be used to eliminate it.

Atheist Group Calls for Investigation into University's Christian Football Coach

http://www.christianpost.com/news/atheist-group-accuses-clemson-football-program-of-christian-worship-117988/

Dabo Swinney, head football coach at Clemson University and an outspoken Christian, brought in a Christian chaplain to lead chapel services, devotionals, and Bible studies. When the Freedom From Religion Foundation heard about Swinney's actions, they complained that the university was endorsing Christian worship and demanded an examination of Swinney's practices.

School Bans Religious T-Shirts

http://www.rawstory.com/rs/2014/04/15/religious-oregon-teens-wear-gay-is-not-ok-shirts-to-school-to-protest-lack-of-straight-day/

On the National Day of Silence, an awareness event focused on highlighting harassment of LGBT individuals, several students at Oregon City High School wore T-shirts reading "Gay Is Not Ok" in protest, citing their religious beliefs against homosexuality. School authorities commanded the students to turn the T-shirts inside out or remove them.

School Officials Prohibit Advertisements for Christian Student Club

http://articles.orlandosentinel.com/2014-04-11/news/os-christian-club-lawsuit-florida-school-20140411_1_school-leaders-liberty-counsel-2013-2014-school-year
http://www.dailycommercial.com/news/article_354cf7da-67d8-57af-ac8b-d219e920d63a.html

The Fellowship of Christian Athletes (FCA) club at Mount Dora High School in Mt. Dora, Florida, was prohibited from posting announcements or promotions for the club through forums such as the school's billboards, public address system, and website, even though other student clubs were allowed to advertise on those same forums. With the help of a religious liberties group, the Mount Dora FCA filed a lawsuit against the school for its unconstitutional discrimination, and the school agreed to grant the FCA equal access.

Transgender Student Files Complaint Against Christian College for Refusing Request to Live in Male Dormitory

http://www.kgw.com/news/Transgender-George-Fox-student-told-he-cant-live-in-male-dorms--253942041.html

Jayce, a sophomore student at George Fox University in Newberg, Oregon, decided to undergo a female-to-male sex transition and consequently requested to live with other male students in male housing. When the Christian university denied her request due to its religious beliefs, Jacye filed a formal complaint against the university, alleging sex and gender discrimination in violation of Title IX. The university refused to abandon its religious beliefs.

Parent Complains About Invitations to Easter Egg Hunt

http://www.christianpost.com/news/muslim-parents-upset-over-eggstravaganza-easter-egg-hunt-invite-children-got-at-school-117429/

After receiving permission from several local public schools, Cherry Hill Presbyterian Church in Dearborn, Michigan, sent flyers home with children that advertised the church's Easter egg hunt. When Majed Moughni, a Muslim attorney and the father of two public school students, saw the invitations, he complained of a "serious violation of church and state."

Elementary Student Commanded to Stop Praying Over Her Lunch

http://www.nydailynews.com/news/national/florida-girl-claims-stopped-praying-lunch-article-1.1742858

http://blog.libertyinstitute.org/2014/04/outrage-school-stops-5-year-olds_4798.html

Five-year-old kindergarten student Gabriella Perez bowed her head and prayed before she ate during every lunch period at Carillon Elementary in Oviedo, Florida. However, a lunch supervisor told Gabriella that she was not allowed to pray and that praying was not good. Liberty Institute sent a letter to the school explaining Gabriella's constitutionally protected right to pray, but the family decided to take Gabriella out of the hostile environment to homeschool her instead.

After-School Program Supervisor Tries to Take Bible Away from Student

https://www.aclu.org/religion-belief/aclu-tn-protects-students-right-read-bible-school

A supervisor for Canon County's REACH after-school program told an elementary student that he could read any book but the Bible in their program. When the student refused to stop reading his Bible, the supervisor attempted to take the Bible away from him. The ACLU of Tennessee sent a letter to REACH explaining the student's constitutional right to read his Bible.

School Confiscates Religious Valentine's Day Cards

http://www.adfmedia.org/News/PRDetail/8987

At Floyd R. Shafer Elementary School's celebration of "Friendship Day" (aka Valentine's Day), a first-grade student brought cards that recognized St. Valentine's historical influence on the holiday and included John 3:16. When Principal William Mudlock saw the cards, he told the parents that it could be offensive to others and ordered them to be removed. A religious liberties group stepped in and filed a lawsuit on the student's behalf against the school for its discrimination.

Student Denied College Admission Due to Religious Beliefs

http://aclj.org/school-prayer/aclj-files-lawsuit-on-behalf-of-student-denied-college-admission-because-of-his-faith

Brandon Jenkins applied for the Community College of Baltimore County's (CCBC) Radiation Therapy Program with competitive credentials and having scored the maximum number of points allowed during the observation portion of the application process. However, when asked what was most important to him during the interview portion, Jenkins stated that the most important thing was God. As a result, the school denied his admission to the program, with Program Director Adrienne Dougherty stating, "I understand that religion is a major part of your life and that was evident in your recommendation letters, however, this field is not the place for religion. We have many patients who come to us for treatment from many different religions and some who believe in nothing at all. If you interview in the future, you may want to leave your thoughts and beliefs out of the interview process." Jenkins contacted a religious liberties organization, who filed a lawsuit on Jenkins's behalf for the discriminatory treatment.

Professor Faces Job Discrimination After Becoming a Christian

http://www.wnd.com/2014/03/university-stung-by-jury-verdict-in-retaliation-case/

http://www.charismanews.com/us/44262-710-000-the-cost-of-discriminating-against-a-christian-professor

The University of North Carolina–Wilmington denied a professor a promotion because he became a Christian. Professor Mike Adams was an atheist when he was hired to teach at the university in 1993. The university celebrated Adams for his atheist viewpoints. However, Adams became a Christian in

2000. Since 2000, Adams has written nationally syndicated articles with a Christian viewpoint. Adams earned multiple awards from the university, received excellent reviews from students, and published the greatest number of articles among his colleagues. Nonetheless, the university denied Adams his promotion and told Adams that he was subject to investigation. In June, Adams was awarded $710,000 in damages for the university's discriminatory treatment.

Elementary Students Chastised for Distributing Coins with Religious Message

http://www.christianpost.com/news/calif-teachers-reprimand-students-bible-verse-coins-legal-group-demands-apology-116613/

Two students from Desert Knolls Elementary School in California were chastised for distributing religious coins during recess and other noninstructional times. The coins contained the verse John 3:16 and the question, "Where will you spend eternity?" A teacher told the two students that she hated the coins. One student's coins were confiscated. A religious law firm demanded that the school apologize for how the teachers treated the boys and for violating their religious rights.

Bowdoin College Disfellowships Bowdoin Christian Fellowship

http://www.nytimes.com/2014/06/10/us/colleges-and-evangelicals-collide-on-bias-policy.html?emc=edit_th_20140610&nl=todaysheadlines&nlid=59743270&_r=1

http://www.patheos.com/blogs/thoughtlife/2014/03/vanderbilt-part-two-religious-liberty-is-imperiled-at-bowdoin-college/

http://spectator.org/articles/57996/god-and-sexuality-bowdoin

http://bowdoinorient.com/article/9029

School officials at Bowdoin College accused the Bowdoin Christian Fellowship of discrimination in the selection of leaders for the organization. The Christian group requires that group leaders not engage in homosexual conduct. Dean of Students Tim Foster told on-campus organizations that not allowing LGBTQ students to participate or hold a leadership position in an organization is considered discrimination. Bowdoin College drafted an agreement stating that Bowdoin Christian Fellowship could not discriminate against LGBTQ students when assigning leadership positions. The two ministers who led the group refused to sign the agreement and subsequently resigned from the organization. Bowdoin is in the process of discontinuing Bowdoin Christian Fellowship's association with the school.

FFRF Complains About Access to Florida Schools

https://ffrf.org/news/news-releases/item/20227-ffrf-blasts-governmental-ties-with-church

Freedom From Religion Foundation (FFRF) sent a letter to two Florida School districts complaining that the high schools are engaging in religious activity. FFRF and the Central Florida Freethought Community claimed that the high schools in both districts discriminated against atheists who wanted to distribute freethinking materials to students. Both atheist groups claim that the schools allowed prayer sessions for athletes, clothes with bible verses, and weekly religious services at Apopka High School.

Philadelphia School Disciplines Security Officer for Following Religious Dress Requirements

http://www.usatoday.com/story/news/nation/2014/03/06/philadelphia-schools-beards-bias/6111505/

http://www.justice.gov/opa/pr/2014/March/14-crt-235.html

The U.S. Department of Justice filed a lawsuit on behalf of school security officer Siddiq Abu-Bakr against a Philadelphia school district. Siddiq and similar individuals suffered religious discrimination when the district instituted a dress code that prohibited police officers and security officers from having beards longer than one-quarter inch. Siddiq notified his supervisor that he could not follow the new dress code because it interfered with his Islamic beliefs. As a result, Siddiq received a written reprimand for violating the policy.

Coach Fired Because of His Religious Obligations

http://www.northjersey.com/news/former-teaneck-hs-rowing-coach-may-sue-over-dismissal-1.659267

Pastor Clemens Reinke was also the high school rowing coach of Teaneck High School. Reinke was fired because he could not attend Sunday matches on account of his pastoral obligations. Following his termination, parents of the rowing team filed complaints against the school board for improper termination, and Pastor Reinke may file his own lawsuit against the school district.

Coach Told to Stop Praying and Stop Sharing His Faith

http://www.nydailynews.com/news/national/n-high-school-football-coach-caught-baptizing-players-article-1.1601977

Mooresville High School Coach Hal Capps was prohibited from sharing his faith with students after Freedom From Religion Foundation discovered a Twitter video in which Capps attended the baptism of several students.

School administrators told Capps he could no longer instigate team prayers. Throughout the controversy, precipitated by a demand letter from FFRF, players expressed their support for their coach and their determination to continue team prayer.

Public School Students Told Not to Participate in Charity Work

http://americanhumanist.org/news/details/2014-02-minnesota-public-school-told-to-end-field-trips-to-c

Public school students in New Hope, Minnesota, assembled nutritional meals for impoverished children overseas. The students worked with a religious charitable organization, Feed My Starving Children. Upon learning of this arrangement, the American Humanists Association sent a threatening letter to school officials, demanding that the district stop participating with the charitable program.

Purdue University Rejects Donor's Plaque Because It Referenced God

http://blog.libertyinstitute.org/2014/02/purdue-university-rejects-reference-to.html

When Purdue University asked Dr. McCracken to supply the language to dedicate a conference room on a plaque, he chose an inscription to honor his parents, "To those who seek to better the world through the understanding of God's physical laws and innovation of practical solutions." Purdue refused his use of "God's physical laws" out of a concern that it would be seen as an endorsement of religion. After Liberty Institute intervened and legal action was threatened, Purdue University allowed McCracken to use his language on his plaque.

Nativity Scene in Fertile, Minnesota, Challenged by Freedom From Religion Foundation

http://ffrf.org/legal/other-legal-successes/item/20286-ffrf-prevents-nativity-scene-from-returning-to-school-cafeteria-february-28-2014

Freedom From Religion Foundation wrote a letter to the Board of Education in Fertile, Minnesota, complaining about a Nativity scene in a school cafeteria. After receiving the demand letter, the district temporarily removed the display and then put it back after a school board vote. The district's attorney decided that, in the future, the Nativity scene will not be displayed without other holiday décor.

Atheist Group Demands Religious Poster Torn Down in Classroom

http://ffrf.org/legal/other-legal-successes/item/20178-religious-poster-becomes-picture-thing-of-the-past-february-21-2014

Freedom From Religion Foundation demanded that a poster with a religious message be removed from Bernard Campbell Middle School in Lee's Summit, Missouri. The district ensured that the poster, which quoted Scripture, was taken down.

Iowa State University Remove Bibles from Campus Hotels

http://www.adfmedia.org/files/IowaStateUniversityLetter.pdf

After receiving a threatening demand letter from Freedom From Religion Foundation, Iowa State University pulled all Bibles from guest rooms on campus. FFRF claimed that the presences of these Bibles constituted a violation of the Establishment Clause.

Pro-Life Group Restricted by School District

http://www.thenewstribune.com/2014/02/19/3057104/wilson-high-student-claims-school.html

Student leaders in the Wilson Students for Life club contend that its group is not receiving fair treatment by school administrators. It has not been allowed to host a day of silence or a candlelight vigil. Furthermore, while the club has displayed some posters, still others have been prohibited because of their strong pro-life message. Wilson Students for Life argue that its message cannot be censored just because it is controversial.

Teacher Attacked for Showing Parts of Creationism Videos

http://www.elkharttruth.com/news/schools/2014/02/19/Concord-High-biology-teacher-accused-of-teaching-creationism.html

High school biology teacher Ryan Culp presented multiple origin theories, including creationism, which he presented through video clips. When the Freedom From Religion Foundation learned of Culp's presentation, FFRF sent a threatening demand letter to Concord Community Schools Superintendent Wayne Stubbs asserting that it is illegal even to present the creationist point of view in public schools.

Group Demands Historic School Tear Down Cross from Top

http://www.foxnews.com/us/2014/02/12/group-wants-kansas-school-to-remove-cross-from-top-building/

Americans United for Separation of Church and State sent a threatening letter to school administrators in Kansas, demanding a cross be removed from the top of Spearville Elementary School. Built in 1925 as a Catholic school, the building was transferred to the local public school district in 1975.

Humanist Group Objects to Pledge of Allegiance

http://americanhumanist.org/system/storage/2/06/d/5023/Matawan-Aberdeen_Regional_School_District_Letter.pdf

The American Humanist Association (AHA) sent a demand letter to Matawan-Aberdeen Regional School District in Aberdeen, New Jersey, to stop the daily practice of reciting the American Pledge of Allegiance. Objecting to the phrase "Under God" in the pledge, AHA alleged that this daily practice of recitation constitutes a violation of the New Jersey Constitution. If AHA's demands are not met, it threatened litigation.

School Secretary Not Allowed to Assist After-School Christian Club in Any Way

http://ffrf.org/legal/other-legal-successes/item/20182-good-news-club-permission-slips-no-longer-handled-by-teacher-january-28-2014

After receiving a demand letter from Freedom From Religion Foundation, the Seminole County School Board decided that an elementary school secretary would not be permitted to even collect permission slips for an after-school club because the club included Christian content.

School Bans Religious Group from Advertising in School Flyer

http://ffrf.org/legal/other-legal-successes/item/20184-%E2%80%9Call-pro-dad%E2%80%9D-meetings-no-longer-advertised-in-public-school-flyer-january-28-2014

"All Pro Dad" is a fatherhood program that uses a football theme to advocate for the importance of fatherhood. Following a letter from the Freedom From Religion Foundation, White Bluffs Elementary School has banned "All Pro Dad" from advertising in its all-school flyer because "All Pro Dad" programming includes religious content.

Atheist Group Demand Removal of Religious Symbols in Classroom

http://ffrf.org/legal/other-legal-successes/item/20183-ffrf-remove-religious-symbols-in-elementary-classroom-january-14-2014

Decorations in an elementary school classroom in Giles County, Tennessee, included religious images. After Freedom From Religion Foundation (FFRF) sent a demand letter to Giles County Superintendent, school administrators forced all teachers to remove religious symbols from their classrooms.

UNDENIABLE: THE SURVEY OF HOSTILITY TO RELIGION IN AMERICA

Teacher Forced to Remove Religious Poster in Her Classroom
http://ffrf.org/legal/other-legal-successes/item/20181-illegal-poster-removed-from-texas-classroom-january-9-2014
Freedom From Religion Foundation (FFRF) sent a letter to Rusk Independent School District in Texas, demanding a high school teacher remove a poster from her classroom that included a Bible verse. The school district acquiesced to FFRF's demands, and the teacher was forced to remove the poster.

Atheist Group Attacks Christmas Sign Outside of School
http://ffrf.org/legal/other-legal-successes/item/19881-ffrf-takes-down-religious-sign-at-west-virginia-school-january-3-2014
During Christmas season, the marquee for Buffalo Elementary included the message, "Wise Men Still Seek Him." Sending a demand letter, Freedom From Religion Foundation (FFRF) successfully intimidated the school district's superintendent into removing the holiday message.

Ex-Employee Sues Catholic School Because of its Religiously Informed Employment Policies
http://www.bostonglobe.com/metro/2014/01/29/dorchester-man-files-discrimination-against-catholic-school-says-lost-job-because-was-gay-married/oKswVITMsOrruEbhsOsOeN/story.html
Fontbonne Academy, a Roman Catholic girls' prep school, hired Matthew Barrett as the food services director. When the school learned that Mr. Barrett was married to another man, it rescinded its offer of employment. Sponsored by the Sisters of St. Joseph of Boston, this school affirms the Catholic church's teaching on sexuality and marriage. Still, Barrett, represented by GLAD counsel, filed a formal complaint with the Massachusetts Commission Against Discrimination in an attempt to coerce the school to violate its employment policies as a religious school.

FFRF Condemns Church's Invitation to Christmas Activities
http://ffrf.org/legal/other-legal-successes/item/19879-ffrf-ends-religious-advertising-in-ohio-elementary-school-december-23-2013
When the Freedom From Religion Foundation (FFRF) received word that South Bloomfield Elementary School in Ashville, Ohio, permitted the distribution of invitations to a local church's Christmas event, it wrote a letter of complaint to the superintendent. The superintendent told the FFRF that he would review the district's distribution policy.

226   FIRST LIBERTY

ATTACKS IN THE SCHOOLHOUSE

Christian School Pressured Out of Voucher Program Because of Religious Beliefs

https://www.au.org/blogs/wall-of-separation/equal-education-nc-christian-school-rejects-vouchers-after-discrimination

Myrtle Grove Christian School in Wilmington, North Carolina, had been approved to receive funds through the state's "Opportunity Scholarship" program. However, when gay activists discovered that the school refused to enroll LGBT students due to its religious beliefs, they vehemently protested the school's approval. The school succumbed to the pressure and voluntarily withdrew from the scholarship program.

Coaches Told to Cease Involvement in Prayers

http://ffrf.org/legal/other-legal-successes/item/19944-coaches-reigned-in-on-prayer-at-nc-high-school-december-20-2013

The Freedom From Religion Foundation sent a letter to the superintendent for South Central High School in Winterville, North Carolina, requesting a reminder to all coaches not to associate themselves with any prayers. The district's attorney confirmed its compliance.

School Choir Told "No Christmas Carols"

http://blog.libertyinstitute.org/2013/12/anderson-high-school-choir-members.html

For several years, members of the Anderson High School Choir in Austin, Texas, sang Christmas carols and other seasonal music at private homes. However, an attorney for the district advised against the Christmas carols because of a misconception that including religious songs would be an Establishment Clause violation. Accordingly, Austin I.S.D. administrators discouraged members of the Anderson High School Choir from singing any Christmas carols. Liberty Institute responded by sending a letter that assured administrators of the constitutionality of students' engaging in private speech through singing religious songs.

School Attempts to Block Christian Student Club

http://blog.libertyinstitute.org/2013/12/long-island-school-says-christian-clubs.html

http://blog.libertyinstitute.org/2014/05/under-new-threat-clients-religious-club.html

When John Raney, a student at Ward Melville High School in Setauket, New York, applied to form a Christian club, school administrators simply ignored his application for more than two months. Only when Raney's mother asked the principal about her son's application did the student learn why his club had been denied. Religious clubs, according to school administrators, are illegal in New York public schools. John then contacted Liberty Institute, who sent the school officials a letter warning them of the risk of legal action. The school district reversed their decision within seven hours of receiving the demand letter, and the club currently makes a positive impact in the community by fighting a growing problem of teen drug use and suicide.

Christian Group Reprimanded for Mentioning God During School Event
http://ffrf.org/legal/other-legal-successes/item/19872-ffrf-halts-proselytizing-group%E2%80%99s-access-to-families-at-public-school-december-19-2013
Points of Light (PoL), a Christian service organization, hosted a barbecue at a "Back to School Night" alongside other school activities at Frick Middle School in Oakland, California. However, when the Freedom From Religion Foundation heard that PoL had mentioned God during the event, it sent a letter to Oakland Unified School District Superintendent Gary Yee complaining about PoL's activity. Consequently, the school district rebuked PoL for its statements and informed them that they could not promote Christianity while on campus.

Atheist Group Scares School Away from Holding Graduation Ceremony at Local Church
http://www.cantonrep.com/article/20131218/NEWS/131219242
http://www.cantonrep.com/article/20140601/News/140609985
When the Freedom From Religion Foundation found out that Hoover High School held graduation ceremonies at a local church auditorium, it sent a demand letter that claimed such a practice violated the Constitution by forcing people into a church, and instructed the school to find a new location. The students started a petition to keep the graduation at the church, but school officials decided to move the ceremony to a local civic center instead.

Atheist Group Bullies School Superintendent into Removing Personal Nativity Scene
http://ffrf.org/legal/other-legal-successes/item/19877-ffrf-takes-down-nativity-scene-at-ohio-school-district-december-18-2013
The Freedom From Religion Foundation sent a letter to Judith Robinson, superintendent of Green Local Schools in Ohio, demanding that she remove the Nativity scene displayed in her office window. Robinson immediately complied.

Elementary Student Instructed to Remove Religion from Award-Winning Speech

http://tampa.cbslocal.com/2013/12/16/controversy-over-5th-graders-religion-speech/

After fifth-grade student Zachary Golob-Drake won an award for a speech about the history of using religion to justify murder, he was scheduled to present the speech to the fourth and fifth grade classes of his own school. However, the assistant principal stripped him of his award and told him that he had to rewrite the speech, remove the religious references, or not compete. Following a long conversation with Golob-Drake's mother, his award was returned, and permission slips detailing the speech were given to the other parents to decide whether to let their children attend.

Band Director Prohibited from Any Affiliation with Student Prayers

http://ffrf.org/legal/other-legal-successes/item/19943-band-director-no-longer-directing-prayer-at-sc-high-school-december-12-2013

The band director at a high school in Rock Hill School District Three in Rock Hill, South Carolina, gave a signal to his students to begin performances, which started with prayer. The Freedom From Religion Foundation frowned on this action and labeled it a constitutional violation in a letter to the school district. The school's legal counsel informed the FFRF that the band director was instructed to cease signaling the start because of its association with the opening prayer.

School Forbids Flyers with Bible Verses

http://www.adfmedia.org/News/PRDetail/8691

When a seventh-grade student at Robert E. Clark Middle School in Kansas City, Kansas, posted flyers promoting a "See You at the Pole" event, a school counselor told the student that the fliers were illegal due to a district-wide policy that banned the distribution of religious materials. The school then removed and destroyed the flyers. A religious liberties group stepped in to defend the student's constitutional religious freedoms. The school removed the ban on distributing religious materials, and the lawsuit was dropped.

School Administrators Hide Christmas Cards and Suppress Teachers' Religious Freedoms

http://blog.libertyinstitute.org/2013/12/in-school-in-troubling-case-of-blatant.html

http://blog.libertyinstitute.org/2013/12/liberty-institute-restores-religious.html

Brooklet Elementary School in Brooklet, Georgia, had a long tradition of displaying Christmas cards on the hallways of the school. Mysteriously, the cards disappeared after Thanksgiving break when administrators reportedly ordered their relocation away from the students' view, which came after a demand from Americans United for Separation of Church and State. School officials insisted they were merely following the law. However, reports surfaced that teachers were ordered to walk away from student-led prayer and remove Bible verses or religious sayings from their email signatures. Following an intervention by Liberty Institute, the Bulloch County Board of Education issued a notice supporting religious liberty, but persisted in its disallowance of religion in email signatures.

ACLU Threatens School for Playing Christmas Carols
http://www.charismanews.com/us/41862-sc-school-bans-religious-christmas-carols-even-without-mention-of-christ
York Preparatory Academy, a public charter school in South Carolina, decided to prohibit students from playing "Joy to the World" and "O Come, All Ye Faithful" after receiving a mass letter from the ACLU threatening legal action against any school that allowed Christmas carols in school productions. After protest from students and parents, the school contacted a religious liberties group, who rebutted the ACLU's misleading demand letter. After being properly informed, the school decided to include the songs in its holiday concert and removed the ban.

Catholic School Derided for Adhering to Religious Beliefs
http://bigstory.ap.org/article/catholic-school-fires-gay-teacher-drawing-protest
When a teacher at Holy Ghost Preparatory School told administrators that he was going to obtain a marriage license with his same-sex partner, the school released him from employment in accordance with its religious beliefs about homosexual conduct. Consequently, the public lashed out at the school on social media, and several alumni announced the discontinuation of their financial support.

Antireligion Group Ends Prayers at Department Thanksgiving Celebration
http://ffrf.org/legal/other-legal-successes/item/19728-ffrf-ends-prayers-during-employee-meetings-at-north-carolina-education-lottery-december-6-2013
The Freedom From Religion Foundation heard that a department within the North Carolina Education Lottery (NCEL) prayed before their annual Thanksgiving celebration and sent a letter condemning the practice. The NCEL responded by eliminating all prayers and religious activities at employee functions.

School Commanded to Eliminate Creationism from Gym Class

https://www.aclu.org/religion-belief/aclu-ohio-warns-public-school-against-allowing-local-clergy-teach-creationism-gym

The Lebanon School District in Lebanon, Ohio, allowed gym classes to be led by an organization called "His Pins," a program headed by local clergy who teach creationism alongside archery. The ACLU of Ohio opposed the class due to its religious content and demanded that the school cancel the program.

School Choirs Participate in Christmas Concert Despite Atheist Groups' Complaint

http://seattle.cbslocal.com/2013/12/05/aclu-protests-high-school-choirs-singing-in-church-concert/

School choirs from Kalispell High School and Whitefish High School in Kalispell, Montana, accepted an invitation to contribute in the "Peace on Earth Community Christmas Celebration," a Christmas concert held at a local Mormon church. The ACLU and the FFRF immediately protested, claiming that such involvement violated the Establishment Clause. The schools chose to participate anyway.

FFRF Tells School to Quit Praying Before Meetings

http://www.presstelegram.com/social-affairs/20131203/national-group-asks-bellflower-unified-school-board-to-stop-prayers-at-meetings

Bellflower Unified School District in Los Angeles, California, has a tradition of opening school board meetings with prayer. The Freedom From Religion Foundation (FFRF) heard about the practice and sent a demand letter commanding its cessation. The district refused to comment or acknowledge the letter.

School Faculty Told to Quit Praying

http://ffrf.org/legal/other-legal-successes/item/19755-faculty-barred-from-religious-extracurricular-at-new-york-school-december-3-2013

The Freedom From Religion Foundation sent a letter to Greer Rychcik, the superintendent of Hyde Park School District in New York, requesting her to tell all faculty members to stop all participation in student prayer groups. Rychcik agreed to send along a reminder to remain neutral towards religion.

Antireligion Group Condemns Religious Youth Motivational Speaker

http://ffrf.org/news/news-releases/item/19286-ffrf-probes-sexist-texas-school-speaker

When the Freedom From Religion Foundation heard that a popular religious motivational speaker was scheduled to present at several high schools in

Texas, it launched an investigation to uncover anything that would facilitate an argument for keeping him out of the schools.

Elementary Student Ordered to Remove God from Poem
http://radio.foxnews.com/toddstarnes/top-stories/school-orders-child-to-remove-god-from-poem.html
A first grade girl at West Marion Elementary School in North Carolina wrote a poem to read at a school assembly for Veteran's Day that honored her two Vietnam War veteran grandfathers. However, when school officials discovered that the poem contained references to God, they ordered the child to remove the references.

University Removes Bibles from Guest Rooms
http://ffrf.org/legal/other-legal-successes/item/19941-ffrf-ousts-bibles-from-university-of-wisconsin-extension-lodging-december-1-2013
When the Freedom From Religion Foundation discovered that the University of Wisconsin-Extension kept a Gideon Bible in each of the guest rooms in its conference center, it sent a letter demanding the removal of the Bibles. The university caved and confirmed that the Bibles would be promptly removed.

FFRF Condemns Christian Football Coach's Mentoring
http://ffrf.org/news/news-releases/item/15113-ffrf-claims-victory-in-ridgeland-school-coach-complaint
Mark Mariakis, head football coach at Ridgeland High School, drove his football players to pregame meals served at a local church, encouraged attendance at a summer Christian football camp, and permitted the team's adoption of a chaplain. The Freedom From Religion Foundation heard about Coach Mariakis's actions and demanded that the school district superintendent halt his involvement. The superintendent responded by confirming the discontinuation of the team chaplain and any involvement in religious activities, but refused to stop serving pregame meals at the church.

West Virginia University Professor Reprimanded for Pro-Life Involvement
http://blog.libertyinstitute.org/2013/11/west-virginia-university-school-of.html
Dr. Byron C. Calhoun, M.D., a West Virginia University School of Medicine Professor and Vice Chairman of the Department of Obstetrics and Gynecology at the West Virginia University Hospital's Charleston Division, volunteered his personal time to act as a national medical advisor for the National Institute of Family and Life Advocates, a pro-life advocacy group, due to his religious convictions on the sanctity of life. After Dr. Calhoun's involvement received media attention, the university threatened him with a written, professional

reprimand. However, under the threat of legal action by Liberty Institute, the university backed off and claimed it never officially filed the reprimand against Dr. Calhoun despite having provided him with a copy.

Atheist Organization Axes Graduation Ceremony Held in Local Church
http://ffrf.org/legal/other-legal-successes/item/20180-ffrf-ends-graduations-in-church-november-21-2014
The Lewis Center for Educational Research Academy for Academic Excellence, a small charter school in Apple Valley, California, held its graduation ceremonies in a local church. The Freedom From Religion Foundation learned of the school's practice and ordered the school to cease holding the ceremonies in any sanctuaries, stating that the practice unconstitutionally forced individuals into church. The school informed the FFRF that the graduation ceremonies would be moved into their newly built gymnasium in the future.

Student Forced to Choose Between God and Graduation
http://www.redstate.com/diary/goppolitx/2013/11/20/cuba-new-mexico-high-school-student-forced-to-choose-between-graduation-and-god/
Liberty Thompson, a devout Seventh-day Adventist and a senior at Cuba High School in Cuba, New Mexico, was on track to be the valedictorian of her class and have enough college credits to graduate high school with an associate degree. However, Thompson found out that the school changed the day of graduation from Friday to Saturday, which is Thompson's Sabbath day. Thompson and her father attempted to appeal the change to the Cuba Independent Schools' school board, but the board refused to let either speak about the issue at all and threatened to arrest Thompson's father or ban him from campus. When the story went public, the board agreed to at least hear the appeal, but insisted that no changes would be forthcoming.

Freedom From Religion Foundation Purges Meal Blessings at School Meetings
http://ffrf.org/legal/other-legal-successes/item/19551-no-more-blessings-at-mandatory-employee-meetings-in-south-carolina-school-district-november-19-2013
Berkeley County School District served lunch at its annual in-service meetings for transportation employees, and a worker said a prayer over the food. The FFRF heard about the prayer and wrote a demand letter condemning the action. The school district consequently agreed to discontinue any prayers in the future.

Humanist Group Bullies Small Schools into Cancelling Annual Christmas Toy Drive

http://townhall.com/columnists/toddstarnes/2013/11/18/school-cancels-christmas-toy-drive-after-humanists-threaten-to-sue-n1748653/page/full
http://www.9news.com/news/article/365198/188/School-drops-Operation-Christmas-Child-after-lawsuit-threat

East Point Academy and SkyView Academy, small charter schools in South Carolina and Colorado, regularly participated in Operation Christmas Child, an annual toy drive for underprivileged children that is sponsored by Samaritan's Purse, an international Christian relief and evangelist organization. Even though the schools' involvement was completely voluntary and nonreligious, the American Humanist Association (AHA) threatened the schools with a lawsuit. Rather than risk a legal battle with the superiorly funded AHA, both principals had no choice but to cancel the program instead of fighting an AHA lawsuit.

College Campus Bus Driver Forced to Resign for Praying

http://www.nj.com/news/index.ssf/2013/11/rutgers_students_rally_for_beloved_bus_driver_who_says_he_lost_his_job_for_praying.html

Stan McNeil, a beloved bus driver for a company contracted by Rutgers University, prayed for a woman in a wheelchair before she rode on the bus. The interaction was captured on video; and, upon seeing the recording, the bus company told McNeil to resign. When students took to social media to call for McNeil's reinstatement, the bus company claimed that McNeil's resignation stemmed from a failure to use the required number of straps to secure the disabled student's wheelchair.

School Pressured into Removing Jesus Painting

http://www.dispatch.com/content/stories/local/2013/11/15/Muskingum-County-Jesus-painting-removed.html

A student at John Glenn High School in New Concord, Ohio, complained about a "Good Shepherd" painting of Jesus located in the school's office. The ACLU also threatened the school district with a lawsuit unless they removed the picture. The school district caved beneath the threats and ordered that the painting be moved to a local church.

Arizona School Axes School Board Meeting Opening Prayers

http://www.azcentral.com/community/mesa/articles/20131112mesa-school-board-ends-opening-prayer-custom.html

The Mesa Public Schools governing board decided to end all opening prayers before public meetings after the board's legal counsel advised them that they would lose imminent lawsuits if the practice continued.

Florida School Districts Adopt Discriminatory Textbook

http://www.wftv.com/news/news/local/hundreds-prepare-protest-against-islam-chapter-vol/nbhJt/
Along with several other Florida school districts, Volusia County School District adopted a world history textbook that dedicates a large portion of its teaching to Islam, while excluding other religions.

School Bus Driver Fired for Praying with Students

http://www.startribune.com/local/south/230757861.html?page=all&prepage=1&c=y#continue
George Nathanial, a pastor in Richfield, Minnesota, also drove school buses for a company contracted by a local school district. During the bus rides, Nathaniel led prayers with and for the students. Complaints began to surface from the school district, and the bus company commanded Nathaniel to quit praying. However, Nathaniel continued his prayers, and the bus company consequently terminated his employment.

Humanist Group Tries to Stop Teacher from Attending Club Meetings

http://americanhumanist.org/news/details/2013-11-humanists-file-suit-over-weekly-prayers-in-missouri
http://www1.komu.com/news/student-in-prayer-suit-against-fayette-district-speaks-out/
The Fellowship of Christian Students Club (FCSC) was permitted to hold weekly prayer meetings in a teacher's classroom before classes began at Fayette High School in Missouri. The teacher often sat in on the meetings, much to the consternation of the American Humanist Association (AHA). The AHA filed a lawsuit claiming that the teacher's indirect involvement in the FCSC's meetings constituted a reckless disregard of other students' constitutional rights. Additionally, the AHA complained about a Bible that the teacher had on her desk. The school district stated that it "will vigorously defend against any claim that the District has taken actions which violate any person's First Amendment rights."

Atheist Group Condemns Student-Led Prayers at School Pep Rally

http://ffrf.org/legal/other-legal-successes/item/19734-rallies-at-oklahoma-high-school-will-include-pep-but-no-prayer-november-4-2013
When the Freedom From Religion Foundation heard that faculty members at Alva High School in Alva, Oklahoma, allowed student-led prayer circles

at school pep rallies, it wrote a demand letter that denounced the practice. In response, Superintendent Steve Parkhurst pointed out that the prayers were voluntary and student-led, but he affirmed that faculty members were reminded not to participate.

School Sued for Allowing Students to Give Their Testimonies

http://americanhumanist.org/news/details/2013-11-mississippi-high-school-student-victorious-in-lawsui

After administrators of Northwest Rankin High School in Flowood, Mississippi, allowed several students to give their Christian testimonies in front of the student body, the American Humanist Association filed a complaint in federal court alleging that the school violated the First Amendment's Establishment Clause. The U.S. Southern District Court of Mississippi handed down a judgment that required the school to implement a new policy on religious activities at school.

Freedom From Religion Foundation Criticizes Student-Led Bible Reading

http://ffrf.org/legal/other-legal-successes/item/19550-ffrf-ends-prayers-during-morning-announcements-in-alabama-high-school-october-31-2013

Hokes Bluff High School in Etowah County, Alabama, opened school days with student-led reading of Scripture and announcements over the school's intercom system. The FFRF wrote a demand letter to Superintendent Alan Cosby that condemned the practice and called for its termination.

School Tells Student "No Bibles at School"

http://aclj.org/free-speech-2/victory-elementary-school-kids-can-bring-bibles-to-school

A fifth grader in the Los Angeles Unified School District was told by his teacher that he could not read his Bible or bring it to school. The student's mother contacted a religious liberties group for help, and the group showed the school how its policy violated the student's First Amendment rights. The principal reversed the unconstitutional rule and permitted the student to bring his Bible to school and read it outside of class.

Atheist Group Attempts to Intimidate Schools After Their Choirs Sing Hymns

http://ffrf.org/news/news-releases/item/19015-public-school-choruses-are-not-church-choirs

Four public school choirs in south-central Pennsylvania agreed to perform in a musical event held at a local Presbyterian church called the Choral Festival. The FFRF found out that the concert included several religious songs and consequently sent demand letters to all four schools claiming constitutional violations. However, the attorneys for the school district denied any wrongdoing and rebuked the FFRF for their mischaracterization of First Amendment law.

Atheist Group Succeeds in Banning Bibles and Candy Canes from Elementary School

http://ffrf.org/news/news-releases/item/18957-ffrf-halts-tenn-teacher-bible-distribution-proselytizing

The Freedom From Religion Foundation wrote a demand letter to the Franklin County School District after it found out that teachers in one of the district's elementary schools had handed out Bibles and candy canes with the story of its Christian origin attached. An attorney for the district confirmed that the practices would be halted immediately.

ACLU Mass-Mails Condemnation of Prayer to Hundreds of Schools

http://wkms.org/post/aclu-tn-advises-schools-game-day-prayers
http://blogs.tennessean.com/politics/2013/tenn-gop-urges-school-districts-to-ignore-aclu-letter/

The ACLU of Tennessee sent a letter to 135 Tennessee public schools that denounced prayer before football games and told school authorities that such an activity is unconstitutional.

School Attacked for Hosting Christian Speaker

http://www.pressherald.com/news/ACLU_asks_Biddeford_schools_to_apologize_for_religious_presentations.html?pagenum=full

After Pastors John and Debbie Phillips' niece was killed in the infamous Columbine High School shooting, they founded Life Choices Ministries (LCM), an organization that makes presentations focused on tolerance and respect. Believing that an LCM event would benefit students, Biddeford Schools Superintendent Jeremy Ray authorized the Phillips to present in Biddeford schools. However, the ACLU of Maine discovered LCM's Christian origins and consequently demanded that the school district apologize for subjecting students to "overtly religious presentations." Ray apologized if anyone was offended, but stood firm on the permissibility of LCM's presentation.

Freedom From Religion Foundation Halts School Lunch Ministry

http://ffrf.org/news/news-releases/item/19140-ffrf-halts-proselytizers-at-school-lunches-october-29-2013

The FFRF wrote a demand letter to school officials at Pedro Menendez High School in St. Augustine, Florida, in order to eliminate local youth pastors' practice of visiting with students during the lunch hour. The school consequently "terminated [the pastors'] standing invitation to visit the school at lunchtime."

Pregame Prayers Condemned by Anti-Religion Group
http://ffrf.org/legal/other-legal-successes/item/19622-prayers-are-dropped-from-pregame-routine-in-oregon-high-school-october-29-2013
When a complaint regarding pregame prayers at Aloha High School football games in Oregon reached the Freedom From Religion Foundation, it wrote a letter accusing the school district of violating the Establishment Clause of the First Amendment. The school principal eliminated all prayers and faith-based activity before games.

Teachers Ordered to Remove Religious Shirts
http://ffrf.org/legal/other-legal-successes/item/19873-ffrf-stops-teachers-from-wearing-%E2%80%9Cjesus-is-my-hero-shirts%E2%80%9D-october-23-2013
Teachers at the Butchel Community Learning Center in Akron, Ohio, joined in celebrating school spirit by wearing donated T-shirts that promoted the school's athletic program. However, the Freedom From Religion Foundation complained to the school superintendent that the shirts were inappropriate because they also contained messages such as "God's Got Our Back." The school district confiscated the shirts and returned them to the donor.

School Cuts Invocation Pursuant to Atheists' Demands
http://ffrf.org/legal/other-legal-successes/item/19611-ffrf-prevents-future-prayers-and-discrimination-at-ohio-high-school-october-22-2013
The Freedom From Religion Foundation wrote a demand letter to the superintendent of Western Brown High School in Mt. Orab, Ohio, after hearing that there had been a prayer during the National Honor Society induction ceremony at the school. Superintendent Peggy McKinney denied any wrongdoing, but ultimately agreed to drop all invocations from future ceremonies.

School Refuses to Allow Prayer by Military Chaplain During Veterans Day Ceremony
http://www.poconorecord.com/apps/pbcs.dll/article?AID=/20131021/NEWS90/310210319
American Legion Post 311 regularly participated in Wallenpaupack Area High School's Veterans Day ceremony. Every year, Post 311 led the ceremony, which included an opening prayer from the group's chaplain. However, District Superintendent Michael Silsby informed Post 311 Commander William

Kemmett that a prayer would not be allowed this year after the district received a complaint from the Freedom From Religious Foundation about prayer in schools. Post 311 decided to take a stand for their religious beliefs and withdrew from the ceremony.

Atheist Group Bullies School into Banning Christmas Carols
http://ffrf.org/legal/other-legal-successes/item/19741-religious-teachings-will-be-prohibited-during-music-classes-at-michigan-elementary-school-oct-16-2013
Every year, students at Emmons Lake Elementary School in Caledonia, Michigan, put on a holiday concert at Christmas. When the Freedom From Religion Foundation heard from a third party complainant that some of the songs contained traditional Christian themes, they immediately contacted Superintendent Randy Rodriquez to object. The school district assured the FFRF that they would address the situation, and the original complainant confirmed that the traditional carols had been barred.

Wisconsin High School Attempts to Suspend School Choir's Christmas Concerts
http://www.wausaudailyherald.com/article/20131031/WDH01/310310273/West-choir-director-says-he-directed-suspend-Master-Singers
http://dailycaller.com/2013/10/14/wausau-school-superintendent-backs-down-in-confused-war-on-christmas/
Wausau West High School has an elite choir group called the Master Singers that performs at the school's winter concert and in other venues. School authorities informed Choral Programs Director Phil Buch that the choir must either sing five secular songs for each religious song in their performances or sing no religious music at all. Consequently, Buch decided to disband the group. The community rose up in protest against the school's restrictions on the choir, causing the school to retract its position and allow the Master Singers to resume their scheduled performances as originally planned.

School Tells Student That Writing About God Is Not Allowed
http://radio.foxnews.com/toddstarnes/top-stories/school-tells-child-she-cant-write-about-god.html
http://blog.libertyinstitute.org/2013/10/10-year-old-shelby-county-school.html#more
When Erin Shead, a ten-year-old student at Lucy Elementary School in Millington, Tennessee, was given an assignment to write about someone she idolized, she decided to write about God. However, after turning in her paper, Shead's teacher told her that she could not write about God, but

instead approved Shead's second choice: Michael Jackson. Additionally, the teacher told Shead that she had to take her paper about God home because it could not remain on school property. Liberty Institute stepped in to inform the school district of Shead's constitutional freedom to talk about God in school. The school authorities consequently allowed Shead to turn in her original paper, which was awarded an A.

Football Coach Instructed to Not Participate in Prayer
http://ffrf.org/legal/other-legal-successes/item/19876-ffrf-helps-end-coach-led-prayer-october-15-2013
Football players at West Linn High School in Tualatin, Oregon, consistently circled together for prayer at their football games. Assistant Coach Art Williams regularly joined the players in their practice until the Freedom From Religion Foundation took action. The FFRF wrote a demand letter to Superintendent William Rhodes calling for the immediate termination of Coach Williams's prayers. The school district adhered to the FFRF's directive and ordered Coach Williams to abstain from joining the players in their prayers.

Teacher Ordered to Remove Pledge of Allegiance Poster Because of Its Reference to God
http://ffrf.org/legal/other-legal-successes/item/19135-teacher-freedom-%E2%80%98comes-from-god%E2%80%99
A social studies teacher at Big Rapids High School in Michigan displayed a poster that included the message that "our freedom ultimately comes from God" alongside the Pledge of Allegiance. The Freedom From Religion Foundation complained to Superintendent Tim Haist about the reference to God, and the teacher was ordered to remove the poster.

Antireligion Organization Shuts Down "See You at the Pole" Event
http://ffrf.org/legal/other-legal-successes/item/19293-ffrf-ceases-see-you-at-the-pole-event-october-14-2013
The principal and a teacher at Columbian High School in Tiffin, Ohio, helped organize the "See You at the Pole" event at their school. The Freedom From Religion Foundation immediately complained to Don Coletta, the district superintendent, about the school authorities' involvement. Coletta buckled under the FFRF's pressure and promised to prohibit such conduct in the future.

High School Football Coach Commanded to Cease Prayers

http://www.tampabay.com/blogs/gradebook/atheist-group-calls-on-pasco-school-district-to-end-football-coach-led/2147304

Zephyrhills High School football coach Reggie Roberts regularly led his players in prayer with the support of his team. When Superintendent Kurt Browning found out, he sent a memo to the entire school district ordering all coaches to abstain from engaging in prayer in their official capacities. The Freedom From Religion Foundation also followed up after hearing about Roberts's prayers, insisting that Browning put a permanent end to such actions.

University Blocks Peaceful Pro-Life Demonstration

http://www.americanfreedomlawcenter.org/case/center-for-bio-ethical-reform-inc-et-al-v-dennis-r-black-et-al/

The Center for Bio-Ethical Reform, Inc. (CBR), a California-based pro-life organization, partnered with the State University of New York at Buffalo (SUNY-Buffalo) chapter of Students for Life to bring CBR's Genocide Awareness Project (GAP) to the university campus. CBR's GAP is a traveling exhibit that parallels abortion to other historically recognized genocide events using graphic photomurals that unveil the atrocities of abortion. When CBR requested approval to use a location outside of the university Student Union building, university officials initially balked and refused to grant permission, even though other groups regularly used the location as a forum for similar activities. After being shown that such discrimination violated the First Amendment, the university reluctantly gave its consent to CBR. However, when CBR put up its display, a mob of SUNY-Buffalo students blocked the exhibit with umbrellas and bed sheets. The university refused to intervene, despite repeated requests from CBR and the mob's explicit violation of university regulations. Consequently, CBR filed a lawsuit against SUNY-Buffalo for its violation of CBR's First Amendment rights. A U.S. Federal Magistrate recommended a denial of SUNY-Buffalo's motion to dismiss, and the case is pending before the U.S. District Court for the Western District of New York.

ACLU Demands School Ban Gideons International

http://www.crossville-chronicle.com/local/x1836125005/BOE-OKs-settlement-with-ACLU

A teacher from Brown Elementary in Crossville, Tennessee, allowed members of Gideons International to come into the classroom and give Bibles to the students. When word of the distribution reached the ACLU of Tennessee, it wrote a demand letter to the Cumberland County Board of Education.

In response, the board agreed to a settlement that banned "Gideons International, or any other organization not solely composed of and led by students" from distributing any religious material during school hours.

Atheist Group Stops After-School Prayer Group

http://ffrf.org/legal/other-legal-successes/item/18835-ffrf-stops-school-sponsored-prayer-group-at-tennessee-elementary-september-24
Love Fellowship Baptist Church in Chattanooga, Tennessee, hosted a group that walked the halls in Hardy Elementary School after hours to pray for the school. Several school administrators, teachers, and students voluntarily joined the group. The Freedom From Religion Foundation heard about the group and complained about the practice in a demand letter sent to the school district's lawyer. The school responded by disallowing the group to continue its after-school prayers.

Florida School Tells Student that Wearing Cross Necklace Is Against School Policy

http://aclj.org/school-prayer/victory-school-allows-student-wear-cross-necklace
When a middle school student in Florida wore a cross necklace to school, the student's teacher informed him that the necklace was not allowed. In response, the student's father contacted a religious liberties group for help. The group provided the father with legal council that enabled him to show the legality of the cross necklace to the school principal, and the school consequently retracted its discriminatory stance.

School Attempts to Prohibit Teacher Participation in "See You at the Pole"

http://www.pacificjustice.org/1/post/2013/09/pji-attorneys-warn-school-district-not-to-silence-teacher-prayers-before-school.html
Bakersfield City School District (BCSD) sent a bulletin to all of the principals in its district that claimed that teachers could not participate in "See You at the Pole" events (nationally recognized, annual, student-led gatherings for prayer before school at the schools' flagpoles). Religious liberty attorneys urged the BCSD to retract their statement and noted that "teachers do not lose their rights to act as citizens and exercise their First Amendment freedoms when they are off the clock."

California School Restricts Local Church's Legal Distribution of Materials

http://aclj.org/school-prayer/victory-school-district-grants-equal-access-religious-speech
A church in California runs a state-approved after-school program called Release Time Religious and Moral Instruction. However, when the church

attempted to distribute informational flyers about the program, a local school district limited the church's distribution while giving other, nonreligious organizations free rein to hand out their materials. The church then reached out to religious liberty attorneys and was able to convince the school district to amend its discriminatory policy and give equal access to religious organizations.

School Considers Eliminating Prayer from Parent Teacher Organization Meetings

http://www.sewaneemessenger.com/front/index.php?id=1162925891841636726
The Franklin County School Board and the North Lake Parent Teacher Organization in Tennessee regularly opened their meetings with prayer. Upon discovering this practice, the Freedom From Religion Foundation ordered the Board and the PTO to end such practices. The board then scheduled a special meeting that allowed members of the community to listen in to the discussion about the FFRF's demands. Although the majority of the board supported continuance of the prayers—to the demonstrated approval of the community attendees through a standing ovation—a lone member of the board and the board's legal council advised a mere moment of silence in order to avoid the threat of litigation.

Atheist Group Demands Prohibition of Student-Led Prayer Before Football Games

http://www.timesfreepress.com/news/2013/sep/06/south-pittsburg-football-prayer-time-challenged/
South Pittsburg High School in Tennessee allows a student-led pregame prayer and worship service on the football field before all home football games called "Meet Me at the 50." When the Freedom From Religion Foundation received an anonymous complaint about the events, it wrote a demand letter to Marion County Superintendent of Schools Mark Griffith calling the practice unconstitutional. Griffith stated that the school had done nothing wrong and responded by filing suit to discover the complainant's identity.

Atheist Group Condemns Graduation Ceremony Due to Location in Local Church

http://ffrf.org/legal/other-legal-successes/item/18751-ffrf-halts-graduation-ceremony-at-church-september-3-2013
Hoover High School in North Canton, Ohio, regularly held graduation ceremonies at the nearby Faith Family Church. The Freedom From Religion Foundation wrote a demand letter to the school superintendent alleging

that this obligated students and their families to enter a church and was therefore unconstitutional. Pushed away from the church location through the FFRF's letter, the school began to seek another venue for future graduation ceremonies.

Freedom From Religion Foundation Intimidates School into Excluding Prayer

http://www.kxii.com/news/headlines/Complaint-stops-prayer-at-Pottsboro-football-games-221725621.html

When the Freedom From Religion Foundation found out that Pottsboro High School opened its football games with a prayer led by a local pastor, they sent a letter to the school superintendent demanding the cessation of the practice. The school bowed to the FFRF's request and exchanged the prayer for a moment of silence.

Atheist Organization Condemns Football Coach's Invitation to Worship Service

http://ffrf.org/news/news-releases/item/18633-ffrf-protests-church-service-sponsored-by-ark-school-and-coach

A high school football coach in Bryant, Arkansas, extended an open invitation on Facebook to a preseason worship service at a local church. When the Freedom From Religion Foundation learned of the invitation, they sent a demand letter to the school superintendent calling for the cancelation of the service, condemning it as "trampling" on the Constitution.

Freedom From Religion Foundation Opposes Vouchers for Lower Income Religious Families

http://ffrf.org/news/news-releases/item/18309-dangerous-wisconsin-voucher-scheme-proceeds

http://ffrf.org/news/news-releases/item/18609-where-is-the-%E2%80%98choice%E2%80%99?-catholic-schools-win-big-in-wis-voucher-scheme

When the Wisconsin legislature proposed a bill to expand private school vouchers for lower income families, the Freedom From Religion Foundation labeled the program as "dangerous" and "appalling" and called for Wisconsin citizens to reject the proposal. The Wisconsin legislature ignored the FFRF and passed the bill, giving disadvantaged religious families the opportunity to choose private education.

Freedom From Religion Foundation Attacks Prayer at High School Graduation

http://ffrf.org/legal/other-legal-successes/item/18685-ffrf-drops-minister-led-high-school-graduation-prayers-august-20-2013

When a student reported that Wallenpaupack Area High School in Hawley, Pennsylvania, allowed a local minister to lead an invocation and benediction at the school's graduation ceremony, the Freedom From Religion Foundation protested to the school superintendent that such actions were unconstitutional and called for their elimination. The school confirmed that they would "no longer have religious rituals as part of the commencement ceremony."

University Dismisses Newly Hired Bishop for Biblical Beliefs

http://www.theamericanconservative.com/dreher/no-african-christians-apply-dartmouth/

Dartmouth University hired James Tengatenga, a prominent bishop from the Anglican Church in Malawi, Africa, to run a foundation for spirituality, ethics, and social justice. After Bishop Tengatenga's appointment, university officials realized that the Anglican Church opposed same-sex "marriage" and that Tengatenga had criticized the Episcopal Church's election of an openly homosexual bishop. Consequently, the university dismissed the bishop before he began his job.

Atheist Group Pressures School to Remove Ten Commandments Poster

http://ffrf.org/legal/other-legal-successes/item/18836-ffrf-complaint-removes-ten-commandments-poster-from-school-library-august-13-2013

When the Freedom From Religion Foundation heard that the Blytheville High School library in Arkansas had a poster of the Ten Commandments hanging near the library checkout station, they complained that the poster violated the Establishment Clause and demanded its removal. Although the school initially resisted, it eventually took the poster down.

Freedom From Religion Foundation Attacks University's Faith-Based Dormitory

http://blog.al.com/montgomery/2013/10/bibles_before_beer_in_faith-ba.html
http://ffrf.org/news/news-releases/item/18312-ffrf-calls-troy-university-dorms-illegal

When the Freedom From Religion Foundation found out that Troy University allowed a private, nonprofit organization to sponsor a dormitory for students of any religion who want to incorporate faith into their collegiate experience, the FFRF demanded that the plans for the housing facility be discontinued. Liberty Institute stepped in to defend the university from the FFRF's accusations.

School Authorities Ignore Anti-Semitic Bullying

http://www.bostonglobe.com/metro/regionals/south/2013/08/10/parents-say-son-was-target-anti-semitic-attacks-carver-middle-high-school/vFloVCjNHBMIPrLXjiuVJN/story.html

Parents of a Jewish junior high school student sued Carver school district in Massachusetts after district officials ignored continued harassment and physical abuse against their son from schoolmates. The harassment included beatings, name-calling, derogatory references to the Holocaust, and a swastika drawn outside of the student's house. This case is ongoing.

University Bans Prayer from Commencement Ceremony

http://ffrf.org/legal/other-legal-successes/item/18563-graduation-prayer-now-a-thing-of-the-past-at-lsu-august-7-2013

The Freedom From Religion Foundation complained to the president of Louisiana State University A&M that the university's practice of allowing a Catholic priest to open and close graduation ceremonies with prayer violated the Constitution. The university responded by discontinuing the prayers.

University Forbids Intelligent Design Theory in Science Classes

http://www.huffingtonpost.com/2013/08/01/ball-state-intelligent-design_n_3688857.html?utm_hp_ref=college

Jo Ann Gora, president of Ball State University, announced that the university would no longer allow professors to include intelligent design as part of their curriculum due to a complaint from the Freedom From Religion Foundation that such teaching violated the "separation of church and state."

School District Discriminates Against Christianity and Judaism in Curriculum

http://radio.foxnews.com/toddstarnes/top-stories/school-defends-textbook-calling-muhammad-gods-messenger.html

Brevard Public School District approved the use of a world history textbook for an advanced placement class that disparages Christianity and Judaism while promoting Islam. Additionally, students are given lessons on the Koran and the five pillars of Islam while all other religions are ignored. After local board members and politicians raised concerns, the issue was placed under review by the school board.

School Attempts to Discriminate Against Christian After-School Club

http://www.lc.org/index.cfm?PID=14100&PRID=1357

Child Evangelism Fellowship (CEF) operated a Christian after-school ministry for children called Good News Club at Cranberry Elementary School in Cleveland, Ohio, during the 2011–2012 school year. The following year, the school began charging CEF over sixty-five dollars per hour to use the school facilities, while still allowing other groups, such as the Boy Scouts of America, to use the facilities free of charge. CEF refused to submit to the discriminatory treatment and filed a lawsuit against the school district.

ACLU Attempts to Stop Student-Led Prayer at Football Games

http://blog.alliancedefendingfreedom.org/2013/07/24/michigan-schools-try-to-silence-prayer/

The ACLU attempted to shut down prayers after football games in Bloomfield Hills School District in Michigan by alleging that a football coach was leading the prayers. Upon investigation, the school district discovered that the prayers were entirely student led and verbally agreed to allow the practice to continue.

ACLU Attacks the Distribution of Gideon Bibles in Kentucky Schools

http://blog.alliancedefendingfreedom.org/2013/07/22/blocking-the-bible-in-kentucky/

The ACLU of Kentucky sent a letter to 174 public school superintendents throughout the state of Kentucky, threatening possible lawsuits in the coming school year if they allow The Gideons International to distribute Bibles to students on campus.

Freedom From Religion Foundation Criticizes School's Graduation Policy

http://blog.libertyinstitute.org/2013/07/protecting-students-religious-freedom.html

The Wisconsin-based Freedom From Religion Foundation attacked the Lexington-Richland School District 5 in South Carolina because it allows students to make opening and closing remarks at graduation with the freedom to choose their own messages, and the school district prohibits discrimination against students' religious messages. Liberty Institute stepped in to insure that student speakers retain the freedom to choose their own messages at graduation, free from religious discrimination. Furthermore, Liberty Institute attorneys endorsed revamping the school district's policy regarding invocations before board meetings to ensure that the policies are in compliance with South Carolina law and U.S. Supreme Court precedent. The school board gave its initial approval of the policy changes.

Atheist Group Attempts to Intimidate Community Members into Cancelling Scheduled Prayers for Local School District
http://ffrf.org/news/news-releases/item/18238-ffrf-takes-on-alabama-school-district-%E2%80%9Cprayer-caravan%E2%80%9D-daily-prayers
http://ffrf.org/news/news-releases/item/18268-ffrf-reports-additional-violations-in-cullman-county-ala
After discovering that school district leaders and community members voluntarily planned on visiting different schools in the local district to pray for the upcoming school year before classes began, the Freedom From Religion Foundation demanded that the school district superintendent cancel the prayers. The school superintended refused, and the prayers continued as planned. FFRF then attempted to bully the school district by another route, sending a second demand letter to another school district leader that called for the cancellation of the prayers and the banning of pastors from school grounds and discontinuation of using churches as meeting places for various school functions.

Anti-Religion Group Attacks Minister's Thanksgiving Lunch Prayer
http://ffrf.org/legal/other-legal-successes/item/18386-ffrf-students-can-give-thanks-without-a-god-july-29-2013
In Mount Vernon, Ohio, Pleasant Street Elementary School celebrated the 2012 Thanksgiving holiday with a special lunch at the school. After hearing that a minister gave a prayer of thanks before the meal, the Freedom From Religion Foundation struck the school with a letter demanding that such prayer never happen again. The Norwalk City School District superintended complied and confirmed that such prayer would no longer be permitted.

College Student Ordered to Hide Cross Necklace
http://blog.libertyinstitute.org/2013/07/university-official-orders-student-to.html
Audrey Jarvis, a 19-year-old liberal arts major at Sonoma Statue University, was working at a student orientation fair when her supervisor told her to hide her cross necklace because it "might offend others, it might make incoming students feel unwelcome...." Jarvis, a devout Catholic, was so upset by the incident that she left the student fair. Liberty Institute assisted Ms. Jarvis in seeking a religious accommodation from Sonoma State University, and the university has apologized for the supervisor's actions, saying that they were "completely wrong."

School District Pressured into Removing Bible Verse from Principal's Office

http://ffrf.org/legal/other-legal-successes/item/18348-principal%E2%80%99s-office-no-place-for-bible-quotes-says-ffrf-july-19-2013

In San Bernardino, California, the Riley Elementary School principal had a Bible verse framed in his office. The Freedom From Religion Foundation received word of the Bible verse and immediately complained to the San Bernardino City Unified School District superintendent. The school district responded by removing the Bible verse from the principal's office.

Elementary School Pressured into Removing Cross From School Office

http://ffrf.org/legal/other-legal-successes/item/18171-ffrf-downs-cross-at-texas-school-july-15-2013

Upon hearing that Brock Elementary School in Brock, Texas, had a framed cross in one of the school offices, the Freedom From Religion Foundation complained to the school superintendent that this display excluded non-Christians and asked that the school remove cross. The school complied and responded: "The cross was located in the elementary office and removed. Have a BLESSED day!"

Antireligion Groups Blast Mother for Praying for School Safety

https://www.au.org/blogs/wall-of-separation/safety-check-woman-praying-on-nh-school-steps-without-permission-could-have

http://ffrf.org/legal/other-legal-successes/item/18170-no-preaching-visitors-allowed-on-new-hampshire-school-property-july-12-2013

When New Hampshire mother Lizarda Urena heard that bullets had been found at Concord High School where her children attended, she made a habit of visiting the campus at the beginning of the school day to pray for the safety of the faculty, staff, and students. After word of Urena's actions got out, Americans United for Separation of Church and State condemned the mother herself as the "obvious security issue," and the Freedom From Religion Foundation sent a letter to the school district superintendent demanding that Urena be banished from the school grounds. The school complied and refused to allow Urena to continue her prayers on school property.

Antireligion Group Bullies School into Barring Student-Led Prayer

http://ffrf.org/legal/other-legal-successes/item/18165-ffrf-action-drops-prayers-from-michigan-high-school-graduation-july-11-2013

After students led prayer at a Ross Beatty Junior/Senior High School graduation ceremony in Cassopolis, Michigan, the Freedom From Religion Foundation complained to the school, claiming that the students' actions violated the Constitution. The school said that it would share these concerns with the student advisor that oversaw graduation events, stating, "We do not anticipate a recurrence [of the prayers]."

Freedom From Religion Foundation Denounces Teacher's Christian Posters
http://ffrf.org/legal/other-legal-successes/item/18335-religious-posters-aren%E2%80%99t-in-kansas-public-school-anymore-july-11-2013
When the Freedom From Religion Foundation found out that a math teacher in McPherson, Kansas, hung several Christian posters in his math classroom, they contacted the school superintendent and requested that the teacher be punished for forcing his religion on students. The school acquiesced to the demand, confirming that the teacher was disciplined and had a note placed in his personal file regarding the situation.

Atheist Organization Condemns Historical Patriotic Song
http://ffrf.org/legal/other-legal-successes/item/18183-religious-song-sung-no-more-at-california-school-july-10-2013
An elementary school in Rancho Cordova, California, highlighted the classic song "America (My Country, Tis of Thee)" as the song of the month. The Freedom From Religion Foundation demanded that the school cease promoting the song because it referred to God in some of the lyrics. The school submitted and ended the use of the song.

Freedom From Religion Foundation Intimidates School into Banning Bible Circulation
http://ffrf.org/legal/other-legal-successes/item/18334-ffrf-ends-bible-handouts-in-washington-high-school-july-10-2013
After members of Gideons International handed out Bibles to students at Cascade School District in Everett, Washington, the Freedom From Religion Foundation sent a letter to Cascade School District Superintendent Steve McKenna threatening a lawsuit unless McKenna barred the distribution of Bibles at the school. McKenna responded by yielding to the threat and stating, "The situation was unfortunate and should not have occurred."

Historical Constitution Class Condemned by Atheist Group Because of Religious Content
http://ffrf.org/legal/other-legal-successes/item/18144-ffrf-helps-to-call-off-unconstitutional-constitution-classes-in-ohio-july-4-2013
The President of the Springboro Community City School Board of Education scheduled summer classes on the U.S. Constitution taught by The Institute on the Constitution, a Christian organization that teaches the Biblical influence

on the United States' formation, and The National Center for Constitutional Studies, a group dedicated to teaching about the origins of the United States Constitution. The Freedom From Religion Foundation sent a letter demanding the cancellation of these classes because they asserted that the United States was founded on Christian principles. The school responded by abandoning the classes.

Freedom From Religion Foundation Quashes Graduation Prayer in Arkansas School
http://ffrf.org/legal/other-legal-successes/item/18180-haas-hall-academy-has-graduation-prayers-no-more-july-2-2013
The Freedom From Religion Foundation intimidated the superintendent of Haas Hall Academy in Fayetteville, Arkansas, into banning prayer at the school's graduation ceremonies pursuant to a local resident's complaint. In their response, the school confirmed, "There will be no prayer at the upcoming Haas Hall Academy graduation."

Atheist Group Demands Removal of Church Banner
http://ffrf.org/legal/other-legal-successes/item/18336-church-banner-banned-from-public-school-grounds-july-1-2013
The Freedom From Religion Foundation sent a letter to the Moreno Valley Unified School District superintendent demanding that the school remove a banner advertising a church that met on the school grounds on Sundays, claiming that the banner violated the school's legal obligation to remain neutral towards religion. The school complied with the request.

Basketball Coach Required to Cease Any Involvement with Pregame Prayer
http://ffrf.org/legal/other-legal-successes/item/18164-supreme-court-precedent-takes-down-b-ball-court-prayer-july-1-2013
The Freedom From Religion Foundation called for the superintendent of Monticello High School in Kentucky to instruct a basketball coach to abstain from all participation in pregame prayer at basketball games, regardless of whether students initiated or led the prayer. The school acted according to the request.

EEOC Investigates Firing of Teacher for Giving a Bible to a Student
http://blog.libertyinstitute.org/2013/06/thanks-to-liberty-institutes-pressure.html
Walt Tutka, a substitute teacher in New Jersey, was fired by the Phillipsburg School District for handing a Bible to a student who asked for it. When the student was the last to enter through a door, Mr. Tutka said, "The first shall

be last, and the last shall be first." The student repeatedly inquired about the origin of the phrase. Eventually, Mr. Tutka found the quote in a pocket New Testament and showed it to the student. The student then commented that he did not own a Bible, so Mr. Tutka offered the pocket Bible to the student. The school district then fired Mr. Tutka. With help from Liberty Institute, Mr. Tutka filed a charge of discrimination against the school district with the U.S. Equal Employment Opportunity Commission (EEOC). Without conducting the required review, the EEOC dismissed Mr. Tutka's complaint. After Liberty Institute pressured the EEOC to perform the required investigation and discovered evidence that the school district fired Mr. Tutka because of his membership in Gideons International, the EEOC reopened its investigation and has requested that Mr. Tutka and the school district enter mediation.

Valedictorian Silenced During Speech for Sharing His Faith

http://blog.libertyinstitute.org/2013/06/joshua-ids-officials-violate-state-and.html

Remington Reimer, valedictorian of Joshua High School in Joshua, Texas, planned to give his valedictorian address and then get ready to attend the U.S. Naval Academy. When Reimer began to speak about his faith during his valedictorian address, however, that was all put at risk. Texas law prohibits schools from editing valedictorian addresses, but as soon as Reimer began to speak about liberty and his faith, school officials cut his microphone. Furthermore, the principal of Joshua High School threatened to send a letter to the U.S. Naval Academy to ruin Reimer's reputation in retaliation for Reimer's speaking about his faith. Following a demand letter from Liberty Institute, school officials apologized to Reimer and provided assurances that no further discrimination against student religious speech will occur in the future.

Atheist Group Nearly Ruins Fifth-Grade Musical

http://www.tylerpaper.com/article/20130523/NEWS08/130529905
http://www.kiiitv.com/story/22453344/thousands-show-support-of-school-play-in-god-we-trust

E.J. Moss Intermediate School's fifth grade class in Lindale, Texas, prepared for over five months to put on a musical, "In God We Trust." The musical connects the faith of important historical figures from the United States founding to the national motto, "In God We Trust." Just days before they were set to perform, a Wisconsin-based atheist group threatened legal action against the school unless certain parts of the play were removed. As a result, some students lost their parts entirely because there was no time to replace the script. A local Baptist church spent $1,600 to rent out the school auditorium for a second showing of the musical so the students could perform the entire show they had worked so hard on all year. Thousands in the community showed up to support the students, with about 900 having to sit in overflow rooms to watch on live feed or outside where they could only hear the show.

Arkansas School to Cancel Sixth-Grade Graduation Because of Prayer
http://www.christianpost.com/news/arkansas-school-district-cancels-graduation-rather-than-allow-prayer-95674/
After receiving complaints from the Wisconsin-based Freedom From Religion Foundation, the Riverside School District in Lakeside, Arkansas, decided to cancel its sixth-grade graduation rather than allow prayer at the graduation.

Student Prays at Graduation Despite Objections
http://www.huffingtonpost.com/2013/05/28/lincoln-high-school-prayer-graduation-kentucky_n_3347203.html
Despite formal objections by six students, Student Body Class President Jonathan Hardwick prayed in "Jesus' name" during Lincoln Country High School's graduation ceremony. Principal Tim Godbey publically noted that, while faculty cannot publically pray on school grounds, students are permitted to voice prayers. Hardwick received a standing ovation from parents and students upon the completion of his prayer.

School Forced to Remove Ten Commandments
https://www.au.org/church-state/julyaugust-2013-church-state/people-events/oklahoma-student-foils-school-posting-of-ten
http://www.huffingtonpost.com/2013/05/15/ten-commandments-oklahoma-muldrow_n_3279658.html
The Freedom From Religion Foundation found out that a high school in the small town of Muldrow, Oklahoma, had copies of the Ten Commandments posted on classroom walls. Immediately, the FFRF threatened the school with a lawsuit if the Ten Commandments were not removed. Despite strong support from the community in favor of keeping the Ten Commandments in the school, the district decided to yield to the threat in order to forgo costly legal proceedings.

Ohio College Agrees to Change Policy Banning Signs at Student-Led Religious Freedom Rally
https://www.thomasmoresociety.org/2013/03/12/free-speech-case-settled-over-sinclair-community-college-violations/
Sinclair Community College in Dayton, Ohio, used a restrictive speech policy

to ban its students from bringing signs to "Stand Up for Religious Freedom" rally. After a federal lawsuit was filed to protect student speech, the school agreed to change its policies.

ACLU and Freedom From Religion Foundation Sue to Remove Student-Owned Jesus Portrait from Ohio School
http://stateimpact.npr.org/ohio/2013/04/03/jackson-city-schools-remove-painting-of-jesus/
http://thetandd.com/lifestyles/faith-and-values/ohio-school-board-votes-to-keep-jesus-portrait-up/article_710897ba-76f7-11e2-9356-001a4bcf887a.html
A community school in Jackson, Ohio, permits each student organization to hang a portrait of a person that holds special significance to that group. A Christian student organization hung a portrait of Jesus in that school in 1947. The portrait hung there for sixty-six years without any objections, acquiring historic significance to the Jackson students and alumni. The portrait is inscribed with the name of the student organization claiming ownership. Nevertheless, the Freedom from Religion Foundation labeled this student speech an "egregious violation," and, joining forces with the ACLU, filed a federal lawsuit against the small Ohio school district. With limited resources and the prospects of an expensive legal attack from FFRF and the ACLU, the school district was forced to remove the historic portrait. The school lamented that it could not afford to fight a protracted legal battle over the portrait.

Community College Bans Employees from Sending Religion-Related Emails to Each Other
http://ffrf.org/legal/other-legal-successes/item/15156-ffrf-stops-community-college-violation-aug-22-2012
Peralta Community College in Oakland, California, issued a sweeping policy prohibiting its employees from talking about religion with one another on school email accounts and forcing employees to remove any religious quotes from email signatures.

Alabama Schools Will Not Teach Students about the History of Easter and Christmas
http://ffrf.org/legal/other-legal-successes/item/17331-ffrf-helps-end-ala-church%E2%80%99s-religious-school-assemblies-march-11-2013
Houston County Schools in Alabama held assemblies right before Easter and Christmas break to teach the students about the history and cultural significance of these two nationally-celebrated holidays. An atheist organization was outraged that students would learn why these holidays

exist. In an effort to suppress any mention of religion in public schools, the organization attacked simple history lessons about culturally important public holidays. The schools submitted to the atheists' demands and canceled the assemblies.

Florida College Bans Gideons from Graduation Ceremonies

http://ffrf.org/legal/other-legal-successes/item/17529-ffrf-ensures-secular-graduation-ceremonies-at-a-fla-college-march-6-2013
St. John River State College banned the Gideons from attending graduations and peacefully passing out pocket New Testaments after the Freedom From Religion Foundation complained of the "exclusionary distribution of bibles."

Florida College Student Suspended for Refusing to Stomp on "Jesus"

http://www.libertyinstitute.org/pages/florida-atlantic-university-student-suspended
A professor at Florida Atlantic University required the students in his class to write "Jesus" on a piece of paper and then stomp on the paper. Ryan Rotela, a Mormon student in the class, refused to stomp on the paper because of his religious beliefs. Rotela then reported the incident to university officials. Instead of protecting Mr. Rotela's religious liberty rights, however, the university officials brought academic charges against Rotela and suspended him. Following a legal demand from Liberty Institute, the university reversed its decision, apologized to Rotela, expunged the academic charges, and agreed to allow Mr. Rotela to take the class from a different professor.

Atheist Group Outraged Teacher Agreed to Students' Requests for Her to Sing a Religious Song

http://www.timesfreepress.com/news/2013/feb/08/religious-song-sparks-complaint/
Heather Moorman is a science teacher at Lakeview Middle School in Ringgold, Georgia, but outside the classroom she is a Christian recording artist. One day while in class her students requested that she sing one of her songs, and Ms. Moorman generously agreed. The Freedom From Religion Foundation caught wind of this and sent a demand letter to "halt this egregious abuse of power" alleging that Ms. Moorman's compliance with the students' requests was "interfering with the rights of students" by imposing her religion on students and "making non-Christian ... students into outsiders." The school's investigation revealed it was an isolated event and took no disciplinary action against Ms. Moorman. Nevertheless, FFRF celebrated this nonevent as "end[ing] Georgia middle school teacher's religious songs."

Pennsylvania School District Denies Equal Access to Religious Club
http://www.pennlive.com/midstate/index.ssf/2013/02/bible_class_fight_christian_gr.html
When the Good News Club, a Christian student club, wanted to start an after-school program at Foose Elementary School in Harrisburg, Pennsylvania, the school responded that the club would have to pay a $1,200 annual fee to use the school's facilities because the club is religious. Other nonprofit organizations are granted free use of the school facilities after school. The Good News Club filed a lawsuit against the school district to be treated fairly.

Arizona Education Association Fights Voucher Program for Special-Needs Students
http://azstarnet.com/news/local/education/precollegiate/judge-upholds-arizona-schoolvoucher-plan/article_75f6a2b2-4845-11e1-8e51-001871e3ce6c.html
A state trial court upheld Arizona's new voucher program for special-needs students, which provides these students with the opportunity to receive private educations. The Arizona Education Association had challenged the voucher program because money could go to religious schools under the program.

School Bans Teachers from Mentioning Religion in Personal Biographies
http://ffrf.org/legal/other-legal-successes/item/17343-ffrf-cleans-up-jackson-tennessee%E2%80%99s-school-district-website-jan-22-2013
The Jackson-Madison County School District in Jackson, Tennessee, asked its teachers for biographical information for the district's website. As would be expected in a diverse selection of teachers, some of the teachers found religion important to their lives and incorporated this into their biographies. The Freedom From Religion Foundation accused these teachers of "push[ing] religion on a captive audience" and demanded that the "religious messages be scrubbed" from the biographies. The school district responded by requiring all teachers to remove any religious elements from their personal biographies.

Oklahoma School Bullied into Replacing Christmas Songs with "Secular Winter-Themed Songs"
http://ffrf.org/legal/other-legal-successes/item/17345-ffrf-calls-out-religious-songs-and-bullying-at-oklahoma-grade-school-jan-11-2013
The Freedom From Religion Foundation threatened Sulphur Elementary School in Sulphur, Oklahoma, for including Christmas songs referencing the historical reason for Christmas in the school's December play. FFRF claimed

that references to "a baby boy" as the "reason for the season" are "divisive" and the Christmas songs should be replaced with generic "secular winter-themed songs." The school submitted to the FFRF's demand.

High School Denies Equal Treatment to Teacher; Issues Sweeping, Unqualified Order to Cleanse Classroom of Any and All Religious Content
http://www.buffalonews.com/apps/pbcs.dll/article?AID=/20130110/
CITYANDREGION/130119944/1002
Cheektowaga Central School District in New York permits teachers to display messages reflecting personal beliefs and interests that are not part of school curriculum, unless those beliefs and interests relate to religion. The district threatened to fire Joelle Silver if she did not remove all vestiges of religion from her classroom. The materials motivating this threat include personal sticky notes on her desk reminding her of religious verses, one encouraging poster (among many) not referencing God but quoting a religious figure encouraging students to hold firm to beliefs and act in love, a quote from President Reagan discussing the historical theme of God and country, and a prayer box in her room used for the school's Bible Study Club. Ms. Silver complied with all requests and then filed a lawsuit in federal district court to end the school's discriminatory practice.

Antireligion Group Intimidates School into Silencing Student-Led Prayers
http://ffrf.org/legal/other-legal-successes/item/17339-ffrf-reminds-utah-school-
there-is-no-need-to-honor-prayer-at-national-honors-society-jan-7-2013
The Freedom From Religion Foundation celebrated a victory over squashing student-led prayers at a Utah High School. FFRF sent a demand letter to the school's superintendent after two student-led prayers occurred at a National Honor Society Induction Ceremony. In response, the superintendent reiterated to school principals that student-led prayers would not be tolerated at school events.

Atheist Opposition to "Merry Christmas, Charlie Brown" Cancels School Field Trip
http://charlotte.cbslocal.com/2012/12/05/church-calls-off-charlie-brown-
christmas-show-amid-controversy/
Students in Little Rock, Arkansas, were planning to take a field trip to see "Merry Christmas, Charlie Brown," a stage adaptation of the classic "A Charlie Brown Christmas." The school explained to parents that the play "would enhance [their] child's creative imagination in the area of dramatic arts." The school also provided notice that the play contained religious themes.

As a result of the opposition to the students' being allowed to see the play, the play was canceled due to safety concerns.

Atheist Group Threatens School for Teaching Two Songs that Mention God in Music Class
http://www.christianpost.com/news/atheist-group-demands-ny-school-district-remove-songs-mentioning-god-from-curriculum-79929/
The Freedom From Religion Foundation threatened the Shenendehowa Central Schools of Clifton Park, New York, because the school district's music class includes two songs that mention God in their lyrics. The school district refused to change its curriculum, noting that the songs "were used appropriately to teach specific musical concepts, and as the basis for secular classroom activities." FFRF did not follow through on its threats against the school district.

Mississippi Cheerleaders Banned from Writing Bible Verse on Run-Thru Banners
http://ffrf.org/legal/other-legal-successes/item/16175-a-mississippi-high-school-will-no-longer-promote-religious-banners-at-sporting-events-oct-22-2012
Cheerleaders at Stone High School in Mississippi wrote a Bible verse on their run-through banner instead of encouraging violence against the other team. The school received a complaint that someone had to look at a quotation from the Bible. Within less than a week, the school assured the complainant that it would not happen again.

Group Demands School Band Stop Playing "God Bless America"
http://www.metrowestdailynews.com/news/x521650947/Group-lodges-complaint-about-God-Bless-America-in-Wayland
The Freedom From Religion Foundation demanded that the Wayland High School band in Wayland, Massachusetts, stop playing "God Bless America" on Pearl Harbor Day and Memorial Day. The FFRF's letter to the school stated that playing "God Bless America" "sends a message to students that the school is endorsing and compelling belief in a god." The school did not acquiesce to the group's demands.

Texas School Prohibits Student from Handing Out Invitations to Church Event
http://www.beaumontenterprise.com/news/article/Lawsuit-dropped-against-Nederland-ISD-3663947.php
A Nederland, Texas, public elementary school prohibited a third-grade student from distributing invitations to a church event. The student's father filed suit

on his son's behalf but dropped the suit when the school district agreed not to discriminate against any religious or nonreligious private student-to-student speech, as long as the speech does not disrupt educational activities.

Freedom From Religion Foundation Stops Prayer at Minford, Ohio, Schools

Bonnie Gutsch, "FFRF halts Ohio high school prayers," Freedom from Religion Foundation, available at http://ffrf.org/legal/challenges/ffrf-halts-ohio-high-schoolprayers/ (accessed May 19, 2012)
High school assemblies and graduations in Minford, Ohio, have included prayer as a tradition for years. On February 25, 2011, the Freedom From Religion Foundation sent a letter to school officials demanding they stop the practice. The school officials complied.

Catholic School Threatened with Lawsuit for Firing Teacher for Religious Reasons

The News-Sentinel, "Fort Wayne-South Bend diocese denies teacher's discrimination allegations," available at http://www.news-sentinel.com/apps/pbcs.dll/article?AID=/20120425/NEWS/120429677/1005/FOOD (Apr. 25, 2012)
A Catholic school in Ft. Wayne, Indiana, fired Emily Herx for undergoing in vitro fertilization (IVF) despite Catholic beliefs opposed to the procedure. Herx had signed an agreement when she began teaching at the school that said she would recognize and follow Catholic teachings. Herx filed suit against the school for firing her for undergoing the IVF treatment.

Owasso, Oklahoma, Schools Prohibited Christian Organization from Distributing Information

http://www.fox23.com/news/local/story/Settlement-reached-in-lawsuit-against-Owasso/1HRD9EtuVEaUb43OFoYU8Q.cspx
Owasso Public Schools banned members of a Christian organization from handing out information to students and teachers. Once Owasso Kids for Christ filed suit, the parties reached a settlement in which religious organizations were allowed to put flyers on a bulletin board and an information table, and the school paid $20,000 in attorney's fees.

Freedom From Religion Foundation Stops Alabama Community's Tradition of Bible Stories at Schools

http://www.al.com/living/index.ssf/2012/02/bible_man_okd_by_jackson_count.html
For thirty-five years, Jackson County, Alabama, invited "Bible Man" to visit its schools and share Bible stories with elementary school students. In December of 2012, the Freedom From Religion Foundation filed a complaint forcing the

community to stop this tradition at one of its schools and to silence organized prayer for football players at a local church. The Jackson County community is determined to find a way to keep their community traditions.

ACLU Investigates School Because It Scheduled Motivational Speakers Through the Fellowship of Christian Athletes
http://www.columbiamissourian.com/stories/2012/01/01/aclu-objects-missouri-school-districts-religious-speakers/
The ACLU investigated a school because it scheduled motivational speakers sponsored by the Christian Fellowship of Athletes. The ACLU obtained school emails in search of any information sufficient to raise First Amendment complaints. It ended up singling out the district guidance counselor's email about the speakers because it made religious references, and also the FCA student members for handing out cards at the school's baseball stadium advertising "Field of Faith." The ACLU had to settle with merely warning the school that it risked violating the First Amendment's Establishment Clause.

Iowa State University Bans Students from Exploring Biblical Insights into Business Management
http://www.iowastatedaily.com/news/article_70ce5c96-4096-11e1-ac1d-0019bb2963f4.html
Despite implementation by successful businesses such as Hobby Lobby and Chick-fil-A, and the growing interest in spirituality's role in successful businesses, Iowa State University, joined by the ACLU, derailed a plan for its students to examine biblical insights into business management. After the course was first approved, twenty faculty members objected to it, purporting to be concerned about academic rigor, and that it would violate the Establishment Clause.

School Forced to End Discrimination Against Religious Groups
http://onenewsnow.com/legal-courts/2011/12/21/christian-club-recognized
A Long Island, New York, school in the Hicksville Union Free School District refused to recognize religious student groups in violation of the Equal Access Act, which prohibits discrimination against religious student organizations in public schools. The principal of the school told one student group, "I don't care if other schools have Christian clubs. I don't want one at this school." After a lawsuit was filed, the school reversed its decision and agreed to recognize student religious organizations in compliance with the Equal Access Act.

Residents and Teachers Prohibited from Praying at School Flagpole Following Letter from the Freedom From Religion Foundation

http://jacksonville.com/news/metro/2011-12-16/story/clay-school-board-rescinds-injunction-against-pastor

Freedom From Religion Foundation complained to a Jacksonville, Florida, school about privately-organized, weekly prayers around its flagpole before school begins, which had occurred for the previous twelve years. In response, the county school board requested the prayers to stop. When the prayers continued, the school board placed an injunction against the minister leading them, making it illegal for him to visit any of the district's schools—even to visit his grandchildren. The injunction was only lifted after the pastor promised to stay off of campuses.

University Forces Nursing Students to Participate in Abortions

http://www.nj.com/news/index.ssf/2011/12/umdnj_settles_with_nurses_over. html

The University of Medicine and Dentistry of New Jersey adopted a policy that requires all nursing students to participate in abortion procedures, even if it is against their religious convictions. A group of nurses filed suit against the university in November 2011, alleging Fourteenth Amendment and medical personnel rights violations. The case settled, and the nurses may now refuse to participate in abortions for religious reasons.

Student Suspended for Identifying as a Christian and Stating Views on Homosexuality

http://www.foxnews.com/us/2011/09/22/texas-school-punishes-boy-for-opposing-homosexuality/

Dakota Ary, an honors student in Fort Worth, Texas, mentioned to a friend during German class that he is a Christian and that he believes homosexuality is wrong. The comment was a result of the German teacher's discussion of homosexuality with the class and the teacher's displaying of a picture showing two men kissing. The teacher overheard Ary's comment and became irate. The teacher then sent Ary to the principal, who suspended Ary for three days. After the school was confronted with its discrimination against Ary's Christian beliefs, it rescinded his punishment.

Freedom From Religion Foundation Stops Official School Prayer, Sparking Protest

Lynn Lampkin, "'Prayer Protest' Held at Hernando Football Game," FOX Memphis, available at http://www.myfoxmemphis.com/dpp/news/Mississippi/prayer-protest-held-at-hernando-football-game-rpt-20110826 (Aug. 26, 2011)

School officials in Desoto County, Mississippi, stopped the practice of leading prayer sessions over the high school football stadium PA system after receiving a threatening letter from Freedom From Religion Foundation. Students and their families protested the end of prayer by shaving their heads and carrying signs pledging allegiance to Christianity. Crowds began to gather around the flagpole during Friday night football games to pray.

California School Fundraiser Prohibits Religious Inscriptions on Bricks

http://www.foxnews.com/us/2011/06/14/california-school-district-cancels-fundraiser-after-submission-scripture/

The Desert Sands Unified School District in California held a fundraiser in which donors could purchase bricks or benches. Purchasers were allowed to have the brick engraved with a message. The school district did not allow two donors to install bricks with Bible verses inscribed on the bricks. The two donors filed suit claiming unconstitutional viewpoint discrimination in a public forum. The claims were based on the Free Speech Clause, the Equal Protection and the Due Process Clauses of the Fourteenth Amendment, the Free Exercise Clause, and the Establishment Clause. The school district rescinded the fundraiser and returned the raised funds.

Freedom From Religion Foundation Opposes Minister Praying at Graduation

http://www.ffrf.org/uploads/legal/gilescounty_letter.pdf

Freedom From Religion Foundation sent a letter of complaint to Giles County, Tennessee, school for inviting a minister to pray at the kindergarten graduation ceremony.

ACLU Sued School for Holding Graduation Ceremonies in a Methodist-Owned Auditorium

Lauren Green, "New Jersey School and ACLU Compromise of Graduation at Christian-Owned Site," FoxNews.com, available at http://www.foxnews.com/us/2011/05/26/new-jersey-high-school-aclu-compromise-grnew-jersey-school-aclu-compromise/ (May 26, 2011)

The ACLU sued Neptune High School in Neptune, New Jersey, after the school decided to continue with its seventy-year tradition of holding its graduation ceremonies at the Great Auditorium of the Ocean Grove Camp

Meeting Association, a Methodist organization. The ACLU settled with the school, agreeing to cover any religious symbols in the Great Auditorium.

High School Class President Threatened with Arrest for Praying at Graduation

Liberty Counsel, "Hampton High School Graduates Choose Prayer at Ceremony," available at http://www.lc.org/index.cfm?PID=14100&PRID=1071 (May 24, 2011)
The class president of Hampton High School wanted to pray at her graduation. The principal of the school, however, said that any students who attempt to pray would be stopped, escorted from the building by police, and arrested. After receiving a demand letter, the school reversed its policy.

ACLU Threatens School into Removing Graduation Prayer, Student Prays Anyway

Liberty Counsel, "Graduation Continued With Prayer in Louisiana," available at http://www.lc.org/index.cfm?PID=14100&PRID=1070 (May 23, 2011)
Following a complaint and a threat from the ACLU, Bastrop High School in Bastrop, Louisiana, replaced the traditional graduation prayer with a "Moment of Silence." Senior Laci Rae Mattice, however, led the audience in the Lord's Prayer despite her instructions to lead the "Moment of Silence."

FFRF Stops Algebra Teacher from Praying with Students

Freedom From Religion Foundation, "FFRF halts prayer in high school algebra class," available at http://ffrf.org/legal/challenges/ffrf-halts-prayer-in-high-school-algebra-class/
A Lenoir City, Tennessee, student complained to the Freedom From Religion Foundation (FFRF) that his former Algebra II teacher prayed with students before their final exams. FFRF wrote a letter to the superintendent. The school's superintendent stopped the prayers, and the teacher apologized in writing.

ACLU Threatens School for Holding Graduation Ceremonies in a Church Building

Liberty Counsel, "Texas Graduation Gets Free Offer of Help from Liberty Counsel Against ACLU Threat," available at http://www.lc.org/index. cfm?PID=14100&PRID=1068 (May 19, 2011)
Irving Independent School District holds their graduation ceremonies at The Potter's House, a nondenominational church, which is used because it can seat more persons than any school-owned facility. The ACLU threatened to sue the school if it did not change locations.

Complaints Against School for Churchmembers' Offering to Pray with Students Before AP Test

http://www.wsbtv.com/news/news/prayer-at-test-site-continues-despite-schoolcompl/nFB8b/

Students at a Georgia high school took an AP test at a local church due to overcrowding concerns at the school. When they arrived, church members were there offering to pray with students before the test. Some parents and students were offended and complained to the school that students were subjected to voluntary opportunities for prayer.

ACLU Attacks the Distribution of Gideon Bibles in Tennessee School

http://www.aclu.org/religion-belief/aclu-tennessee-stops-unconstitutional-bible-distribution-white-county-school

A parent complained after a Gideon Bible was distributed to her daughter during school. The ACLU stepped in and settled the case with the school. Bibles can now only be distributed when paired with nonreligious materials, contact with religious distributors is limited, the religious texts are not emphasized over the nonreligious texts, and clear disclaimers of school endorsement are posted at the distribution site.

Los Angeles Unified School District Banned a Fifth Grader from Performing a Christian Song at a Talent Show

http://www.adfmedia.org/News/PRDetail/4612

The Los Angeles Unified School District in California prohibited a fifth-grade student from performing a Christian song at an elementary school talent show. After the student got a temporary restraining order against the school district, the district changed its position and permitted the student to sing the song.

Freedom From Religion Foundation Threatened Polk County, Florida, with a Lawsuit if the Polk County School Board Continued to Pray at Meetings

http://www.newschief.com/article/20110205/NEWS/102055127/1021/news01?p=1&tc=pg

The Freedom From Religion Foundation threatened a lawsuit against the Polk County School Board if the board continued to pray at its meetings. In response, the board added a disclaimer to its board meeting agendas, which reads, "Voluntary invocation may be offered before the opening of the School Board meeting by a private citizen. The views or beliefs expressed in the invocation have not been reviewed nor approved by the School Board, and the Board is not allowed, by law, to endorse the religious beliefs or views of this, or any other speaker."

Freedom From Religion Foundation Stops Graduation Prayers in McNairy County

Letter from Charlie Miskelly to Rebecca Markert, available at http://www.ffrf. org/uploads/legal/McNairy%20County%20Schools%20TN.pdf (Jan. 27, 2011)

The McNairy County School district had a practice of hosting student-led prayers over loudspeakers at graduation ceremonies. The Freedom From Religion Foundation wrote a letter stating that "the Supreme Court has struck down prayer at public high school graduations." After receiving two complaints, the school stopped the tradition.

School Under Attack for Saving Money by Holding Graduation in a Church

http://www.ajc.com/news/news/local/cherokee-fight-over-graduations-at-churches-could-/nQncH/

A Cherokee County, Georgia, public school holds its graduation ceremony in a church. Americans United for Separation of Church and State spoke out against the practice, claiming that holding graduation ceremonies in a church violated the students' constitutional rights. The school claims, however, that it holds graduation in the church because it saves tens of thousands of dollars. A similar secular venue would be much more expensive, and the school gym would not accommodate all of the attendees.

Univ. of Wisconsin-Madison Denied Funding to Student Group That Is "Too Religious"

http://www.speakupmovement.org/Map/CaseDetails?Case=240

The University of Wisconsin-Madison Roman Catholic Foundation (UWMRCF) was denied funds from the student activity fee funding on the grounds that the organization was "too religious." The UWMRCF appealed to the Student Judiciary. The Freedom From Religion Foundation pressured the Student Judiciary to withhold funding, but the Student Judiciary reversed the university's decision and granted the funding.

West Virginia University–Parkersburg Removes Prayer from Graduation Ceremony Despite Overwhelming Support

http://www.speakupmovement.org/Map/CaseDetails?Case=266

West Virginia University–Parkersburg decided to remove prayer from the nursing school graduation ceremony even after students voted overwhelmingly in support of including the prayer.

Professor Fired for Teaching Catholic View of Homosexuality in "Introduction to Catholicism" Class

http://www.foxnews.com/us/2010/07/09/university-illinois-reinstates-instructor-fired-catholic-beliefs/

Dr. Kenneth J. Howell, an adjunct professor at the University of Illinois, was fired from his position after a lecture on the Catholic view of homosexuality set off a firestorm of "insensitivity" complaints on campus. Although Dr. Howell had given the same lecture for nearly ten years to his Introduction to Catholicism class this was the first time it had sparked such debate. After Dr. Howell's attorneys sent a letter to the university threatening legal action if Dr. Howell's First Amendment rights were not respected, the university agreed to reinstate him as a member of the faculty.

Students Prohibited from Wearing Religious Jewelry

Jay Sekulow, "Free Speech Victory in CO: School OK's Student Cross," ACLJ, available at http://aclj.org/school-prayer/free-speech-victory-in-co-school-ok-s-student-cross (Oct. 18, 2010)

Students at Mann Middle School in Colorado Springs were told that they could no longer wear religious jewelry because some people at the school were "offended" by the display. Cainan Gostnell regularly wore a cross necklace to school. Concerned by the new rule, Gostnell sought legal assistance to preserve his right to wear the cross. After receiving a demand letter, the school assured Gostnell that he would not be punished.

Religious Education Program Stops In-School Classes Following Threat of Lawsuit

http://www.journalgazette.net/article/20100826/LOCAL04/308269981

The Weekday Religious Education program has been in Ft. Wayne, Indiana, for over sixty years and has been providing in-school classes for twenty. When a lawsuit was filed against the program, however, the program closed down the in-school instruction. Weekday Religious Education now only exists as an after-school program.

Students Told to Stop Their "Christian" Actions

Liberty Counsel, "Students Told to Cease 'Christian' Acts," available at http://www.lc.org/index.cfm?PID=14102&AlertID=1149 (June 24, 2010)

A group of Christian high school students in Roswell, New Mexico, distributed rocks with Bible verses painted on them and food, hot chocolate, and candy canes. The school did not object until the students distributed rubber models of preborn babies with Bible verses written on them. School officials confiscated all of the models and told the students that they needed to stop their "Christian" actions. Twenty-five of these students were later given detention for putting donuts with religious messages in the school's teachers' lounge.

Principal and Athletic Director Criminally Charged for Praying Over a Meal

Christina Leavenworth, "Pace High School's Frank Lay retires," FOX10tv.com, available at http://www.fox10tv.com/dpp/news/pace-high-schools-frank-lay-retires (May 21, 2010)

Pace High School Principal Frank Lay and Athletic Director Robert Freeman were charged with criminal contempt because they prayed over a meal. The ACLU had received an injunction prohibiting school employees from promoting religion at school events. Lay and Freeman were found not guilty of violating the injunction.

Miami University of Ohio Discriminates Against Religious Clubs in Distributing Funds

Alliance Defense Fund, "Speak Up: Miami University of Ohio," available at http://www.speakupmovement.org/Map/CaseDetails?Case=217

Miami University of Ohio used a two-tiered system to unevenly distribute funds to student clubs depending upon the club's mission. All religious groups were funded out of a limited fund of approximately $10,000. Nonreligious groups were funded out of a general fund of $350,000. Furthermore, restrictions were placed on money from the limited fund that did not exist on money from the general fund. After being sued over this two-tiered system, the university eliminated the funding system and granted a more equitable distribution of funds to all student groups.

School Agrees to End Discrimination Against Student Speech

http://oldsite.alliancedefensefund.org/userdocs/EBVoluntaryDismissal.pdf

A Pennsylvania school barred a student from wearing a pro-life T-shirt that read, "Abortion is not Healthcare." After the student sued the school for state and federal violations, the school ended its policy prohibiting student expression promoting a particular religious denomination, sect, or viewpoint.

College Student Penalized for Choosing to Write About Religious Poem

Alliance Defense Fund, "Speak Up: Tarrant County College," available at http://www.speakupmovement.org/Map/CaseDetails?Case=231

Bethany Roden, a student at Tarrant County College in Texas, was assigned to write a response paper on two poems of her choice for an English composition class. Roden chose poems with religious themes and incorporated her religious beliefs into her essay. Her professors penalized her for including religious themes in her essay. Upon receiving a demand letter, the college changed Roden's grade from a B to an A.

School Officials Confiscate Drawing of Jesus on the Cross and Recommend Psychological Testing

Brad Puffer, "Taunton, Mass. boy sent home from school for Jesus drawing," NECN, available at http://www.necn.com/Boston/New-England/2009/12/15/Taunton-Mass-boy-sent-home/1260897625.html (Dec. 15, 2009)

The parents of a second-grader at Maxham Elementary School in Taunton, Massachusetts, criticized public school officials after their son was sent home from school for drawing a picture of Jesus dying on the cross. School faculty confiscated the student's drawing and recommended psychological testing. School officials denied the claims and said an examination was never issued. The boy's parents said the second grader had scenes of Jesus' crucifixion on his mind after visiting a Catholic shrine with his parents.

Minnesota Schools Leave American Legion Out of Veterans Day Because of Prayer

Mary Jane Smetanka, "Bloomington schools, Legion part ways over prayers at flag," Star Tribune, available at http://www.startribune.com/local/west/69720847. html?page=1&c=y (Nov. 10, 2009)

Bloomington School District in Minnesota cut the American Legion out of its traditional Veteran's Day ceremony because the American Legion had said a prayer during the ceremony in the past. In response, The American Legion withheld $30,000 in scholarships normally given to the schools, and other organizations refused to participate in the ceremony because of the school district's treatment of The American Legion.

EEOC Tells Catholic College It Must Cover Contraceptives in Its Health Insurance

Charlotte Allen, "The Persecution of Belmont Abbey," The Weekly Standard, available at http://www.weeklystandard.com/Content/Public/ Articles/000/000/017/093aasuz.asp?page=1 (Oct. 26, 2009)

When an employee of Belmont Abbey College, a private college established by Benedictine monks, discovered the college's health care policy provided for contraceptives and abortion services, the college president immediately moved to harmonize the policy with Catholic teaching. Eight faculty members objected and filed a complaint with the Equal Employment Opportunity Commission. After initially ruling in support of the college, the EEOC then reversed its opinion and declared the college *had* engaged in gender discrimination by denying oral contraceptives to its female employees.

High School Cheerleaders Prohibited from Using Religious Banner

http://www.chattanoogan.com/2009/9/29/159917/Attorney-Says-Students-Can-Make-Bible.aspx
Cheerleaders at Lakeview-Fort Oglethorpe High School in Fort Oglethorpe, Georgia, made a banner saying "Commit to the Lord" that the football team burst through as they ran out onto the field. After several years, a parent complained about the banner and, to avoid litigation, the school ended its practice.

Ohio University Refuses to Recognize Christian Student Organization

Alliance Defense Fund, "Speak Up: Wright State University," available at http://www.speakupmovement.org/Map/CaseDetails?Case=252
Wright State University (WSU) in Ohio refused to recognize Christian Bible Fellowship (CBF) as a student club. WSU said that recognition was denied because CBF required voting members to abide by Articles of Faith and because CBF refused to include nondiscrimination terms in its constitution. After receiving demand letters, the university allowed CBF to keep faith-based membership and exempted the group from the nondiscrimination policy.

Texas A&M Rejects Christian Organization for Requiring Members to Be Christian

Alliance Defense Fund, "Speak Up: Texas A&M University," available at http://www.speakupmovement.org/Map/CaseDetails?Case=230
Texas A&M University refused to approve Freshman Leaders in Christ's (FLIC) constitution unless it removed a provision that required members to be Christian. After receiving a demand letter, Texas A&M allowed FLIC to remain a student organization and keep their constitution.

Pennsylvania School Refused Recognition of Good News Club

http://religionclause.blogspot.com/2009/01/pennsylvania-good-news-club-flyer-case.html
The Good News Club was blocked from becoming an official club by Haverford, Pennsylvania, public schools. After a suit was filed against the school district, however, a settlement was reached in which the Good News Club would become an official school club and the school district would pay attorney's fees.

Community College Implemented Prohibitive Rules for Distributing Religious Literature

http://religionclause.blogspot.com/2009/01/suit-challenging-yuba-community. html

Yuba Community College in California prohibited the distribution of religious material unless the school first approved the material and the material was only distributed during certain hours. Following a lawsuit, the school agreed to change the rules to allow students to share religious material on campus.

Student Penalized for Mentioning Jesus in a Christmas Poem

Liberty Counsel, "Sixth-Grader Penalized For Mentioning Jesus in His Christmas Paper at School," available at http://www.lc.org/index. cfm?PID=14102&AlertID=934 (Dec. 18, 2008)

An eleven-year-old student in Hattiesburg, Mississippi, was penalized for mentioning Jesus in a Christmas poetry assignment. His teacher asked him to submit a rewrite of the poem. Upon being overruled by the principal, the teacher then refused to display the students' poems as promised.

California School District Bans Good News Clubs from Distributing Flyers to Students

Liberty Counsel, "School District Complies With Demand To Allow Christian Club Announcements," available at http://www.lc.org/index. cfm?PID=14100&PRID=676 (Apr. 2, 2008)

The Carmel United School District in Carmel, California, prohibited the Good News Club, a Christian student organization, from distributing flyers advertising the club because the school district said that allowing these flyers would be an endorsement of Christianity. After receiving a demand letter, the school district reversed its policy.

California School Board Denies Credit for Community Service Hours Performed at Church

Liberty Counsel, "School Board Settles Lawsuit By Amending Policy and Accepting Student's Community Service Hours at Church," available at http://www.lc.org/ index.cfm?PID=14100&PRID=658 (Jan. 29, 2008)

The Long Beach District School Board denied credit to a student for community service hours performed at his church. Threatened with a lawsuit, the school board granted the credit and rewrote the policy to allow service at both secular and religious organizations in accordance with the First Amendment.

Student's Religious Artwork Removed from School Mural

Doug Huntington, "Girl's Cross Put Back into School Mural," Christian Post, available at http://www.christianpost.com/news/girl-s-cross-put-back-into-school-mural-27748/ (Jun. 2, 2007)

Thompson Junior High School in Oswego, Illinois, had the school's art department create a mural for the school. Each student in the art club was given a piece of the mural to work on. The principal ordered Melissa Yates' piece to be covered with blue paint, however, because she had drawn a cross on her piece. Following receipt of a demand letter, the school reversed its policy and allowed Yates' cross to be restored to the mural.

Third-Grade Student Stopped from Reading Bible During "Reading Time"

Thomas More Law Center, "Thomas More Law Center Ensures Right Of Third-Grade Student To Read Bible In Public School," available at http://www.thomasmore. org/qry/page.taf?id=19&_function=detail&sbtblct_uid1=3&_nc=45ac96639e2 d94aafe24cc62ceddb5a1 (July 23, 2007)

Third-grade student Rhajheem Haymon was told that he could not read his Bible during quiet reading time. After receiving a demand letter laying out the reasons why Rhajheem should be allowed to read his Bible, the school reversed its policy.

Arkansas High School Bans Graduation Prayer and Religious Commencement Speaker

Liberty Counsel, "Annual 'Friend or Foe' Graduation Prayer Campaign Finishes Fifth Successful Season," available at http://www.lc.org/index. cfm?PID=14100&PRID=588 (Jul. 17, 2007)

Administrators of Omaha High School in Omaha, Arkansas, told graduating seniors that they could not pray at their graduation or choose a youth ministry leader as the commencement speaker. After one of the seniors sought legal assistance, the school reversed its decision and allowed both prayer and the students' choice of commencement speaker.

High School Valedictorian Prohibited from Praying During Graduation Speech

Al Sullivan, "God not allowed Valedictorian pulls speech rather than remove prayer," Hudson Reporter, available at http://www.hudsonreporter.com/pages/ full_story/push?article-God+not+allowed+Valedictorian+pulls+speech+rather+ than+remove+prayer%20&id=2412697 (Jul. 12, 2007)

Jeremy Jerschina, the valedictorian of his class, submitted his valedictorian speech, which included a prayer, to school officials prior to his graduation ceremony from the Bayonne High School. School officials reviewed the speech and told Jerschina that he could not pray or reference his religious beliefs. Rather than give the speech without the prayer, Jeremy refused to give any valedictorian speech.

Michigan School Bans Choir from Singing "The Lord's Prayer" at Graduation

Dr. Kendall Harmon, "Choir Told Not to Sing 'The Lord's Prayer' at Graduation," available at http://www.kendallharmon.net/t19/index.php/t19/article/3172/ (May 26, 2007)

In memory of a fellow student who had died, the Comstock Park High School's choir wished to sing "The Lord's Prayer" at the school's graduation, which was being held in a church building. Although the choir had already performed this song at a benefit, school officials, acting on legal advice, would not let them perform the song. Because of the song's religious content, the school's legal counsel advised, "Don't go there."

Students Suspended for Praying in Cafeteria

Gundrun Schultz, "12 Washington State High School Students Suspended for Public Prayer Group," LifeSiteNews.com (Mar. 6, 2007)

A group of high school students started a before-school prayer meeting in the cafeteria. The school wanted the students to meet in a classroom where they would not be seen by other students. After the group insisted on praying in the cafeteria, they were suspended.

School Stops Second Grader from Giving Valentine's Day Bibles

Liberty Counsel, "School Admits Error and Allows Student To Give Bibles To His Friends," available at http://www.lc.org/index.cfm?PID=14100&PRID=552 (Feb. 21, 2007)

The day before Valentine's Day, Adam Prevette, a second grader at Roaring Elementary School in Wilkesboro, North Carolina, brought Bibles to school for two of his friends. His teacher told him that he could only give the Bibles if he brought enough for everyone, so the following day Adam brought Bibles as Valentine's Day gifts for his classmates. However, when he brought them the teacher then stated that Adam was not allowed to hand out the Bibles. Following multiple meetings, the school principal agreed to allow Adam to distribute the Bibles and apologized that he had been prevented.

Pennsylvania Schools Demand Fees from Religious Club

Liberty Counsel, "Religious Club Gains Equal Access to Pennsylvania Public Elementary Schools," available at http://www.lc.org/index. cfm?PID=14100&PRID=545 (Jan. 26, 2007)

Child Evangelism Fellowship (CEF) had been holding Good News Clubs in two elementary schools in Clinton County, Pennsylvania, for a number of years. At one point, CEF was advised that, unlike other groups, they would have to pay a fee for the use of school facilities. They were first told that they would be charged a fee because CEF was not local. After CEF showed that it had a local office, they were told that CEF must pay because the Good News Clubs were "sectarian." After receiving an attorney's letter, the school superintendent informed CEF they would not impose a fee.

New Jersey School Bans Good News Club After Discovering Club Is Christian

Liberty Counsel, "School District Reverses Decision and Grants Christian Club Equal Access to Facilities," available at http://www.lc.org/index. cfm?PID=14100&PRID=16 (Jan. 17, 2007)

After learning that the Good News Club teaches morals and character development from a Biblical perspective, the principal of Minue Elementary School in Carteret, New Jersey, tried to block club meetings on the school premises. The principal first refused to allow flyers to be sent home to inform parents about the club, and then told the club they could not use school premises, even though they paid the usage fee. After receiving an attorney's letter, the school attorney informed the club that they could meet and distribute flyers.

Milwaukee School Limits Number of Students Who May Attend Bible Club

Liberty Counsel, "Milwaukee Public Schools Remove Cap on Good News Clubs," available at http://www.lc.org/index.cfm?PID=14100&PRID=14 (Jan. 11, 2007)

Hi-Mount Elementary School in Milwaukee, Wisconsin, limited the number of school children who could attend the Good News Club and refused to allow permission slips to be sent home to parents, informing them about the club and requesting permission for their children to attend. Good News Club coordinators tried unsuccessfully on numerous occasions to resolve the issue and were forced to file a lawsuit to convince the district to end the discrimination.

School Makes Bible Club Start an Hour After School

Liberty Counsel, "Milwaukee Public Schools Remove Cap on Good News Clubs," available at http://www.lc.org/index.cfm?PID=14100&PRID=14 (Jan. 11, 2007)
Congress Street School in Milwaukee refused to allow its Good News Club to meet until an hour after the end of the school day. Secular clubs were permitted to begin immediately after school. After correspondence with attorneys, the school ended its discriminatory practice.

Ohio Schools Refuse to Allow Bible Club to Distribute Information and Permission Slips

Liberty Counsel, "Ohio School District Halts Discrimination Against Good News Clubs," available at http://www.lc.org/index.cfm?PID=14100&PRID=13 (Jan. 10, 2007)
Good News Clubs in Stow, Ohio, were denied the right to distribute information and parent permission slips to students. Since the parents were not informed of the opportunities to send their children to the after-school Bible clubs, attendance would be limited. After attorneys threatened to take legal action, the schools reversed their decision.

Connecticut School District Requires Extra Fees from Bible Club

Liberty Counsel, "Good News Clubs Return to Connecticut Schools," available at http://www.lc.org/index.cfm?PID=14100&PRID=10 (Jan. 4, 2007)
Wolcott School District in Wolcott, Connecticut, had always charged Good News Clubs only the minimal charges that are applicable to local nonprofit organizations, such as the Boy Scouts. When the Good News Clubs applied to use school facilities for the 2006–07 school year, however, district officials insisted that the Good News Clubs must be charged higher fees as a "non-Wolcott" organization. Following an attorney's letter, the Wolcott School District reversed its decision.

Brown University Suspends Religious Student Organization

FIRE, "Brown University: Wrongful Suspension of Religious Student Group," available at http://thefire.org/case/728.html
Brown University officials suspended a Christian student group, the Reformed University Fellowship. Brown's Office of the Chaplains and Religious Life gave unclear reasons for the suspension. After weeks of public pressure, the Brown administration sent a letter to Reformed Uniformed Fellowship allowing the group to re-affiliate.

School Prohibits Elementary Students from Handing Out Flyers for Vacation Bible School

Montana News Association, "School District Reverses Policy Banning Religious Literature," available at http://www.montanasnews.tv/articles.php?mode=view&id=5249 (Aug. 29, 2006)

Gabriel and Joshua Rakoski, students at Hollymead Elementary School, asked to hand out flyers about a Vacation Bible School. The school district's policy prohibited the "distribution of literature that is for partisan, sectarian, religious or political purposes," and the students' teacher did not allow them to distribute the flyers. Following a demand letter stating that the policy was unconstitutional, the school district changed its policy.

University of Mary Washington Bans All Religious and Political Student Groups

Alliance Defense Fund, "Speak Up: University of Mary Washington," available at http://www.speakupmovement.org/Map/CaseDetails?Case=233

Robert Simpson wanted to start a Christian group on campus at the University of Mary Washington, but the university required that he agree to their nondiscrimination policy and refused to recognize any religious or political group. After receiving a demand letter, the university changed its policies so as to not violate the right to free association or free speech.

High School Cancels "Diversity Day" Instead of Including Christians

http://www.lc.org/pressrelease/2006/nr032206.htm

The Viroqua High School planned a "diversity day" in order to showcase the viewpoints of various religious groups, sexual orientations, and nationalities, but stated that Christian groups and former homosexuals would be excluded. After a legal organization intervened on behalf of the excluded groups, the school district cancelled the event entirely rather than include them.

Fourth Grader Prohibited from Bringing Candy Canes with Story of Jesus to School

Religion Clause, "Student Can Give Classmates Candy Canes with Jesus Story Attached," available at http://religionclause.blogspot.com/2005/12/student-can-giveclassmates-candy.html (Dec. 16, 2005)

Jaren Burch, a fourth-grader in Mansfield, Texas, tried to take candy canes that were attached to a story about Jesus to a class party, but his teacher told him that he would not be allowed to do so. After receiving a demand letter regarding Jaren's First Amendment rights, school officials reversed their position, allowing him to bring the candy canes with the stories.

Community College in New York Prohibits Christian Student Group

Alliance Defense Fund, "Speak Up: North Country Community College," available at http://www.speakupmovement.org/Map/CaseDetails?Case=213

Tammy Snyder, a student at North Country Community College in Saranac Lake, New York, attempted to start a Christian student group on campus. To advertise, Ms. Snyder hung flyers around campus, careful to respect school policy regarding the creation of a student organization. On three separate occasions campus officials removed Ms. Snyder's flyers, informing her that her organization would violate the separation of church and state. After being sent a demand letter, the college reversed its position and allowed Ms. Snyder to establish the club.

Sophomore Suspended for Distributing Religious Pamphlets at School

Kelly McCarthy, "Student suspended for passing out religious material," Student Press Law Center, available at http://www.splc.org/news/newsflash.asp?id=1083 (Sept. 30, 2005)

Samantha Weatherholtz, a sophomore at Fort Defiance High School in Virginia, was suspended for three days for passing out religious pamphlets. Following the suspension, complaints caused the school to revise its speech policy.

Middle School Students Stopped from Praying at the Flagpole

Jim Brown, "School Reverses Decision on Student Prayer Rally," Christianity.com, available at http://www.christianity.com/news/religiontoday/1360179/ (2005)

Three students at a middle school in Barnegat, New Jersey, met at the flagpole and started to pray. A school administrator stopped the students, telling them that they could not participate in "See You at the Pole," that their prayers were creating a "disturbance," and they must stop mixing school and religion. Upon being threatened with a lawsuit, the school reversed its decision and allowed a "do over" prayer meeting.

Texas School District Demands Fees from Bible Club

Grapevine-Colleyville I.S.D. surprised Students Standing Strong (SSS), a student-led Bible study club, on a Friday with an ultimatum that it must sign away its right to be a student club and pay fees in order to hold its previously approved club meeting the following Monday. Other, non-Christian clubs were not given the same ultimatum. After a demand letter was sent, the school district agreed to allow SSS to meet without signing an additional form or paying additional fees.

Principal Stops Performance of Song That Might Mention God

Liberty Counsel, "Kindergarten Class Permitted To Sing Song That Principal Deemed To Be Religious," available at http://www.lc.org/index.cfm?PID=14100&PRID=463 (June 3, 2005)

At an end-of-the-year ceremony, a kindergarten class at Terrytown Elementary School in Terrytown, Louisiana, wished to sing "I Can't Give Up Now," written by Mary Mary. The school principal did not wish to allow the class to perform the song because, even though the song does not mention God, she interpreted the word "he" in the song as referring to God. The principal changed her position and allowed the song only following the threat of a lawsuit and pressure from parents.

Middle School Student Punished for Distributing Church Flyers

Student Press Law Center, "Florida School District Settles Suit with Student Who Challenged Distribution Policy," available at http://www.splc.org/news/newsflash. asp?id=950 (Feb. 11, 2005)

Christine Curran, an eighth-grader at Driftwood Middle School in Hollywood, Florida, took flyers for a church youth conference to pass out at school. Although she was passing them out between classes, school policy required that the flyers be approved by a school official, and Christine was told she would be "written up." After a lawsuit was filed, the school district agreed to rewrite the policy.

College Bans Christian Organization from Showing *The Passion of the Christ*

FIRE, "Indian River Community College: Ban on 'The Passion of the Christ' and Repression of Free Speech," available at http://thefire.org/case/661.html

Indian River Community College (IRCC) in Fort Pierce, Florida, prohibited the Christian Student Fellowship from showing *The Passion of the Christ*. IRCC claimed the prohibition was consistent with its policy prohibiting the showing of R-rated movies. However, IRCC had previously allowed the viewing of an R-rated film, *Welcome to Sarajevo,* as well as the performance of a skit called "F**king for Jesus." After facing intense media scrutiny, IRCC administrators overturned the prohibition.

Muslim Student Suspended for Wearing Head Covering

https://www.rutherford.org/publications_resources/on_the_front_lines/pr492

Nashala Hearn, an eleven-year-old Muslim girl in the Muskogee Public School District, was suspended twice for wearing a head covering, since the school district's dress code did not allow "hats, caps, bandannas, plastic caps, and hoods on jackets." After a lawsuit was filed criticizing the dress code as unconstitutional, the school district changed the code to allow for religious exceptions.

Principal Removes "Christian" from Student Organization's Name
David Limbaugh, Persecution, How Liberals Are Waging War Against Christianity *50–51 (HarperCollins Sept. 7, 2004)*
A Panama City, Florida, principal changed the name of one Bible club from "Fellowship of Christian Students" to "Fellowship of Concerned Students" without conferring with student members. The principal also prohibited the organization from advertising.

Teacher Prevents Kindergarten Student from Giving Out Jellybeans with Religious Poem to Classmates
Rutherford Institute, "Institute Called On to Defend Kindergartner's Right to Religious Expression!" available at https://www.rutherford.org/publications_resources/on_the_front_lines/pr473 (Feb. 9, 2004)
A teacher prevented a kindergarten student from giving out bags of jellybeans along with a religious poem entitled "The Jelly Bean Prayer" to classmates. The school's policy permitted students to distribute secular gifts but not religious gifts.

Schools Refuse to Count Religious Volunteer Work for Graduation Requirement
Rutherford Institute, "School Officials Discriminate Against Religious Puppeteers, Deny Community Credit for Volunteering at Vacation Bible School," available at https://www.rutherford.org/publications_resources/on_the_front_lines/pr454 (Oct. 6, 2003)
Montgomery County Public Schools in Maryland require sixty hours of community service as a prerequisite to graduation. Students who worked at a Vacation Bible School on an Indian Reservation were not permitted to count that time toward their hourly requirement. Attorneys intervened and the students were permitted to count the hours, but, unfortunately, the policy remains and continues to discriminate against students who participate in religiously based community service.

Iowa School Refuses Access to Fellowship of Christian Athletes
http://www.alliancedefendingfreedom.org/News/PRDetail/860
The South Tama Community School District in Iowa refused the Fellowship of Christian Athletes (FCA) access to school facilities, so an FCA member complained. Only after a demand letter was sent to the school district did

the district back down and change their policy to stop discriminating against religiously affiliated groups.

Rutgers University Re-Recognizes Christian Student Group

InterVarsity and Rutgers, "InterVarsity and Rutgers Joint Statement," available at http://www.intervarsity.org/news/intervarsity-and-rutgers-joint-statement (April 1, 2003)

In 2002, Rutgers University denied official status to the InterVarsity Multi-Ethnic Christian Fellowship (InterVarsity) because InterVarsity did not follow the university's nondiscrimination policy. InterVarsity sought to select members who upheld the group's Christian beliefs, a practice deemed discriminatory by the university. After InterVarsity filed suit, Rutgers agreed to recognize the organization and grant it the same privileges available to other university-sanctioned organizations.

University of North Dakota Refuses to Recognize Christian Medical and Dental Association

Alliance Defense Fund, "Speak Up: University of North Dakota," available at http://www.speakupmovement.org/Map/CaseDetails?Case=208

The University of North Dakota refused to officially recognize the school's chapter of the Christian Medical and Dental Association (CMDA). Without formal recognition, the CMDA was barred from receiving funding and publicizing its meetings. The university denied CMDA the right to fully function because the group restricts membership to those who adhere to the association's Christian beliefs. After a lawsuit was threatened, the university recognized CMDA and changed its policy to recognize the rights of religious organizations to maintain their religious integrity.

Texas Tech Defends Professor who Discriminates Against Religious Students

Lisa Falkenberg, "Policy Involving Evolution Prompts Federal Inquiry," Associated Press, Jan. 29, 2003, BC cycle

A Texas Tech professor discriminated against students on the basis of their religion. The university stood behind the professor, saying the professor's policies were not in conflict with those of Texas Tech.

UNC Threatens Christian Student Group for Not Allowing Non-Christian Leaders

Jim Brown, "After Legal Threat, UNC Allows InterVarsity Ministry to Remain on Campus," Agape Press, available at http://thefire.org/public/pdfs/4811_2875.pdf (Jan. 7, 2003)

An administrator at the University of North Carolina at Chapel Hill threatened to strip InterVarsity Christian Fellowship (IVCF) of funding because of IVCF's refusal to allow non-Christians to serve in leadership roles. After being threatened with a lawsuit, UNC allowed IVCF to continue as an officially recognized student organization.

Teacher Throws Away Students' Bibles and Threatens to Call CPS

David Limbaugh, Persecution: How Liberals are Waging War Against Christianity 45 (Regnery Pub. Jan. 1, 2003)

A schoolteacher at Lynn Lucas Middle School near Houston, Texas, threw away two students' Truth for Youth Bibles and took the students to the principal's office where she threatened to call Child Protective Services on their parents for permitting them to bring their Bibles. Later, at the same school, different officials threw away a student's book cover showing the Ten Commandments, claiming the Ten Commandments are hate speech and could offend students.

Elementary Student Told She Cannot Read Religious Book As Her Favorite Book About Christmas Traditions

http://www.freerepublic.com/focus/f-news/724609/posts

A second-grade teacher at Northwest Elementary School in Massachusetts, as part of a class project, asked students to bring books to class about their Christmas traditions. Laura Greska, a second-grader, brought a book called "The First Christmas," but her teacher stopped her from reading it because it was religious. A lawsuit was filed against the school district for violating Laura's First Amendment rights.

School Prohibits Students from Distributing Candy Canes with "Jesus Loves You"

Catholic League, "2002 Report on Anti-Catholicism: Education," available at http://www.catholicleague.org/education-9/ (Dec. 31, 2002)

School officials in Reno, Nevada, prohibited students in a Bible club from distributing candy canes with the message "Jesus Loves You" attached to them. After the club sought legal assistance, the school reversed its policy.

Teacher Prevents Kindergarten Student From Praying Before Snacks

Frank J. Murray, "Federal Court Hears Lawsuit Over Kindergarten Christian; New York Schools May Relent, May Let Tot Say Grace at Meals," Washington Times, *April 12, 2002*

Kindergartner Kayla Broadus prayed, "God is good. God is great. Thank you, God, for my food," with two classmates at her school in Saratoga Springs, New York, at the snack table before they ate their snack. Her teacher silenced the prayer, scolded Kayla, and informed the school's lawyer. A lawsuit ensued over the child's prayer.

College Students Passing Out Religious Cards Threatened with Arrest

Adrian Sainz, "Miami-Dade Community College, students settle free-speech suit," Jacksonville.com, available at http://jacksonville.com/tu-online/apnews/ stories/061402/D7K56C984.html (Jun. 14, 2002)

Students at Miami-Dade Community College tried to distribute business-sized cards to other students on campus. Each card had a number for people to call where they could hear a recorded message about Jesus Christ. Campus security officers approached and told the students that they couldn't pass out the cards. Later, the students returned to resume handing out their cards and were approached by security guards and an administration official. When the students tried to leave, more security officers and a police officer were summoned to threaten the students with arrest. A lawsuit had to be filed to protect the students' rights.

University Prohibits Student Organization from Hosting Event with Prayer and Invitation to Follow Christ

Alliance Defense Fund, "Speak Up: University of Texas-Pan American," available at http://www.speakupmovement.org/Map/CaseDetails?Case=226

The University of Texas-Pan American did not allow a student group, Chi Alpha, to host an event at which a guest speaker would lead prayer and have a call to follow Christ. After receiving a demand letter, the university allowed the event to be held.

Students Told They May Paint Panels at School So Long As None Reference God or Jesus

https://www.rutherford.org/publications_resources/on_the_front_lines/pr411

When students at the Boca Raton School District in Florida were permitted to paint panels around the high school, members of the Fellowship of Christian Athletes were told that they could not paint messages with references to

God or Jesus. The members and their parents were forced to file a lawsuit against the school to stop the discrimination.

ACLU Attempts to Remove "God Bless America" Sign Posted at School Following 9/11

Ryan McCarthy, "School Rallies to Retain Sign; The ACLU Says the Message 'God Bless America' Divides Kids by Religion and is Unconstitutional," The Sacramento Bee (Oct. 6, 2001)

In the wake of Sept. 11, 2001, Breen Elementary School posted a sign that said "God Bless America." The ACLU intervened in an attempt to have the sign removed, calling it a clear violation of the U.S. and California constitutions.

Elementary Student Prevented from Handing Out Religious Valentine's Day Cards

Freedom Forum, "Wisconsin School Board: Girl May Hand Out Religious Cards," available at http://www.freedomforum.org/templates/document. asp?documentID=14741 (Aug. 29, 2001)

Morgan Nyman, a second-grader at Cushing Elementary School in Delafield, Wisconsin, was told by school officials that she could not hand out her Valentine's Day cards because they contained religious messages and would violate the separation of church and state. The school district changed its position and apologized after a lawsuit was filed on Morgan's behalf.

Third Grader Forced to Turn Shirt That Says "Jesus Christ" Inside Out

Bangor Daily News, "School Cool to Girl's 'Jesus' Sweatshirt," available at http://news.google.com/newspapers?nid=2457&dat=20010214&id=ea5JAAAAIBAJ&sjid=eg4NAAAAIBAJ&pg=4209,3647441 (Feb. 14, 2001)

Gelsey Bostick, a third-grader at Asa Adams School in Orono, Maine, was required to wear her shirt inside out because it had the words "Jesus Christ" on it. The principal defended the actions and stated that it was a matter of the shirt being interpreted by the students as bearing swear words. After a legal center intervened on Gelsey's behalf, the school reversed its position.

Middle School Student Prevented from Wearing Cross Necklace

Freedom Forum, "Alabama School District Settles Dispute Over Cross Necklace," available at http://www.freedomforum.org/templates/document. asp?documentID=11770 (Mar. 1, 2000)

Kandice Smith, a sixth-grader at Curry Middle School in Jasper, Alabama, wore a cross necklace to school and was told by her principal that if she did not conceal it she could be suspended. The school dress code barred jewelry worn outside of clothing. The school only reversed its position after a lawsuit was filed on Kandice's behalf.

Valedictorian Told He Must Give "Secular" Speech
Alliance Defense Fund, "ADF Achieves Victory for Valedictorian," available at http://www.alliancedefensefund.org/Home/ADFContent?cid=2736
Matthew Reynolds, the valedictorian at HLV Junior-Senior High School in Victor, Iowa, wished to express his faith and attribute his success to faith in Jesus Christ in his graduation speech. However, although Matthew planned to begin by clarifying that his views were not the views of the school or the administration, the school principal told Matthew that he must make his speech "secular." Following an attorney's letter explaining the law and Matthew's rights, the principal allowed Matthew to give the speech as he intended.

Student Told She Cannot Tell Her Friends About Her Church Youth Group
Alliance Defense Fund, "Student Can Now Share About Her Youth Group," available at http://www.alliancedefensefund.org/Home/ADFContent?cid=3176
In Flagstaff, Arizona, sixth-grader Caitlin Ribelin was told that she was not allowed to give information about her church youth group to her friends, since school policies did not allow religious materials. After a lawsuit was filed on her behalf, the school changed its policy to allow all literature to be treated the same on school campuses.

Elementary School Student Punished for Praying Before Meals
Joan Little, "City Schools Issue Rules About Students, Religion," St. Louis Post-Dispatch, *July 11, 1996, at 2B*
Elementary school student Raymond Raines was "caught" praying over his meal at his elementary school. He was lifted from his seat and reprimanded in front of all the other students, then taken to the principal who ordered him to cease praying in school.

School Administrators Worry About Students Reading Bibles During Lunch Breaks
Barbara Vobejda, "School Officials Weigh Sachs' Ruling on Religious Gatherings," Washington Post, *Dec. 8, 1984 at B3*
Maryland's Attorney General ruled that Catonsville High School students could continue their informal religious activity of gathering to read the Bible during their Thursday lunch hours. School administrators were worried about the ruling because they feared it would create problems in a "sensitive area."

FIRST LIBERTY

ATTACKS AGAINST CHURCHES AND MINISTRIES

Supreme Court Upholds Right of Religious Organizations to Select Their Own Spiritual Leaders

Hosanna-Tabor Evangelical Lutheran Church & School v. EEOC, 132 S. Ct. 694 (2012)

Cheryl Perich, a teacher at Hosanna-Tabor Lutheran School, was fired for threatening to sue the school after she was asked not to return because she had narcolepsy. Perich sued under the Americans with Disabilities Act. The school argued its right to hire or fire Perich based on the "ministerial exception," which legally protects the rights of churches and ministries to select their religious leaders without government interference. During oral argument at the Supreme Court, the government argued that there is no ministerial exception, allowing the government to regulate who a church may hire or fire as its religious leaders. The Supreme Court upheld the ministerial exception and specified that government regulation of the hiring and firing of ministers would violate both the Free Exercise Clause and the Establishment Clause.

Freedom From Religion Foundation Sues to Restrict Federal Funds from Faith-Based Charities

Hein v. Freedom From Religion Foundation, 551 U.S. 587 (2007)

The Freedom From Religion Foundation filed a lawsuit against the White House claiming the Establishment Clause bars faith-based charities from receiving government funding. In a 5-4 decision, the U.S. Supreme Court ruled that an atheist organization lacked taxpayer standing to challenge a White House conference that informed both faith-based and secular organizations about federal funding for programs that help the poor.

City Council Holds Emergency Meetings to Keep Out Unwanted Church

Church of the Lukumi Babalu Aye, Inc. v. City of Hialeah, 508 U.S. 520 (1993)

The Church of the Lukumi Babalu Aye sought to set up a church in Florida. The church practices Santeria, a religion that incorporates animal sacrifice into its religious practices. Upon hearing of the church's plan to develop a church in the city, the city council held an emergency meeting and passed ordinances to prevent the church from practicing the animal sacrifice, an essential part of the church's free exercise. A lawsuit had to be filed to protect the church's right to free exercise.

New York City Attempts to Sow Confustion About Pregnancy Resource Centers

Evergreen Association, Inc. v. City of New York, 740 F.3d 233 (2d Cir. 2014)

New York City enacted a law that would compel "pregnancy service centers" to post signs about services they do not provide, distracting from the messages those organizations want to communicate. A federal district court found that the definition of "pregnancy service centers" was overly vague and that the ordinance was subject to strict scrutiny and not narrowly tailored. The U.S. Court of Appeals for the Second Circuit affirmed most of the district court's ruling but held that the government could likely require signage stating whether a center has medical staff.

Township Burdens Small Church That Wants to Open Seminary

First Korean Church of New York, Inc. v. Cheltenham Tp. Zoning Hearing Bd., No. 12-1917, 2013 WL 362819 (3d Cir. 2013)

In 1996, First Korean Church in Cheltenham Township, Pennsylvania, purchased property to use as a church and seminary. While the township allowed educational and religious uses in the property owned by the church, the township refused to allow the seminary because the church had not sought authorization from the state to operate the seminary. In 2003, Cheltenham Township enacted an ordinance that required churches to apply for a variance. When First Korean Church sought the variance, the township denied the application. The township also burdened the small church with high taxes. First Korean Church brought a lawsuit in an attempt to obtain relief but was denied relief by a Federal District Court in Pennsylvania and by the U.S. Court of Appeals for the Third Circuit. The U.S. Supreme Court has also denied review.

Baltimore Requires Pregnancy Resource Centers to Post Misleading Information

Greater Baltimore Ctr. for Pregnancy Concerns, Inc. v. Mayor & City Council of Baltimore, Nos. 11-1111 and 11-1185, 2013 U.S. App. LEXIS 13607 (4th Cir. 2013) (en banc)

Baltimore's city council passed an ordinance that compelled limited-service pregnancy centers, such as those maintained by religious organizations, to post signs stating that they do not provide or make referrals for abortion or birth control services. Claiming the church's free speech, free exercise of religion, and equal protection rights were violated, the Roman Catholic Congregation, Inc., and the Greater Baltimore Center for Pregnancy Concerns, Inc., sued the city. The district court held that the ordinance violated the centers' free speech rights, but the Fourth Circuit Court of Appeals, en banc, said that the district court erred in its handling of the case and ordered the district court to reconsider the case.

Bible Camp Forced to Sue for Right to Build

Eagle Cove Camp & Conference Ctr., Inc. v. Town of Woodboro, Wis., 734 F.3d 673 (7th Cir. 2013)

Eagle Cove Camp and Conference Center sought to construct a Bible camp on land that they owned in Woodboro, Wisconsin. When Eagle Cove applied for permission to build the camp, the city continually denied their requests, alleging that the camp could not conform to local zoning requirements. Finally, Eagle Cove brought a lawsuit, but both the district court and the court of appeals found for the city.

Florida Town Attempts to Block Expansion of Synagogue by Declaring It a Historical Landmark

Temple B'Nai Zion, Inc. v. City of Sunny Isles Beach, Fla., 727 F.3d 1349 (11th Cir. 2013)

Reformed Jewish synagogue Temple B'Nai Zion in Sunny Isles, Florida, had plans to expand their facilities due to their growing congregation. Instead, the Sunny Isles City Commission voted to classify Temple B'Nai Zion's land as historic and blocked the planned expansion. Temple B'Nai Zion filed a lawsuit challenging the city's blocking of the expansion. The lawsuit is ongoing.

County in Maryland Repeatedly Attempts to Stop Church Construction

Reaching Hearts Int'l, Inc. v. Prince George's County, 478 Fed. Appx. 54 (4th Cir. 2012)

The county of Prince George, Maryland, denied Reaching Hearts International Church clearance to build a new church. The suit, which began in 2008 against the county for opposing the construction of a new building, continued on as the county denied the district court's order to provide water and sewage lines to the property. The district court also affirmed a jury award of $3.7 million in damages for the church. The church filed another suit against the county in July of 2011 seeking to enforce the order to supply water and sewage lines and claiming that the resistance is due to a personal vendetta of one of the county councilmen. The Fourth Circuit affirmed the district court's decision in favor of the church.

Mississippi Town Tries to Stop Church from Moving into Abandoned Downtown Property

Opulent Life Church v. City of Holly Springs, MS, No. 12-60052 (5th Cir. 2012)
The Opulent Life Church in Holly Springs, Mississippi, wanted to move into a larger facility as it had nearly outgrown its present meeting place. Once the church found a new property, however, it also discovered that the city would not grant a permit for the church to move into the new property without getting permission of sixty percent of all property owners within a one-quarter mile radius of the proposed site—a requirement that applied only to churches and to no other type of facility or business. Liberty Institute filed a lawsuit against the City of Holly Springs on behalf of the Opulent Life Church for violating the Constitution and the Religious Land Use and Institutionalized Persons Act, which prohibits zoning ordinances from discriminating against churches. The case settled, and Opulent Life Church is now free to move into its new property.

Lawsuit Stops City from Giving Land to Religious School in Exchange for Use of Athletic Facilities

Wirtz v. City of South Bend, 669 F.3d 860 (7th Cir. 2012)
South Bend, Indiana, transferred some land to St. Joseph's Catholic School in exchange for having use of the school's athletic facilities. Taxpayers sued to stop the transfer, claiming that granting land to a religious school for occasional use of the school's athletic facilities violated the Establishment Clause. A federal district court granted an injunction to stop the transfer. South Bend eventually requested and was granted a modification to the injunction to allow it to sell the property, which it did to the school. The city then appealed the initial injunction, but the appeal was dismissed as moot and untimely.

Seven-Sky Challenges Obamacare for Forcing Purchase of Insurance

Seven-Sky v. Holder, 661 F.3d 1 (D.C. Cir. 2011)
Seven-Sky challenged the Patient Protection and Affordable Care Act (Obamacare) claiming it exceeded Congressional Commerce Clause authority and violated the Religious Freedom Restoration Act because the mandate to purchase insurance was a mandate to violate Seven-Sky's religious belief that purchasing insurance expresses skepticism in God's ability to provide. The courts held the act does not exceed Commerce Clause authority and that it does not violate the Religious Freedom Restoration Act.

Texas Town Bans Church from Commercial Property
The Elijah Group, Inc. v. The City of Leon Valley, Texas, 643 F.3d 419 (5th Cir. 2011)
Leon Valley, Texas, prohibited a church from meeting on property that was zoned for businesses. The Fifth Circuit held that this violated the Religious Land Use and Institutionalized Persons Act's (RLUIPA) requirement that churches be treated on "equal terms" with other organizations. The church was then allowed to meet on the property, and the city agreed to pay $250,000 in legal fees to the church.

FFRF Sues to Stop Tax Exemption for Ministers' Housing
Freedom From Religion Foundation, Inc. v. Geithner, 644 F.3d 836 (9th Cir. 2011)
Plaintiffs challenged the parsonage exemption, which provides a tax exemption for "ministers of the gospel." Ministers are able to receive allowances, which are not considered taxable income under the statute. Suit was filed under California law and federal law. The state defendants were granted their Motion to Dismiss, but the federal defendants were not.

San Diego County Attempts to Stop Church from Using Recreational Building for Church Service
Guatay Christian Fellowship v. County of San Diego, 670 F.3d 957 (9th Cir. 2011)
http://www.pacificjustice.org/press-releases/county-drops-bid-toturn-church-into-bar
The Guatay Christian Fellowship used a recreational building in a trailer park as a space for church services for twenty-two years before the County of San Diego attempted to stop the use because the church did not have a permit to use the building as a recreational facility. The Ninth Circuit dismissed the church's RLUIPA and constitutional claims against the county on the grounds that they were not ripe because the church still had not applied for a permit. The county eventually granted a permit to the church to allow continued operations.

Lawsuit Attempts to Stop Rescue Mission from Requiring Religious Participation
Intermountain Fair Housing Council v. Boise Rescue Mission Ministries, 657 F.3d 988 (9th Cir. 2011)
The Intermountain Fair Housing Council and two individuals filed suit against Boise Rescue Mission Ministries alleging that the mission was in violation of the Fair Housing Act and that it engaged in religious discrimination by holding chapel services and requiring guests in the discipleship program to participate in religious programs. The district court ruled in favor of the

mission, a homeless shelter that receives no government funding and provides free and voluntary services. The Ninth Circuit affirmed.

City of Yuma Attempts to Block Church from Meeting in Former Department Store

Centro Familiar Cristiano Buenas Nuevas Christian Church v. City of Yuma, 651 F.3d 1163 (9th Cir. 2011)

A church in Yuma, Arizona, purchased an old department store to use as a new church building. Yuma required that religious organizations receive a permit to use a building for religious purposes. The city denied the permit, claiming that it wanted to convert the part of the city where the department store was located into an entertainment district, and no bars, nightclubs, or liquor stores could be within 300 feet of a church. The Ninth Circuit held that under the Religious Land Use and Institutionalized Persons Act (RLUIPA), the city could not single out a church for discrimination in zoning restrictions.

City Attempts to Keep Church from Meeting in Industrial Use Area

International Church of Foursquare Gospel v. City of San Leandro, California, 673 F.3d 1059 (9th Cir. 2011)

San Leandro, California, denied a rezoning application and a conditional use permit to a church, and the church sued claiming violations of the Religious Land Use and Institutionalized Persons Act (RLUIPA), the First Amendment, and the Fourth Amendment. The district court granted summary judgment to the city. The Ninth Circuit reversed the lower court, however, holding that the lower court erred when it held as a matter of law that a city does not impose a substantial burden in violation of RLUIPA when its use permit process is neutral and of general applicability. The Ninth Circuit also held that the city did not prove that its interest in preserving an area for industrial use was compelling, and a fact issue remained whether the city used the least restrictive means to achieve its interests.

Lawsuit Attempts to Stop County from Providing Loans to Church for Low-Income Housing

Glassman v. Arlington County, Virginia, 628 F.3d 140 (4th Cir. 2010)

In 2004, First Baptist Church of Clarendon in Arlington County, Virginia, proposed a plan to build a ten-story tall building on church property with the bottom two floors being used as the church and the upper eight floors being used for apartments, including some low-rate and moderate-rate apartments. Arlington County approved these plans and provided loans to finance the construction of the apartments. Glassman sued the county claiming that this involvement violated the Establishment Clause. A federal district court and the Fourth Circuit Court of Appeals both held that the county's involvement did not advance the First Baptist Church of Clarendon's faith, thus there was no violation of the Establishment Clause.

San Francisco Issues Anti-Catholic Resolution
Catholic League for Religious and Civil Rights v. San Francisco, 624 F. 3d 1043 (9th Cir. 2010) (en banc)
Cardinal William Levada told Catholic adoption agencies to stop placing children with homosexual couples. The City of San Francisco issued an anti-Catholic resolution, calling Cardinal Levada's statement "hateful" and "discriminatory" and calling on him to rescind his request. The Catholic League and two individual Catholics sued San Francisco for violating the Establishment Clause. An eleven-judge panel of the Ninth Circuit Court of Appeals ruled in favor of the city, concurring with the decision by the district court to dismiss the case.

Church Sues for Right to Expand Building
Rocky Mountain Christian Church v. Board of County Commissioners of Boulder County, Colorado, 613 F.3d 1229 (10th Cir. 2010)
When Rocky Mountain Christian Church and School applied for a permit in 2004 to expand its building, Boulder County rejected its application. Evidence at trial showed that the county applied zoning ordinances non-neutrally. The church sued and won at the federal district court, which held that the county had violated the Religious Land Use and Institutionalized Persons Act. The Tenth Circuit Court of Appeals affirmed.

Lawsuit Challenges Unconstitutional Pittsburgh Law Regulation Protesting of Abortions
Brown v. City of Pittsburgh, 586 F.3d 263 (3d Cir. 2009)
The United States Court of Appeals for the Third Circuit found that a Pittsburgh law requiring protesters to remain 15 feet from hospital entrances and 8 feet from hospital patrons while within 100 feet of a hospital is unconstitutionally overbroad and vague. The law was passed in an effort to keep pro-life demonstrators away from hospital patrons that may be seeking an abortion.

Louisiana Police Officer Threatens Preachers with Arrest
World Wide Street Preachers Fellowship v. Town of Columbia, 591 F.3d 747 (5th Cir. 2009)
A police officer in Columbia, Louisiana, arrested one street preacher and threatened others with arrest for preaching on state property. The officer

told the preachers, "You cannot picket, boycott, on state property or right-of-way." The U.S. Court of Appeals for the Fifth Circuit affirmed the district court's holding that the police officer violated the street preachers' First Amendment rights, but refused to hold the city of Columbia liable because the city did not have a custom or practice of prohibiting street preachers.

Atheist Group Sues to Stop Funds for Cleanup in Detroit from Going to Church

American Atheists, Inc. v. City of Detroit, 567 F.3d 278 (6th Cir. 2009)
St. John's Episcopal Church entered into a contract with the City of Detroit Development Authority to improve its exterior appearance in order to enhance the city's image prior to the 2006 Super Bowl and to spur economic development in the area. The contract provided for reimbursement of half of the church's expenses, up to $180,000. After the American Atheists filed suit against the city, city officials withheld the reimbursement promised to the church. The Sixth Circuit held that the city's revitalization program did not violate the Establishment Clause or the Michigan Constitution.

Former Employee Sues Ministry for Holding to Religious Beliefs

Pedreira v. Kentucky Baptist Homes for Children, Inc., 579 F.3d 722 (6th Cir. 2009)
Kentucky Baptist Homes for Children (KBHC) is a Christian organization that provides assistance to abused children. Due to its religious beliefs, KBHC has a policy against supporting homosexual conduct. Accordingly, KBHC terminated one of its employees, Alicia Pedreira, after discovering her active lesbian conduct. Pedreira sued KBHC for holding to its religious beliefs, but the United States Court of Appeals for the Sixth Circuit found in favor of KBHC. Pedreira then tried to cut KHBC's government funding, stating that it violated the Establishment Clause. A settlement ensued that allowed KHBC to keep its funding but subjected them to intense scrutiny regarding any religious activity.

Christian Peer Support Group Cannot Encourage Looking to God at Mandatory Meeting

Milwaukee Deputy Sheriffs' Association v. Clarke, 588 F.3d 523 (7th Cir. 2009)
The Seventh Circuit Court of Appeals held that inviting a Christian peer support group to mandatory police officer meetings where the speakers encouraged the officers to look to God for guidance was a violation of the Establishment Clause.

Town of Gilbert Discriminates Against Religious Signs
Reed v. Town of Gilbert, 587 F.3d 966 (9th Cir. 2009)
A Gilbert, Arizona, sign ordinance discriminated against certain signs based on the content of the signs. According to the code, religious assembly signs were required to be smaller in size, fewer in number, and displayed for much less time than similar nonreligious signs. The ordinance also allowed ideological and political signs to be posted without a permit, whereas a permit was required to post religious assembly signs. A federal district court denied an injunction against the sign ordinance. The U.S. Court of Appeals for the Ninth Circuit, in a two-to-one decision, upheld the discriminatory ordinance.

County Attempts to Ban Rabbi from Having Religious Services in His Home
Konikov v. Orange County, 276 Fed. Appx. 916 (11th Cir. 2008)
Rabbi Joseph Konikov was ordered by county code enforcement officials to stop holding prayer meetings in his home, alleging that he was in violation of local laws prohibiting "operating a synagogue or any function related to a synagogue and/or church services..." He was ordered to stop the prayer meetings or face daily fines totaling nearly $56,000. Only at the Court of Appeals were the ordinance and fines overruled.

City Bans Church from "Religious Use" of Property in Commercial District
Digrugilliers v. Consolidated City of Indianapolis, 506 F.3d 612 (7th Cir. 2007)
A Baptist church was told the church's "religious use" of its property violated the city's zoning code, which prohibited "religious use" of property in a commercial district. City officials told the church it would need to obtain special permission to use the building for religious purposes and threatened the church with a lawsuit, fines of up to $2,500 for each violation, and court costs.

Town Changes Zoning Ordinance to Exclude Churches
Petra Presbyterian Church v. Village of Northbrook, 489 F.3d 846 (7th Cir. 2007)
Following a purchase of property by a church, Northbrook changed the zoning ordinance to prevent churches from operating within its zone. The town obtained an injunction to prevent the church from meeting. The district court held that the church failed to show that the altered zoning ordinance burdened the church's exercise of religion even though they had to meet elsewhere. After an appeal, the appellate court affirmed the district court's ruling.

City of Boise Prohibits Religious Activities at Homeless Shelter
Community House, Inc. v. City of Boise, 490 F.3d 1041 (9th Cir. 2007)
Boise, Idaho, leased a homeless shelter to a nonprofit Christian organization,

which provided voluntary chapel services and other religious activities at the shelter. The city then barred religious activities from the shelter. The organization filed a lawsuit to protect its right to conduct religious activities at the shelter. A federal district court granted an injunction prohibiting the city from banning religious activities at the shelter, but the Ninth Circuit Court of Appeals reversed, saying that there should be no religious activities at the shelter, even if participation is voluntary.

San Francisco Police Prohibit Religious Sound Amplification While Permitting Others
Rosenbaum v. City and County of San Francisco, 484 F.3d 1142 (9th Cir. 2007)
Rosenbaum and Livingston had been sharing the Gospel message using amplified sound in the streets and parks of San Francisco since 1978. Beginning in 1995, however, many of their permit applications for sound amplification were either denied or issued with significant restrictions. San Francisco police arrested Livingston on numerous occasions in response to hecklers' complaints about the content of Livingston's message. On one occasion, police issued a citation against Livingston but refused to cite persons from 'Reckless Records,' who were using an eighty-watt amplifier fifteen feet away from Livingston without a permit. On more than a dozen occasions, the city denied permits requested by Rosenbaum and Livingston. A lawsuit was filed, and the Ninth Circuit failed to sanction this unlawful discrimination, issuing a ruling in favor of the San Francisco officials.

School Excludes Nativity Scenes While Permitting Menorahs and Star and Crescents
Skoros v. City of New York, 437 F.3d 1 (2d Cir. 2006)
A Catholic parent objected to a policy of excluding a Nativity scene from the schools' holiday displays while permitting menorahs, the Star and Crescent, and Christmas trees. A lawsuit was filed to remedy the exclusion of the Nativity scene. The court determined that it was appropriate to exclude the Nativity scene as it was still a religious symbol while the others had become secularized and that a child would not perceive an endorsement of Judaism or Islam or a disapproval of Christianity. The Second Circuit affirmed the district court's ruling.

Lawsuit Seeks Equal Access for Religious Worship Use at Library
Faith Center Church Evangelistic Ministries v. Glover, 462 F.3d 1194 (9th Cir. 2006)
Contra Costa County, California, allows educational, cultural, or community-

related meetings at its library, but explicitly prohibits religious worship. Faith Center Church sued for access to the library, but the Ninth Circuit held that excluding religious worship is a permissible exclusion from the forum.

Cheyenne Stops Church from Operating Daycare in Residential Area
Grace United Methodist Church v. City of Cheyenne, 451 F.3d 643 (10th Cir. 2006)
The City of Cheyenne denied a nonprofit church's request for a variance to operate a daycare in a residential zoning area. The district court ruled and an appellate court affirmed the exercise of a daycare was not a sincere exercise of the church's religion and that the city properly denied the church's daycare request in the interest of the health, safety, and welfare of citizens.

Lawsuit Attempts to Oust Leadership of Hindu Temple
Hindu Temple Society of North America v. Supreme Court of the State of New York, 142 Fed. Appx. 492 (2d Cir. 2005)
Six individuals sued the Hindu Temple Society of North America, a house of worship they rarely attended, asking to be put in charge of the leadership of the Temple. They wanted to restructure the Temple's governing board and asked the court to place them in a position of authority within the Temple. After a four-year battle, the New York Court of Appeals ruled in favor of the Hindu Temple, granting them their right to order their worship as they deemed fit.

Officers Used Misleading Information to Remove Students from Christian Boarding School
Heartland Academy Community Church v. Waddle, 427 F.3d 525 (8th Cir. 2005)
Chief Juvenile Officers for the state of Missouri were upset with the teaching of a Christian boarding school. The officers conspired to use misleading information to obtain a removal order and then sent in juvenile authorities and armed law enforcement officers to remove 115 of the school's students. The Eighth Circuit Court of Appeals held that the seizures were unreasonable under the Fourth Amendment and that the officers violated the school's procedural due process and freedom of association.

FFRF Sues to Limit Access to Faith-Based Halfway House
Freedom From Religion Foundation v. McCallum, 324 F.3d 880 (7th Cir. 2003)
The Freedom From Religion Foundation filed a lawsuit to prevent correctional authorities from directing inmates to the Faith Works halfway house because that halfway house incorporates Christianity into its program.

Church Association Sues Chicago Over Zoning Laws
Civil Liberties for Urban Believers v. City of Chicago, No. 01-4030, 2003 U.S. App. LEXIS 24176 (7th Cir. 2003)
Civil Liberties for Urban Believers (CLUB), an association of forty Chicago-area churches, sued the City of Chicago arguing that the city's zoning laws placed an undue burden on churches and were thus in violation of the Constitution, Illinois' Religious Freedom Restoration Act, and RLUIPA. The appellate court ruled against CLUB, continuing to make it difficult for Chicago churches to build and expand within the city.

Separationist Groups Sue Texas for Working with Faith-Based Charities
American Jewish Congress v. Bost, 37 Fed. Appx. 91 (5th Cir. 2002)
"Separation of church and state" groups sued the State of Texas in federal district court for its charitable choice program. The lawsuit was an attempt to strike down the charitable efforts of several businesses and churches involved in a program to move people off welfare roles into paying jobs.

Town Revokes Permit for Church to Hold Worship Services
Amandola v. Town of Babylon, 251 F.3d 339 (2d Cir. 2001)
Romans Chapter Ten Ministries, Inc. had obtained a permit to use Babylon's Town Hall Annex to hold worship services, but when an angry resident called the city to complain about the facilities being used for church services, the town revoked the permit. The church had to file a lawsuit to protect their right to access the community facilities and to end the religious discrimination. The Second Circuit held that revocation of the permit violated the First Amendment.

Lawsuit Attempts to Stop Montgomery County's Religious Accommodation
Ehlers-Renzi v. Connelly School of the Holy Child, 224 F.3d 283 (4th Cir. 2000)
An ordinance in Montgomery County, Maryland, accommodated churches by exempting them from acquiring a special permit before constructing a school on church property. A lawsuit was filed to attempt to strike down the law. The Fourth Circuit held that the ordinance did not violate the Establishment Clause.

Church Prohibited from Showing Religious Film at Senior Center
Church on the Rock v. City of Albuquerque, 84 F.3d. 1273 (10th Cir. 1996)
Albuquerque, New Mexico, prohibited Church on the Rock from showing a religious film at a senior center or passing out Bibles to people at the center. Church on the Rock sued to be able to show the film and distribute Bibles. A federal district court found for the city, but the Tenth Circuit reversed, holding

that Albuquerque had engaged in unconstitutional viewpoint discrimination against the church.

Village Blocks Diocese's Plans to Build Cemetery

The Roman Catholic Diocese of Rockville Ctr. v. The Incorporated Vill. of Old Westbury, No. 09-CV-5195(PKC) (E.D.NY. Sept. 3, 2015)

The Roman Catholic Diocese of Rockville Centre's plans to create a cemetery have been repeatedly blocked by a Long Island village since 1994. The diocese claims that the village imposed arbitrary and unreasonable burdens preventing it from using the property for its intended religious purpose. Judge Pamela K. Chen has allowed the diocese's case to continue.

Phoenix Threatens to Shut Down Home Bible Study

Salman v. City of Phoenix, No. CV-12-01219-PHX-JAT (D. Ariz. Aug. 27, 2015)

A Phoenix, Arizona, Bible study in a private home may be forced to close. The city has applied its building code to the thirty-five person Bible study to require the home to meet the building requirements applied to churches. The owners of the home have brought suit to allow their private Bible studies to continue.

Church Told to Close Over Permit Requirements After Ten Years

Church of Our Lord & Savior Jesus Christ v. City of Markham, No. 15 C 4079 (N.D. Ill. Aug. 19, 2015)

After operating in the same location for ten years without issue, the Church of Our Lord and Savior Jesus Christ received a summons requiring it to close because it had not received a conditional use permit. The church sued the city of Markham, Illinois, under Illinois' Religious Freedom Restoration Act and the federal Religious Land Use and Institutionalized Persons Act. A federal district court declined to dismiss the case.

New Jersey Bars Catholic Cemetery from Selling Its Own Headstones

Roman Catholic Archdiocese of Newark v. Christie, No. 3:2015cv05647 (D.N.J., filed July 20, 2015)

Targeting the Archdiocese of New Jersey, the state of New Jersey barred any religious organization that controls a cemetery from selling memorials, vaults, or mausoleums. In response, the Institute for Justice on behalf of the Archdiocese filed a lawsuit to protect its right to sell headstones for its private community on its private property. The law was passed after the local headstone industry group lost a lawsuit against the church the year before.

Former Teacher Sues Catholic School for Holding to Catholic Beliefs

Dollar v. Trs. of Mount de Sales Acad. Inc., No. 5:2015-cv-00253 (M.D. Ga., filed June 29, 2015)

Flint Dollar, a music teacher at Mount de Sales Academy Catholic school in Macon, Georgia, was fired after informing the school that he planned to enter into a same-sex marriage. The school released a statement that it was committed to upholding the Catholic teaching on marriage, and same-sex marriage goes against Catholic doctrine. Dollar filed a federal lawsuit against the school.

San Diego Forces Church Off of Property with Zoning Change

San Diego Christian Worship Center Church, Inc. v. City of San Diego, No. 37-2015-00017917-CU-OR-CTL (San Diego Sup. Ct., filed May 28, 2015)

The San Diego Christian Worship Center in Kearny Mesa opened in 1995 and has since invested over $700,000 in improvements to its property. In 2014, however, city planners decided to change the zoning in which the church property sits to exclude the church. The San Diego Christian Worship Center filed a lawsuit against the city to avoid being forced off its property. The litigation is ongoing.

Jury Fines Catholic School $1.9 Million for Enforcing Moral Code of Conduct

Herx v. Diocese of Fort Wayne—S. Bend, Inc., No. 1:12-CV-122 RLM, 2015 U.S. Dist. LEXIS 3047 (N.D. Ind. Jan. 12, 2015)

A jury found that the Roman Catholic Diocese of Fort-Wayne-South Bend must pay $1.9 million to a St. Vincent de Paul Catholic School teacher who was fired for undergoing in vitro fertilization. Even though the jury was instructed that Catholic doctrine views the procedure as gravely immoral, the jury penalized the school for firing the teacher under its faith-based code of conduct. The judge lowered the amount to $403,608.

Bayview, Texas, Bans Church and Religious School from Operating on Their Own Property

Cornerstone Church by the Bay v. Town of Bayview, Texas, No. 1:14-cv-00126 (S.D. Tex., filed Jul. 22, 2014)

Cornerstone Church in Bayview, Texas, was gifted property, which it sought to use as a church and religious school. Bayview refused to allow the property to be used as a church or religious school, however, and the Bayview Board of Aldermen voted unanimously to ban churches and schools from the area where Cornerstone's property sits, despite allowing nonreligious institutions in the same area. Liberty Institute filed a lawsuit against Bayview, Texas, and a U.S. district court judge issued a preliminary injunction blocking Bayview from enforcing their zoning ordinance against the property.

Atheist Groups Sue to Block Tax-Exempt Status for Churches and Parsonages

American Atheists v. Shulman, No. 2:12-cv-00264 (E.D. Ky. May 19, 2014)
http://religionclause.blogspot.com/2014/05/court-rejects-atheists-attack-on-church.html
http://www.atheists.org/document.doc?id=34
Several atheist groups filed a lawsuit challenging tax-exempt status for churches and the tax exemption for parsonages. The court held that the plaintiffs did not have standing because they never applied for the religious status that would allow them to receive such benefits.

Muslim Congregation Denied Zoning Permit for Worship Center

Am. Islamic Ctr. v. City of Des Plaines, No. 13-6594, 2014 WL 1243870 (N.D. Ill. Mar. 24, 2014)
http://articles.chicagotribune.com/2013-09-17/news/chi-lawsuit-des-plaines-zoning-denial-violates-muslim-groups-religious-freedom-20130916_1_mosque-american-islamic-center-religious-freedom
A Bosnian Muslim congregation requested that the City of Des Plaines, Illinois, rezone a building in a manufacturing district to accommodate a new mosque. The city council refused the request, citing safety and traffic concerns due to the industrial nature of the area. The mosque filed a lawsuit against the city for discriminatory treatment. An Illinois federal district court found in favor of the city council on the grounds of legislative immunity.

Santeria Priest Targeted for Prosecution Because of His Religious Beliefs

Badillo v. Amato, 2014 U.S. Dist. LEXIS 10210 (D.N.J. Jan. 28, 2014)
A New Jersey district court judge held that Jorge Badillo, a Santeria priest, may proceed with his First Amendment and Fourth Amendment claims against Chief Amato of the Society for the Prevention of Cruelty to Animals (SPCA). Amato had entered Badillo's property without permission or warrant and found animals used in Badillo's religious practices. Badillo contends that Amato had targeted his property for inspection and prosecution because of Badillo's religious beliefs.

New Orleans Arrests Pastor for Preaching During Gay Pride Festival

Gros v. New Orleans City, No. 12-2322 (E.D. La. Dec. 16, 2013)
In 2011, the city of New Orleans passed a law that prohibited loitering or congregating on Bourbon Street "for the purpose of disseminating any social,

political, or religious message between the hours of sunset and sunrise," while still allowing other forms of expression. In 2012, Pastor Paul Gros of Vieux Carre Assembly of God Church was arrested during the Southern Decadence gay pride festival over the Labor Day weekend. A federal district court found that New Orleans violated Pastor Gros's constitutional rights.

FFRF Sues to Stop Parsonage Exemption
Freedom from Religion Found., Inc. v. Lew, No. 11-cv-626 (W.D. Wis. Nov. 22, 2013)
Arguing unconstitutional discrimination, the Freedom From Religion Foundation sued to stop tax exemptions for a minister's parsonage allowance. A federal district court ruled in favor of the FFRF, but the case is on appeal.

New Jersey Community Attempts to Block Construction of Mosque
Al Falah Center v. City of Bridgewater, CIV.A. 11-2397 MAS (D.N.J. Sept. 30, 2013)
A Muslim group in Bridgewater, New Jersey, purchased unrestricted property in order to build the Al Falah Center, a mosque that they had been planning for over ten years. When word of their submitted building application became public, however, the community became hostile to the plans. The city council then rushed to pass an amended zoning ordinance that would block any houses of worship on Al Falah's newly purchased property and rejected the Al Falah Center's application. Al Falah filed a lawsuit asking for injunctive relief from the city council's discriminatory treatment. A federal judge ruled in favor of the mosque and ordered the council to reconsider Al Falah's application without factoring in the newly enacted ordinance. The city has appealed the decision to the U.S. Court of Appeals for the Third Circuit.

Department of Natural Resources Denies Assistance to Religious Preschool
Trinity Lutheran Church of Columbia, Inc. v. Pauley, No. 2:13-cv-04022, 2013 WL 5567166 (W.D. Mo. Sept. 26, 2013)
Trinity Lutheran Church is a Missouri church that operates a day care and preschool facility called the Learning Center. To improve the Learning Center's playground, Trinity Lutheran Church applied for the Scrap Tire Program, a program run by the Department of Natural Resources Solid Waste Management Program that awards competitive grants to qualifying organizations in order to purchase recycled materials to improve playgrounds. Trinity was initially selected as a grant recipient, but the grant was revoked when the Department of Natural Resources determined that funding Trinity contravened its policy against subsidizing religious organizations. Trinity sued

the department head for the discriminatory policy, but a Missouri federal district judge upheld the policy.

St. Louis Prohibits Church from Meeting in Large Tent and Arrests Four

New Life Evangelistic Ctr., Inc. v. City of St. Louis, No. 4:12-CV-1077-HEA, 2013 WL 4517765 (E.D. Mo. Aug. 26, 2013)

New Life Evangelistic Center in St. Louis, Missouri, erected a large tent on its property to host worship services and provide for the needs of the homeless. Claiming that the tent posed an immediate danger to public health, safety, and welfare, the City of St. Louis issued an emergency condemnation of the property and sent police officers to disburse the people conducting the services, arresting four persons for occupying a condemned building. This case is pending.

Ministry Leader Accused of "Crimes Against Humanity" for Opposing Homosexual Conduct

Sexual Minorities Uganda v. Lively, No. 12-CV-30051-MAP, 2013 WL 4130756 (D. Mass. Aug. 14, 2013)

Abiding Truth Ministries is a Christian organization that defends the biblical view of marriage in the United States and around the globe. Scott Lively, president of Abiding Truth Ministries, was haled into court by a Ugandan LGBTI advocacy group who claimed that Lively's support of biblical marriage constituted "harsh and frightening" persecution of the LGBTI community in Uganda and demanded the termination of Lively's ministry. A federal district court in Massachusetts has agreed to hear the case, stating, "[M]any authorities implicitly support the principle that widespread, systematic persecution of individuals based on their sexual orientation and gender identity constitutes a crime against humanity that violates international norms."

City of Elgin Attacks Ministry That Provides Mobile Pregnancy Services

Life Ctr., Inc. v. City of Elgin, Ill., 13 C 1759, 2013 WL 4029148 (N.D. Ill. Aug. 8, 2013)

The Life Center (TLC) runs a mobile facility that operates in the commercial parking lots of consenting businesses and provides pregnancy services along with Christian literature to women in need. The City of Elgin, Illinois, amended its ordinances to include a limiting temporary land use provision and attempted to shut the ministry down. Instead, TLC fought back, and a federal judge called Elgin's "effort to curtail private entities from providing free and valuable services to its young women ... ill-advised," and held that the city's amendments were unconstitutionally vague and overbroad.

Geneva College Sues for Right to Not Facilitate Abortifacient Coverage
Geneva College v. Sebelius, No. 2:12-207, 2013 U.S. Dist. LEXIS 85107 (W.D. Penn. June 18, 2013)
Geneva College, a Presbyterian college, filed suit over objections to being required by the Patient Protection and Affordable Care Act's HHS mandate to cover contraceptives that it considers abortifacients, which would be in violation of its religious beliefs. The college claims these requirements violate the Religious Freedom Restoration Act, the First and Fifth Amendment, and the Administrative Procedures Act. A federal district court granted a preliminary injunction stopping enforcement of the mandate against the college.

Los Angeles Refuses to Allow Orthodox Congregation to Meet in Residential Area
Congregation Etz Chaim v. City of Los Angeles, No. 10-1587 (C.D. Cal. May 15, 2013)
In 1996, the City of Los Angeles, California, denied the request of Congregation Etz Chaim, an Orthodox Jewish synagogue, to meet in a residential home for church purposes. Etz Chaim refused to give in to the discriminatory refusal, choosing instead to fight back in federal court. After a legal battle lasting more than fifteen years, federal judges ruled that the city's imposition of land-use regulations against Etz Chaim violated federal law by intruding on their free exercise of religion. The city finally agreed to settle the lawsuit by paying Congregation Etz Chaim $950,000.

City of Naperville Refuses to Grant Permit for Islamic Center
Irshad Learning Ctr. v. County of DuPage, No. 10-cv-2168, 2013 U.S. Dist. LEXIS 47094 (N.D. Ill. Mar. 29, 2013)
An Islamic center was denied a zoning permit in Naperville, Illinois. The center sued Naperville for violating the Religious Land Use and Institutionalized Persons Act (RLUIPA), the Religious Freedom Restoration Act (RFRA), and the U.S. Constitution. The center asserted that it was being treated differently from nonreligious organization and other religious organizations. The U.S. District Court for the Northern District of Illinois found that Naperville had substantially burdened the Islamic center's free exercise of religion and violated both RLUIPA and RFRA.

Catholic Television Network Sues to Not Be Forced to Cover Birth Control

Eternal Word Television Network, Inc. v. Sebelius, No. 2:12-501 (N.D. Ala. Mar. 25, 2013)

Eternal Word Television Network, a Roman Catholic media network, filed a lawsuit challenging the Patient Protection and Affordable Care Act and the HHS mandate's requirement that the organization provide health insurance that covers contraceptives, abortifacients, and sterilization products for its employees. A federal district court dismissed the lawsuit because the HHS mandate's final language was not yet complete.

Catholic Business Sues Over Obamacare's Mandatory Birth Control Drug Coverage

Legatus v. Sebelius, 901 F. Supp. 2d 980 (E.D. Mich. Oct. 31, 2012)

Legatus, an organization of Catholic business and professional leaders; Daniel Weingartz, a Catholic; and Weingartz Supply Company, a for-profit Catholic business, filed suit against the Patient Protection and Affordable Care Act's mandate that businesses provide health insurance that covers birth control and some types of abortion pills even though Catholics oppose the use of any form of contraception. A federal district court granted a preliminary injunction stopping enforcement of the mandate against Weingartz and the Weingartz Supply Company. The case is now on appeal to the Sixth Circuit.

City of Medina Issues Moratorium on Church Construction

Woodridge Church v. City of Medina, No. 11-275, 2012 U.S. Dist. LEXIS 87687 (D. Minn. June 25, 2012)

Woodridge Church filed plans with the city of Medina, Minnesota, to expand its church. The city refused to approve the plans, issuing a one-year moratorium on church construction and creating a new zoning district to include the church with recommended square footage limits to the size of buildings and their footprints. The church withdrew its request and filed suit based on several statutory and constitutional grounds. The case settled.

Philadelphia Attempts to Stop Churches from Feeding the Homeless

Chosen 300 Ministries, Inc. v. City of Philadelphia, No. 2:12-3159 (E.D. Penn., filed June 5, 2012)

Philadelphia relocated an art collection to the downtown area and enacted new regulations that closed down a church's program of feeding homeless people outdoors in public parks. A group of churches filed a complaint claiming the new regulations were designed to stop the food programs in violation of the churches' First Amendment free speech rights as well as rights created by Pennsylvania's Religious Freedom Protection Act. The group of churches claims the city targeted religiously sponsored feeding programs, while creating exceptions for other nonreligious activities.

Village Attempts to Prevent Catholic Church from Using Land as a Cemetery

Roman Catholic Diocese of Rockville Centre, New York v. Incorporated Village of Old Westbury, No. 09 cv 5195, 2012 U.S. Dist. LEXIS 56694 (E.D.N.Y. Apr. 23, 2012)

The Roman Catholic Diocese of Rockville Center, New York, bought land to use as a cemetery. The village fought to keep the church from using the land as a cemetery. The diocese is suing the village for Religious Land Use and Institutionalized Persons Act, free exercise, and equal protection violations.

Village of Bolingbrook Refuses to Allow Church to Build on Its Rental Property

Liberty Temple Full Gospel Church, Inc. v. Village of Bolingbrook, No. 11-2173 (N.D. Ill. Apr. 12, 2012)

The Liberty Temple Full Gospel Church in Bolingbrook, Illinois, sued under the RLUIPA because the city refused to let it build a church on its rental property based on the absence of a zoning designation on the city map. The district court denied the city's motion for summary judgment, allowing the case to proceed to trial.

City of Kelso Attempts to Stop Religious Education Center

Victory Center v. City of Kelso, 2012 WL 1133643 (W.D. Wash. April 4, 2012)

The Kelso Church of Truth bought land on which the church planned to build an educational center called the Victory Center. The City of Kelso, Washington, opposed construction of the building, claiming that the building would be a community center and that the land was not zoned for such a building. The district court dismissed the church's federal and state constitutional claims, but preserved its Religious Land Use and Institutionalized Persons Act (RLUIPA) claims. The church plans to move forward with the RUILPA claims.

Village of Woodbury Attempts to Keep Out Jewish Community Via Zoning Laws

Village of Kiryas Joel, New York v. Village of Woodbury, New York, No. 7:11-8494 (S.D.N.Y. Mar. 29, 2012)

The town of Kiryas Joel, New York, an Orthodox Jewish Hasidic village, sued the nearby town of Woodbury, New York, for changing zoning laws in an attempt to discriminate. The Jewish community was in the process of expanding into Woodbury when the city officials changed the zoning laws regulating the population density in the area so that the Jewish community could no longer continue the expansion.

Christian School in Ohio Banned from Using Its Buildings

Tree of Life Christian School v. City of Upper Arlington, 2012 WL 831918 (S.D. Ohio Mar. 12, 2012)

Upper Arlington, Ohio, refused to grant a Christian school a permit to use its building, prohibiting the school from operating. Upper Arlington allowed day-care facilities to operate in the same zone, however. Tree of Life Christian School sued under the Religious Land Use and Institutionalized Persons Act (RLUIPA).

States Sue to Stop Federal Government from Mandating Coverage of Birth Control

State of Nebraska v. U.S. Department of Health and Human Services, No. 4:12-3035 (D. Neb., filed Feb. 23, 2012)

The attorneys general of South Carolina, Texas, Florida, Ohio, Oklahoma, and Nebraska filed suit against the U.S. Department of Health because of recent legislation requiring insurance to cover birth control. The attorneys general claim that the legislation violates the Religious Freedom Restoration Act, freedom of speech, freedom of association, and the free exercise of religion. The attorneys general are bringing the suit both on behalf of their states and the people of their states.

Connecticut Town Prevents Jewish Group from Restoring Historic Building

Chabad Lubavitch of Litchfield County, Inc. v. Borough of Litchfield, Connecticut, 853 F. Supp. 2d 214 (D. Conn. Feb. 17, 2012)

The U.S. District Court for the District of Connecticut granted summary judgment against a Jewish organization's Religious Land Use and Institutionalized Persons Act (RLUIPA) and Free Exercise Clause claims. The organization alleged that the Borough of Litchfield discriminated against the organization based on religious grounds by denying its application to restore and add to a historic building. The Court held that the statute preventing the expansion did not substantially burden the free exercise of the organization's religion because it is neutral and not applied arbitrarily.

City in Georgia Limits Expansion of Scientologist Church

Church of Scientology of Georgia, Inc. v. City of Sandy Springs, Georgia, 2012 WL 500263 (N.D. Ga. Feb. 10, 2012)

The City of Sandy Springs granted a conditional approval of the Church of Scientology's rezoning application but refused to allow expansion of the church for lack of parking. The church brought a suit claiming violations of the First Amendment and the Religious Land Use and Institutionalized Persons Act (RLUIPA). While the court held that the city did not violate the equal terms provision or the exclusion and limits provision of RLUIPA or the church's substantive due process rights under Georgia's constitution, it held that there remained material fact issues as to whether the city's conditional approval imposed a substantial burden on the church's religious exercise and whether the city acted with discriminatory purpose.

Santa Fe County, New Mexico, Refuses to Allow Religious Group to Build New Temple
O Centro Espirita Beneficente Uniao do Vegetal v. Board of County Commissioners of Santa Fe County, No. _____ (D.N.M., filed Feb. 2, 2012)
Santa Fe County, New Mexico, denied a religious group, O Centro Espirita Beneficente Uniao do Vegetal (UDV), permits needed to build a new temple outside of Santa Fe city limits. UDV sued, claiming that the denial is because some members of the community are opposed to the church.

City of Alpharetta Denies Application for Islamic Center to Expand
Islamic Center of North Fulton, Inc. v. City of Alpharetta, Georgia, No. 1:10-1922 (N.D. Ga. Jan. 25, 2012)
The City of Alpharetta, Georgia, denied an application by an Islamic Center to expand its facilities. The center filed a lawsuit under the Religious Land Use and Institutionalized Persons Act (RLUIPA), but the district court found in favor of the city.

Dallas Ordinance Limits Ministry that Provides Food for the Homeless
Big Hart Ministries Association, Inc. v. City of Dallas, 2011 WL 5346109 (N.D. Tex. Nov. 4, 2011)
Big Hart Ministries Association, which provides food for the homeless in Dallas, Texas, brought suit against the City of Dallas, alleging that a Dallas ordinance that requires Big Hart to have a pre-approved location for food distribution violates the Texas Religious Freedom Restoration Act. A federal district court refused the city's motion to dismiss the case.

New Jersey Requires Retirement Center to Include Nonchurch Member on Board
Wiley Mission v. State of New Jersey, Department of Community Affairs, No. 10-3024, 2011 U.S. Dist. LEXIS 96473 (D.N.J. Aug. 25, 2011)
The Wiley Mission, which operates a continuing care retirement center (CCRC) for senior citizens, pushed back at a New Jersey statute that requires

all CCRCs regulated by the state to include a non-church member on the board. The Wiley Mission was told a failure to add a nonchurch member to its board would result in the organization losing its license to operate in the state. The Wiley Mission alleged the statute violated the organization's First Amendment and Equal Protection rights. The U.S. District Court agreed in part, saying a strict scrutiny analysis applies when looking at the church's freedom of association claims. The court held "the department presents no evidence that the statute is narrowly tailored to protect senior citizens" and granted the plaintiffs summary judgment on the freedom of association issue.

Church Denied Clearance to Construct New Building in Prince George, Maryland
Reaching Hearts Int'l, Inc. v. Prince George's County, 2011 WL 3101801 (D. Md. July 22, 2011)
The city of Prince George, Maryland, continues to deny Reaching Hearts International Church clearance to build a new church. The suit, which began in 2008 against the city for opposing the construction of a new building, continues on as the city denied the district court's order to provide water and sewage lines to the property. The district court also affirmed a jury award of $3.7 million in damages for the church. The church filed another suit against the city in July of 2011 seeking to enforce the order to supply water and sewage lines and claiming that the resistance is due to a personal vendetta of one of the city councilmen.

City of Phoenix Attempts to Limit Ringing of Church Bells
St. Mark Roman Catholic Parish Phoenix et al. v. City of Phoenix, Arizona, No. 2:09–1830 (D. Ariz. Apr. 19, 2010)
A federal district court in Arizona permanently enjoined the City of Phoenix from enforcing its noise ordinance against noises arising from religious expression, such as the ringing of church bells, holding that enforcing the noise ordinance against such noises violated the First and Fourteenth Amendments to the U.S. Constitution and Arizona's Free Exercise of Religion Act.

City of Montgomery Requires Permit to Engage in Religious Protest
Bethel v. City of Montgomery, No. 2:04-743, 2010 WL 996397 (M.D. Ala. Mar. 2, 2010)
Preachers challenged a city ordinance in Montgomery, Alabama, requiring people to obtain a permit before participating in public assembly, such as religious protests. A magistrate judge found the ordinance to be

constitutionally permissible and recommended the case be dismissed with prejudice.

Evangelists Arrested in San Antonio for Peacefully Preaching on Public Sidewalks
Muniz v. City of San Antonio, No. 5:10-00749 (W.D. Tex. 2010)
Jose Muniz was cited and Todd Leibovitz was arrested and jailed overnight for peacefully preaching and distributing free religious literature on public sidewalks in San Antonio. Liberty Institute represented Muniz and Leibovitz in a lawsuit against the city of San Antonio. The case settled for approximately $15,000 and the city's agreement that peacefully preaching and distributing free religious literature are constitutionally protected activities.

City in Georgia Imposes Additional Requirements on Churches
Christ Liberty Family Life Center v. City of Avondale Estates, Georgia, No. 1:10-02326 (N.D. Ga. 2010)
A city zoning ordinance prohibits churches from being located in a certain area of town. Christ Liberty's property was in that particular area, and its ministries were hindered because it was stopped from meeting on the leased property. Libraries and other organizations are not required to obtain the "conditional use permit" that churches in the town are required to obtain.

Town of Greensborough Attempts to Delay Permit for Church
Fortress Bible Church v. Feiner, 734 F.Supp.2d 409 (S.D.N.Y. 2010)
Fortress Bible Church sued the town of Greensborough, New York, under the Religious Land Use and Institutionalized Persons Act (RLUIPA) because of intentional delays in granting a land-use permit for the church and because of hostility toward the church. The court held in favor of the church, ordering the town to grant the permit.

Court Reverses Decision and Agrees Church Is Entitled to a Special Permit
Grace Church of Roaring Fork Valley v. Board of County Commissioners of Pitkin County, Colorado, 742 F.Supp.2d 1156 (D. Colo. 2010)
A federal court initially rejected a Colorado church's Religious Land Use and Institutionalized Persons Act (RLUIPA) claim in 2007. When the case was finally about to go to trial in 2010, however, the court reversed its order and found in favor of the church on the grounds that it was entitled to a special permit. The court also found, however, that any religious hostility that occurred was merely coincidental and that the church was not entitled to any damages.

City of Elgin Drives Homeless Ministry from City

Family Life Church v. City of Elgin, 561 F. Supp. 2d 978 (N.D. Ill. Jun. 18, 2008)

H.E.L.P.S., a Christian homeless ministry operating out of a church building in Elgin, Illinois, was told that the city required the church to obtain a building occupancy permit and zoning permission to keep the ministry open. Elgin's city manager informed them that a conditional use permit would also be necessary and told them that the chances of obtaining one from the city council were "a million to one." After the city drove the organization from the Family Life Church, H.E.L.P.S. began ministering at a camp twenty minutes outside the city, on weekends at other churches, or on their bus. The district court held that the city's actions did not violate the First Amendment.

Lawsuit Attempts to Stop Federal Funds to Marriage Education Workshops

Christianson v. Leavitt, 482 F. Supp. 2d 1237 (W.D. Wash. Mar. 20, 2007)

The Northwest Marriage Institute provides both biblically-based and secular marriage education workshops throughout the Pacific Northwest. Over the past two years, the institute has been awarded three federal grants, enabling it to provide the secular workshops at no charge to low-income families. None of the funds were used for the biblically-based workshops. Nevertheless, Americans United for Separation of Church and State, representing thirteen Washington taxpayers, filed a lawsuit seeking to force the institute to repay the funds it had received and block all future funds.

ACLU and AUSCS Sue to Stop Support for Faith-Based Life Skills Program for Inmates

Moeller v. Bradford County, No. 3:CV-05-0334, 2007 U.S. Dist. LEXIS 7965 (M.D. Penn. Feb. 5, 2007)

A faith-based program located in Bradford County that provided construction skills, life skills, and mentoring to incarcerated persons came under attack from an ACLU and AUSCS lawsuit that sought to stop support of the program.

New York State Bans Renting Buildings for Religious Services

Relevant Church v. Egan, No. 7:07-00327 (N.D.N.Y. 2007)

Relevant Church requested to rent the Dulles State Office building for Easter services. New York State officials denied the request, claiming that renting to a church would violate the "separation of church and state" and that state policy prohibited religious services in its buildings. After the church's attorneys filed suit, officials reversed their decision and allowed the church to use the building. Officials also changed the state policy to allow religious services in state office buildings.

Town in New Jersey Bans Religious Use of Public Square
Care and Share Ministry v. Village of South Orange, No. 2:07-00758 (D.N.J. 2007)
Members of a South Orange, New Jersey, Christian ministry called "Care and Share" wanted to hold an event at a public square, where members would perform skits, live music, and puppet shows for local children. Village officials denied Care and Share access to the public square, saying only public or nonreligious private groups would be allowed to use the space. Though South Orange officials denied Care and Share's request, they granted the request for use of public space by an organization known as "Road Devils, NJ." The Road Devils event included public consumption of alcohol, live bands using vulgar language with electronic sound equipment, and female mannequins dressed only in underwear. After a lawsuit was filed, South Orange officials backed down and said they would not discriminate against a religious organization based on viewpoint.

Texas Town Attempts to Kick Student Ministry Out of Its Property
Collegiate Community Outreach v. City of Denton, No. 4:07-00564 (E.D. Tex. 2007)
Collegiate Community Outreach (CCO) is a religious ministry located in a residential area close to the University of North Texas campus. The City of Denton, Texas, told the ministry they could no longer operate out of their current property because they were in violation of zoning laws. After CCO filed a lawsuit, the city reversed its decision.

Town Forces Church to Meet Outside City Limits in Temporary Building Without Heat
Lighthouse Christian Center, Inc. v. City of Reading, No. 06-1979, 2006 U.S. Dist. LEXIS 54988 (E.D. Penn. Jul. 26, 2006)
The Lighthouse Christian Center wanted to lease a building within Titusville's C-1 commercial zone. However, the Titusville zoning code did not allow churches, but permitted theaters, clubs, lodges, bars, and amusements in its commercial districts. Lighthouse was forced outside the City of Titusville, where it rented a temporary building that lacked heat and insulation. After a lawsuit was filed, the city settled and agreed to amend the zoning code.

Religious Organizations Prohibited from Listing Staffing Requirements
Geneva College v. Chao, No. 2:06-01663 (W.D. Penn. 2006)
Members of Geneva College and the Association of Faith-Based Organizations (AFBO) were denied access to post-employment opportunities because of a governmental "nondiscrimination policy" prohibiting the listing of religious

staffing requirements. After a lawsuit was filed, the federal government and the Commonwealth of Pennsylvania conceded that the policy did not apply to Geneva College or AFBO's members, and they are no longer prohibited from posting job listings.

National Day of Prayer Event Barred from City Hall Meeting Room
Barkey v. City of Idaho Springs, Colorado, No. 1:06-01209 (D. Colo. 2006)
A coordinator for the National Day of Prayer and others planned to observe the event in a park area outside of Idaho Springs, Colorado's city hall, but reserved the council's meeting room in case of inclement weather. After rain forced the group inside on the day of the event, a city administrator informed them of a city policy barring use of the space for religious purposes. After a lawsuit was filed, city officials decided to close the city council chambers for general use by the public, and the city constructed a new room to be used by the public as a meeting room, including religious groups.

City in Texas Bans Religious Meetings in Homes But Permits Other Meetings
Grace Community Church v. City of McKinney, No. 4:04-251 (E.D. Tex., filed Jul. 16, 2004)
The City of McKinney, Texas, had an ordinance that prohibited religious meetings in a home in a residential neighborhood. Grace Community Church was told by the City of McKinney that the church could no longer meet in a home despite equally sized, non-religious groups being allowed to do the same. A lawsuit was filed on behalf of the church, alleging a violation of the church's right to meet in the pastor's home under federal law.

Tucson Denies Reimbursement Funds for Religious City Event
Gentala v. City of Tucson, 325 F. Supp. 2d 1012 (D. Ariz. Nov. 7, 2003)
Patricia and Robert Gentala applied for reimbursement for coverage of city costs for a National Day of Prayer event. The city denied the funds, although it routinely offered funding to similar groups. The Gentalas sued, and a federal district judge ruled against the Gentalas. The Ninth Circuit en banc affirmed. Shortly after the final decision of the Ninth Circuit, the U.S. Supreme Court decided *Good News Club v. Milford Central School,* which held that it is a violation of the right to free speech to deny a group access to government facilities because the group was communicating a religious message. The Gentalas filed a petition to the Supreme Court. The Supreme Court remanded the case to be reconsidered in light of the *Good News Club v. Milford Central School* ruling. Finally, in 2003, the federal district court ruled

that Mr. Gentala could not be discriminated against because of the religious message of the event.

Town's Unwritten Policy Prohibits Religious Use of Community Center
Moore v. City of Van, Texas, 238 F. Supp. 2d 837 (E.D. Tex. Jan. 7, 2003)
Van, Texas, had an unwritten policy prohibiting groups from using the Van Community Center if the use was for a religious purpose. Citizens wanting to use the center for religious purposes sued the city. A federal district court held that Van's policy was unconstitutional.

Maui Denies Small Church Permit to Build on Its Own Land
Hale O Kaula Church v. The Maui Planning Commission, No. 01-00615, 2003 U.S. Dist. LEXIS 24510 (D. Haw. Jul. 18, 2003)
Hale O Kaula, a small congregation on Maui, applied for a building permit to construct a church on five acres of agricultural land it had purchased years earlier. Despite having granted similar permits to other secular and religious organizations, the Maui Planning Commission refused to allow Hale O Kaula to build. As a result, both the church and the Justice Department filed separate lawsuits on the grounds that the Religious Land Use and Institutionalized Persons Act (RLUIPA) had been violated. The county argued that RLUIPA was unconstitutional and attempted to have the cases dismissed. The court ruled in favor of Hale O Kaula, finally allowing the church to build.

Houston Attempts to Take Historic Churches' Private Property
Latter Day Deliverance Revival Church v. Hous. Hous. Auth., No. 01-15-00790-CV (Tex. Ct. App. Dec. 1, 2015)
The Houston Housing Authority threatened to use eminent domain to take the property of two historic churches that have been ministering to the Houston's Fifth Ward for over eighty years. The Latter Day Deliverance Center uses the land threatened by the city for ministry activities, such as setting up youth centers, food pantries, and providing educational assistance to the community. After Liberty Institute brought suit on behalf of the churches, the city dropped its threat to bulldoze one church and dismissed eminent domain proceedings against another.

Teacher Sues Christian School for Abiding by Its Faith-Based Standards
Richardson v. Nw. Christian Univ., No. 15CV20442 (Or. Ct. App. Aug. 4, 2015)
Northwest Christian University in Eugene, Oregon, terminated a teacher, Coty Richardson, for planning to have a child out of wedlock with her boyfriend of twelve years. School officials notified the teacher that the school expects teachers to be role models for the students, and her cohabitation and

pregnancy out of wedlock are incompatible with the school's mission. In response, Richardson filed suit against the school.

ACLU Sues California County for Recognizing Christian Ministry
Lavagetto v. County of Calaveras, No. 15-cv-40665 (Cal. Sup. Ct., filed Feb. 18, 2015)
Calaveras County in California passed a resolution honoring the work of the "Door of Hope," a Christian-operated pregnancy center. The ministry is focused on "strengthening the lives of women and young women in Calaveras County by inviting them to test and see for themselves the many blessings that can come from living the teachings of Christ." The American Civil Liberties Union (ACLU) filed suit, and the Calaveras County Board voted to repeal the resolution.

Neighbor Sues Small Jewish Congregation
Schneider v. Gothelf, No. 429-04998-2013 (Tex. Dist. filed Dec. 17, 2013)
Congregation Toras Chaim is a small Orthodox Jewish congregation that meets in a home in the community where the congregants live so that they can walk on the Sabbath. David Schneider, a neighbor of the congregation, filed a lawsuit to stop the congregation from meeting in the home and demanded several thousand dollars from the congregation. Schneider did not file suit against non-Jewish businesses in the community. Schneider then took over the homeowners' association in the community and brought the association into the lawsuit against the congregation, after several years of amicable relations between the congregation and the homeowners' association. Liberty Institute represented Congregation Toras Chaim, and won a victory for the small congregation.

Town in New Jersey Restricts Orthodox Jewish Meetings in Home
554 Queen Anne Rd., Inc. v. Teaneck Bd. of Adjustment, No. L-12194-10 (N.J. Super. Ct. Law Div. Aug. 26, 2013)
Etz Chaim of Teaneck, an Orthodox Jewish synagogue in Teaneck, New Jersey, hired Rabbi Daniel Feldman and gave him a house to live in. When Rabbi Feldman began conducting services in his living room, his neighbors protested, and the city required Rabbi Feldman to apply for zoning approval in order to continue the services. However, the Teaneck Board of Adjustment placed numerous conditions on the zoning approval, and the synagogue filed a lawsuit. A New Jersey court upheld all of the board's restrictions.

YMCA Denied Religious Exemption to Property Tax Assessments

Larimer Cnty Bd. of Comm'ns v. Colo. Prop. Tax Adm'r, 2013 Colo. App. LEXIS 507 (Colo. App. Apr. 11, 2013)

A Colorado state appellate court vacated an order from the Board of Assessment Appeals misapplying state law to deny the Young Men's Christian Association (YMCA) a religious exemption to property tax assessments.

Town in Maine Taxes Church Property More than Other Nonprofit Organizations' Property

Aldersgate United Methodist Church v. City of Rockland, Maine, et al., No. CV-12-020 (Super. Ct. Me., Mar. 20, 2013)

Aldersgate United Methodist Church in Rockland, Maine, filed suit against the city for taxing churches differently than it does other benevolent charities and nonprofit organizations. Rockland only allows churches to get tax exemptions for their main buildings and not for their parsonages or other buildings. Other nonprofit organizations, however, receive tax exemptions for all of their buildings. Following the lawsuit, the church was granted tax exemptions for all of its buildings.

Catholic Business Sues for Protection from State Law Requiring Contraceptive Coverage

Yep v. Ill. Dep't of Ins., No. 2012 CH 5575 (Dupage Co. IL Cir. Ct., Jan. 15, 2013)

An Illinois state trial court issued a temporary restraining order protecting a Catholic-owned business from state law requiring contraceptive coverage in its health care plans to employees. The court held that the law imposes a substantial burden on the free exercise of religion.

Marathon, Michigan, Denies Tax Exemption to Muslim Summer Camp

Camp Retreats Found., Inc. v. Township of Marathon, 2012 WL 1698379 (Mich. App. May 15, 2012)

A Michigan tax tribunal found that a Muslim summer camp was not a charity or entitled to a tax exemption because the camp prohibited trespassing and the primary purpose of the camp was to be a place for sports and recreation for children. However, the Michigan state appellate court reversed the decision, finding that the camp's offering of sports and recreation did not nullify the fact that its main purpose was to provide Islamic children with a religious experience at the camp.

City of Hartford Attempts to Block Jewish Group from Using Property

Chabad Chevra, LLC v. City of Hartford, No. 106003847, 2011 Conn. Super. LEXIS 3204 (Conn. Super. Ct. Dec. 15, 2011)

The city of Hartford, Connecticut, attempted to prevent a Jewish group from using its own property for religious purposes. A Connecticut trial court reversed the city's zoning order, and the city decided not to appeal.

ACLU Challenges Proposed Amendment Reversing Ban on Religious Funding

Shapiro v. Browning, No. 11-CA-1892 (Fl. Cir. Ct. Dec. 13, 2011)

A proposed Florida amendment that eliminates a ban on taxpayer money being used to fund religious organizations has been placed before voters. The ACLU challenged the ballot language, and the court held that the amendment was unconstitutional and could not be placed on the ballot.

Court Permits Lawsuit to Determine Whether Pastor Was Fired

Errgong-Weider v. United Congregational Church of Norwalk, 2011 WL 5842378 (Super. Ct. Conn. Oct. 25, 2011)

The Superior Court of Connecticut denied a motion to dismiss a lawsuit brought by a pastor against the church that attempted to fire him by vote of its members. The court held that it was proper for it to determine if the pastor was effectively terminated by the vote according to corporation laws. The court held that the church's own constitution and bylaws will be taken into consideration in making the decision.

Michigan Zoning Board Blocks Religious Organization

Great Lakes Society v. Georgetown Charter Township, 2011 WL 1600496 (Mich. Ct. App. Apr. 28, 2011)

A religious organization's application for a special use permit required for churches was denied by the city zoning board because the proposed building was to serve people in the community and was not for public worship. The board then amended its street-frontage requirements to specifications that the religious organization's property did not meet, and then denied the organization's request for variance. The Michigan court rejected Religious Land Use and Institutionalized Persons Act (RLUIPA) and constitutional challenges and upheld the zoning board's denial.

Mosque Denied Use of Residence as Place of Worship

Islamic Cultural Ctr. of Monticello, Inc. v. Village of Monticello, 29 Misc. 3d 1223 (A) (NY Sup. Ct. Nov. 17, 2010)

The New York Supreme Court in Sullivan County found that there was no

Religious Land Use and Institutionalized Persons Act (RLUIPA) violation in denying a permit for a mosque to use a single-family house as a place of worship. The mosque bought the house and a lot across the street from the house to use as a place of worship, even though the property was zoned for residential purposes. The city took several years to process the special use permit submitted by the mosque, but eventually denied the permit. The court denied the RLUIPA claims brought by the mosque because there was no evidence that the mosque was being treated differently from any other religious institution.

Anti-Religious Group Sues to Block Contracts with Faith-Based Halfway Houses

Council for Secular Humanism, Inc. v. McNeil, 44 So. 3d 112 (Fla. Dist. Ct. App. 1st Dist., Apr. 27, 2010)
The Council for Secular Humanism sued the state of Florida and two faith-based halfway houses that provided reintegration assistance to recently released prisoners. The Council for Secular Humanism challenged the state's contracts with the two halfway houses, asserting that any payment to the halfway houses constituted payment to a church. The trial court found for the state. The case has been appealed.

Christian School in Los Angeles Shut Down Pending Permit

County of Los Angeles v. Sahag-Mesrob Armenian Christian School, 188 Cal. App.4th 851 (Cal. App. 2010)
Los Angeles insisted that Sahag-Mesrob Armenian Christian School obtain a special use permit in order to operate. The city refused to allow the school to operate while it was waiting for the permit application to be processed. The school filed suit under the Religious Land Use and Institutionalized Persons Act (RLUIPA), but the appellate court ruled in favor of the city, holding that the refusal to let the school operate while the permit was pending was not a substantial burden on the school.

ACLU Sues to Stop Arizona's Tuition Scholarship Program

Green v. Garriott, 212 P.3d 96 (Ariz. App. Mar. 12, 2009)
The ACLU and others filed suit to declare Arizona's corporate tax credit tuition program unconstitutional because it allowed tuition scholarships to be used at private religious schools. The lawsuit, an attempt to discriminate against religious schools rather than grant them equal treatment, was dismissed by the court.

City of Sinton Bans Ministry to Misdemeanor Offenders
Barr v. City of Sinton, 295 S.W.3d 287 (Tex. 2009)
Pastor Barr's Christian organization, which provides housing and religious instruction to men who have been released from prison for misdemeanor offenses, was completely banned by the City of Sinton, Texas, from existing anywhere within its city limits. In a landmark decision, the Texas Supreme Court applied the Texas Religious Freedoms Restoration Act to rule in favor of Barr.

City's Planning and Zoning Commission Attempts to Keep Out Buddhist Temple
Cambodian Buddhist Society of Connecticut, Inc. v. Planning and Zoning Commission of the Town of Newtown, 941 A.2d 868 (Conn. 2008)
Pong Me and the Cambodian Buddhist Society of Connecticut purchased property in the city of Newtown, Connecticut, on which it planned to build a Buddhist temple. The city's Planning and Zoning Commission denied them a building permit, arguing that the Asian architecture, potential noise, and possible high volume of cars near the temple would disrupt the harmony of the surrounding neighborhood. Using the Religious Land Use and Institutionalized Persons Act and a Connecticut religious freedom law, the society took the city to court. In 2008, the Connecticut Supreme Court ruled in favor of the city, banning the society from building its temple.

Texas Demands State Approval of Religious Curricula at Seminaries
HEB Ministries, Inc. v. Texas Higher Education Coordinating Board, 235 S.W.3d 627 (Tex. 2007)
Texas passed a law forcing all seminaries to get state approval of their curriculum, board members, and professors. Tyndale Seminary was fined $173,000 by the state for using the word "seminary" and issuing theological degrees without government approval. A suit had to be filed to prohibit the government's attempts to control religious training. Both the district court and the court of appeals upheld the law. Finally, after nine years of suffering and losses, the Texas Supreme Court reversed and held that the law violated the First Amendment and the Texas Constitution.

Tax Exemption for Teachers at Nonreligious Schools Extended to All Teachers
Anchorage Baptist Temple v. Coonrod, 166 P.3d 29 (Alaska 2007)
The Alaska Superior Court ruled that teachers of parochial schools could continue to receive tax exemptions. Teachers at nonreligious schools had

already received tax exemptions before the legislature extended the privilege to religious schoolteachers.

Woman Sues Church, Pastor, and Elders for Using Church Discipline
Westbrook v. Penley, 231 S.W.3d 389 (Tex. 2007)
A member of a church had an unbiblical relationship and desired to divorce her husband without a biblical reason. She refused to repent of her sin, and the church, through its church disciplinary process according to the book of Matthew, sent a letter to the congregation informing them of the member's lack of repentance and the unacceptability of her behavior. She sued the church, the elders, and the pastor, dragging secular courts into an internal church matter. The state Supreme Court unanimously held for the church.

Church Member Sues Church to Stop Church Discipline
Doe v. Watermark Community Church, No. 05-06-00763-CV, 2006 Tex. App. LEXIS 10362 (Tex. App.—Dallas 2006)
A judge prohibited Watermark Community Church in Dallas, Texas, from engaging in religious speech in following Jesus' words in Matthew 18. The church was sued by a member who sought to stop the church disciplinary process. A restraining order was issued against the church, prohibiting the leaders from speaking about sin and from following the Matthew 18 model of restoring a member to the body of Christ. The restraining order was ultimately reversed and the case dismissed on appeal.

Parishioner Sues Church for Expressing Its Religious Beliefs About Her Actions
Kliebenstein v. Iowa Conference of the United Methodist Church, 663 N.W.2d 404 (Iowa 2003)
A parishioner at Shell Rock United Methodist Church sued her church for referring to her divisive actions as acting within "the Spirit of Satan." The Iowa Supreme Court's decision to allow such a suit violated the First Amendment rights of the church to speak about behavior from a biblical perspective.

Court Denies Church Right to Exclude Trespassers
Church of Christ in Hollywood v. The Superior Court of Los Angeles County, 121 Cal. Rptr. 2d 810 (Cal. App. 2002)
Former church member Lady Cage-Barile began to intimidate and harass members of the church and interrupt and disrupt Bible studies, so the church informed her she was no longer welcome on church property. When the church sought an order barring Cage-Barile, the court denied it, and the

church was forced to go to the California Court of Appeals to enforce its right to exclude trespassers from church premises.

Catholic Hospital Allows Sterilization After ACLU Threatens to Sue
http://www.nationalreview.com/corner/catholic-hospital-sterilization-aclu-lawsuit-threat-ian-tuttle
The American Civil Liberties Union (ACLU) on behalf of Rachel Miller threatened to sue a Dignity Health Catholic hospital in Redding, California. The hospital initially refused to allow a doctor to conduct a sterilization procedure in its facilities because Catholic doctrine teaches that voluntary sterilization is gravely immoral. After the ACLU threatened to sue, the hospital allowed the procedure to go forward.

Door County, Wisconsin, Bans Church from Displaying Cross at Easter Service Following Letter from FFRF
http://www.greenbaypressgazette.com/story/news/local/door-co/news/2015/06/05/group-objects-cross-washington-island-park/28554453/
For decades, the Bethel Evangelical Free Church in Door County, Wisconsin, held an outdoor Easter service at a county park. For the service, the church erected a white wooden cross. When the Freedom From Religion Foundation (FFRF) learned that the church displayed the cross, they sent a letter to the county demanding that the county prohibit the display. The county, in response to the letter, told Bethel Evangelical Free Church that they may no longer display a cross during their outdoor Easter service.

La Grange, Illinois, Attempts to Require Permit for Churches' Outdoor Activities
http://www.chicagotribune.com/suburbs/la-grange/news/ct-dlg-church-permit-tl-0618-20150610-story.html
La Grange, Illinois, proposed a zoning change that would require churches to receive a special use permit to engage in any outdoor activities, including things like scouting groups, that are not deemed "part of the congregation's mission." Community pastors challenged the zoning ordinance, noting that churches, not the city, know better what is and what is not part of a church's mission.

FFRF Intimidates Florida Town to Cancel Soccer Event Because of Church's Participation
https://ffrf.org/news/news-releases/item/23182-ffrf-breaks-up-church-city-partnership
Casselberry, Florida, had planned to partner with a local church to hold

a "Friday Fun Day" soccer event. The town cancelled the event, however, after receiving a letter from the Freedom From Religion Foundation (FFRF) objecting to the town's working with a church. FFRF complained that someone from the church might share a religious message during the event.

FFRF Forced County Commission to Rescind Their $3,000 Grant to Ministry

http://ffrf.org/news/news-releases/item/21751-ala-commission-rescinds-3-000-faith-grant-to-baptist-ministry

An Alabama county commission approved a grant to a Christian men's ministry at Covington Baptist Association whose purpose was "to get more men to church." The county quickly received a complaint from Freedom From Religion Foundation, warning them against government support to their chosen ministry. The Alabama commission was forced to rescind their $3,000 grant to the ministry.

FFRF Attacks "Ark Encounter" Theme Park

https://ffrf.org/news/news-releases/item/21800-ffrf-urges-irs-to-investigate-noahs-ark-theme-park

The Freedom From Religion Foundation is demanding that the IRS investigate the tax-exempt status of two nonprofit organizations that own and operate a Noah's Ark-themed park being built in Williamstown, Kentucky.

Freedom From Religion Foundation Blocked in Attempt to Ban Parsonage Exemption

http://www.jsonline.com/blogs/news/282602101.html

The Internal Revenue Service permits tax-free housing to ministers, an exemption known as the "parsonage exemption." This exemption was created to avoid unfair treatment of ministers whose churches do not own their own parsonage and to recognize that a minister often works from home. The Freedom From Religion Foundation (FFRF) filed a lawsuit to have the parsonage exemption declared unconstitutional. The U.S. Circuit Court of Appeals for the Seventh Circuit held that FFRF lacked the kind of concrete harm needed to challenge the parsonage exemption.

Government Questions Tax-Exempt Status of Schools That Support Traditional Marriage

https://www.lifesitenews.com/opinion/how-the-federal-government-may-put-christian-schools-out-of-business

During oral arguments in *Obergefell v. Hodges,* the U.S. Solicitor General indicated that religious schools that believe in traditional marriage may lose their tax-exempt status. Responding to a question from Justice Alito,

Solicitor General Donald Verrilli stated that the tax-exempt status of such religious schools "is going to be an issue."

ACLU Sues Christian Child-Care Facility

http://www.springfieldnewssun.com/news/news/crime-law/mom-says-she-was-fired-for-pregnancy/nWZ3H/

Inside Out, a Christian child-care facility in Ohio, settled claims that it fired an employee who is a single mother after she told them she was pregnant. However, Inside Out President William Stout denied the organization discriminated against pregnant workers and said she was not fired; instead she quit her job in "good terms." Inside Out does have policies of conduct based on Biblical principles, including prohibiting "sexual relations outside the covenant of marriage," but "we do not discriminate against people for being pregnant," Stout said.

City in California Bans Church from Feeding Homeless

http://finance.yahoo.com/news/harbor-missionary-church-files-emergency-191118521.html

For six years, Harbor Missionary Church has provided clothing, food, showers, counseling, and other support to thousands of homeless residents of the City of Ventura, California, through "Operation Embrace." Harbor Missionary Church extended compassion and love toward the homeless persons who sought shelter on church property, and regarded this practice as a central tenet of the church's beliefs. Unexpectedly, city officials in Ventura demanded the church obtain a condition use permit, in addition to its church permit, to continue its ministry. When the church applied, the city denied its request. After denying the church a permit to continue its ministry, police and code-enforcement officers arrived without warning and searched the church to ensure that it was no longer ministering to and feeding the homeless. Harbor Missionary Church filed a lawsuit in federal district court alleging that the permit denial violated the church's right to free exercise of religion under the First Amendment and under the Religious Land Use and Institutionalized Persons Act (RLUIPA). After several appeals and failed mediation, the dispute between the city of Ventura and Harbor Missionary Church is ongoing, but the church is requesting an emergency injunction so it can reopen "Operation Embrace" until a final decision is reached in its broader federal religious freedom case.

Upper Arlington, Ohio, Bans Christian School from Office Building
http://www.thisweeknews.com/content/stories/upperarlington/
news/2015/04/30/sixth-circuit-hears-tree-of-life-appeal.html
Tree of Life Christian School purchased a 15.8 acre office building in Upper
Arlington, Ohio, to serve between 500 and 900 students and employ
approximately 100 persons. Upper Arlington, however, has so far refused
to allow the school to meet in the office building, citing the city's zoning
ordinance. A religious liberties organization filed a lawsuit challenging Upper
Arlington's use of its zoning ordinance under the Religious Land Use and
Institutionalized Persons Act. While Tree of Life Christian Schools lost at
the district court, the school has appealed to the U.S. Court of Appeals for
the Sixth Circuit.

**ACLU Sues Department of Health and Human Services to Force Catholic
Relief Agencies to Refer for Abortions**
http://townhall.com/columnists/robertknight/2015/04/14/aclu-to-catholics-
give-abortions-to-immigrant-children-n1984725
The American Civil Liberties Union (ACLU) filed a lawsuit against the U.S.
Department of Health and Human Services as part of an effort to force Roman
Catholic relief agencies to refer immigrants for abortions and contraceptives,
in violation of Catholic religious beliefs.

**Auburn, New York, Declares Church's Music Camp Not Part of Church's
Mission**
http://blog.libertyinstitute.org/2015/04/victory-city-of-auburn-drops-cease-
and_24.html
First Presbyterian Church in Auburn, New York, hosted a summer music
camp as an outreach to children in the community. Auburn, New York,
however, ordered the church not to hold the camp, stating that the music
camp was not part of the church's mission. First Liberty Institute represented
the church against the city's demands, noting that the city's ban violated the
First Amendment and the federal Religious Land Use and Institutionalized
Persons Act. The city withdrew its order against the church and permitted
the church to host its camp.

Catholic Diocese Forced to Pay Almost $2 Million After Firing Teacher for Immoral Conduct

http://dailysignal.com/2014/12/29/former-catholic-school-teacher-fired-violating-catholic-teaching-awarded-1-95-million-mostly-hurt-feelings/?utm_source=twitter&utm_medium=social

Roman Catholic religious doctrine rejects in vitro fertilization (IVF) treatments as sinful. Emily Herx, a junior high school teacher at St. Vincent de Paul School in Fort Wayne, Indiana—part of the Catholic Diocese of Fort Wayne–South Bend—underwent IVF treatment. Because of Herx's IVF treatment, her teaching contract was not renewed. Herx sued the diocese, arguing that her termination was sex discrimination because male employees who received vasectomies—also prohibited by Catholic doctrine—were not terminated. Herx was awarded almost $2 million.

Maryland County Reduces Fees on Churches Only in Exchange for "Green" Ministries and Sermons on Environmentalism

https://www.washingtonpost.com/local/md-politics/churches-receive-stormwater-fee-discounts-by-starting-green-ministries-sermons/2014/11/16/7bbb94e4-6914-11e4-b053-65cea7903f2e_story.html

Maryland applies a "stormwater remediation fee" to all property owners, including churches. Prince George's County, however, will reduce those fees on churches if the churches will agree to preach environmentally focused sermons and start "green" ministries.

Houston Mayor Annise Parker Subpoenas Pastors' Sermons

http://www.foxnews.com/opinion/2014/10/14/city-houston-demands-pastors-turn-over-sermons.html

Annise Parker, Houston's first openly lesbian mayor, subpoenaed all sermons that dealt with homosexuality, gender identity, or Annise Parker from five area pastors. Following an outcry over the subpoenas, Mayor Parker withdrew the subpoenas.

Fairfax County Attacks Right to Assemble for Religious Study

http://washingtonexaminer.com/virginia-county-takes-aim-at-home-bible-studies-freedom-of-assembly/article/2548301

Lawmakers in Fairfax County, Virginia, drafted an ordinance that would limit the number of persons one could have in a home. The ordinance prohibits a person from having more than forty-nine persons in a home and from having forty persons meet more than three times every forty days. The ordinance specifically listed religious groups as one of the targets of the law.

Preachers Arrested for Preaching in a Train Station
http://www.alliancealert.org/2014/05/15/evangelist-jailed-after-preaching-the-gospel-at-public-train-station-found-not-guilty/
http://christiannews.net/2013/02/23/evangelists-arrested-for-preaching-at-nj-train-station-still-facing-jail-time-as-trial-continues/
Preachers Robert Parker and Don Karns were arrested by two police officers for preaching in the Princeton Train Station. The preachers spent three hours in jail for preaching at the train station where they had been preaching for five years. They were both acquitted.

City Orders Church to Stop Serving the Homeless
http://www.courthousenews.com/2014/05/19/67971.htm
http://religionclause.blogspot.com/2014/05/rluipa-suit-challenges-citys-refusal-to.html
http://www.scribd.com/doc/225626795/Harbor-Church-v-Buenaventura-Complaint
Harbor Missionary Church sued the City of Ventura after the city told them to stop serving the homeless in the city's downtown, The church owns downtown property which it uses to provide childcare services, meals, clothes, and showers. The Stanford Law School Religious Liberty Clinic is representing the church.

Crisis Pregnancy Centers Under Attack for Christian ideals
http://www.centerforinquiry.net/opp/news/center_for_inquiry_urges_ohio_lawmakers_to_drop_resolution_honoring_crisis_/
Center for Inquiry (CfI) wrote a letter to the members of Ohio House Committee on Health and Aging in protest of a resolution that would recognize the work of pregnancy resource centers. CfI believes that pregnancy resource centers advance narrow Christian values.

News Website Removes Church's Advertisement
http://townhall.com/columnists/toddstarnes/2014/04/18/why-did-a-news-outlet-cancel-this-churchs-easter-ad-n1826297
The Journey Church (TJC) in New York paid Capital New York (CNY), a New York City news organization, to run an advertisement campaign for TJC's Easter Sunday services. Only days before Easter weekend, CNY told the church that it was implementing a new company-wide policy prohibiting the running of any religious-affiliated campaigns and cancelled the church's advertisements. When members from TJC began to investigate, CNY reversed its decision and reinstituted the campaign.

Homeless Ministry Halted by City Ordinance

http://townhall.com/columnists/toddstarnes/2014/04/28/is-hud-threatened-by-a-christian-groups-plan-to-expand-its-mission-n1830556

City Gospel Mission (CGM) provided food and shelter to the homeless population of Cincinnati for over 80 years. After CGM began moving its growing ministry to a new building, the insurance company reported that the building was subject to the Fair Housing Act, which prohibited CGM from choosing to whom it could provide shelter. Although Cincinnati officials agreed to waive the restriction, the Federal Department of Housing and Development refused to do so, putting CGM's expansion on indefinite hold.

Pastor's Homeless Feeding Ministry Shut Down

http://www.christianpost.com/buzzvine/alabama-pastor-barred-from-feeding-the-homeless-without-pricey-food-truck-permit-video-117827/

Rick Wood, pastor at the Lord's House of Prayer in Oneonta, Alabama, handed hot dogs and water bottles from his truck to homeless individuals in the community. One day, police stopped Pastor Wood for operating a food truck without a permit. Pastor Wood vowed to continue his ministry, but the cost of a permit could put him out of business.

Church Ordered to Remove Patriotic Billboard

http://sacramento.cbslocal.com/2013/12/28/nevada-county-church-ordered-to-remove-support-our-troops-sign/

When Simple Truth Church (STC) covered an old billboard with a new sign that contained an American flag and the message, "Support Our Troops," the officials of Nevada County, California, ordered STC to remove the sign. Even though the previous sign stood for twenty years without issue, the officials claimed that STC needed a permit to make any changes to the billboard.

Church Battles for Legal Building Permits

http://www.libertyinstitute.org/pages/issues/in-the-church/light-of-the-world-church

When Light of the World Gospel Ministries in Nebraska needed to expand its facilities, it purchased lots surrounding its existing church. However, the church met opposition as it sought various permits to make use of its new property. Assisted by Liberty Institute, Light of the World Church convinced the village board to approve its final building permit in January 2014.

Church Nativity Scene Stolen

http://bringmethenews.com/2013/12/11/nativity-scene-figurines-stolen-from-st-joseph-church-returned-anonymously/

Vandals stole multiple pieces from the Nativity scene that the Church of St. Joseph in St. Joseph, Minnesota, erected annually during the Christmas season. The pieces were put back after the pastor made a public plea for their return.

Group Demands a Halt to Proposed Funding for Christian Organization

https://www.au.org/blogs/wall-of-separation/win-for-the-wall-au-letter-convinces-county-officials-in-washington-state

Pierce County Council in the state of Washington proposed a budget that would give $7,000 to Child Evangelism Fellowship (CEF), a Christian ministry that runs after-school programs for children. Americans United for Separation of Church and State discovered the proposal and threatened the County with litigation unless CEF was removed from the budget. The county complied and struck CEF's funding.

City Attempts to Block Women's Ministry

http://aclj.org/long-awaited-victory-christian-womens-ministry

Candlehouse Teen Challenge, a Christian ministry to women battling addictions, approached the town of Vestal, New York, about its intention to purchase land for its facilities. Town officials initially agreed to the proposed use, but denied Candlehouse's applications after local residents opposed the ministry's plans. Candlehouse refused to stand for the discrimination and reached out to a religious liberties group for assistance. After a five-year battle that culminated in a federal jury trial, the court ruled in favor of Candlehouse and authorized the ministry's establishment.

Homeless Feeding Ministry Threatened with Closure

http://www.newsreview.com/chico/food-handout-in-jeopardy/content?oid=12029958

http://www.chicoer.com/news/ci_24560672/orchard-church-feedings-continue-chico-move-near-city

For more than five years, Orchard Church, located in Chico, California, regularly supplied pizza to homeless individuals at the Chico City Plaza. One day, authorities informed the church that they would either need to cease their ministry entirely or apply for a permit to continue. With the help of a religious liberties organization, the church sought and was granted a permit. However, opposition from local business owners caused the church to agree to relocate the ministry from the plaza to the Chico Municipal Center.

Christian Ministry Workers Threatened with Jail Time for Serving Local Homeless and Elderly

http://blog.libertyinstitute.org/2013/11/pennsylvania-christian-ministry.html

For over five years, Isaiah 61 Ministries, a well-established, nonprofit Christian ministry in Harrisburg, Pennsylvania, served their local community by providing weekly meals, toiletries, clothing, and other forms of assistance to homeless men and women, as well as to the poor and elderly. Then, without warning, the Dauphin County Commissioners threatened to arrest ministry workers and volunteers if they continued their ministry on county property. Liberty Institute stepped in and sent a demand letter to the Dauphin County officials informing them of their unconstitutional conduct and requesting that the workers be permitted to continue their acts of Christian charity on public property.

Pro-Life Group Prohibited from Participating in Annual Christmas Parade

http://www.mlive.com/news/grand-rapids/index.ssf/2013/11/right_to_life_refused_entry_in.html

Right to Life, a pro-life advocacy group from Grand Rapids, Michigan, applied to participate in the city's annual Art Van Santa Parade. The group's float featured children in Santa hats and a smaller banner that read, "Life: A Precious Gift." The city rejected the group's application on the grounds that their float was "not neutral," even though the exact same float was approved the year before.

Local Residents Attempt to Block Repairs to Historic Church

http://mvgazette.com/news/2013/11/25/judge-denies-injunction-block-use-cpa-money-church?k=vg53457a2ab97cc&r=1

Several residents in Oak Bluffs, Massachusetts, filed a lawsuit in an attempt to prohibit the city from restoring the stained glass windows in Trinity Methodist Church, a historic local parish. A superior court judge rejected the plaintiffs' allegations that the city's restorations were an unconstitutional endorsement of religion and permitted the repairs.

City Counsel Attempts to Block Christian Homeless Shelter

http://www.adfmedia.org/News/PRDetail/8653

Lighthouse Rescue Mission in Hattiesburg, Mississippi, applied for a zoning amendment to allow overnight shelter for women and children in its newly purchased building. Citing zoning ordinances, the city counsel rejected the application. However, Lighthouse filed a lawsuit against the illegal zoning regulations, and the city agreed to settle the case and grant Lighthouse all of its requests.

Maryland Church Denied Utilities for New Building
http://www.gazette.net/article/20130916/NEWS/130919403/1124/montgomery-county-pays-125-million-to-settle-with-church&template=gazette
Bethel World Outreach Ministries wanted to build an 800-seat church in Montgomery County's agricultural preserve, but the county denied the church's water and sewage permits. Bethel sued the county, and the county settled with Bethel by agreeing to pay $1.25 million in exchange for Bethel's selection of different property.

Homeless Ministry Told to Choose Between Jesus and Government Funding
http://www.foxnews.com/opinion/2013/09/09/usda-tells-christian-charity-to-kick-jesus-to-curb/?test=latestnews
For over thirty years, the Christian Service Center (CSC) in Lake City, Florida, supplied Bibles, prayer, and food to the homeless. However, during a contract renegotiation with the USDA, a government representative informed CSC that they would no longer receive government food unless they took down all religious décor, discontinued Bible distribution, and ended prayers. CSC refused to change their ministry and consequently was not able to renew their contract for USDA assistance.

Man Sues Church for Noise from Church Bells
http://www.providencejournal.com/breaking-news/content/20130903-narragansett-man-sues-catholic-episcopal-churches-over-bell-ringing-video.ece
Narragansett, Rhode Island, resident John Davaney sued St. Thomas More Catholic Parish because he claimed that the church's bells chimed too often, prohibiting him from quietly enjoying his property and ruining his marriage.

City Police Threaten to Arrest Church Group for Feeding the Homeless
http://www.lovewinsministries.org/2013/08/feeding-homeless-apparently-illegal-in-raleigh-nc/
For six years, Love Wins Ministries (LWM) conducted a feeding program for the homeless every weekend outside of a city park in Raleigh, North Carolina. One morning, Raleigh police arrived and, without explanation, commanded the ministry members to disband or be arrested. After complying with police orders, LWM engaged in a fight with the Raleigh Police Department and City Council to resolve the situation. Following several months of negotiation

coupled with enormous public pressure, the city finally agreed to provide LWM with a warehouse to continue their ministry to the homeless.

Church Defaced With Satanic Symbols
http://www.wtop.com/120/3411879/Hail-Satan-sprayed-in-Latin-on-century-old-Va-church
A century-old church in Danville, Virginia, was spray-painted with satanic symbols and the Latin phrase for "Hail Satan." Local authorities took the vandalism under investigation.

ACLU Threatens Oklahoma City for Leasing Facilities from a Church to Use as a Wellness Center
http://blog.libertyinstitute.org/2013/08/liberty-institute-commends-oklahoma.html
Oklahoma City decided to provide health and wellness centers for active seniors in the city. The centers would be operated by the nonreligious, nonprofit Healthy Living, Inc. The city decided that the best location for one of these centers would be in property owned by the Putnam City Baptist Church. The ACLU, however, sent Oklahoma City a threatening letter opposing the city's purchase or lease of property from the church. Attorneys from Liberty Institute reviewed the ACLU's letter and informed the city that not only were the ACLU's claims unfounded but that rejecting the property solely because it was owned by a church would constitute impermissible hostility to religion.

Sidewalk Sunday School Banned from Public Park
http://www.adfmedia.org/News/PRDetail/8315
Voices of Mercy Outreach Ministries obtained permission to use a public park for its Sidewalk Sunday School ministry, but was subsequently banned from the park after being notified by the Recreation and Park Commission for the Parish of East Baton Rouge that the ministry had violated a policy prohibiting the religious use of parks operated by the commission, even though at least one other religious group was permitted to use the park. The dispute was settled, and the commission agreed to amend its policies and allow the group to meet at the park.

Atheist Group Tries to Deny Christian Ministry Equal Access to Public Services
http://www.lc.org/index.cfm?PID=14102&AlertID=1592
North Miami loans a sound truck, event staff, and other public property to nonprofit organizations. Following its neutral policy, North Miami will loan the equipment regardless of whether the organization is religious. Mission

Miami, a religious nonprofit organization, planned a National Day of Prayer event and sought to borrow the equipment from North Miami. Shortly thereafter, a city councilman and the Freedom From Religions Foundation pressured the council to reverse its decision and exclude Mission Miami from the nonprofit services. The North Miami City Council rejected the calls for religious discrimination and reapproved Mission Miami's right to participate in neutral city services.

Virginia Denies Equal Treatment to Sikhs and Criminalizes Marriages by Unlicensed Ministers

http://www.aclu.org/religion-belief/fairfax-judge-strikes-down-law-licenses-perform-marriages

A Virginia law prohibited unordained ministers from officiating marriages unless they pay a $500 fee. Sikhism is a nonhierarchical religion without ordained clergy. Under the Virginia state law, marriages cannot be legally performed under a Sikh minister without the additional fine. A judge ruled that both of these requirements are unconstitutional because applicants were treated differently based on whether or not their religions had ordained ministers. A Virginia appellate court held that this statute violated the Equal Protection Clause of the U.S. Constitution. In addition, the statute made it a criminal offense for a minister not licensed by the state to use the word "marriage" in a religious ceremony, in violation of the Free Exercise Clause of the U.S. Constitution.

Atheist Group Threatens Lawsuit to Coerce YMCA to Facilitate Promotion of Atheist Beliefs

http://christiannews.net/2013/02/07/humanist-group-threatens-to-sue-ymca-chapter-for-refusing-to-provide-booth-space-at-spring-festival/

The Summerville, South Carolina, Young Men's Christian Association (YMCA) hosts a spring festival. In accordance with its historic mission to promote Christian discipleship, the YMCA rejected an application from a local atheist organization, opposed to the YMCA's mission, to have a booth at the YMCA's festival. The American Humanist Association threatened lawsuits, heavy fines, and jail time if the YMCA did not allow an organization dedicated to promoting atheism at the spring festival.

California City Agrees to Settlement After Blocking Construction of Islamic Worship Center

http://www.justice.gov/opa/pr/2013/February/13-tax-147.html

An Islamic Center in Lomita, California, applied for a permit to replace its existing buildings with one worship center. The city unanimously denied the permit, citing traffic concerns, even though a traffic study concluded that the construction would improve traffic flow in the area. The Department of Justice filed a lawsuit against Lomita for substantially burdening religious rights to worship. The city agreed to a settlement in which it will expedite a new application for the Islamic Center, train its employees about religious discrimination, and periodically report to the Justice Department.

Massachusetts Governor Takes Aim at Parsonage Exemption
http://religionclause.blogspot.com/2013/02/mass-governors-income-tax-proposal.html
Massachusetts Governor Deval Patrick published his 2014 tax plan, which includes a proposal to eliminate the historic parsonage exemption. Under this exemption, clergy of all faiths are able to receive tax-exempt housing allowances.

County Delays Permitting Church to Build Cross on Its Property
http://www.lc.org/index.cfm?PID=14100&PRID=1285
Lutheran Church of the Cross of Porte Charlotte, Florida, attempted for six years to erect a sixty foot cross on its eleven-acre property. Charlotte County prevented the cross from being erected by misclassifying it as a sign instead of a structure or art work, which meant the cross was too tall to meet the criteria for signs. Before making its erroneous classification, the county expressed concern about how the church's cross, on the church's private property, might be perceived by non-Christians. After a law firm stepped in to defend the church, the county reclassified the cross and issued a permit for its construction.

ACLU & *Los Angeles Times* Advocate Against Religious Exemptions
http://www.latimes.com/news/opinion/editorials/la-ed-enda-employment-non-discrimination-act-20130502,0,2410499.story
http://www.aclu.org/lgbt-rights/employment-non-discrimination-act-statement
The *Los Angeles Times* Editorial Board advocated for a significantly reduced religious exemption to a federal nondiscrimination bill for self-identified transgendered persons and individuals in same-sex relationships. The editorial suggested that all religious organizations other than houses of worship should be forced to employ transgendered persons and individuals in same-sex relationships, citing the ACLU for the idea that protecting religious educational institutions or ministries would be unacceptable. The *Los Angeles Times* and ACLU are conspicuously silent about the need to protect closely-

held and family-owned businesses operating according to religious mission statements.

FEMA Denies Disaster Relief to Churches Devastated by Superstorm Sandy
http://www.breitbart.com/Big-Government/2013/03/21/Bill-To-Provide-Sandy-Relief-To-Houses-of-Worship-Stalled-in-Senate
http://www.huffingtonpost.com/2013/02/13/sandy-aid_n_2679410.html
Superstorm Sandy, the second-costliest storm in U.S. history, devastated communities throughout the Northeast. Among the ruins were many churches and houses of worship. Federal funds were allocated to help the communities rebuild, but FEMA refused to allow any funds to be used to repair houses of worship. In response, the U.S. House of Representatives voted overwhelmingly to end FEMA's religious discrimination. Following opposition from the ACLU, Americans United for Separation of Church and State, and *The New York Times,* the bill stalled in the Senate, and the churches have been denied any assistance.

Man Plans to Murder Family Research Council Employees Because of the FRC's Stance on Homosexuality
http://www.huffingtonpost.com/2013/04/22/family-research-council-shooter-sentence_n_3132634.html
A man planned to mass murder the employees of four religious organizations and then smear Chick-fil-A sandwiches on the employees' faces because of their opposition to same-sex "marriage." After shooting the security guard at the Family Research Council, however, the man was subdued.

Christian Pastor Pressured to Withdraw from Inaugural Benediction for Preaching Christian Sexual Ethics
http://usnews.nbcnews.com/_news/2013/01/10/16449097-pastor-nixed-from-obama-inaugural-over-anti-gay-remarks
On January 9, 2013, President Obama announced that Louie Giglio would give the inaugural benediction. That same day, Thinkprogress.org dug up a twenty-year-old sermon Mr. Giglio gave on homosexuality, in which he communicated the Christian belief that homosexuality is a sin. Mr. Giglio withdrew from giving the inaugural benediction 48 hours later due to the fervent outcry from pro-homosexual groups, citing his concern that these groups would use the inauguration to advance their political agendas. President Obama's Inaugural Committee issued a statement approving of Mr. Giglio's departure because his beliefs did not reflect the President's vision of an inclusive America.

Riverside County Bans Churches from Locating in Wine Country

http://www.faith-freedom.com/news/preliminary-victory-for-calvary-chapel-bible-fellowship/

http://www.opposingviews.com/i/religion/wine-country-vintners-church-we-dont-want-your-kind-out-here

Since 1999, Riverside County, California, has banned churches from locating in the Temecula Wine Country. When the pastor of the only existing church in Temecula Wine Country spoke with some of the vintners in the region, he was told, "We don't want your kind out here." Following the threat of litigation, the county began considering amendments to its zoning regulations to allow houses of worship into the wine country.

Court Stops Construction of Tennessee Mosque Despite City Approval

http://www.wsmv.com/story/18646518/murfreesboro-mosque-stopped-by-judge

The Murfreesboro Islamic Center was within three months of completion when a chancellor court ruled that not enough public notice was given before the zoning commission approved construction. The Plaintiffs have been fighting the mosque's construction, fearing that it is a "sharia compliant" organization. The county has the option of reapproving the building as long as it gives proper notice of the public meeting. As of now, the mosque has not been reapproved.

IRS Asked to Investigate Church Due to Alleged Political Statements in Sermons

http://www.au.org/files/pdf_documents/2012-05-hager-hills.pdf

On May 21, 2012, Americans United for Separation of Church and State wrote to the IRS contending that the pastor of Hager Hill Freewill Baptist Church violated federal tax law by intervening in an election where he told his congregation that "he wants to see President Barack Obama removed from office." The pastor made this statement while discussing the President's comments affirming his policy backing same-sex "marriage," a policy antithetical to the church's religious belief on the biblical conception of marriage.

Evangelist Prohibited from Distributing Religious Tracts at Cheese Festival

http://religionclause.blogspot.com/2012/05/suit-challenges-limits-on-evangelists.html

Police stopped an evangelist from passing out religious tracts at the Sorrento Cheese Italian Heritage Festival in Buffalo, New York, even though members of other organizations such as the Air Force and schools were allowed to pass out pamphlets. The evangelist sued, seeking an injunction allowing him to pass out his tracts as well as for costs and nominal damages. In the suit, he claimed the actions of the city violated due process and his First Amendment rights.

City Settles with a Buddhist Center for $900,000 After Denying Permit to Build a Temple

http://religionclause.blogspot.com/2012/05/california-city-settles-rluipa-suit.html

The Walnut, California, Planning Commission denied a Buddhist Zen Center's application for a conditional use permit to build a temple in 2008. After the Buddhist Zen Center and the Department of Justice filed a suit under the Religious Land Use and Institutionalized Persons Act (RLUIPA), the city settled with the Department of Justice and the center for $900,000.

ACLU Attempts to Force County to Discriminate Against Religious Festival

http://www.wdtv.com/wdtv.cfm?func=view&section=Fox-10&item=Prosecutor-Commission-Legal-Funding-Jesus-Fest269

The ACLU attempted to force Harrison County, West Virginia, to discriminate against a religious festival in its grant distribution. The County Prosecuting Attorney refused to discriminate, noting that the grant funding process was neutral towards religion.

Pittsfield Township Denies Michigan Islamic Academy's Application for Rezoning

http://www.annarbor.com/news/director-of-american-islamic-council-calls-pittsfields-rationale-against-islamic-school-neo-jim-crow/

The Pittsfield Township Board of Trustees denied the Michigan Islamic Academy's application for rezoning, which would have allowed the academy to build a new school on property it purchased. The academy claimed it received assurances from the township prior to purchasing the land that they would be able to rezone as long as they followed the procedures for rezoning. The academy claims violations of the Religious Land Use and Institutionalized Persons Act (RLUIPA) and the First and Fourteenth Amendments.

Gettysburg, Pennsylvania, Declares Civil War Chapel to be an "Eyesore" Weeks After Awarding It the City's Beautification Award

United States Christian Commission v. Gettysburg

John Wega built a reconstruction chapel like those used by the U.S. Christian Commission during the Civil War. Mere weeks after being presented with Gettysburg's beautification award, the reconstruction Civil War chapel was declared an eyesore by the borough. Gettysburg attempted to force the chapel out of the town's square. Once it became apparent that the chapel had a legal right to remain, arsonists set fire to the chapel's Bibles, burning down the chapel and several nearby structures. Wega is now working to rebuild the chapel.

Minnesota Church Settles RLUIPA Case for $500,000 and Land

http://www.startribune.com/local/west/136353248.html (Dec. 28, 2011)
The city of Wayzata, Minnesota, and the Unitarian Universalist Church of Minnetonka agreed to settle a RLUIPA case brought against the city by the church. The city dropped the zoning issues and sold the church three acres of land on which to build a new building and also agreed to pay $500,000 in damages and fees. The church claimed religious discrimination in the suit, while the city merely said that they were worried about the noise the church would create.

Illinois Severs Ties with Catholic Charities over Adoption to Homosexuals

http://articles.chicagotribune.com/2011-11-15/news/ct-met-catholic-charities-foster-care-20111115_1_civil-unions-act-catholic-charities-religious-freedom-protection
The state of Illinois ended its historic relationship with Catholic Charities, which was the first organization to inspire child welfare services in that state, because the organization would not adopt children to homosexual couples. Adopting to homosexual couples would violate well-established Roman Catholic Church doctrine. Although Catholic Charities was willing to refer homosexual couples to other adoption agencies, the state refused to accommodate them. Ironically, this religious-based discrimination is in response to the Religious Freedom Protection and Civil Unions Act. The Act, when combined with state antidiscrimination laws, requires homosexual civil unions to be treated like marriages, but only provides protection to religious clergy who decline to officiate a civil union. Two-thousand children will now have to transition to new agencies.

Indiana Civil Rights Commission Brings Full Force of State Power Against Small Religious Association

http://www.christiannewswire.com/news/1227913200.html
The Indiana Civil Rights Commission (ICRC) asserted authority over a group of nine homeschool families that had formed an organization to provide religious-based social interaction for their children. A discrimination claim was filed with the ICRC when one of the families requested a special diet

for its child to avoid allergy concerns and the organization determined it would be safer if the child's family prepared the meal. ICRC asserted jurisdiction to investigate and penalize the small, religious association—an organization without any employees, offering no goods, services, or public accommodations, powered by volunteers and donations. The conflict has forced the group to temporarily disband pending a final resolution and has exhausted its small repository of donations.

Dallas Central Appraisal District Denies Tax Exemption to Church that Meets Outside
http://www.libertyinstitute.org/video/romanian-orthodox-church-dallas/
A group of Romanian immigrants saved their money to buy a plot of land to worship on and to eventually—once they could afford it—build a church on. The Romanian Orthodox congregation met on the property one Sunday each month for a worship service. The Dallas Central Appraisal District, however, began taxing the property, asserting that the land was not being used for religious purposes because there was no church structure built on the land.

Interfaith Retreat Center Prevails After Initial Zoning Discrimination
https://www.rutherford.org/publications_resources/tri_in_the_news/southwest_virginia_county_relents_approves_permit_for_interfaith_spiritual
An interfaith retreat center in Grayson County, Virginia, was denied a special use permit for its property. The leader believed the denial was due to discrimination against the center's philosophy. After the center filed a complaint with a state court, the Grayson County Board of Supervisors granted the center's permit request.

Mormon Church Sues Texas City over Denial of Permit
http://religionclause.blogspot.com/2011/11/mormon-church-sues-texas-city-to.html
A Mormon church in Mission, Texas, sued the city over its refusal to issue a permit for the church to construct a new building. The church claims that the city purposefully changed the voting rules for issuing permits so that the church would not receive a permit. The church filed the suit under RLUIPA, the Texas Religious Freedom Restoration Act, and the free exercise and due process clauses of the Constitution.

California Museum Permits Pro-Evolution Documentary but Stops Pro-Intelligent Design Documentary

http://www.evolutionnews.org/2011/08/california_science_center_pays050081.html

The California Science Center cancelled a showing of a documentary that supported Intelligent Design theory. The following week, however, the museum showed a documentary supporting evolutionary theory. A lawsuit alleging religious discrimination was filed, and the California Science Center agreed to pay $110,000 in damages in the settlement of the suit.

Idaho City Discriminates Against Churches in Zoning Laws

http://www.kboi2.com/news/local/123491194.html

The city of Mountain Hope, Idaho, specifically singled out religious groups for exclusion in its zoning law. No Limits Christian Ministries brought suit under the Religious Land Use and Institutionalized Persons Act. The city responded by modifying its zoning ordinance to treat churches fairly.

City Forced to End Zoning Discrimination Against Religious Organization

http://www.justice.gov/usao/nys/pressreleases/May11/airmontsettlementpr.pdf

The Village of Airmont, New York, denied a permit to a religious organization to build a Jewish educational facility. The U.S. Attorney's Office settled a lawsuit with the village to amend its zoning code and to end its discrimination against the group.

Library Prohibits Christian Author from Holding Book Discussion

http://ilenevickministriestn.blogspot.com/2011/01/whats-it-going-to-take-in-us-christians.html

Ilene Vick, author of *Personality Based Evangelism,* filed suit against Putnam County after the library refused to let her use the library's room to lead a discussion on her book. In the suit that followed, the judge ordered the library to never again refuse access to its facility to a Christian.

Church Brings RLUIPA Suit in Illinois

http://religionclause.blogspot.com/2010/12/hispanic-congregation-sues-illinois.html

The Rios de Agua Viva church filed a lawsuit under the Religious Land Use and Institutionalized Persons Act (RLUIPA) against Burbank, Illinois, for requiring it to file for a special use permit to use a restaurant as a meeting place. The church alleges that other, nonreligious institutions do not have to apply for the special permits.

County Admits in Settlement It Targeted Church with Legislation

http://thedailyrecord.com/2010/11/18/anne-arundel-county-to-pay-325m-to-riverdale-baptist/

Anne Arundel County, Maryland, agreed to a settlement with the Riverdale Baptist Church in which the county would allow the church to build a school and pay $3.25 million in damages. The RLUIPA litigation started in 2008 when the county passed litigation targeting the church's proposed construction of a new school after initially approving the school's zoning application. In the settlement, the county admitted that it purposely timed the litigation so that it would not affect other private schools.

Michigan Church Wins RLUIPA Settlement

http://www.dailytribune.com/article/20101102/NEWS/311029991/church-asks-court-to-strike-down-hazel-park-zoning-law

The Salvation Temple in Hazel Park, Michigan, settled a lawsuit it filed against the city for not allowing it to move into a building zoned for commerce or industry. The restriction on the church was prohibitive because there were no other properties available that could house the church. In the settlement, the city allowed the church to move into a vacant commercial building.

Group Challenges the Nonprofit Status of a Christian Ministry for Opposing Same-Sex "Marriage"

http://religionclause.blogspot.com/2010/10/au-asks-irs-to-investigate-church.html

Americans United for Separation of Church and State wrote a letter to the IRS claiming a Christian organization in Sioux City, Iowa, was in violation of its nonprofit status. The organization, Cornerstone World Outreach, campaigned to local churches and asked them to preach against same-sex "marriage" in the weeks leading up to Iowa's Supreme Court elections so that people would vote against the justices that legalized same-sex "marriage."

Libraries Censor Religious Discussion

http://americanlibrariesmagazine.org/news/02172010/florida-man-sues-two-libraries-religious-discrimination

http://www.wnd.com/2010/08/191129/

Several public libraries across the county have banned the discussion of religious books and the holding of religious seminars in their facilities.

Dallas Prohibits Church from Hosting a Christian School in Its Building

Eric Nicholson, "Council Says 'No' to Coram Deo; Liberty Institute Lawyer Claims Violation of Federal Law," Preston Hollow People, *available at http://www. prestonhollowpeople.com/2010/06/23/council-says-no-to-coram-deo-liberty- institute-lawyer-claims-violation-of-federal-law/ (Jun. 23, 2010)*

Dallas, Texas, prohibited Hillcrest Church from hosting a Christian school, Coram Deo Academy, in its building, citing traffic concerns. The school, however, was already housed on the same street, just down the block from the church.

Arizona Town Prohibits Home Churches or Bible Studies in Single-Family Neighborhoods

http://www.azcentral.com/community/chandler/articles/2010/03/15/20100315 religion-ban-private-homes-gilbert.html

An Arizona town ordered the Oasis of Truth Church to end its services in its pastor's home because its city zoning code made it illegal to hold church-sponsored activities in single-family homes. After an appeal was filed and the media began to focus on the issue, the town reversed its decision and modified its zoning laws to permit Bible studies and small worship services in single-family neighborhoods.

Federal Agency Backtracks After Barring Religious Worship in Public Housing Complex

http://www.dallasnews.com/news/community-news/dallas/ headlines/20100305-Church-services-are-back-on-at-5879.ece

After initially barring religious worship services in public housing facilities due to Establishment Clause concerns, the Dallas Housing Authority (DHA) reversed its decision. A DHA spokesman explained that the incident was caused by a misinterpretation of federal guidelines.

Los Angeles Bars Evangelism on Sidewalks Near Courthouses

http://www.adfmedia.org/News/PRDetail/3731
http://oldsite.alliancedefensefund.org/userdocs/MianoComplaint.pdf

The City of Los Angeles prohibited anyone from approaching another person about education and counseling, among other things, within 100 feet of courthouse doors, unless the other person consents. This was interpreted as making it illegal for an evangelist to peacefully share the Gospel to willing members of the public who passed by on sidewalks next to the unused emergency exits of a courthouse.

Richmond Changes Ordinance to Protect Religious Speech

http://www2.timesdispatch.com/news/2010/feb/05/suit05_20100204-223008-ar-11567/

Two street evangelists were confronted six different times by Richmond, Virginia, police who wanted them to end their public preaching. Some of the officers threatened the preachers with invented violations. After the evangelists sought legal assistance to protect their free speech rights, the Richmond City Council recognized the problems in its law and proposed a new noise ordinance to end its unconstitutional discrimination against religious speech.

Church Zoning Application Revoked in New Jersey

http://www.northjersey.com/news/bergen/87635227_Property_owner__Ridgefield_Park_at_odds_over_building_s_use.html?c=y&page=1

After approving a zoning variance to house a church in the back of a two-story Dunkin Donuts / Baskin Robbins building, a New Jersey town rescinded its approval. The property owner said that there was no concrete reason for the denial.

Religious Group Forced to Limit Expansion

http://www.northjersey.com/news/crime_courts/031210_Settlement_between_Englewood_synagogue_neighborhood_group_limits_outdoor_events_indoor_expansion_.html?c=y&page=1

After nearly a decade of legal disputes, a New Jersey town settled with a community group over a synagogue and the synagogue's plans to expand existing facilities and use tents for events on its property. The settlement allowed the synagogue to expand and use tents, but set restrictions on when and how tents can be used and prohibited future expansion for six years.

ACLU Opposed Connecticut Town's Allowing Salvation Army to Collect Funds at Festival

http://religionclause.blogspot.com/2009/12/group-complains-about-citys-favoritism.html

Meriden, Connecticut, hosts the Festival of Silver Lights every year, which is a large attraction. In 2009, the ACLU complained because Meriden gave the Salvation Army the exclusive right to collect funds at the festival. The ACLU claimed that this showed that the city favored a religious institution. The funds, however, only went towards the charity's social services.

Texas City Stops Church's Plans for a Halfway House

http://www.kwtx.com/home/headlines/59321097.html?site=full

The city of Bellmead, Texas, denied the Church of the Open Door a zoning permit to build a halfway house. After the church began working on opening the halfway house, the city passed a provision prohibiting the construction of halfway houses within a thousand feet of any home, school, or park. The parties settled the lawsuit when the city agreed to pay the church $550,000.

San Diego Refuses to Grant Permit to Church Because of Community Plan

http://www.utsandiego.com/news/2009/Apr/25/rancho-bernardo-grace-church-gets-right-to-stay/

Grace Church of North County applied to San Diego for a ten-year permit to use space in Rancho Bernardo industrial park. The city refused to grant the permit because including the church in the industrial park was inconsistent with the community plan. The church sued the city under the Religious Land Use and Institutionalized Persons Act (RLUIPA). San Diego agreed to pay $950,000 in damages.

City in Florida Uses Zoning Ordinance to Block Outreach Center

http://articles.sun-sentinel.com/2009-04-28/news/0904270567_1_chabad-posner-city-s-insurer

Cooper City, Florida, refused to let Chabad Rabbi Shemul Posner open his outreach center because of zoning restrictions. Eventually, the Rabbi had to move the outreach center in order for it to be opened. In the suit that followed, a jury awarded the Rabbi $325,750 in damages on a RLUIPA claim and $470,000 in attorney's fees.

City in Pennsylvania Denies Church Permission to Use Park for the National Day of Prayer

Norwin Star, "Church to Use Park for Prayer Day," available at http://aclj.org/aclj/the-norwin-star-monroeville-pa---church-to-use-park-for-prayer-day- (Apr. 24, 2008)

Members of the Suburban Community Church in Monroeville, Pennsylvania, requested permission to use a public park for the National Day of Prayer, but were denied access. The church sought legal assistance, which sent a demand letter to the borough explaining the constitutional rights of the church to use the park. The letter asked for a statement in writing that the church would be allowed to use the park. Following receipt of the letter, the borough's council met and voted unanimously to allow the church to use the park.

Pennsylvania Borough Denies Church Permission to Use Park for the National Day of Prayer

Patti Dobranski, "Religious Freedom Bolstered in Irwin," Pittsburgh Tribune-Review, *available at http://aclj.org/aclj/tribune-review-pittsburgh-pa---religious-freedom-bolstered-in-irwin (Apr. 15, 2008)*

The Borough of Westmoreland, Pennsylvania, denied Suburban Community Church permission to use a public park for a National Day of Prayer event. The borough stated that they would not allow the park to be reserved for religious purposes. After receiving a demand letter, one of the borough's council members denied that the borough prohibited the church from reserving the park. After being notified that the council's prohibition was recorded on tape, the borough's council unanimously approved the church's request to use the park.

City of Plano Bans Church from Reserving Council Chambers Unless It Includes Other Faiths

Free Market Foundation, "Free Market Sues City of Plano for Preventing Pastor from using Council Chambers on National Day of Prayer," available at http://freemarketblog.wordpress.com/2008/03/14/free-market-sues-city-of-plano-for-preventing-pastor-from-using-council-chambers-on-national-day-of-prayer/ (Mar. 14, 2008)

The City of Plano prohibited an all-Christian alliance from renting its facilities for the National Day of Prayer, insisting that other faiths be required to share the space as a condition for use.

City in Texas Uses Zoning Ordinance to Delay Church

Elizabeth Langton, "Texas: Duncanville church says city zoning decision violates U.S. law," Dallas Morning News (Feb. 8, 2008)

The City of Duncanville, Texas, was using zoning laws to discriminate against Templo Bautista to deny the congregation the ability to hold services. After purchasing a building in the downtown area, the church was told a special use permit would be required in order to begin using the building for services. Templo Bautista applied for the permit, paid the necessary fees but was still denied use of the building because one landowner was opposed to the church's location. After multiple hearings at the city council, the church was finally allowed to occupy the building and to hold church services.

NFL Threatens Churches Showing the Super Bowl on Big Screens
Jacqueline L. Salmon, "NFL Pulls Plug On Big-Screen Church Parties For Super Bowl," Washington Post, *available at http://www.washingtonpost.com/wp-dyn/ content/article/2008/01/31/AR2008013103958.html (Feb. 1, 2008)*
The NFL demanded that Fall Creek Baptist Church in Indianapolis, Indiana, cancel its advertised Super Bowl party. In addition to objecting to the church's use of the words "Super Bowl" in promotions, the league objected to use of any screen larger than fifty-five inches and disliked the church's plans to show a video highlighting the Christian testimonies of Colts coach Tony Dungy and Chicago Bears coach Lovie Smith.

Tax Assessor Refused Parsonage Exemption For Parsonage Not Adjacent to Church
Liberty Counsel, "Church Challenges Constitutionality of Property Tax Assessment," available at http://www.lc.org/index.cfm?PID=14100&PRID=564 (Apr. 13, 2007)
A Bay County's property appraiser, Rick Barnett, developed a new standard for determining whether to grant tax exemptions to church property. Barnett was the only Florida property appraiser to refuse to exempt church parsonages that are not adjacent to houses of worship. Barnett denied Faith Christian Family Church's application for a tax exemption on its parsonage and assessed property taxes on the property. The church was forced to file a lawsuit.

Full Gospel Powerhouse Church of God in Christ Denied Tax Exemption After Building Burns
http://www.wnd.com/2006/08/37571/
An African-American church bought a church building that subsequently burned down. The tax appraisal district denied them a tax exemption because they could no longer meet on the property for services and assessed back taxes for non-use because of the fire. There were other churches, however, with open land not being used that were granted exempt status. The church was forced to file a lawsuit to protect its very existence.

Florida Town Revokes Permit for Orthodox Jewish Synagogue
Liberty Counsel, "City of Hollywood, Florida, To Pay $2 Million To Synagogue for Zoning Discrimination," available at http://www.lc.org/index. cfm?PID=14100&PRID=77 (Jun. 30, 2006)
An Orthodox Jewish Synagogue moved into two houses and started remodeling the houses into a synagogue, angering neighbors. A zoning board granted the synagogue a permit, but just fifty-three days later, the city commissioners voted to revoke the special permit, citing zoning issues.

A lawsuit was filed and the case was eventually settled, with the city agreeing to rewrite their codes.

Biblical Museum and Theme Park Struggle for Tax Exemption
Liberty Counsel, "Holy Land Experience Wins Final Round of Property Tax Exemption Battle," available at http://www.lc.org/index.cfm?PID=14100&PRID=73 (Jun. 16, 2006)
The Holy Land Experience is a living biblical museum that conveys its religious message through teaching, preaching, dramatic enactments, special music, performances, and multimedia presentations. After almost four years of litigation, the Orange County Circuit Court issued an order stating the property on which The Holy Land Experience sits is exempt from ad valorem taxation. Despite this ruling, the county property appraiser continued to refuse to recognize The Holy Land Experience as tax-exempt. The museum was eventually forced to file for contempt of court for this blatant violation of a court order.

County in Virginia Bans Church Service from Barn
Liberty Counsel, "Virginia County Bucking Against Cowboy Church," available at http://www.lc.org/index.cfm?PID=14100&PRID=61 (May 10, 2006)
A private landowner agreed to allow The Cowboy Church of Virginia to conduct services on his property in Bedford County, Virginia. After a few months, the landowner received a Notice of Violation, stating that his barn could not be used for religious services and that his property wasn't zoned for religious meetings.

City in California Denies Church Permit Because Officials Believe the Church to be a Cult
https://www.rutherford.org/publications_resources/on_the_front_lines/pr537
The Church of the Light bought some land in Ontario, California, after determining that the property was zoned so that it could be used for religious assembly. However, the city passed an ordinance requiring new churches to obtain a permit before building, and five days after the ordinance was passed, Ontario's Development Advisory Board denied the church's permit, claiming the denial was based on allegations that the church was a cult. A lawsuit was filed to protect the church's rights to build their church.

City Limits Church's Land Use to Keep Out Large Churches
Iglesia de Oracion y Alabanza v. City of Mesquite
A Pentecostal church in Mesquite, Texas, was told by the city that it could

only use one acre of its ten-acre lot to build its church because the city did not want any big churches in the area.

Church Prevented from Meeting Because of Lot Size
Plano Vietnamese Baptist Church v. City of Plano
A Vietnamese Baptist church in Plano, Texas, was told by the city that it could not use a former church building it had purchased for a house of worship because the lot on which the church building was located was not two acres or more in size. The church appealed the city's decision to the district court, which permitted the church to use the building.

Ohio Library Prohibits Christian Group from Meeting to Discuss Traditional Marriage Unless Advocates of Homosexual Marriage Also Present
http://www.lc.org/index.cfm?PID=14102&AlertID=461&printpage=y
A Christian group requested access to a community room in the Newton Falls Library in Youngstown, Ohio, for a meeting about the biblical perspective of traditional marriage. The library director denied the request because the library's policy required that any time a "controversial subject" was discussed, the opposing viewpoint must also be presented. The policy was revised only after a lawsuit was filed.

Town in Texas Overrides Its Own Expert to Block Church
Templo La Fe v. City of Balch Springs
The city council of Balch Springs, Texas, prevented Templo La Fe from building a church on its own land. The city's experts on the Planning and Zoning Commission voted unanimously to approve the building, but four city council members decided to override their own experts. The church was forced to file a lawsuit, and only after the Department of Justice opened an investigation did the city settle the lawsuit and allowed the church to proceed with its plan to build.

Churches Banned from Renting School Facilities in Peabody, Massachusetts
American Center for Law and Justice, "Peabody, MA Clearing Way for Religious Organizations to Use Facilities," available at http://aclj.org/aclj/aclj-reaches-agreement-with-city-of-peabody-ma-clearing-way-for-religious-organizations-to-use-facilities (Feb. 7, 2005)
Beverly Church of the Nazarene and the Living Hope Church of the Nazarene sued the city of Peabody, Massachusetts, for not renewing a contract to use public school facilities for religious services. School officials told the churches that they could no longer use the school because doing so was a violation

of the "separation of church and state." The city and the churches settled, allowing the churches to continue using the facilities.

Washington Town Censors Announcement Posted on a Public Board Regarding Showing of the *Jesus* Film

Liberty Counsel, "City of Aberdeen Backs Down From Censoring an Announcement on a Public Reader Board Regarding the Private Showing of the Jesus Film," available at http://www.lc.org/index.cfm?PID=14100&PRID=395 (Jan. 5, 2005)
Child Evangelism Fellowship of Pacific Harbors, Washington, inquired about posting an announcement on a public reader board about a public showing of the *Jesus* film. The organization was told that because of the "separation of church and state," the city could not permit the word "Jesus" to be posted on the board. After receiving an attorney's letter pointing out the unconstitutionality of this policy, the city allowed the posting.

City in Texas Discriminates Against Church's Roof Design

The City of Plano, Texas, attempted to prevent the WillowCreek Fellowship Church from opening because of the slant of the church's roof, even though no ordinance existed relating to the angle of the roof and despite the fact that the roof of a school down the street from the church had an identical angle. Only after threat of a lawsuit under RLUIPA did the city relent and permit the church to open.

Indiana Town Prohibits Distribution of Religious Literature in Public Parks

Rutherford Institute, "Rutherford Institute Attorneys File Suit Against Lebanon City Parks Officials For Banning Distribution of Religious Literature," available at https://www.rutherford.org/publications_resources/on_the_front_lines/pr421 (Apr. 28, 2003)
A minister and a church member from Grace Baptist Church were prohibited from distributing religious literature in a public park in Lebanon, Indiana, though the minister had distributed materials in the park for years. A lawsuit was filed to protect the minister's rights.

School District Evicts Church in the Middle of the Church's Lease

ReligiousTolerance.org, "Rental of Public School & Library Facilities by Religious Groups," available at http://www.religioustolerance.org/ps_pra7.htm (Mar. 15, 2003)
Reunion Church leased an empty high school on Sunday mornings for services, but the Dallas I.S.D. evicted the church in the middle of the lease, claiming that renting their facilities to a church violates school board policy.

Reunion Church filed a lawsuit challenging their eviction, and the school district reversed its decision.

Organization Banned from Using Library for Meeting About American History and the Ten Commandments

Beverly Goldberg, "Christian-Rights Group Sues over Nixed Library Meeting," American Libraries Magazine, *available at http://americanlibrariesmagazine. org/news/01202003/christian-rights-group-sues-over-nixed-library-meeting (Jan. 20, 2003)*

Liberty Counsel, a Christian civil rights legal defense organization, was denied access to the Dunedin Public Library near Tampa, Florida. Liberty Counsel wanted to use a community meeting room for a meeting relating to America's Christian History and the influence of the Ten Commandments. After Liberty Counsel sued, the Dunedin Public Library changed its policy to settle the lawsuit.

School Ordered to Stop Leasing Space to Church

Alliance Defense Fund, "Pennsylvania township changes position, agrees to allow churches to rent school facilities," available at http://www.alliancedefensefund. org/Home/ADFContent?cid=4148

Quakertown Community School District officials were informed by a zoning officer to stop leasing space to Harvest Community Fellowship Church because the church was using space at the school to hold a Sunday church service. The church's use qualified as "principal use" of the facilities, even though the church only used the facilities for a few hours on Sundays. Under the unmodified zoning code, only one principal use can be made of a property without obtaining a variance. The church had to seek help from attorneys to correspond with the township officials until they agreed to amend the zoning code.

Library Refuses Access to Religious Groups

http://www.ala.org/ala/alonline/currentnews/newsarchive/2002/july2002/ texaslibrary.cfm

The public library in Mitchell County, Texas, denied Rev. Seneca Lee access to a room in which he planned to hold a meeting about political and social issues from a Christian perspective. A library policy prevented religious groups from using the meeting room. Only after a lawsuit was filed did the library change their policy of discriminating against religious groups.

Allen, Texas, Refuses to Lease Property for Church Use But Leases to Secular Groups

The City of Allen denied Cottonwood Creek Baptist Church the right to lease property for church use, even though the city had previously allowed secular groups to lease the same space. The ordinance applied by the city targeted churches for unfair treatment and exclusion. After a lengthy discussions with the church's attorneys, the city finally allowed the church to lease the space.

Texas Town Bans Churches from Meeting in City-Owned Buildings

The city of Terrell, Texas, prohibited the Purpose Life Church from meeting in a city owned building, saying, "Local governments are not allowed to have church activities in a city-owned building. This is consistent with city policy. The city has denied these types of requests of other church events. We are governed in this area by both state and federal law." Only after attorneys filed a lawsuit and the Department of Justice investigated the city did the city settle the lawsuit and pay damages to the church.

New York City Prohibits Bible Study in Community Center

Alliance Defense Fund, "Almost a Year after the Tragic Attack on America, Pastor Wins Right to Hold Bible Study for Residents in New York City...," available at http://www.christianrights.org/Alliance%20Defense%20Fund/ADF%205.htm

Following the September 11 attacks, a New York City pastor wanted to use the Woodside Community Center, located in a public housing development, to host a Bible study for New Yorkers. The pastor was denied his request because religious services (unless connected to a family-oriented event like a wedding) were prohibited. A lawsuit was filed to prevent the community center from treating religious groups differently from other groups.

FIRST LIBERTY

ATTACKS IN THE MILITARY

ACLU Sues Virginia Military Institute over Prayers Before Meals
Bunting v. Mellen, 541 U.S. 1019 (2004)
The U.S. Court of Appeals for the Fourth Circuit ruled that cadets at Virginia Military Institute (VMI) could no longer join together to pray before meals. The American Civil Liberties Union filed a lawsuit against VMI on behalf of two students who believed that the prayers violated the U.S. Constitution. The case was appealed to the Supreme Court, but the court refused to hear the case.

FFRF Sues to Remove World War II Memorial
Freedom from Religion Found., Inc. v. Weber, No. 13-35770, 2015 U.S. App. LEXIS 15399 (9th Cir. Aug. 31, 2015)
After World War II, Army soldiers from the 10th Mountain Division sought to honor their fallen brothers with a monument in the style of religious shrines they had seen on battlefields in Europe. The Freedom From Religion Foundation brought suit to challenge this historic war memorial, known as "Big Mountain Jesus," located near Kalispell, Montana. The U.S. Court of Appeals for the Ninth Circuit held that the memorial is constitutional, affirming that the Constitution does not compel the government to purge cultural or historic symbols from the public sphere merely because they are religious.

Veterans Memorial on Mt. Soledad Ordered Torn Down
Trunk v. City of San Diego, No. 13-57126 (9th Cir. 2015)
The Mount Soledad Veterans Memorial Cross in San Diego, California, has stood since 1954 as a symbol of the selfless sacrifice of our nation's veterans. The memorial displays photos and names of over 3,500 American veterans along with diverse religious and secular symbols. In January 2011, a federal court of appeals ruled that the memorial gives onlookers the impression of government endorsement of religion and therefore violates the Establishment Clause. The veterans memorial was saved when the memorial and the land upon which it sits were transferred to private owners.

Marine Court-Martialed for Refusing to Remove Bible Verse from Desk
United States v. Sterling, No. 201400150, 2015 CCA LEXIS 65 (N-M.C.C.A. Feb. 26, 2015)
Lance Corporal Monifa Sterling, a Marine stationed at Camp Lejune in North Carolina, printed her favorite Bible verse, "No weapons formed against me shall prosper," and posted it in her workspace. Although other service members were permitted to keep personal items on their desks, Sterling was

ordered to remove the verse. After she did not remove the verse, it was torn down and she was court-martialed. Liberty Institute and former U.S. Solicitor General Paul Clement are representing Sterling in her appeal to protect the religious liberties of those who serve our country.

Catholic Priest Prevented from Providing Religious Services on Military Base

Leonard v. U.S. Department of Defense, No. 1:13-cv-1561 (D. D.C. Apr. 30, 2014)
http://kdvr.com/2013/10/14/priest-employed-by-government-claims-shutdown-violates-religious-freedom/
Father Ray Leonard is a Catholic priest under contract with the U.S. Government to provide Catholic services at the Kings Bay Naval Submarine Base in Georgia. During the government shutdown stemming from congressional failure to reach a federal government funding agreement, Leonard was instructed to cease his religious undertakings. Other religions and denominations were allowed to continue their religious practices. The military base locked Father Leonard out of his office, denied his access to articles of Catholic faith, and threatened him with arrest if he attempted to continue his religious activities. After Father Leonard brought a lawsuit against the base for its religious discrimination, the base immediately lifted its restriction but sought to have Father Leonard sign an atypical contract that would ruin the lawsuit.

Humanist Group Sues to Eliminate Veterans Memorial in Lake Elsinore, California

American Humanist Association v. City of Lake Elsinore, No. 5:13-cv-00989 (C.D. Cal. July 16, 2013)
The city of Lake Elsinore, California, set up a five-foot tall black granite slab with a white silhouette of a soldier kneeling before a cross along with several other crosses and a Star of David in the background as a veterans memorial. The American Humanist Association brought a lawsuit challenging the memorial because it included a cross. A federal district court in California held that the design violates both the Establishment Clause and the California Constitution. In June of 2014, the city council approved a new memorial featuring a soldier kneeling before a gun instead of a cross.

AUSCS Sues to Force Removal of Veterans Memorial from King, North Carolina

Hewett v. City of King, North Carolina, No. 1:12-1179 (M.D.N.C. filed Nov. 2, 2012)
The American Legion Post 290 of King, North Carolina, contributed to the

design and construction of a veterans memorial in King, N.C., that includes a silhouette of a soldier kneeling before a cross-shaped headstone. Americans United for Separation of Church and State filed a lawsuit against the city of King alleging that the memorial violates the U.S. and North Carolina constitutions because it contains religious imagery and sits on public land. The American Legion, represented by Liberty Institute, intervened in the case to defend the memorial.

MRFF Sues to Stop National Prayer Luncheon
Mullin v. Lt. Gen. Gould, No. 1:11-247 (D. Colo. Feb. 9, 2011)
The Military Religious Freedom Foundation (MRFF) and several U.S. Air Force Academy faculty members filed suit seeking to enjoin a National Prayer Luncheon. The keynote speaker was a retired Vietnam-era Marine who is known for his evangelistic speaking. Even though attendance was not mandatory, the MRFF claimed that the command structure encouraged attendance to an extent amounting to coercion. A federal district court dismissed the lawsuit because the plaintiffs did not have standing to bring the suit.

Reverend Veitch Sues Navy Following Multidenominational Services
Veitch v. England, 471 F.3d 124 (D.C. Cir. 2006)
Reverend D. Philip Veitch, a Navy chaplain, refused to participate in multidenominational services and eventually resigned. Veitch sued the Navy, arguing that his First Amendment rights were violated. The appeals court ruled that Veitch's resignation was voluntary and affirmed the lower court's decision granting summary judgment to the defendants.

"God Bless the Military" Sign Under Attack
http://chaplainalliance.org/site/wp-content/uploads/2015/09/2015-09-25-Chaplain-Alliance-News-Release.pdf
Following the 9/11 terrorist attacks, a Marine Corps base in Hawaii posted a sign that reads "God bless the military, their families and the civilians who work with them." The sign has come under attack by a group that wants it to be moved to the base's chapel. In response, the Chaplain Alliance for Religious Liberty issued a statement defending the constitutionality of the sign. According to the statement, "God bless our military" is a slogan similar to the official national motto, "In God We Trust," which courts have repeatedly upheld. The Chaplain Alliance also commented that since the founding of our country, every president has publicly called on God to bless America.

War Memorial May Be Separated from Others over Christian Symbol
http://m.columbiatribune.com/news/local/boone-county-commission-hears-opinions-on-war-memorial-ahead-of/article_b9fff70f-d21b-537e-bf2b-5e5cfdb1f327.html

The Boone County Commission in Missouri proposed to move its Operation Desert Storm memorial from the county's courthouse lawn to a local cemetery. The memorial has been the center of controversy due to its Ichthus Christian fish symbol. The parents of Sterling Wyatt, who was killed on duty in Afghanistan, spoke at the meeting to urge the council to keep the memorial in place alongside the county's other war memorials.

Air Force Base Criticized for Advertising Christian Event
http://christianfighterpilot.com/2015/07/31/mikey-weinstein-attacks-air-force-for-gospel-explosion/

The Cannon Air Force Base was criticized for sending out information about an optional Christian event. Advertisements for a "Gospel Explosion" event in a chapel were distributed in the same manner as for any other activity at the base, such as standup comedy shows or golf tournaments. One non-commissioned officer sent an email letting people know about the event and requesting that people spread the word.

MRFF Calls for Zero Tolerance for Christian Military Chaplains
http://www.militaryreligiousfreedom.org/2015/06/62615-mikeys-op-ed-mrff-demands-ouster-of-all-homophobic-military-chaplains/

Mikey Weinstein is the president of the Military Religious Freedom Foundation. However, far from advancing religious freedom, the group is self-described as "the only organization devoted solely to fighting the scourge of fundamentalist Christian extremism." Weinstein has published an op-ed demanding all chaplains who believe that homosexuality is a sin must be forced out of military service. In his words, they are "cretinous sentinels of vile prejudice and hate-mongering bigotry," and "the Department of Defense must expeditiously cleanse itself of the intolerant filth that insists on lingering in the ranks of our Armed Forces."

MRFF Attacks Air Force Christian as National Security Threat
http://www.christianexaminer.com/article/air.force.senior.master.sgt.story.of.family.medical.trip.to.mexico.draws.censorship.threat/48287.htm

Every year, Air Force Master Sergeant Larry Gallo takes his family over the Christmas holidays on a nine-day medical mission trip to Mexico, Guatemala, or Honduras. "Seven years ago my family and I started giving up our commercial Christmases to do something different," Gallo said. "Since then, we never looked back. These trips allow everyone to slow down and realize that some of the stress we put on ourselves is uncalled for once we put things into perspective." It is such a great story of selflessness and sacrifice that the online publication for the Air Force Reserve Command used it as its weekly feature article. However, the Military Religious Freedom Foundation (MRFF) demanded it be taken down because it was a "shameless and incredibly prominent and public promotion" of religion on official Air Force websites. Mikey Weinstein, MRFF founder and president, went so far to say that the article "emboldens our Islamic enemies because we look like Crusaders and it enrages our Islamic allies."

Sikh Student Denied Entry into the ROTC

http://jurist.org/paperchase/2014/11/aclu-sues-us-army-for-denying-sikh-student-enrollment-in-rotc.php

The United States Army refused to allow Iknoor Singh, a Sikh college student, to enlist in the Reserve Officer Training Corps (ROTC) program unless he shaved his beard, removed his turban, and cut his hair. The student sought a religious exemption from the Army grooming regulations in order to enroll in the ROTC program. The Army denied his request because they believed the accommodation would undermine readiness, unit cohesion, standards, health, safety, and discipline. The Army then stated the request could not be accommodated until the student was an enlisted member, but in order to enlist, he would first have to comply with the grooming regulations. Iknoor Singh sued, claiming violations of the Religious Freedom Restoration Act, and won in a federal district court. After three years of fighting the Army's policy, the prospective officer can now pursue a career in military intelligence without violating his religious beliefs.

Department of Veterans Affairs Bans Native American Religious Practice

http://blog.libertyinstitute.org/2015/07/update-us-department-of-veterans.html

Since 2008, a VA medical center in Kansas has permitted its veterans who follow a Native American faith to hold religious meetings in a sweat lodge. In March of 2015, however, a supervisor at the VA medical center told the spiritual leader of the sweat lodge that they could no longer hold services. The medical center then suspended the leader of the sweat lodge and forbade him from contacting members of the sweat lodge. First Liberty Institute sent a demand letter to the Department of Veterans Affairs to protect the religious liberty rights of the veterans who follow the Native American faith. The medical center offered, instead, to replace the religious service with a showing of the movie Trail of Tears. Hiram Sasser, an attorney at First Liberty Institute, called this an "offensive attempt to pacify a clearly disregarded religious minority."

Navy Chaplain Almost Fired for Following Religious Beliefs

http://www.foxnews.com/opinion/2015/09/04/navy-exonerates-chaplain-accused-being-anti-gay.html

Wes Modder, an Assemblies of God chaplain in the Navy who had served with the Navy SEALs, was given a "detachment for cause" letter because he conducted his pastoral counseling in accordance with the religious beliefs of the Assemblies of God. Chaplain Modder's commanding officer recommended firing Chaplain Modder from the Navy. First Liberty Institute and WilmerHale represented Chaplain Modder and defended his right to follow his religious beliefs in his pastoral counseling. Navy Personnel Command rejected the commanding officer's request and cleared Chaplain Modder of any wrongdoing.

MRFF Demands Court-Martial for General Who Spoke at a National Day of Prayer Event

http://www.airforcetimes.com/story/military/2015/05/15/group-wants-two-star-court-martialed-for-speech/27317903/

The Military Religious Freedom Foundation called for Air Force Maj. Gen. Craig Olson to be "aggressively and very visibly brought to justice for his unforgivable crimes and transgressions" of speaking at a National Day of Prayer Task Force event in which Maj. Gen. Olson credited God for his accomplishments in the Air Force. Maj. Gen. Olson also asked the audience to pray for Defense Department leaders and troops.

Navy Recruit Training Command Limits Religious Services for Non-Liturgical Religious Groups

http://www.navytimes.com/story/military/2015/05/06/mikey-weinstein-ron-crews-boot-camp-druid-some-religious-services-denied/70905518/

The Navy Recruit Training Command has denied access to religious services for "non-liturgical" religious groups, including the Church of Christ, Unitarian-Universalists, Buddhists, and Druids.

MRFF Demands End to Phrase, "Have a Blessed Day"

http://www.christianexaminer.com/article/military.personnel.banned.from.telling.visitors.to.have.a.blessed.day/48532.htm

Gate guards at Robins Air Force Base in Georgia sometimes used the phrase, "Have a blessed day," when greeting persons at the gate. Mikey Weinstein, founder and president of the Military Religious Freedom Foundation (MRFF), contacted the unit commander for base security forces and demanded that gate guards be prohibited from using the word "blessed." The commander for base security complied with the demand.

Department of Defense Refuses to Permit Sikhs to Wear Religious Attire
http://christianfighterpilot.com/2014/12/30/sikhs-continue-calls-for-military-service/#more-30654
The Department of Defense refuses to permit Sikhs to participate in the U.S. Armed Forces while following the religious dress required by their faith. One hundred and five members of the House of Representatives and fifteen senators sent letters to the Department of Defense urging an update of the DoD's dress code to permit Sikhs to participate in the armed forces without being required to violate their religious beliefs.

Army Veteran Suspended for Seeking Religious Liberty Legal Assistance
http://www.pacificjustice.org/press-releases/updatehospital-that-silencedgod-bless-americaresponds-with-more-censorship
Boots Hawks, a twenty-year U.S. Army veteran, joined Dameron Hospital's Quality Management office in Stockton, California, after retiring from the military. One day, Hawks was ordered to remove the phrase "God Bless America" from his email signature block. Hawks complied, but told his supervisors that he would like to seek legal counsel regarding the situation. In response, Hawks was put on two days' leave for "insubordination." A religious liberties group came to Hawks's aid, but the hospital only changed the discipline to paid leave. Moreover, the hospital refused to back down from its stance on Hawks's email signature, but instead decided to institute a new policy with a mandatory standardized signature block for all employees.

Virginia Governor Vetoes Bill Protecting Pastors' Religious Beliefs
http://www.alliancealert.org/2014/04/22/chaplains-encourage-va-legislators-to-override-governors-veto/
The Virginia legislature passed SB 555, which prohibits the government from censoring the sermons of Virginia National Guard chaplains. However, Governor Terry McAuliffe vetoed the bill.

MRFF Condemns Government Involvement in National Day of Prayer
http://christiannews.net/2014/04/19/u-s-military-not-backing-down-after-group-urges-withdrawal-from-national-day-of-prayer-event/
The Military Religious Freedom Foundation sent a letter to the Pentagon demanding that government officials abandon all association with the

National Day of Prayer. The U.S. Military responded by making clear its intention to continue its participation in the observance.

Air Force Officials Remove Bible Verse from Cadet's Whiteboard
http://www.theblaze.com/stories/2014/03/12/some-air-force-cadets-so-angry-over-what-happened-with-bible-verses-on-campus-they-have-staged-a-revolt/#
A cadet at the U.S. Air Force Academy in Colorado Springs, Colorado, wrote a Bible verse on the personal whiteboard posted on his door, but officials removed the verse after receiving complaints that the mere presence of the verse was offensive. When other cadets rose up in protest by writing Bible verses on their own whiteboards, the Military Religious Freedom Foundation wrote a letter to the U.S. Air Force Academy demanding that the verses be removed. Liberty Institute responded by pointing out the cadets' religious rights.

Sikhs Seek Permission to Practice Religion
http://articles.chicagotribune.com/2014-03-10/news/sns-rt-us-usa-defense-sikh-20140310_1_sikhs-turbans-new-policy
In March, 105 lawmakers signed a bipartisan letter asking the Pentagon to allow Sikhs to wear beards, long hair, and turbans while serving in the military. The lawmakers argued that stiff regulations on religious apparel hinder Sikhs from serving in our nation's armed forces.

Humanist Group Attacks Nearly-90-year-old Peace Cross
http://www.libertyinstitute.org/document.doc?id=153
For almost ninety years, a cement cross stood at an intersection in Bladensburg, Maryland, without issue. The memorial honors the forty-nine residents of Prince George's County who died in service during World War I. In February 2014, the American Humanist Association filed a lawsuit in attempt to have the memorial removed. In May 2014, the American Legion, represented by Liberty Institute, filed a motion to intervene to save the memorial.

Group Demands Removal of On-Base Christmas Displays
http://www.foxnews.com/us/2013/12/19/nativity-scenes-removed-from-guantanamo-dining-halls-after-complaints/
http://radio.foxnews.com/toddstarnes/top-stories/air-force-will-not-remove-holiday-display.html
http://www.foxnews.com/opinion/2013/12/09/air-force-removes-nativity-scene/
The Military Religious Freedom Foundation (MRFF) demanded that military bases around the country remove displays that reference the religious story behind Christmas.

Air Force Pressured to Punish Trainer for Christian Affirmation
http://www.jta.org/2013/11/21/news-opinion/united-states/air-force-academy-wont-discipline-trainer-who-pledged-to-proselytize?utm_source=twitterfeed&utm_medium=twitter
After Allen Willoughby, an Air Force athletic trainer, stated in a personal letter that he would continue to share Jesus with anyone he came in contact with, the Military Religious Freedom Foundation called on the Air Force Academy to punish Willoughby for his affirmation. The Air Force refused to hand down any discipline, stating that Willoughby spoke in his personal capacity and not for the Air Force Academy.

Chaplains Forced Out of Veterans Affairs Training Program
http://www.foxnews.com/opinion/2013/11/11/veterans-affairs-forced-chaplains-from-program-for-quoting-scripture-praying-in/
Two Baptist chaplains enrolled in a one-year Clinical Pastoral Education program that is mandatory for anyone desiring to work as a chaplain in a VA hospital. During the program, they were repeatedly subjected to harassment by the program leader and commanded to stop quoting the Bible and praying in Jesus' name. The chaplains refused to do so, ultimately resulting in the dismissal of one chaplain and the withdrawal of the other. The Conservative Baptist Association of America has filed a lawsuit on behalf of the chaplains.

Group Demands the Termination of Air Force Policy Analyst Due to Christian Beliefs
http://www.lgbtqnation.com/2013/11/group-demands-dismissal-of-ex-gay-therapist-from-air-force-academy-staff/
Mike Rosebush, a former vice president of Focus on the Family and clinical member of NARTH (The National Association for Research & Therapy of Homosexuality), was hired by the Air Force Academy as a Senior Operations Research Analyst for the Academy's Center for Character and Leadership Development. When the Military Religious Freedom Foundation found out about Rosebush's background, they immediately demanded his termination.

Military Briefings Identify Evangelical Christians as National Threats
http://blog.libertyinstitute.org/2013/10/shocking-new-allegations-of-hostility.html
http://www.breitbart.com/Big-Peace/2013/10/25/Breaking-New-Military-Docs-Raise-Possibility-Obama-Admin-Burying-Scandal-on-Anti-Christian-Material
In an email, a lieutenant colonel at Fort Campbell in Kentucky advised his officers to be on guard against soldiers who might be affiliated with Christian

organizations, which he described as "domestic hate groups" similar to Neo-Nazis and the KKK. Meanwhile, soldiers attending a pre-deployment briefing at Fort Hood reported that the briefing stated that evangelical Christians and Tea Party members are "tearing the country apart" and are threats to the United States. Soldiers at Camp Shelby in Mississippi were informed that the American Family Association is classified as a hate group and that anyone contributing to such organizations would be subject to punishment under the Uniform Code of Military Justice. Liberty Institute launched an investigation into this matter. While the military camps either denied the allegations or dismissed them as isolated incidents, soon after Liberty Institute's investigation, Army Secretary John McHugh sent out a branch-wide memo ordering leaders to stop characterizing evangelical Christians and related groups as threats.

Group Coerces Air Force into Changing Official Oath Due to Reference to God

http://blog.libertyinstitute.org/2013/10/in-public-arena-last-week-we-reported.html

The Military Religious Freedom Foundation (MRFF) threatened to sue the Air Force Academy unless it abolished the phrase "so help me God" from the end of the official oath. Additionally, the MRFF demanded the removal of a 29-year-old poster of the original oath. While the Air Force initially resisted removing the reference entirely, the phrase has officially been made optional.

San Antonio Air Force Base Reports Numerous Incidents of Religious Persecution

http://www.foxnews.com/opinion/2013/09/30/airmen-say-air-force-is-punishing-evangelical-christians/

Village Parkway Baptist Church in San Antonio, Texas, held an open-forum meeting for airmen at the nearby Lackland Air Force Base to discuss ongoing religious hostility. At the meeting, airmen reported multiple confrontations surrounding their religious liberties, including officers being commanded to openly affirm homosexuality, a military member being written up for having his Bible out despite open acceptance of a Muslim prayer rug, a cadet being required to repeat Basic Training for admitting he was a Christian, and many more.

Farsi Linguist in U.S. Army Harassed by Anti-Muslim Slurs

Fellow soldiers in the U.S. Army harassed Naida Hosan because her name sounded Islamic to them. The harassment included calling her "Sgt. Hussein" and asking what God she prayed to. It got so bad that she legally changed her name to Naida Christian Nova. Ms. Hosan is a Catholic, and after her family immigrated to the United States, her father changed the family name—to avoid discrimination—from Hosein to Hosan, short for the word "hosanna" that he heard so often in church.

Air Force Master Sergeant Punished for Christian Beliefs

http://www.libertyinstitute.org/pages/issues/in-the-public-arena/liberty-institute-defends-airman-persecuted-for-his-faith

http://www.foxnews.com/opinion/2013/09/06/air-force-cracking-down-on-christians/

Senior Master Sergeant Phillip Monk, a 19-year Air Force veteran at Lackland Air Force Base in San Antonio, returned from deployment and found that he had a new commander who was an open lesbian. Sergeant Monk's commander asked Sergeant Monk what he thought about same-sex "marriage." Sergeant Monk initially refused to answer, stating that his views on same-sex "marriage" were irrelevant to his job. When Sergeant Monk's commander insisted that he tell her what he thought, Sergeant Monk affirmed that he believed in the biblical view of marriage. Sergeant Monk's commander then relieved him of his duties and had him reassigned, despite Sergeant Monk's spotless record. When Sergeant Monk reported the retaliatory religious discrimination, Air Force investigators charged him with the crime of making false official statements. Liberty Institute stepped in to assist Sergeant Monk. The Air Force dropped their charges and awarded Sergeant Monk the Meritorious Service Medal.

Army Chaplain's Assistant Rebuked for Religious Beliefs on Biblical Marriage

http://nation.foxnews.com/2013/08/06/fox-exclusive-airman-faces-punishment-her-religious-beliefs

http://www.theblaze.com/stories/2013/08/06/army-chaplain-assistant-reportedly-threatened-with-reduction-in-pay-and-rank-over-facebook-post-calling-homosexuality-a-sin/

After a young Army chaplain's assistant posted a message on her personal Facebook page about the biblical view of homosexuality, she was rebuked by her commanding officer for "creating a hostile and antagonistic environment in the unit" and ordered to remove the Facebook post or face the Uniform Code of Military Justice, which entailed demotion in both rank and pay. While choosing to remain anonymous, the chaplain's assistant vowed to defend herself in court if necessary.

DOJ Defunds Young Marines Group for Emphasizing the "Love of God and Fidelity to Our Country"

http://blog.libertyinstitute.org/2013/07/doj-violates-law-to-defend-young-marines.html

The Bossier Parish Young Marines and Youth Diversion program is a program for at-risk youth that the Bossier Parish Sheriff's Office in Bossier, Louisiana, has operated for over ten years. The program had received federal funds to purchase uniforms and supplies, but the U.S. Department of Justice (DOJ) and the Louisiana Commission on Law Enforcement denied funds for the program after a DOJ audit of the program noted its "special emphasis on the love of God and fidelity to our country." Liberty Institute sent a demand letter on behalf of the Bossier Parish Sheriff's Office seeking a reversal of the DOJ's decision.

Military Seeks to Punish National Guard Veteran for Stance on Biblical Marriage

http://townhall.com/columnists/toddstarnes/2013/07/11/airman-punished-for-objecting-to-gay-marriage-in-military-chapel-n1638648

http://www.pointofview.net/site/News2?page=NewsArticle&id=23298&news_iv_ctrl=1181

Technical Sergeant Layne Wilson, a 27-year veteran of the Utah Air National Guard, wrote a letter objecting to the performance of gay weddings in West Point chapels. Lieutenant Colonel Kevin Tobias responded to Wilson's email, informing him that his letter constituted a failure to "maintain a standard of professional and personal behavior that is above reproach," even though the Defense of Marriage Act was still the law at the time of the letter. Additionally, the Air National Guard terminated Wilson's six-year reenlistment contract, replacing it with a one-year extension. Wilson took action against the religious discrimination, and his six-year contract was reinstated.

Atheist Group Seeks to Stop Spiritual Assistance for Recovery from Dept. of Veterans Affairs

http://ffrf.org/news/news-releases/item/18275-don%E2%80%99t-subject-us-veterans-to-%E2%80%98spiritual-healing%E2%80%99

The U.S. Department of Veterans Affairs (VA) notes that recovery of health includes treatment of mind, body, and spirit, and provides veterans with VA chaplains if they desire spiritual guidance. The Freedom From Religion Foundation already lost a 2006 lawsuit complaining about the provision of chaplains to aid recovery. Nonetheless, the FFRF continued its seven-year war against the VA's provision for its veterans by sending a letter to Eric Shinseki, the Secretary of the Veterans Affairs, demanding that the VA eliminate any association with religion or spirituality.

Military Chaplain Forced to Remove Christian Blog Post

http://radio.foxnews.com/toddstarnes/top-stories/chaplain-ordered-to-remove-religious-essay-from-military-website.html

Lieutenant Colonel Kenneth Reyes, a chaplain for the Joint Base Elmendorf-Richardson in Alaska, wrote a column on the origin of the phrase "There is no such thing as an atheist in a fox hole," concluding the essay with a reflection on his own faith. When the Military Religious Freedom Foundation found out about the column, they accused Reyes of embarking on an "anti-secular diatribe" and demanded that the article be removed and that Reyes be punished for his essay. The base commander subsequently ordered the removal of the piece.

Atheist Group Tries to Silence Prayer in the Navy

http://ffrf.org/news/news-releases/item/17785-sailors-forced-to-hear-shipboard-prayer

The Freedom From Religion Foundation (FFRF) issued a demand letter to the Secretary of the Navy insisting that any and all ship-wide prayers be stopped. According to the FFRF's complaint, prayers are broadcast throughout the entirety of a naval ship, thus subjecting sailors to "coercive" activities. No resolution has come to the matter.

President Obama Opposes Religious Protection for Soldiers

https://www.redstate.com/toddstarnes/2013/06/12/obama-strongly-objects-to-religious-liberty-amendment/

http://www.whitehouse.gov/sites/default/files/omb/legislative/sap/113/saphr1960r_20130611.pdf

John Fleming, a Louisiana state representative, proposed an amendment to the National Defense Authorization Act to protect the religious rights of soldiers amid growing hostility. Although the proposal received bipartisan support, the Obama administration "strongly objected" to the amendment, stating that it would have a "significant adverse effect on good order, discipline, morale, and mission accomplishment."

Former Serviceman Criticizes the Prevalence of Christianity in the Armed Forces

http://www.centerforinquiry.net/uploads/attachments/For_God_and_Country_Parco.pdf

A former Air Force Lieutenant Colonel wrote a thirty-five page paper criticizing the influence that "fundamental" Christianity has on the armed forces and calling for regulations that would restrict servicemen's abilities to openly express their faith.

United States Air Force Removes "Commando Prayer" from Air Force Plane
http://ffrf.org/legal/other-legal-successes/item/17336-ffrf-removes-prayer-from-us-air-force-plane-march-8-2013
The Freedom From Religion Foundation complained to the United States Air Force that a "commando prayer" on the side of an airplane threatened the religious freedom of nonreligious service members, causing their freedoms to be "trampled upon." The U.S. Air Force bowed to their wishes and removed the prayer.

President Obama Opposes Conscience Protections for Military Chaplains
http://www.alliancealert.org/2013/01/03/chaplain-alliance-calls-on-obama-administration-to-honor-chaplain-protections-passed-by-congress/
http://www.whitehouse.gov/the-press-office/2013/01/03/statement-president-hr-4310
Congress passed a provision with strong bipartisan support that prohibits the armed forces from requiring chaplains to perform "any rite, ritual, or ceremony that is contrary to the conscience, moral principles, or religious beliefs of the chaplain" or from discriminating against a chaplain for that chaplain's refusal to perform such a rite, ritual, or ceremony. President Obama, however, called the provision "ill-advised."

Army Training Materials Label Christians "Extremists," in the Same Category as Al-Qaeda
http://radio.foxnews.com/toddstarnes/top-stories/army-labeled-evangelicals-as-religious-extremism.html
In U.S. Army training materials provided for an Army Reserve unit in Pennsylvania, Evangelical Christians and Catholics were labeled "religious extremists," along with Hamas and Al-Qaeda. After religious groups complained about the presentation, the Army trainer who prepared the material apologized.

Group Demands Court-Martial of General for Promoting Christian Military Marriage Counseling
http://159.54.242.91/news/2012/08/gannett-watchdog-group-says-indiana-national-guard-chief-martin-umbarager-promoted-religion-082112/
The Military Religious Freedom Foundation called for Maj. Gen. R. Martin Umbarger to be court-martialed for promoting Centurion's Watch, a nonprofit

Christian organization that offers marriage counseling to military families. The MRFF also called on the National Guard Bureau to investigate the president of Centurion's Watch as well.

Air Force No Longer Encourages Officers to Attend Chapel

http://religionclause.blogspot.com/2012/04/air-force-drops-course-reading-that.html

The U.S. Air Force recently complied with a letter sent by the Military Religious Freedom Foundation that asked them to remove a reading from the Squadron Officer School course that encouraged officers to attend chapel as a spiritual example to their men.

Navy Chaplain Sued by Military Religious Freedom Foundation for Content of His Prayers

http://www.dallasnews.com/news/religion/20120403-judge-dismisses-lawsuit-against-dallas-based-group-former-chaplain-for-use-of-curse-prayers.ece

The founder of the Military Religious Freedom Foundation, Mikey Weinstein, filed suit against the former Navy chaplain and the chaplaincy of Full Gospel Churches for saying prayers that Weinstein claimed incited threats of violence against him. The district court judge disagreed, however, and dismissed the suit on the grounds that there was no proof of a connection between the prayers and the threats.

Army Removes Cross from Chapel to Avoid Offending Other Faiths

http://radio.foxnews.com/toddstarnes/top-stories/military-crosses-removed-out-of-respect-for-other-faiths.html

The Army dismantled and removed the cross from a chapel at an Army forward operations base in Afghanistan "out of respect for the beliefs of other faiths." Cross-shaped windows on the building were boarded up until they can be replaced. These actions occurred following a complaint from an atheist soldier.

Air Force Pressured to Remove God from Logo

http://christianfighterpilot.com/blog/2012/01/18/atheist-gets-secretive-agency-to-changemotto/

The Military Association of Atheists and Freethinkers (MAAF) successfully removed God from the U.S. Air Force Rapid Capabilities Office (RCO) logo on its official patch. It pressured the RCO into replacing "Doing God's Work" with "Doing Miracles." The MAAF claimed that the logo, which was written in Latin, constituted government establishment of religion in violation of the First Amendment.

Air Force Academy Withdraws Support of Operation Christmas Child

http://www.gazette.com/articles/religious-127840-academy-christmas.html
The Freedom From Religion Foundation wrote a letter to the U.S. Air Force Academy complaining about the support the Academy gives Operation Christmas Child by encouraging cadets to participate in the project. Operation Christmas Child is a charity that sends children Christmas presents along with a religious message. The Academy responded to this letter by no longer directly encouraging the project, and only allowing school chaplains to promote participation.

Military Association of Atheists and Freethinkers Attacks Memorial Cross to Fallen Marines

http://latimesblogs.latimes.com/lanow/2011/11/camp-pendleton-cross-marinesatheists.html
Private parties put up a thirteen-foot cross at Camp Pendleton in memorial of four Marines who died and as a general memorial for all fallen Marines. The Military Association of Atheists and Freethinkers has complained about the memorial.

Obama Administration Fights to Keep Prayer off World War II Memorial

http://www.foxnews.com/politics/2011/11/04/obama-administration-opposes-fdr-prayerat-wwii-memorial/
The Obama administration opposes the World War II Memorial Prayer Act, which would put a copy of Franklin D. Roosevelt's D-Day prayer on the World War II Memorial in Washington, D.C. The administration claims that under the Commemorative Works Act, it is prohibited to put anything on a memorial that will hide part of it. A decision still has not been reached on whether to add the prayer to the memorial.

Army Prohibits Jewish Man from Keeping His Beard and Becoming a Chaplain

http://www.chabad.org/news/article_cdo/aid/1696300/jewish/Faced-With-Chaplain-Shortage-Army-Letting-Rabbi-Keep-Beard-After-All.htm
Rabbi Menachem Stern filed suit against the Army for not allowing him to be in the Army without shaving his beard. As a Chabad rabbi, Menachem's beard carries important religious significance. The rabbi claimed that the Army's refusal to let him keep his beard was a violation of his equal protection rights. The Army eventually relented, allowing Stern to keep his beard and enter the reserves.

Groups Oppose Christian Concert at Ft. Bragg, North Carolina

http://religionclause.blogspot.com/2010/09/ft-bragg-christian-concert-draws-church.html

Billy Graham Ministries put on "Rock the Fort" at Ft. Bragg, North Carolina, as it has done at many other military bases. "Rock the Fort" is a Christian music festival that the Army allows to occur on base, but does not pressure soldiers to attend. Americans United for Separation of Church and State and the Freedom From Religion Foundation both wrote letters to the U.S. Army complaining that its allowance of the festival violated the Establishment Clause. The Army let the festival go on as planned.

Military Religious Freedom Foundation Opposes Franklin Graham's Speaking for the National Day of Prayer

http://religionclause.blogspot.com/2010/04/objections-raised-to-pentagons-speaker.html

The Pentagon asked pastor Franklin Graham to speak for the National Day of Prayer. The Military Religious Freedom Foundation complained about this invitation, saying that Graham had offended Muslims in the past. The organization also complained that the National Day of Prayer Task Force, a Christian organization, was too closely tied to the military.

Minister's National Prayer Luncheon Invitation Revoked Because of His Comments on Homosexuality in the Military

http://blogs.cbn.com/thebrodyfile/archive/2010/02/24/exclusive-tony-perkins-disinvited-to-military-prayer-breakfast.aspx

An ordained minister and Marine Corps veteran was punished for speaking out on a topic unrelated to his planned comments at the National Prayer Luncheon at Andrews Air Force Base outside of Washington, D.C. The minister criticized President Obama's call to end "don't ask, don't tell," resulting in his invitation to speak at the National Prayer Luncheon being rescinded. The minister criticized the action as "blacklisting" to suppress unwanted viewpoints.

Honor Guardsman Fired for Saying "God Bless You and This Family, and God Bless the United States of America"

"'God Bless You' Suit Prevails," WorldNetDaily, *available at http://www.wnd.com/2003/08/20198/ (Aug. 8, 2003)*

Military veteran and honor guardsman Patrick Cubbage was fired from the New Jersey Department of Military and Veterans Affairs (NJDMVA) for saying "God bless you and this family, and God bless the United States of

America" to families as he presented a folded flag in honor of a fallen veteran. Though the families did not object to the practice, one of Cubbage's co-guardsmen complained to their supervisor, and Cubbage was warned not to say the blessing to the families. Later, Cubbage gave the blessing to a family after a request from the fallen veteran's son. Shortly thereafter, Cubbage was terminated. Cubbage settled with the NJDMVA for ten months' back pay and his job back.

FIRST LIBERTY

MANAGING EDITORIAL TEAM

Kelly Shackelford, Esq., has been president and CEO of First Liberty Institute (formerly Liberty Institute) since 1997. He is a constitutional scholar who has argued before the United States Supreme Court, testified before the U.S. House and Senate on constitutional issues, and has won a number of landmark First Amendment and religious liberty cases. He was recently named one of the 25 greatest Texas lawyers of the past quarter-century by Texas Lawyer, and is the recipient of the prestigious William Bentley Ball Award for Life and Religious Freedom Defense for his leadership and pioneering work protecting religious freedom. He is on the Board of Trustees of the U.S. Supreme Court Historical Society.

Jeffrey Mateer, Esq., joined First Liberty Institute in 2010 after 19 years in private litigation practice. He now oversees and directs Liberty Institute's legal team. He specializes in religious liberty matters, including free exercise, free speech, RLUIPA and public acknowledgment of religion cases. Mr. Mateer has been honored as a Texas Rising Star and Texas Super Lawyer. He received his undergraduate education at Dickinson College, where he graduated with honors in 1987, and his legal education at Southern Methodist University, where he graduated with honors in 1990.

Justin Butterfield, Esq., graduated from Harvard Law School in 2007. He served as the student coordinator for the Veritas Forum, was a member of the Federalist Society, and was heavily involved with the Harvard Law School Christian Fellowship. A native Texan, Mr. Butterfield completed his undergraduate studies at the University of Texas at El Paso where he graduated *summa cum laude,* with honors, and University Banner Bearer with a bachelor's degree in Electrical Engineering.

The Managing Editorial Team also wish to acknowledge the outstanding contributions of the attorneys, research fellows, and interns at First Liberty Institute, who both know the legal landscape of religious liberty and strive to keep religious liberty as America's first liberty.

ABOUT FIRST LIBERTY INSTITUTE

When it comes to winning big cases for the religious liberty of Americans, First Liberty Institute shines. I have had the privilege of working as part of their team on just such cases. First Liberty Institute's intelligence, quality, and strategy give people of faith the best representation. They care about results, not taking credit, and the result is victories.

—*Paul Clement, 43rd Solicitor General of the United States*

First Liberty Institute (formerly Liberty Institute) is the largest nonprofit legal organization in the United States with the sole mission of protecting religious liberty for all Americans.

First Liberty Institute's vision is to reestablish religious liberty in accordance with the principles of our nation's Founders, who believed that religious liberty was the "first" liberty—the freedom upon which all others are grounded.

First Liberty Institute uses an innovate model in which a staff of top-notch attorneys support a national network of elite attorneys from approximately half of the top 50 law firms in the nation. This legal strategy wins a high percentage of strategic cases to protect religious liberty for millions of Americans. First Liberty Institute uses only the best attorneys from each locality and area of legal specialization (such as appellate law, military law, etc.) to ensure familiarity, expertise, and the best opportunity for a positive outcome.

Our efforts have won victories at all levels, including the U.S. Supreme Court, state supreme courts, federal and state courts of appeals, district courts, administrative courts, and highly favorable settlements.

First Liberty Institute staff attorneys—each one a constitutional and legal expert—also advise members of Congress and state governments on religious liberty law and appear thousands of times in the media each year.

To learn more:
FirstLiberty.org